I0877112

# MY VICTORIAN NOVEL

# MY VICTORIAN NOVEL

## Critical Essays in the Personal Voice

Edited with an Introduction by

Annette R. Federico

Foreword by

Jane Tompkins

UNIVERSITY OF MISSOURI PRESS

Columbia

Copyright © 2020 by
The Curators of the University of Missouri
University of Missouri Press, Columbia, Missouri 65211
Printed and bound in the United States of America
All rights reserved. First printing, 2020.

Library of Congress Cataloging-in-Publication Data

Names: Federico, Annette, 1960- editor, writer of introduction. | Tompkins, Jane P., writer of foreword.
Title: My Victorian novel : critical essays in the personal voice / edited with an introduction by Annette R. Federico ; foreword by Jane Tompkins.
Description: Columbia : University of Missouri Press, 2020. | Includes bibliographical references and index.
Identifiers: LCCN 2019052073 (print) | LCCN 2019052074 (ebook) | ISBN 9780826222077 (hardcover) | ISBN 9780826274434 (ebook)
Subjects: LCSH: English fiction--19th century--History and criticism. | Identity (Psychology) | Interest (Psychology) | Authors and readers. | Books and reading. | Literature--Psychology.
Classification: LCC PR734 .I33 2020 (print) | LCC PR734 (ebook) | DDC 823/.809--dc23
LC record available at https://lccn.loc.gov/2019052073
LC ebook record available at https://lccn.loc.gov/2019052074

∞™ This paper meets the requirements of the American National Standard for Permanence of Paper for Printed Library Materials, Z39.48, 1984.

Typefaces: New Caledonia

For Florence Rose Federico (1925–2019)
In so many ways, my heroine

# Contents

# Foreword

Jane Tompkins

The reading and writing of novels has always been a personal affair. It wasn't until stories about people who were not gods and goddesses or kings and queens came to be regarded as significant and interesting that the novel sprang into existence, in the course of the eighteenth century. The production of novels arose from the premise that what happens to individual human beings—their joys, their fears, their fates—matters. Readers wanted stories that could apply to themselves and writers wanted to write them. It was only with institutionalized ways of talking about literature in the twentieth century that it became off limits to think about what readers felt as they read—rather ironically, since it was seeing personal experience as having value that called the novel into being.

Keeping personal responses to a novel out of critical writing seemed necessary in the 1950s, when English professors were trying to establish literary criticism as a respectable discipline by putting it on a scientific—which is to say, thoroughly objective—basis. This work helped establish English departments as the center of the humanistic enterprise. As critical theory evolved in the following decades, French poststructuralism took over the field, influencing work across the humanities and social sciences. But recently, information technology, along with social and economic factors, has marginalized the humanities in college curricula, and English departments have dwindled in size and influence. The digital humanities' attempt to make literary studies relevant by embracing the computer's statistical virtuosity as an analytical tool has not righted the balance.

Meanwhile, the general desire for stories about people's lives flourishes. In books of fiction and biography, in movies, on TV, online, and in the news, stories about other human beings grab and hold our attention. And now, finally, despite digitalization, literary criticism has caught up with this most basic hunger, that is, the hunger to learn from literature how other people's lives relate to our own. The critics in the present collection write intelligently, vividly, and instructively about how novels have affected the way they live. *My Victorian Novel* marks the moment when acknowledging the primary importance of individual experience in the reading of novels has come of age institutionally and professionally.

When I first wrote the word "novels" in the previous sentence, I typed "navels" by mistake—clearly a Freudian slip. The reproach always launched against people who write about their own experience in response to literature is that it turns criticism into nothing more than adolescent navel-gazing. Readers of this collection will discover that this is untrue. When coming to know oneself is entwined with the reading of great fiction, it deepens our appreciation of the novels themselves and lets us see how they help their readers to understand the world, and their own lives.

Not only do the essays that follow testify to the ways in which literature can affect us personally, but they also offer, as it were, two stories in one: an interpretation of the story the novel tells, and, parallel to it, a story about the person who is writing the essay. Literary criticism as a genre gains from the presence of this second story. What I mean is that the content of these essays, being in every case personal and experiential, produces a familiarity and spontaneity in the writing that make them a pleasure to read and nearly impossible to put down. As Michael Flynn says of Dickens's voice in *David Copperfield*, an autobiographical novel that Dickens tells us he had difficulty separating himself from when he finished it: "[T]he tangibility of that voice made me believe the narrative."

It is the sound of authenticity that makes these essays live. Honesty and intimacy animate the enterprise. There's more at stake here than defending a critical position, establishing one's scholarly credentials, or displaying theoretical competence. The author doesn't write primarily to make a point, although points are made, but to communicate something, an involvement with a book so deep that it has shaped his or her life.

The essays collected here are as different as the personalities and circumstances of the people who wrote them. Supported by the editor's rich and informative introduction, together they expand one's view of how books function in readers' lives, both at particular moments and over time as a reader returns again and again to the same text. Taken as a whole the essays allow us to see something that up to now has usually remained hidden from those of us who read academic writing about literature: namely, how close, personal, and far-reaching the relationship between reader and text can be.

And when the reader is highly trained, she can put her experience into language in a way that enlightens other readers. Nonprofessional readers have all kinds of intense and significant experiences with books, but people who teach and write about novels for a living, having been educated in analysis and in the expression of ideas, are uniquely qualified to make their encounters with books striking and meaningful for others. And when they put their whole selves into it, and what they write becomes moving and memorable for their readers, they become, in a sense, novelists themselves.

When So Young Park tells the story of how, when she was commuting to graduate school in Manhattan, she began rereading *The Newcomes*, a seldom-read 1,000-page novel by Thackeray, on the night of September 11, 2001, and continued to read it one chapter a night from then on because it was the only thing that made her feel safe, I was rapt. She created in me a sense of this novel as a great big fascinating world that one could lose oneself in completely, and she made me want to read it, which I had never dreamed of doing before.

When Lillian Nayder describes her beginnings as a literary scholar doing research on Dickens, the reality of her life and that of the characters she pores over in *The Pickwick Papers* start to mirror each other. She realizes she had felt excluded from the male club of her English department in the same way the servant, Sam Weller, feels excluded from the Pickwick Club. The charm and ease with which she develops the analogy echoes Dickens's own. Her enthusiasm and appreciation for *Pickwick* and the taste of it she gives us made me want to read it, too, for the first time. When a writer brings her own emotions and experiences to bear in responding to a work of literature, her account of that work intensifies because it is her own life as well as the story of some character that is at stake. The sense of urgency this brings to *our* reading comes not just from the personal details of the author's history but also from the new angles of vision it opens on the work in question.

Annette Federico's essay on *Wuthering Heights* provides a powerful and dazzling example of this supercharged effect. Her encounters with Brontë's masterpiece offer simultaneously a meditation on human love and passion, a riveting account of her own coming to consciousness in the context of her early marriage, and a brilliant succession of perspectives on the novel. Though the essay moved me in part because her story parallels mine, its themes apply to practically anyone who has lived, suffered, and thought about it. When you read these essays, I think you'll feel similarly moved and rewarded.

Jane Tompkins
Professor Emerita of English, Duke University

# Acknowledgments

It has been a pleasure, again, to work with everyone at the University of Missouri Press. I especially wish to thank Gary Kass. His candor forced me to more clearly articulate my hopes for this project, and his ongoing encouragement kept those hopes from flagging. Gloria Thomas's copyediting made fifteen different voices sound harmonious. Thanks also to the two outside readers for their exceptionally perceptive, generous, and detailed comments on every essay.

Each contributor to *My Victorian Novel* responded to my invitation to write this different kind of criticism with unexpected optimism, delight, and warmth. Thank you for staying with me. You've opened the door a little wider for others who want to reflect on the meaning of what we do as readers, teachers, and writers. I am especially pleased to include Terrance Riley's essay on the Sherlock Holmes stories. In an email to me way back in July, Terry wrote, "This is turning out to be one of the most rewarding projects I have ever worked on." He gave us something close to his heart.

Many colleagues and friends have inspired and encouraged me, by word or by example. Thanks to Dabney Bankert, Pamela Beverage, Erica Cavanaugh, Sharon Cote, Marina Favila, Laurie Kutchins, Laurie Lakebrink, Sofia Samatar, Janine Utell, and Greg Wrenn. I am also enormously grateful to Jane Tompkins, who replied to my fan letter about her book so graciously. It is truly an honor to hold her words here.

Thanks also to the Department of English and the College of Arts and Letters at James Madison University for material and moral support.

Chuck Dotas, bringer of sunflowers, my hand is on my heart. Thank you for all the patient listening and for sharing life's winding path with me.

# MY VICTORIAN NOVEL

INTRODUCTION

# In the Personal Voice

Annette R. Federico

> Yet his object will not always be to explain the work of art. He may seek rather to deepen its mystery, to raise round it, and round its maker, that mist of wonder which is dear to both gods and worshippers alike.
>
> Oscar Wilde, "The Critic as Artist"

*My Victorian Novel* collects essays by fifteen scholars, each about a single British novel that has acquired personal meaning for the essayist—a work that has become entwined with a personal story, or one that has remained elusive or compelling for reasons hard to explain. This book endeavors to bring reading and criticism closer to home by frankly acknowledging that over time we develop relationships with the books we study and teach, and that reflecting on our subjective use of certain works is valid, meaningful, and mentionable. Rereading Victorian fiction for our classes or our scholarship must at some level involve a relaxation of feeling, the evocation of memories, psychic immersion, and moral engagement. By reflecting on our own histories with novels studied, researched, taught, and re-experienced in different contexts, sometimes over many years, the writers in *My Victorian Novel* collectively reveal, with wonderful variation, how an aesthetic object comes to inhabit our personal and pedagogical as well as our critical lives.

The essays collected here, all previously unpublished, are by literary scholars who have dedicated our lives to studying and teaching nineteenth-century fiction and the Victorian world. But these are not conventional scholarly critiques, and the collection does not draw a hard line between interpretation and introspection. They are *essays* in the original sense of the word, *attempts*; they evidence the "action or process of trying or testing"; each is "a sample, an example, a rehearsal."[1] The essay form intertwines self-observation and critical questioning; it represents a space for opportunities, glimpses, openings. Ruth-Ellen Boetcher Joeres has asked whether academic articles can properly be called *essays* since the "great majority of them . . . do not possess the clarifying, communicating effect that essays as a form can create." Unlike an academic article, the essay maintains "a delicate balance between objective and subjective, between certainty and ambiguity," it can "both feel and think," be at the same time "particular and general."[2] The writing in *My Victorian Novel* asks how we might balance the desire to understand a text objectively with more subjective motives, aimed at other kinds of understanding. How might scholarship and publishing change if we loosen the bonds of academic style and approach the task of writing literary criticism more as an essayist would, provisionally, inquisitively, even lyrically?

In "Found in the Details: Essaying the Particular," Boetcher Joeres, a professor emerita of German and women's studies, writes beautifully about the satisfactions of writing a kind of criticism that watches for nuance, that winds its way leisurely through detail, rather than taking the highway to declarations. These are the different mental and stylistic paths of essayist and academic. In his tribute to Sir Frank Kermode after his death in 2010, Verlyn Klinkenborg lamented, "In my years in academia, I had watched the study of literature go down any number of rabbit holes—chasing after theory and ideology and system. The very point of reading and talking about what we read seemed to have been lost in a kind of strangulating self-seriousness and alienation." Kermode, though, "was drawn to the entanglements of the text and its rational mysteries," Klinkenborg noted. "In his many books and essays, he protected the reader's freedom to be interested in whatever was interesting. That meant writing a prose that was never wholly academic and over the years became more and more open to the intersection of literature and the lives we're actually living."[3] Loving entanglements, seeking out intersections between life and reading, protecting the reader's freedom to be interested in whatever is interesting: these are the ideas that underscore and motivate *My Victorian Novel*.

In the past several decades, the methodology of scholarly writing has been concerned chiefly with excavating facts about culture and history; it has been context-driven, symptomatic, determined to show a text's collusion with the subtle workings of social power and privilege. Traditional scholarly writing usually deploys analysis and argumentation, and is driven by faith in the value of objective inquiry—a good thing, certainly! Unbiased inquiry is a time-tested way of arriving at facts about literature and other disciplines, and I greatly value (and rigorously employ) my empirical training in the study of literature. Here, though, the other writers and I are taking a break from argumentation. By refraining from business as usual, we may inadvertently remind our readers that there is more than one kind of question (the cultural-historical one) to ask about the meaning of any literary work, and more than one way of arriving at an understanding about it. Many different kinds of knowledge—aesthetic, creative, psychological, spiritual—glimmer through that heavy backdrop of cultural and historical information.

In a short chapter called "Good Readers and Good Writers," from his great lectures delivered at Wellesley and Cornell in the mid-twentieth century, Vladimir Nabokov claimed the temperament best suited for critical reading is a combination of the scientific and the artistic. Nabokov advocated "an artistic harmonious balance between the reader's mind and the author's mind. We ought to remain a little aloof and take pleasure in this aloofness while at the same time we keenly enjoy—passionately enjoy, enjoy with tears and shivers—the inner weave of a given masterpiece."[4] It is a knack to remain aloof and also be immersed to the point of shivers. As teachers in English departments, we tend to do this almost intuitively in the classroom because we want to model both registers of response for our students. Our published scholarship, though, tends to be more strictly policed, our responses more segregated. Aloofness dominates analysis; shivers are relegated to the acknowledgments—the first place I go when I pick up a scholarly book, no matter what the book's disciplinary focus.[5] The acknowledgments hint at the person inside the scholar, and the immediate tone of voice grounds both reader and author in a specific time and place. Sometimes I am a little bit jealous of other scholars' many friends, loved ones, colleagues, and research funding. But most of the time, I am not so petty. I am genuinely moved by an author's gratitude, her commitment to intellectual labor, her humility. "I could never have written this book without my beloved parents, devoted partner or spouse, students, children, editor, teacher, yoga instructor, therapist, librarian, and dog." So many networks of relationship emerge. They form the social part of reading, just as they do the cooperative aspect of writing criticism. There is the private part, too, of course. But it is a lovely thing when the two, the public and the private, aloofness and shivers, are allowed to come together. "To be quite objective in [literary study] is of course impossible," Nabokov observed. "Everything that is worthwhile is to some extent subjective."[6] And it is just because the subjective makes everything worthwhile that it cannot be banished completely from any pursuit of knowledge. In literary study, there will always be the persistent if muted note of individuality, of a unique self with something to say to another unique self—the steady background hum and conversational appeal of the personal voice.

How personal? For some of the contributors to this book, the desire to share a story about their reading life was the impetus for writing. Andrea Kaston Tange's first memory of reading *Jane Eyre*, for example, is a narrative presented so concretely and movingly that we want to follow her into maturity. Her story is about the necessity of that first innocent reading, before the complexities of life—and of theory—changed and enriched the novel for her. My own essay, on *Wuthering Heights*, is also an intimate story, one about love and self-acceptance. But the essayists' motives for writing and for self-expression vary widely. Some contributors deliberately hold the narrative impulse in check. The energy behind Sara Malton's essay, for example, is undoubtedly personal, a veiled speculation on why it was impossible for her to read *The Return of the Native* for almost twenty years. There is something she is not prepared to bring before an audience, and cannot even fully articulate for herself, yet her close analysis of the novel's "communicative plotting" attests irrepressibly to the enduring strength of this work for her—perhaps because it dramatizes the silencing of women's versions of events, or the public shaming of women that the #MeToo movement has brought to light. Jonathan Farina is virtuosic in his detailed analysis of the language in Thackeray's *Vanity Fair*, but he self-reflexively undercuts the professional pose of mastery, the mask of knowing reserve, in the service of which we are forced to translate our feelings about what we read into academic jargon. People render their personal feelings—their feelings about a novel as well as their feelings about family—into stock expressions and professional idioms, Farina says, rather than coming out directly in honest language. Speech itself, the lyric voice of the critic, may conjure the person behind the prose, as in Catherine Robson's essay on *Bleak House*. Robson's approach to Dickens's novel is well credentialed, and her analysis of character manages to be both brainy and highly imaginative. Her essay feels personal because of her *style*—she does not try to conceal her personality behind academic prose. Her writing has humor, verve, and warmth.

That the essays here are on a rich and varied continuum from the personal to the academic is evidence in itself that trying to stretch our talents as readers and writers beyond professional protocols is an exciting and challenging task. In the past four decades, literary scholarship has had a strong sociological bent. But the definition of scholarship is changing—or at least widening. We seem to be looking for a new vocabulary to describe this next bend in the road, a veering away, perhaps, from contextual frames and the authority of explanations. Rita Felski, one of the most prominent advocates for an alternative to ideological critique, has offered the word "postcritical" to serve "as a placeholder for emerging ideas and barely glimpsed possibilities" of what scholarly writing may be like in the future. "The role of the postcritical," she writes, "is neither to prescribe the forms that reading should take nor to dictate the attitudes that critics must adopt; it is to steer us away from the kinds of arguments we know how to conduct in our sleep."[7] Deidre Shauna Lynch and Evelyne Ender have referred to "a growing enthusiasm for countermodels . . . that sidestep the traditions of critical hermeneutics."[8] Stephen Benson and Clare Connors have introduced the term "creative criticism" as a category for writing that "exploits, distorts, works over, hyperbolises, erases or plays with the conventions of academic critical prose."[9] Amy J. Elias uses the term "rhetorical dialogics" to describe a form of criticism that "presupposes a social and ethical relationship between author and reader." Elias advocates "an underground appreciative criticism (that enemy of professionalized theory)" that deliberately favors description over suspicion.[10] And in an essay about Virginia Woolf, Rebecca Solnit champions "counter-criticism," a kind of writing "that seeks to expand the work of art, by connecting it, opening up its meanings, inviting in the possibilities."[11] Solnit, a journalist and art critic, is eloquent in her call for a more open-ended form of critique:

> This is a kind of criticism that does not pit the critic against the text, does not seek authority. It seeks instead to travel with the work and its ideas, to invite it to blossom and invite others into a conversation that might have previously seemed impenetrable, to draw out relationships that might have been unseen and open doors that might have been locked. This is a kind of

> criticism that respects the essential mystery of a work of art, which is in part its beauty and its pleasure, both of which are irreducible and subjective. The worst criticism seeks to have the last word and leave the rest of us in silence; the best opens up an exchange that need never end.[12]

This call for a criticism of open exchange, of conversation and sharing, implicitly takes the emphasis away from the mastery implied by interpretation and sees each reader's own experience with a text as a valid form of scholarly discourse.

Getting older gives some of us permission to lower our intellectual defenses, and to write how we want, about what we love. In an article written for a special section called "Reading over Time" in *PMLA*, Peter J. Rabinowitz declares that "with age comes confidence. Attitudes that we may have been afraid or embarrassed to assume suddenly become possible." We get to a point where we do not feel compelled to suppress an "increased readiness to shut out trendy criticism that bores us," he writes. In fact, it is a sign of health to remain open to "emotional positions we had once guarded against."[13] But it turns out that being less guarded is still surprisingly hard for most established scholars—it is as though our dissertation director were looking over our shoulder as we write, like Woolf's phantom Angel in the House. Yet, without some degree of emotional commitment, scholarship can feel anemic. Literary criticism, even academic criticism, has its own creative energies, its own writerly intuitions. To write about any work of art invites unanticipated responses and risks. Real writers get this right away, and always have. Zadie Smith, J. C. Hallman, Anne Fadiman, Geoff Dyer, Susan Howe, Anne Carson, Ali Smith, Margaret Atwood, James Wood, and many others confess frankly their acceptance of the allure of literature, its "rational mysteries," in Klinkenborg's words, and that is why their criticism is so stylish, so observant and alive.[14] They do not try to hide their responses from themselves—on the contrary, the critical act may be an excavation of those responses, a voyage in. As Jane Tompkins tells us in her inspiring new book *Reading through the Night*, "Doing literary criticism meant backing up your opinions about a book by pointing to specific passages and describing what it was in them that bore you out. I'd never thought to ask what *in me* caused me to respond as I did." When Tompkins, in her seventies, did begin to ask that question, she embarked on an inner journey that was utterly revelatory.[15]

To teach critical reading and critical thinking is one of the tried and true justifications for the role of English departments in colleges and universities.[16] What would happen if we also taught students how to engage with a literary work aesthetically and subjectively, to see their critical papers as genuinely creative responses to literary works?[17] Maybe we could call it *critical feeling*? There are precedents for this approach to writing about literature and other arts. Eve Kosofsky Sedgwick taught a course for both graduate and undergraduate students called Experimental Literary Writing at Duke University in the 1990s. Angelika Bammer and Anna Grimshaw have taught the interdisciplinary class Experiments in Scholarly Form at Emory University. Jane Rendell, an architectural historian, gives a yearly talk to postgraduate students about how to use "performative and other modes of creative writing" in their theses. German art historian An Paenhuysen teaches a course called Creative Forms of Art Criticism and Writing.[18] I also have offered a writing course at my university titled Creative Criticism, which, with the blessing of the creative writing faculty, was allowed to count toward the requirements for the creative writing minor. While also requiring students to do research in a particular area, these kinds of courses implicitly ask how academic criticism can cultivate, rather than censor, a more writerly voice. They seek to encourage originality and the making of unconventional connections among texts, and they offer a workshop-like space for trying out new forms. They may also, as Elias points out, imply "resistance to the neoliberal university" by forging "new intellectual communities that bring artists and scholars together and that are based on trust and open interchange" instead of the usual disciplinary camps, different silos for creatives and for scholars.[19]

"Reading" has emerged lately as a big topic of discussion—close reading, surface reading, distant reading, flat reading, and just reading. But it may be even more requisite to think about how we *write* about literature now, and for whom, and why. In *The Future of Scholarly Writing*, Bammer and Boetcher Joeres refer to a "writing crisis" in academia, "an uneasy awareness of the fact that established forms of scholarly presentation . . . are no longer adequate to the needs of the contemporary academy, much less to the world of those beyond it."[20] Although *My Victorian Novel* is not specifically about the public role of the humanities, the essays gathered here implicitly engage questions about presentation, performance, and public relevance. Just as any rereading of a well-known novel may suddenly reveal a new vision or a surprising insight, writing without the usual formulas and phrases can open unexpected doors—and invite unexpected audiences to enter in. As the editors of *A Poetics of Criticism* wrote in 1994, "Although the rise of cultural studies in the late eighties and early nineties teased at allowing a new articulation of criticism within the academy, not much has changed in terms of the possible *forms* of criticism. But literary criticism, if it is to achieve greater generative significance as a cultural creation, needs to engage its own fear of writing."[21] The forms of writing in this book are nowhere near the avant-gardism of *A Poetics of Criticism*—but you may occasionally sense the fear. When criticism diverges from the straight line of argumentation, the knowledge presented may seem soft, unanchored to history or facts. Our usual and useful habit of mind wants to grasp the crux of the argument. Readers of the essays collected here may occasionally wonder what the takeaway is. What is the thesis? Where is the actual argument? The middle way between thinking and feeling, between a concentrated focus and a diffused awareness, is a difficult path for seasoned academics to follow. To inflect a scholarly argument with memory, affection, sadness, or humor is to sustain a difficult tension between the personal and the professional voice—and the struggle is often visible in these pages. Almost every contributor mentioned to me that writing his or her essay had been "rewarding," "fun," or "a pleasure" but also that it had been extremely difficult. These fifteen essays, with their variations in tone, purpose, structure, and focus, are, indeed, experiments. They are responses to the symbolic richness of language, the social and moral assumptions we bring to reading, and especially the unpredictability of our own affective tastes and capacities and our psychic involvement. These things are all part of the process of writing literary criticism, though we seldom acknowledge their presence, or their power.

Adopting a more subjective or aesthetic stance in literary criticism may feel strange at first, a bit touchy-feely, and flying without the safety net of supporting quotations, cultural and historical referents, or a habitual theoretical frame can feel disquieting and unprotected. But it may be emotionally and intellectually emancipating as well. The project of writing about one Victorian novel in almost any way we wanted presented these scholars and I with an occasion for writing about something else, something that had been waiting to be seen, understood, and articulated, what the psychoanalyst and essayist Adam Phillips calls "a side effect" of the process of writing.[22] The something else could have been literary—the dynamics of a narrative's design, its imagery, its contexts, metaphors, structure. Or it could have been something more personal, or more universal—education and love, identity and growing up, memory, time, or mortality.

The experiential approach to reading and criticism is not a new development. In *Readings and Feelings: An Introduction to Subjective Criticism*, published in 1975, David Bleich asserted that reading literature "can produce new understanding of oneself—not just a moral here or a message there, but a genuinely new conception of one's values and tastes as well as one's prejudices."[23] And in a book a few years earlier he contended that subjective criticism "assumes that each person's most urgent motivations are to understand himself, and that the simplest path to this understanding is awareness of one's own language system as the agency of consciousness and self-direction."[24] The personal associations that we usually push to the back of our minds as scholars could be clues to new insights—about a work of literature, about history, about the present, and about our own lives. The desire to know something intellectually and also experientially—to know it for oneself—must, to some degree, motivate all humanist inquiries.

Also back in 1975, the psychoanalytic critic Murray M. Schwartz foresaw the vast migration toward theoretical abstraction that would reshape literary study for the next three decades. In an essay titled "Where Is Literature?" Schwartz pointed out, "All criticism of literature originates in our personal experiences of individual works, and all criticism is a transformation of these experiences. This seems obvious, yet, implicitly or explicitly, it is the most frequently denied or avoided aspect of the professional study of literature." Academics, he said, justified their work by pursuing "impersonal contexts or, in one jargon, 'pretexts' for the interpretation of the texts that matter to individual critics."[25] Five years after Schwartz wrote his essay, Jane Tompkins published her influential collection *Reader-Response Criticism: From Formalism to Post-Structuralism*. Tompkins's overview of the development of reader-response criticism was broad and exciting. She included essays by phenomenologists such as Wolfgang Iser and Georges Poulet, the psychoanalytic critic Norman Holland, and structuralists and poststructuralists such as Stanley Fish, Jonathan Culler, and David Bleich. Some of these essays are now considered classics in reader-response theory.

Subjective criticism, though, was around long before Schwartz's essay or Tompkins's book (as she acknowledges in her introduction). In the wake of T. S. Eliot and the New Criticism in the 1930s and 1940s, in the wake of theory in the 1980s, and now in the wake of "the end of theory" in the early twenty-first century, subjective criticism continues to haunt the margins of literary study. In fact, with our eyes turned toward what comes "after" theory and "post" critique, we are liable to forget that strong advocates for experiential criticism have always been part of the academy, and that sometimes it helps to look back before we leap into the future. In the 1920s and 1930s, critics including I. A. Richards, J. W. Harding, and John Dewey each, in different ways, emphasized that reading was first and foremost about the individual's experience with a particular work. The American scholar Louise Rosenblatt was one of the earliest advocates for subjective criticism. Her *Literature as Exploration*, published in 1936, has been "unfairly neglected" by historians of literary criticism, as Wayne Booth laments in his foreword to the fifth edition.[26] *Literature as Exploration* outlines the importance of the reader's orientation toward the literary work and what Rosenblatt later called the "transactional theory" of reading.[27] It is an accessible, clear-eyed argument for the importance of literary study and close reading in modern democracies.

Rosenblatt and the New Critics started on the same path in the prewar years. Both deplored "the neglect of literature as an art resulting from the traditional preoccupation with literary history and 'the message' of the work."[28] But they parted company in their very different understandings of the nature of art. The New Critics treated the text as an autonomous entity that could be objectively analyzed. Rosenblatt believed that the work was delivered, created, or performed in the event of reading. When a reader or critic adopts what she called an "aesthetic stance," she is focused on what is happening during the act of reading. She "listens to herself" while she reads, paying attention to the associations aroused by words and images. Not all features of a text will penetrate the reader's awareness. Rosenblatt referred to the phenomenon of "selective attention": when we read aesthetically, some features of a text will "have a sharp impact, others will be glossed over or stay on the outer fringes of consciousness."[29] Roland Barthes expressed a similar idea, in *Camera Lucida* (1981), when he wrote about the *studium* and *punctum* of looking at a photograph.[30] The aesthetic stance is requisite in the literary encounter. It is the mode of entry. When someone reads a work of imaginative literature aesthetically, he does not automatically screen out matter he is not going to use. Instead, he pays attention to many things at once—to the particular words in their particular arrangement, to sounds, images, and patterns, even to the physical time and place in which the reading occurs. Barthes, of course, wrote beautifully about the phenomenological aspect of reading in *The Pleasure of the Text* (1973), as did Gaston Bachelard in *The Poetics of Reverie* (1960), how the physical memory of reading certain books may inform our reaction to them over time, and several essays in this book dwell on this kind of reading memory.[31] Unlike New Criticism's edict separating the critic from the reader, or any number of other theoretical approaches, from cultural studies to new historicism, that break up a text and then rearrange it according to a pre-existing filter or code, Rosenblatt urged critics of all persuasions to recognize the personal commitments and desires that enter the reading experience. And so "the critic must begin by being a reader. Paradoxically, the contrary is also true: the reader must be a critic." The reader must accept her responsibility to pay attention to "the second stream of response," that mode of listening, sorting, and selecting that is the province of criticism. But the critic must equally recognize that his formal analysis of a text has its roots in the reading experience itself.[32]

To think and write about Victorian novels is to engage with the past. Scholars who study the nineteenth century are committed to finding new knowledge through the methods of historical research and objective analysis. Yet we also have our own histories with these works. Indeed, as Jonathan Farina puts it in his contribution to this book, "No doubt every novel we reread becomes more about our history with it than about itself." There are a hundred questions anyone could ask about the facts of a novel and its historical situation, a hundred arguments we could make for or against certain interpretations. These things are usually at the front of our minds when we are pursuing scholarship, as they must be. But one of the assumptions of this collection is that whenever we fully engage with a work of art, there is almost always a private intuition that guides the interpretation we publish to others. As we read the Victorian past, through historical studies, archival manuscripts, cultural artifacts, or digital tools, we are also always reading past the words on the page into the present, into our own time, and into our own lives.

This brings me to the unique appeal of rereading and writing about nineteenth-century fiction. Why assemble a collection of subjective essays on the Victorian novel? One reason is that Victorian novels are stories about a time and place that feels long ago and far away, so we can unbend our minds a little. And even with their love for convoluted plots, Victorian novelists do not try to trick the reader, or to be underhanded. I may feel that the Victorian author is wiser, more emotionally aware, more intelligent than I am, but I rarely feel he or she is just being clever for the sake of being clever, like a "dryly cerebral" experimentalist, to quote Zadie Smith.[33] The Victorian novel just wants our love. Some postmodern neo-Victorian novelists take this earnestness as a flaw and try to correct, complicate, or ironize it. Others want actually to *write* Victorian novels because they justly admire the form the Victorians shaped and commanded—psychological realism—and because it is a challenge to construct multiple plots or create a convincing Victorian setting (foggy London, wild heath, cathedral town, ghostly manor house). As Smith notes, "That nineteenth-century English novels continue to be written today with troubling frequency is a tribute to the . . . nostalgia we feel for that noble form."[34]

Victorian novels are also uniquely invitational, the definition of reader-friendly reading. "One reason we idolize the nineteenth-century English novel," Smith argues, "is the way its methods, aims and expression seem so beautifully integrated. Author, characters and reader are all striving in the same direction."[35] Just think of those engaging narrators. "Let us then step into the coach with the Russell Square party," says the narrator of *Vanity Fair*, "and be off to the Gardens. There is barely room between Jos and Miss Sharp, who are on the front seat. Mr. Osborne is sitting bodkin opposite, between Captain Dobbin and Amelia." And off we go, squeezed into the coach to Vauxhall. Anthony Trollope liked to make polite introductions. "The reader must now be requested to visit the rectory of Plumstead Episcopi; and as it is as yet still early morning, to ascend again with us into the bedroom of the archdeacon." "I must ask the reader to make the acquaintance of Major Grantly of Cosby Lodge, before he is introduced to the family of Mr. Crawley, at their parsonage in Hogglestock." "We will now pay a visit to the John in question,—a certain Mr. John Eames, living in London, a bachelor, as the intelligent reader will certainly have discovered, and cousin to Miss Grace Crawley." It is great pleasure to be secreted into people's bedrooms and private chambers this way. "I have been pressing my elbows on the arms of my chair, and dreaming that I was standing on the bridge in front of Dorlcote Mill, as it looked one February afternoon many years ago," says our storyteller. "Before I dozed off, I was going to tell you what Mr. and Mrs. Tulliver were talking about, as they sat by the bright fire in the left-hand parlor, on that very afternoon I have been dreaming of."[36] We turn the page and there we are, in the left-hand parlor by the bright fire, listening to Mr. Tulliver talk to Tom about his education. Some people find this technique contrived or cloying, but I wonder if even the coolest readers do not feel a flutter of interest and pleasure. All we have to do listen and imagine: we are being told *a story*.

One thing Victorian novelists never apologize for is the strength of their imaginations. Generally speaking, the Victorian novelist has unquestioned faith in the power of language to bring about a new and concrete reality. Writers such as Eliot and Dickens respect the reader's imaginative hunger and the need for pleasure, but they also require from us some understanding of human psychology and of how society is organized. The Victorian novelist knows how to deploy suspense and to work on our feelings while also communicating an implicit desire for order and for empathy. As contributor Ellen Rosenman confesses in her essay here, the intelligent pleasures of Victorian fiction can be seductive. The length, the language, the intricate plots, the melodrama and suspense, the piling on of detail, the sense of visiting the past—all of these features still possess great appeal for people who like getting lost in a book. Reading *Jane Eyre* for a class she was teaching, says Rosenman, felt like something she would do on vacation; she converted to Victorian literature in midcareer because of the irresistible delight she discovered reading these compelling narratives.

The Victorian novel is indeed irreducible and manifold. It is a form that springs from a time of immense and rapid change, variety, experimentation, and excitement, as well as democratic struggle, moral questioning, and the serious soul-searching triggered by Darwinian theory and other intellectual and material developments. "The history of thought from 1830 on, religious thought, in particular," Walter Houghton pointed out in the 1950s in *The Victorian Frame of Mind*, "is a history of successive blows," as people were exposed to "a constant succession of shattering developments."[37] The important changes in the way human beings were learning to understand themselves and their society were recorded and processed through stories by the very serious artists the nineteenth century produced. So another reason to write about the Victorian novel, outside of the pleasure factor, is that these fictions dramatize how a newly industrialized, democratic, and imperialist society was getting to be arranged, and how individuals experienced the anxieties, triumphs, and injustices of an important era in European social history. And although many of the essays here are about the satisfactions offered by Victorian novels, several recognize the unsettling complexities of nineteenth-century global politics, or see our own world reflected in the blindness or ambition of the Victorians, as well as in the efforts Victorian people made toward resistance, understanding, or sympathy. The midcentury giants who predominate in this collection looked squarely at the quotidian reality of modern society, at servants and sewers, at politics, money, and death. There is usually a dark psychic alley of guilt, loss, or pain that winds its own maze into the narrative, sometimes circling back into the light of closure, sometimes remaining in the background of crime or sexual violence or empire. The Victorian novel sometimes seems like a shallow place, all melodrama and surface, but it has unsuspected depths. Henry James called the mid-Victorian novel a "large loose baggy monster." My own metaphor would be a deep and echoing well, a black tunnel, or a collective psychic reservoir. The Victorian novel is full of modern reverberations, unpleasant realities that needle and pull at the reader, undermining merely abstract or theoretical readings.

In his 1980 study of the period, William E. Buckler observed that in Victorian fiction "[a]ll the human negatives are there: ignorance, poverty, violence, injustice, grossly outmoded institutions, bullishly inept politicians, the decay of spiritual coherence, an explosive tension between the individual and the group, the failure of privilege to assume responsibility, the aggressive determination of incompetence to take over the future." This is a good list, a sadly familiar list. For as Buckler observes, these things "are there . . . because they are always there." Victorian novelists wanted to entertain and delight their contemporaries, but they also felt responsible to respond to or intervene in the concerns of their age, which they knew were "real, individual, threatening, demanding urgent attention," as Buckler claimed, and had to be "dealt with in a real manner that touches real need."[38] A function of the Victorian novel was to humanize the systemic problems of mid-nineteenth-century capitalism. As the philosopher and novelist Iris Murdoch observed, the "nineteenth-century novel . . . was not concerned with 'the human condition', it was concerned with real various individuals struggling in society."[39] (In a mildly disputable generalization, Murdoch also said, "The most obvious difference between nineteenth-century novels and twentieth-century novels is that the nineteenth-century ones are better.")[40] Another philosopher, Richard Rorty, has argued that a novelist such as Dickens was radical not because he had a plan for transforming his society but because he forced his readers "to notice and understand the people they passed on the street."[41] Victorian fiction's commitment to individuals, the overlooked detail and the overlooked person, remains ethically relevant. It is a commitment that underscores and validates the subjective involvement of the contributors to this book, as well as the work they do as teachers of literature.

It may seem counterintuitive to look back to the middle of the twentieth century to get a grip on the nineteenth. Yet intellectuals writing fifty or sixty years ago thought hard about the place of literature in modern society in ways that arguably are parallel to Victorian concerns about the domination of the human subject by social systems and the importance of art and the imagination in people's moral education. Lionel Trilling, especially, wrote astutely about the nineteenth-century sensibility and what had changed by the middle of the twentieth. Trilling argued that for the Victorians, a new novel by Dickens or Thackeray was really an event, not only because it was a form of entertainment, comparable to the latest blockbuster on Netflix or in the cinema, but because the novel showed people their society from a human angle that was overtly moral and didactic, rich in specificities and in problems the reader had to work through. In a 1967 essay, and I quote at length, Trilling wrote:

> Novels are still ceaselessly written, published, reviewed, and on occasion hailed, but the old sense of their spiritual efficacy is ever harder to come by. One thing is certain: to whatever purposes the novel now addresses itself, it has outgrown the activity which, in the nineteenth century and in the early days of the twentieth, was characteristic of the genre, virtually definitive of it, the setting of the values of moral and spiritual life over against the values of the world. This is a confrontation that no longer engages our interest. Which is by no means to say that getting and spending are not of great moment, or that moral and spiritual sensibility have declined. As to the latter, indeed, it flourishes in a way that is unprecedented—it may well be that never before have so many people undertaken to live enlightened lives, to see through the illusion that society imposes, doing this quite easily, without strain or struggle, having been led to the perception of righteousness by

> what literature has told them of social life. Whatever we may do as persons in the world, however we behave as getters and spenders, in our other capacity, as readers, as persons of moral sensibility, we know that the values of the world do not deserve our interest. We know it: we do not discover it, as readers once did, with the pleasure and excitement that the novel generated as it led toward understanding.[42]

Writers have been warning people about the snares of worldly vanities since John Bunyan's *The Pilgrim's Progress* (1678)—a keynote for Thackeray. But the industrial revolution filled Western culture with such unprecedented bounty, offered so much to some while depriving so many others, that a moral sea change occurred before most ordinary individuals could process how the old values were shifting. Something was interfering with the individual's quest for moral and spiritual meaning. *Machinery*, for some Victorian thinkers, was anything that replaced an ideal of human growth, variety, and vitality with something shallow, formulaic, or fake. Thomas Carlyle's "Mammonism" and "Gigmania," Matthew Arnold's "Philistinism," and John Ruskin's "Goddess of Getting-on" all are attacks on the new tendency to value things over human welfare. So Arnold explicitly attached the meaning of "culture" to *being* and *becoming*, and called it "an inward working." In his social criticism, Ruskin repeatedly asserted the value of *being* over *having*: "There is no Wealth but Life." In chapter 3 of *On Liberty*, J. S. Mill wrote, "Human nature is not a machine to be built after a model, and set to do exactly the work prescribed for it, but a tree, which requires to grow and develop itself on all sides, according to the tendency of the inward forces which make it a living thing." Oscar Wilde valued the contemplative life precisely because it is "the life that has for its aim not *doing* but *being*, and not *being* merely, but *becoming*—that is what the critical spirit can give us."[43] These writers deeply understood the modern situation, the intimidating encroachments of mechanization, materialism, abstract theorizing, and social incohesion. They saw the accumulated effects of dehumanization and indifference upon an individual's sense of unique, animate involvement in the everyday world. The overarching theme of many Victorian novels is just this human battle with machinery.

If we have been lucky enough to be born in the middle of the twentieth century, we already know these things, we know it all, we know even too much. We know that material and worldly values are superficial, that capitalist ideology has made those values the only values; we know about neoliberalism's failures; we know that socialization goes all the way down; we know about gender and class ideology, about surveillance and institutional control of the individual subject, just as we know, too, that there is no individual subject. Maybe as scholars we have been a little too knowing?

Lisa Ruddick describes how the most influential scholarship of the past few decades, in its skepticism about liberal individualism, has mistakenly "questioned the ideals of the inner life," or else taught students to "adopt a neutral historicist voice that allows them to handle the inner life—someone else's—as a historicist curiosity, without attributing value to it."[44] Along similar lines, in his 2017 book on the political history of literary criticism, Joseph North argues that after rejecting the New Critics, the Left's concern with "diagnosing" culture ended up undermining efforts to transform it. In the mid-twentieth century, before the neoliberal radicalization of the academy, the study of literature, says North, was part of "the cultivation of aesthetic sensibility, with the goal of more general cultural and political change." But the hermeneutics of suspicion and the dismantling of the idea of a free subject have made the humanistic study of literature (once called, quaintly, "literature appreciation") difficult to justify. North argues that the academic study of literature, as it manifests now in US colleges and universities, may function as a "test case" for an important social question, that of "how and to what extent the societies in which we live allow us to cultivate deeper modes of life."[45]

Trilling, of course, is right. We cannot read a Victorian novel the way a Victorian reader did. For we know too much in other ways. Compared to the world of a middle-class reader settling down with the next installment of *Dombey and Son*, we live in a media-saturated world, inside a never-ending tidal wave of reports of incomprehensible cruelty and injustice, unavoidable images of global misery and environmental catastrophe. And yet, the essays in *My Victorian Novel* reveal how much some Victorian authors knew that we have yet to discover. They created compelling and powerful stories that have endured for nearly two centuries out of the chaos they saw when they held up art's mirror to the modern world. Trying to stay human and nourish an inner life in the face of suffering, injustice, poverty, and oppression is something we may have a slightly better grasp upon from reading the stories Victorian writers created to help expose and combat these things, as best they could. Almost every Victorian novel I can think of is about characters who are struggling to live the life that is inside of them.

What about activism in the academy and the value of objectivity and research? What will be the role of digital humanities in expanding humanistic knowledge? What about historicism and cultural studies? And what about theory? I would never suggest that these approaches or methodologies do not count as scholarship or contribute to knowledge in a given field. I would, especially, never say that theory does not belong in an English class. Theory is what taught me to think. When I was in graduate school in the mid-1980s, it was the heyday of theory, and it was life-changing for me. I unearthed my notebooks from those years recently and was impressed (and maybe appalled) at how *much* theory I had to read. All the important names are there: Jameson, Lukács, Culler, Bakhtin, Benjamin, Barthes, Said, Fish, Foucault. I duly recorded that for a structuralist, "the author must be assumed, because the text didn't spring up like a mushroom, but you just don't get into his human beingness," and noted that Paul de Man believed "the grammarization of rhetoric leads to some kind of truth, but the rhetorization of grammar leads to uncertainty" and that Terry Eagleton was "a Neo-Orthodox Marxist interested in the fabrication of a cultural product, not values or excellence of writing." I had no preparation for the sophistication of these thinkers, absolutely none. At my undergraduate university, I was taught the canon, and that was that. I found these theorists simply mind-blowing. They proposed complex, fascinating answers to questions that intrigued me—about how to define literature, about how to read, and most of all about why studying and writing about literature matters.

In the mid-1980s, the looming job market generated enough panic that I sent my work out very prematurely. When I tried to publish articles on Victorian fiction as a graduate student, I hit a wall of rejections. I had not really internalized theory or the critical methodology that was required to publish professionally. I had simply never been taught to read literature this way before graduate school. One referee for an article wrote that I needed to tie my idea "to a more comprehensive theoretical framework" and suggested Lacan or Cixous. Another wrote that my essay "was really discussing a semiotics of the body" and that I should have read Mary

Douglas and Michel Foucault. Yet another remarked, "The problems of this essay reside in a certain lack of complexity and theorization. There is a tendency here to treat characters as people." For an insecure graduate student, this was the worst kind of put-down. It implied I was a naïve reader, not only theoretically unsophisticated but the kind of reader who, consciously or subconsciously, became personally involved with characters' unfolding personalities, as if I were seeking some kind of relationship with the author or hoping to bring the story into some relevance with my own life. I needed to learn to back away, to think of characters as linguistic constructs, sociological types, or bourgeois subjects—not as real people.

But there were other critical models, other theories about reading that I did not stumble upon until later. In *The Disappearance of God*, published in 1963, J. Hillis Miller expounded, "Criticism demands above all that gift of participation, that power to put oneself within the life of another person. . . . If literature is a form of consciousness the task of the critic is to identify himself with the subjectivity expressed in the words, to relive that life from the inside, and to constitute it anew in his criticism."[46] Thirty years later, after his conversion to deconstruction, Miller had not changed his basic ideas about critical reading. "The reader who sees the text as merely language is not being a competent reader," he argued. "To read a novel properly is to allow oneself to be taken in by the characters, to think of them as if they were real persons, and to speak or write of them as such."[47] The essays included here by Catherine Robson and Deborah Denenholz Morse suggest that treating characters as people is what ropes us into a novel to begin with. Miller's advocacy of "intersubjectivity," a fundamentally accepting critical position, was somewhat out of step by the 1980s and 1990s, the era of the resisting reader and of an explosive new field called cultural studies.[48] In my theory classes, no one wanted to talk about reader-response or the long and respected tradition of subjective criticism initiated by Dewey, Richards, and Rosenblatt. Wayne Booth's work on the ethics of reading also seemed to have lost its authority in those decades. Academia has its fashions and trends, yet some of Booth's justifications and arguments are worth revisiting. In *The Company We Keep*, Booth explained that "a kind of play-acting with characters, or characteristics, a kind of faking of characters, is one of the main ways that we build what becomes our characters. . . . The ideal of purging oneself of responses to persons, the ideal of refusing to play the human roles offered us by literature, is never realized by any actual reader who reads a compelling fiction for the sake of reading it."[49] This release of the self into the fictional world is a very precious ability. Why would we want to discipline or outgrow it? In this one way, perhaps, we might mirror the Victorian reader, for whom, according to Kate Flint, "[r]eading fiction, an activity which combined flexing the imagination with anticipating and reacting to the dynamics of a range of narratives, was a vicarious means of inhabiting other lives, and, potentially, changing one's own."[50]

For Flint and Booth, reading a novel takes stamina. It is a supremely participatory act. Virginia Woolf wrote that "to read a novel is a difficult and complex art. You must be capable not only of great fineness of perception, but of great boldness of imagination if you are going to make use of all that the novelist—the great artist—gives you."[51] But as we all know, it can be hard at times to keep our minds and imaginations awake, refreshed, and well exercised. There are professional pressures, for one thing (publish or perish, they used to say). Then again, Victorian novels are *so* long, *so* descriptive and full of detail, we tend to screen out what we are not going to use in a lecture or a conference paper, perhaps more so in each subsequent reading. Reiterative reading itself can be a liability. Patricia Meyer Spacks observes that "people who teach literature reread the same texts again and again, and get paid for it." That is a blunt job description, and close to reality. There are great rewards in being a professional rereader, but there are also occupational hazards: hubris, smugness, boredom, an attitude of complacency. "As we encounter the same text again and again, it comes to inhabit the deep reaches of the brain," Spacks contends. "Repetition generates belief. Rereading, by virtue of its repetitions, can provide its practitioner with the illusion that she has total possession of a text."[52]

The essays in this collection, each in a different way, try to unmask that pose of total possession. For as every writer here confesses, even when we have written about and taught a novel repeatedly, objectively, in terms of social facts, ideology, biography, theory, or history, it may still feel strange and ungraspable, familiar yet unknown. Our work as readers and critics may be not to master the work but rather to "deepen its mystery," in Wilde's wonderful phrase. Going back to the same works over many years leaves an imprint. Of course it does. For many people outside the academy, to claim that a relationship with literature over the years enriches and deepens a life is simply a given. The popularity of reading memoirs is a celebration of this belief, as is that of books by scholars written for general audiences about the continued relevance of canonical works.[53] To be able to reflect with intellectual curiosity and emotional wonder on the reading experience may be the most important qualification for a literary critic. And encouraging a similar habit of reflection in others may be the most essential thing we do as teachers of literature.

To study a text in its social contexts, as historians or sociologists do, or as a document to be correlated with other evidence concerning the structure of language, or as part of an author's biography produces valuable knowledge. *My Victorian Novel* in no way denigrates such interests. But when these concerns predominate, as Rosenblatt would say, the scholar is functioning not as a literary critic but as a linguist, a historian, a biographer, a sociologist, an archivist. "The term 'literary critic' should be reserved for one whose primary subject is his aesthetic transaction with the text; he reflects on the work of art he has evoked," she asserts. In the first quarter of the twentieth-first century, this sounds like a very conservative definition of literary criticism, and it would disqualify many critical practices today. Yet Rosenblatt's definition is a useful one, and it is a controlling idea behind the fifteen essays here. The classification and analysis of the elements of a text can produce interesting data. But for Rosenblatt, and for the authors here, the data that really matter are "individual personal encounters with texts."[54]

Historicism and cultural studies are here to stay—indeed, every contributor to this book has worked under those critical flags. But maybe a certain tone in criticism is on the wane, one that used to appear in readings of Victorian novels as cultural artifacts like any other or in works that looked for clues to their complicity with capitalism, imperialism, racism, or misogyny. We are now allowed to talk about what these novels have given to us, how they have both challenged and comforted us. Murdoch thought the nineteenth-century novel possessed "a great consoling power . . . a deep relaxing of tension, however alarming or horrible the events which are narrated, because of a sense of the strength of society, and of politics as a natural and ordinary part of the human scene."[55] Whether or not you agree with Murdoch—maybe no work of fiction can adequately address, let alone relax, the tensions of twenty-first-century life—the authorial confidence of the Victorian novel may allow even the anxious modern reader to fall under the trance of the storyteller.

Traditional scholarly writing has its own excitements, and an academic stance structures or informs some of the essays here. But overall the mood is permissive, deliberately so. The open-ended nature of this collection means that not all the authors will engage with their novels in the same way. If there is an underlying theme anchoring these essays, it may be expressed in two simple claims: first, that elements of autobiography have always been part of literary criticism, and second, that writing well about a work of literature is not a science but a truly creative act and a uniquely challenging art form.

Some essays here are built around memories of reading and of growing up with an important novel. Andrea Kaston Tange writes about reading *Jane Eyre* as a child and again as a teenager, and then reexamining her idolization of the heroine when she came to teach the novel to undergraduates. Her changing relationship with *Jane Eyre* is tied to the reframing of feminism over the decades and her understanding that there is no pure or unproblematically heroic feminist politics. Similarly, Deborah Denenholz Morse reflects on her forty-year relationship with *The Duke's Children* and especially her growing sympathy for Lady Glencora. Trollope's novel has become, for Morse, a meditation on mourning, loss, and compromise, as well as a celebration of commitment. Now nearing seventy, she finds that her past readings have, inescapably, become a crucial part of every new reading of the Palliser novels. In his reflection on discovering the Sherlock Holmes stories as a child, Terrance Riley describes how an entirely new way of being in the world was revealed to him. Conan Doyle's hero modeled values and behaviors Riley could see nowhere when he was growing up in Flint, Michigan—curiosity, skepticism, a fascination with science. There existed in the Holmes stories a confident moral environment he was intuitively drawn toward, and it belonged to a faraway land called "England," with its native dispositions toward civility, formality, progress, and fair play.

There are also stories of therapeutic or reparative reading. On the evening of September 11, 2001, So Young Park, then a graduate student in New York City, began rereading *The Newcomes*. Thackeray's 1,144-page tome took her to another world and offered mental sanctuary during a time of extreme turbulence and uncertainty. Through *The Newcomes*, Park began to see how all the threads of her identities—as literature teacher, Korean daughter, and budding Victorianist—could be brought into productive play. For Beverley Park Rilett, *Middlemarch* is the touchstone, the one book she keeps returning to for lessons about the need for sympathy, a reminder about the inscrutability of other people, and even of our own motives. Another Eliot novel, *Daniel Deronda*, represents the mystery at the center of all our reading encounters in Ellen Rosenman's essay. Precisely because this novel falls within the tradition of realism, *Daniel Deronda*'s dislocating representations of human experience have forced Rosenman to rethink the so-called pleasures of reading and the ethical demands that cling to all our reading and to our personal relationships. Sara Malton offers a similar scene of disquieting reading. She implicitly asks why *The Return of the Native*, once so formative to her identity as a scholar, has been impossible for her to reread until now.

Some essays blend academic-style close reading with personal reflection. Jonathan Farina's dissection of the language of exchange in *Vanity Fair* is linked to his own memories of growing up as a stockbroker's son in New York City. It is a lively and perceptive study of the way small talk moves each of us along from day to day in a diverse and competitive world. Similarly, Mary-Catherine Harrison writes about the dissonance she has felt as a Quaker dedicated to activism and social justice and also a teacher of literature, where real-world change feels removed or aestheticized. Her research on the geographical divisions among middle-class and working-class people in Victorian Manchester in Gaskell's *North and South* uneasily reflects her experience of working in Detroit but living in Ann Arbor. In her essay on *Bleak House*, Catherine Robson explores Dickens's depiction of erotic relations, framed around general questions about the ways certain people read novels, and also how they imagine their lives. For Robson, uncovering how Dickens's ninth novel presents the connections between sex and life turns out to be a deeply personal endeavor, not just for herself but, potentially, for all of us.

Other contributors consider how they feel when reading Victorian fiction in the twenty-first century, and especially when teaching Victorian novels to the younger generation. There is a strange sensation of *déjà vu* when we teach a novel that we first read when we were the same age as our current students. Michael J. Flynn asks why his first encounter with *David Copperfield* in college was so different from that of his students. When he first experienced Dickens's novel in the early 1990s, he responded to the emotional cues; his students, though, pick up almost exclusively on the proleptic cues. Flynn's essay ultimately asks what a life story like *David Copperfield* means to Americans living in the age of social media. Similarly, Tom Ue observes how difficult it can be for undergraduates to figure out whose side they are on in Gissing's *New Grub Street*, that of the pragmatic and successful Jasper Milvain or of the suffering idealists Reardon and Biffen, who sacrifice their lives for their art. Ue, an enthusiastic Gissing-ite, shows how a novel of the 1890s anticipates, and uneasily reflects, an utterly twenty-first-century phenomenon: the commercialization of everything.

There are some "inside academia" stories in this collection, too, about the dramas of graduate school and the job search, the insecurities and anxieties, the dreams and frustrations. A particular novel can, literally, shape the trajectory of an entire career. Lillian Nayder tells a story about being a doctoral research assistant. Her unpaid labor on *The Pickwick Papers* left her feeling exploited, but her editorial assignment also set the path for a very successful career as a Dickens scholar. Nayder addresses the challenges she faced, as a young woman scholar, in finding a way into Dickens's novel, which is itself about an exclusively male club. Her experiences of intellectual benefit and also academic exploitation are very closely tied to the subject matter of *Pickwick*. Bram Stoker's *Dracula* is perhaps a rather peculiar favorite, but for Narin Hassan, it is the novel that opened up the Victorian world, led her to choose it as her focus, and inspired her scholarship in areas such as the body and reproduction, Victorian medicine, postcolonial studies, and how spiritual and supernatural practices were filtered through scientific rationality. A practicing instructor of yoga and meditation, Hassan also explores *Dracula* through the lens of contemporary Western fascination with Eastern spiritual and philosophical systems and modern theories of energy and the body. As Hassan ponders her feelings of displacement as the only child of Pakistani diplomats, *Dracula* also becomes a reflection of late-Victorian and contemporary anxieties about foreign peoples and spaces.

Some beloved names are, alas, missing from this collection: Wilkie Collins, Mary Elizabeth Braddon, George Meredith, Robert Louis Stevenson, Lewis Carroll, and New Woman novelists such as Mona Caird, Sarah Grand, and Olive Schreiner. But this is still a pretty diverse group of novels, and they came together without my design, interference, or premeditation. Quite by accident, no two contributors had the same favorite novel, showing how truly individual even a trained literary taste can be. The habit of studious reading is everywhere apparent in these contributions, yet all the scholars here wear their learning lightly. Maybe the most daring thing about these essays is their reluctance to keep the work at arm's length, to situate it (as we are always told to do) and screw it into a frame. Is this a backward move toward phenomenology or reader-response, or a retreat to a less aggressive kind of criticism, maybe even a politically irresponsible kind?

Eve Kosofsky Sedgwick proposes a critical practice that could take its place beside suspicious reading, one that would permit openness to affective responses, to an expression of need, or to a desire for connection. The problem, Sedgwick argues, is not that critics do not read from the "reparative position," for we do, all the time—affective reading is just as attached to concepts of freedom, justice, and survival as ideologically driven readings, and just as eager for knowledge of the world and of human actions. But we lack a critical vocabulary of reparative reading, and we definitely lack some good models of critical reparative *writing*. "The vocabulary for articulating any reader's reparative motive toward a text or a culture has long been so sappy, aestheticizing, defensive, anti-intellectual, or reactionary that it's no wonder few critics are willing to describe their acquaintance with such motives," she says. Yet if critics embrace such practices, we may learn "the many ways selves and communities succeed in extracting sustenance from the objects of a culture."[56]

I do not think that embracing the complex pleasures of reading Victorian fiction and writing about that reading experience is delinquent, quietist, or misguided.[57] On the contrary, I believe it is radically sane and enlightened. I came to this conclusion after reading one of the most important books in my life, Eliot's *Middlemarch*. Among other truths, *Middlemarch* taught me that the "best piety is to enjoy—when you can. You are doing the most then to save the earth's character as an agreeable planet. And enjoyment radiates. It is of no use to try and take care of all the world; that is being taken care of when you feel delight—in art or in anything else."[58]

But now, like Will Ladislaw, I feel I have been impetuous and have gone further than I intended. So, to conclude: the essays here describe a criticism that has its roots in the unfolding relationship between the reader and the book she holds in her hands—in the first moment of contact, in studying and in teaching, and in the ongoing and mysterious presence of a treasured work in the equally mysterious process of living out a life. This is not something that happens in isolation. Talking about our reading lives is communal and ethically meaningful. Almost sixty years ago, Rosenblatt wrote that the reader of a work of literature is "engaged in a creative process at once intensely personal, since the [text] is something lived through, and intensely social, since the text . . . can be shared with others."[59] By inviting critics to share their experiences with one special novel, without the pressure of an analytical agenda, the sociable essays here may restore vitality to the act of literary criticism, and in turn welcome more people to talk about how the stories they have lived through over time have enchanted and transformed them.

## NOTES

1. *Oxford English Dictionary* online, s.v. "essay," https://www.oed.com/view/Entry/64470?rskey=AaUGEM&result=1#eid.
2. Ruth-Ellen Boetcher Joeres, "Found in the Details: Essaying the Particular," 111, 116.
3. Verlyn Klinkenborg, "Frank Kermode," *New York Times*, August 20, 2010, A20.
4. Vladimir Nabokov, *Lectures on Literature*, ed. Fredson Bowers (New York: Harcourt Brace, 1980), 4–5.
5. As does Boetcher Joeres, who admits that she almost immediately gravitates there. "Found in the Details," 113.
6. Nabokov, *Lectures on Literature*, 4.
7. Rita Felski, *The Limits of Critique*, 173; see also Felski's earlier manifesto, *Uses of Literature*.
8. Deidre Shauna Lynch and Evelyne Ender, "Introduction: Time for Reading," 1076.
9. Stephen Benson and Clare Connors, eds., *Creative Criticism: An Anthology and Guide*, 3. Benson and Connors cite sources that deploy the terms "postcriticism, deformative criticism, anarcho-scholasticism, fictio-criticism, visionary criticism" (2). I recommend their anthology for a variety of creative models. They also include a bibliography of twentieth- and twenty-first century works of creative criticism and works about creative criticism.
10. Amy J. Elias, "Context Rocks!," 582, 580.
11. Rebecca Solnit, "Woolf's Darkness: Embracing the Inexplicable," 93.
12. Solnit, "Woolf's Darkness," 93–94.
13. Peter J. Rabinowitz, "Sedimental Education; or, Reading as We Age," 662.
14. See Zadie Smith, *Changing My Mind*; J. C. Hallman, *B. and Me*; Anne Fadiman, *Ex Libris: Confessions of a Common Reader*; Geoff Dyer, *Out of Sheer*

*Rage: Wrestling with D. H. Lawrence*; Susan Howe, *My Emily Dickinson*; Anne Carson, *Eros the Bittersweet*; Ali Smith, *Artful*; Margaret Atwood, *Negotiating with the Dead: A Writer on Writing*; James Wood, *The Broken Estate: Essays on Literature and Belief*.

15. Jane Tompkins, *Reading through the Night*, 97. Tompkins has previously questioned "culturally legitimate sources of knowledge," most notably in the essay "Me and My Shadow" (quoted here, 171) and in her memoir *A Life in School: What the Teacher Learned*.

16. The mission statements of almost all English departments show this to be true. For a thorough unpacking of the practice and history of critical reading, see Michael Warner, "Uncritical Reading."

17. Jane Tompkins argues eloquently for this approach to teaching literature in "Speak, Memory."

18. Eve Kosofsky Sedgwick, "Teaching 'Experimental Critical Writing'"; Angelika Bammer, "Tribal Rites: Academic-Speak and the Promise of Belonging," 62–63; Jane Rendell, "Foreword: L'avant-coup," xx; An Paenhuysen, course description, https://nodecenter.net/course/creative-art-writing.

19. Elias, "Context Rocks!," 585.

20. Angelika Bammer and Ruth-Ellen Boetcher Joeres, eds., *The Future of Scholarly Writing*, 2.

21. Juliana Spahr, Mark Wallace, Kristin Prevallet, and Pam Rehm, eds., *A Poetics of Criticism*, 7.

22. Adam Phillips, *Side Effects*, xi–xv.

23. David Bleich, *Readings and Feelings: An Introduction to Subjective Criticism*, 3–4. Some material in the following paragraphs has appeared in slightly different form in my *Engagements with Close Reading* (Routledge, 2016), chap. 3.

24. David Bleich, *Subjective Criticism*, 297–98.

25. Murray M. Schwartz, "Where Is Literature?," 50.

26. Wayne Booth, foreword to *Literature as Exploration*, by Louise Rosenblatt, vii.

27. Louise Rosenblatt, *The Reader, the Text, the Poem: The Transactional Theory of the Literary Work*. For Rosenblatt, the reader's mental and emotional bearing when experiencing any work of written communication helps to determine its status and its meaning. She identified two positions in *Literature as Exploration*. The *efferent* stance (from the Latin *efferre*, to carry away) is primarily involved with analyzing and summarizing what the reader wants to retain after reading. Attention tends to be focused outward, on how the information in the reading material will be put to use. In the *aesthetic* stance the reader is focused on what is happening during the act of reading.

28. Rosenblatt, *Literature as Exploration*, 289.

29. Rosenblatt, *The Reader, the Text*, 25, 167.

30. Roland Barthes, *Camera Lucida: Reflections on Photography*, trans. Richard Howard, 25–27.

31. Roland Barthes, *The Pleasure of the Text*, trans. Richard Miller; Gaston Bachelard, *The Poetics of Reverie: Childhood, Language, and the Cosmos*, trans. Daniel Russell.

32. Rosenblatt, *The Reader, the Text*, 137.

33. Zadie Smith, "*Middlemarch* and Everybody," 40.

34. Smith, "*Middlemarch* and Everybody," 40.

35. Smith, "*Middlemarch* and Everybody," 33.

36. W. M. Thackeray, *Vanity Fair*, 52; Anthony Trollope, *The Warden*, 63; Anthony Trollope, *The Last Chronicle of Barset*, 19, 140; George Eliot, *The Mill on the Floss*, 8.

37. Walter Houghton, *The Victorian Frame of Mind, 1830–1870*, 67.

38. William E. Buckler, *The Victorian Imagination: Essays in Aesthetic Exploration*, 7.

39. Iris Murdoch, "Against Dryness," 291.

40. Iris Murdoch, "Existentialists and Mystics," 221.

41. Richard Rorty, "Heidegger, Kundera, and Dickens," 78.

42. Lionel Trilling, "James Joyce in His Letters," in *The Moral Obligation to Be Intelligent: Selected Essays*, ed. Leon Wieseltier, 454 (New York: Farrar, Straus & Giroux, 2000).

43. Matthew Arnold, *Culture and Anarchy*, 209; John Ruskin, "Unto This Last," 270; J. S. Mill, *On Liberty*, 87; Oscar Wilde, "The Critic as Artist," 384.

44. Lisa Ruddick, "When Nothing Is Cool," 73.

45. Joseph North, *Literary Criticism: A Concise Political History*, 3, vii.

46. J. Hillis Miller, *The Disappearance of God*, vi.

47. J. Hillis Miller, *Ariadne's Thread: Repetition and the Narrative Line*, 117.

48. Miller, *Disappearance of God*, vi.

49. Wayne Booth, *The Company We Keep: An Ethics of Fiction*, 252, 255–56.

50. Kate Flint, "The Victorian Novel and Its Readers," 31.

51. Virginia Woolf, "How Should One Read a Book?," 260–61.

52. Patricia Meyer Spacks, *On Rereading*, 163.

53. There are many reading memoirs and books about the power of reading: Phyllis Rose's *The Year of Reading Proust: A Memoir in Real Time* (Washington, DC: Counterpoint, 1997); Wendy Lesser's *Nothing Remains the Same: Rereading and Remembering* (New York: Houghton Mifflin, 2002); several by Anne Fadiman, including her edited collection *Rereadings: Seventeen Writers Revisit Works They Love* (New York: Farrar, Straus & Giroux, 2005); Rebecca Mead's *My Life in "Middlemarch"* (New York: Crown, 2014); Ann Bogel's *I'd Rather Be Reading: The Delights and Dilemmas of the Reading Life* (Grand Rapids: Baker, 2018); Jane Tompkins's *Reading through the Night* (2018); and Katharine Smyth's *All the Lives We Ever Lived: Seeking Solace in Virginia Woolf* (New York: Crown, 2019). Nathaniel Philbrick's *Why Read "Moby-Dick"?* (New York: Penguin, 2011); Andrew Kaufman's *Give "War and Peace" a Chance: Tolstoyan Wisdom for Troubled Times* (New York: Simon & Schuster, 2014); and Anne Boyd Rioux's *Meg,*

*Jo, Beth, Amy: The Story of "Little Women" and Why It Still Matters* (New York: W. W. Norton, 2018) defend the continued relevance of three nineteenth-century classics.

54. Rosenblatt, *The Reader, the Text*, 162, 174–75.

55. Murdoch, "Existentialists and Mystics," 222.

56. Eve Kosofsky Sedgwick, *Touching Feeling: Affect, Pedagogy, Performativity*, 150–51. Michael Warner notes that Sedgwick's "reparative reading seems to be defined less by any project of its own than by its recoil from a manically programmatic intensification of the critical. It is not so much a method as a (principled?) avoidance of method." "Uncritical Reading," 18.

57. "You do this kind of work simply because it's the kind of work that you like to do, and the moment you think you're doing it to make either people or the world better, you've made a huge mistake. There's no justification whatsoever for what we do except the pleasure of doing it and the possibility of introducing others to that pleasure. That's it!" Stanley Fish, quoted in Mark Bauerlein, "A Solitary Thinker."

58. George Eliot, *Middlemarch*, ed. Bert Hornback, 140.

59. Louise Rosenblatt, "The Poem as Event," 126.

## WORKS CITED

Arnold, Matthew. *Culture and Anarchy*. Cambridge: Cambridge University Press, 1993.

Atwood, Margaret. *Negotiating with the Dead: A Writer on Writing*. New York: Anchor, 2002.

Bachelard, Gaston. *The Poetics of Reverie: Childhood, Language, and the Cosmos*. 1960. Translated by Daniel Russell. Boston: Beacon Press, 1971.

Bammer, Angelika. "Tribal Rites: Academic-Speak and the Promise of Belonging." In *The Future of Scholarly Writing*, edited by Angelika Bammer and Ruth-Ellen Boetcher Joeres, 57–70. London: Palgrave Macmillan, 2015.

Bammer, Angelika, and Ruth-Ellen Boetcher Joeres, eds. *The Future of Scholarly Writing*. London: Palgrave Macmillan, 2015.

Barthes, Roland. *Camera Lucida: Reflections on Photography*. Translated by Richard Howard. New York: Hill & Wang, 1981.

———. *The Pleasure of the Text*. 1973. Translated by Richard Miller. New York: Hill & Wang, 1975.

Bauerlein, Mark. "A Solitary Thinker." *Chronicle of Higher Education*, May 15, 2011. https://www.chronicle.com/article/A-Solitary-Thinker/127464/.

Benson, Stephen, and Clare Connors, eds. *Creative Criticism: An Anthology and Guide*. Edinburgh: University of Edinburgh Press, 2014.

Bleich, David. *Readings and Feelings: An Introduction to Subjective Criticism*. Urbana: National Council of Teachers of English, 1975.

———. *Subjective Criticism*. Baltimore: Johns Hopkins University Press, 1972.

Boetcher Joeres, Ruth-Ellen. "Found in the Details: Essaying the Particular." In *The Future of Scholarly Writing*, edited by Angelika Bammer and Ruth-Ellen Boetcher Joeres, 111–26. London: Palgrave Macmillan, 2015.

Booth, Wayne. *The Company We Keep: An Ethics of Fiction*. Berkeley: University of California Press, 1988.

———. Foreword to *Literature as Exploration*, 5th ed., by Louise Rosenblatt, vii–xiv. New York: Modern Language Association, 1995.

Buckler, William E. *The Victorian Imagination: Essays in Aesthetic Exploration*. New York: New York University Press, 1980.

Carson, Anne. *Eros the Bittersweet*. Toronto: Dalkey Archive, 1998.

Dyer, Geoff. *Out of Sheer Rage: Wrestling with D. H. Lawrence*. New York: Picador, 2009.

Elias, Amy J. "Context Rocks!" *PMLA* 134.3 (May 2019): 579–87.

Eliot, George. *Middlemarch*. Edited by Bert Hornback. New York: W. W. Norton, 2000.

———. *The Mill on the Floss*. New York: W. W. Norton, 1994.

Fadiman, Anne. *Ex Libris: Confessions of a Common Reader*. New York: Farrar, Straus & Giroux, 1998.

Federico, Annette R. *Engagements with Close Reading*. London: Routledge, 2016.

Felski, Rita. *The Limits of Critique*. Chicago: University of Chicago Press, 2015.

———. *Uses of Literature*. Malden, MA: Blackwell, 2008.

Flint, Kate. "The Victorian Novel and Its Readers." In *The Cambridge Companion to the Victorian Novel*, edited by Deirdre David, 13–35. Cambridge: Cambridge University Press, 2012.

Hallman, J. C. *B. and Me*. New York: Simon & Schuster, 2015.

Houghton, Walter. *The Victorian Frame of Mind, 1830–1870*. New Haven: Yale University Press, 1957.

Howe, Susan. *My Emily Dickinson*. New York: New Directions, 1985.

Lynch, Deidre Shauna, and Evelyne Ender. "Introduction: Time for Reading." *PMLA* 133.5 (October 2018): 1073–82.

Mill, J. S. *On Liberty*. In *Mill*, edited by Alan Ryan. New York: W. W. Norton, 1997.

Miller, J. Hillis. *Ariadne's Thread: Repetition and the Narrative Line*. New Haven: Yale University Press, 1995.

———. *The Disappearance of God*. Cambridge: Harvard University Press, 1963.

Murdoch, Iris. "Against Dryness." 1961. In *Existentialists and Mystics*, edited by Peter Conradi, 287–95. New York: Penguin, 1997.

———. "Existentialists and Mystics." 1970. In *Existentialists and Mystics*, edited by Peter Conradi, 221–34. New York: Penguin, 1997.

North, Joseph. *Literary Criticism: A Concise Political History*. Cambridge: Harvard University Press, 2017.

Phillips, Adam. *Side Effects*. New York: Harper Perennial, 2007.

Rabinowitz, Peter J. "Sedimental Education; or, Reading as We Age." *PMLA* 133.3 (May 2018): 661–66.

Rendell, Jane. "Foreword: L'avant-coup." In *The Creative Critic: Writing as/about Practice*, edited by Katja Hilevaara and Emily Orley, xix–xxii. London: Routledge, 2018.

Rorty, Richard. "Heidegger, Kundera, and Dickens." In *Essays on Heidegger and Others*, 66–82. Cambridge: Cambridge University Press, 1991.

Rosenblatt, Louise. *Literature as Exploration*. 1936. 5th ed. New York: Modern Language Association, 1995.

———. "The Poem as Event." *College English* 26.2 (November 1962): 123–28.

———. *The Reader, the Text, the Poem: The Transactional Theory of the Literary Work*. Carbondale: Southern Illinois University Press, 1994.

Ruddick, Lisa. "When Nothing Is Cool." In *The Future of Scholarly Writing*, edited by Angelika Bammer and Ruth-Ellen Boetcher Joeres, 71–86. London: Palgrave Macmillan, 2015.

Ruskin, John. "Unto This Last." In *The Genius of John Ruskin*, edited by John D. Rosenberg, 229–72. Charlottesville: University of Virginia Press, 1998.

Schwartz, Murray M. "Where Is Literature?" In *Transitional Objects and Potential Spaces: Literary Uses of D. W. Winnicott*, edited by Peter Rudnytsky, 50–62. New York: Columbia University Press, 1993.

Sedgwick, Eve Kosofsky. "Teaching 'Experimental Critical Writing.'" In *The Ends of Performance*, edited by Peggy Phelan and Jill Lane, 104–15. New York: New York University Press, 1998.

———. *Touching Feeling: Affect, Pedagogy, Performativity*. Durham: Duke University Press, 2003.

Smith, Ali. *Artful*. New York: Penguin, 2014.

Smith, Zadie. *Changing My Mind: Occasional Essays*. New York: Penguin, 2009.

———. "*Middlemarch* and Everybody." In *Changing My Mind: Occasional Essays*, 29–41. New York: Penguin, 2009.

Solnit, Rebecca. "Woolf's Darkness: Embracing the Inexplicable." In *Men Explain Things to Me*, 85–108. Chicago: Haymarket Books, 2014.

Spacks, Patricia Meyer. *On Rereading*. Cambridge: Harvard University Press, 2011.

Spahr, Juliana, Mark Wallace, Kristin Prevallet, and Pam Rehm, eds. *A Poetics of Criticism*. Buffalo: Leave Books, 1994.

Thackeray, W. M. *Vanity Fair: A Novel without a Hero*. New York: W. W. Norton, 1994.

Tompkins, Jane. *A Life in School: What the Teacher Learned*. New York: Basic Books, 1996.

———. "Me and My Shadow." *New Literary History* 19.1 (Autumn 1987): 169–78.

———. *Reader-Response Criticism: From Formalism to Post-Structuralism*. Baltimore: Johns Hopkins University Press, 1980.

———. *Reading through the Night*. Charlottesville: University of Virginia Press, 2018.

———. "Speak, Memory." *Chronicle Review*, November 18, 2018.

Trollope, Anthony. *The Last Chronicle of Barset*. London: Penguin, 2002.

———. *The Warden*. London: Penguin, 1982.

Warner, Michael. "Uncritical Reading." In *Polemic: Critical or Uncritical*, edited by Jane Gallop, 13–38. London: Routledge, 2004.

Wilde, Oscar. "The Critic as Artist." In *The Artist as Critic: Critical Writings of Oscar Wilde*, edited by Richard Ellmann, 341–407. Chicago: University of Chicago Press, 1982.

Wood, James. *The Broken Estate: Essays on Literature and Belief*. New York: Picador, 2010.

Woolf, Virginia. "How Should One Read a Book?" In *The Second Common Reader*, 258–70. London: Harcourt Brace Jovanovich, 1986.

CHAPTER ONE

# Identifying as a Reader

Andrea Kaston Tange

## On *Jane Eyre* by Charlotte Brontë

At the age of eight or nine, I discovered what I immediately dubbed "the good shelves" in the school library. I did not know much about how books are shelved. But I did know that on *the good shelves* stood one perfect, engaging book after another, in long rows. When I was in graduate school, and particularly fascinated with Victorian and Edwardian children's literature, I finally figured out that the books on the good shelves were all written by E. Nesbit. It was not that authorship was meaningless to me as a child: everyone knew the "Little House" books were all written by the grown-up Laura, or that Roald Dahl had created both Charlie in his chocolate factory and James in his peach. Noel Streatfeild's "Shoes" books were obviously all by the same person, as both the titles and plots suggested, even though the little girl protagonists changed. But the family in *The Story of the Treasure Seekers* was not the same family I found in *Five Children and It*, and the titles did not imply an immediate connection.[1] It made just as much sense to me as any other system to think that the smiling librarians who checked out books to me several times per week had conveniently decided to group together all the books worth reading.

At some point, I obviously branched out beyond the good shelves, but their precedent made me gravitate toward other books that shared their most salient qualities. In considering the stories I loved most as a child, the ones that I would have shelved in *the good section*, if you will, I recently looked up their dates of publication and realized with a start that I have apparently been a Victorianist since I could read a chapter book. I have fond memories of *Black Beauty* (1877), *A Little Princess* (1905), *The Railway Children* (initially published serially, 1905), *Beautiful Joe* (1893),

*A Girl of the Limberlost* (1909), *Freckles* (1904), *The Little Lame Prince* (1875), *Toby Tyler; or, Ten Weeks with a Circus* (1881), and all the fairy tales of George MacDonald (1867–1882). My elementary school library was rich in the romance of the orphan. I know I read scores of more contemporary books too—detective stories, fantastical ones, and the first book that ever made me sob and sob, *Where the Red Fern Grows* (1961).[2] But the older books drew me in most alluringly to worlds that felt both foreign and familiar, recognizably old-fashioned compared to my own but with problems of siblings and of imagination that felt at once identifiable and transporting.

Without question, so much in those books prepared me for what has become the clearest arc of my reading life: my repeat encounters with *Jane Eyre* (1847). Their manor houses and manners, their self-sufficient children and absent parents, their clothes without zippers, bread-and-milk suppers, carriages, button-boots, and coal fires. Their metaphors. Their prose demanded things of me as a reader—offering language pitched to children without talking down to them, but vocabulary and syntax nearly a century old that *felt* different from other books, though I could not have explained how at the time.

Yet while it may have given me the tools to read Charlotte Brontë's novel at an early age, no collection of books could have poised me to anticipate the meaning that comes from rereading a single book time and again. The good shelves helped me to define myself as a reader, to find the prose styles and tones and narrators that appealed to me, and to begin to understand a period in history. But *Jane Eyre* has stuck with me because it made an intense early impression, one that produced enthralled identification, and then it challenged me, as I grew into a more informed reader, to recognize that even my earliest delight was predicated on systems in which Jane and I were similarly privileged. It would have been impossible for me to think of her as privileged when I first met her—forlorn, ill-treated, derided for being a reader. It was not until I continued to meet her, over time and in new contexts, that I could begin to see beyond her exhilarating heroism to the fact that the limitations of her world are not merely those imposed upon her but also those placed on others, which she by necessity exploits to reach her own version of success. The discomfort I feel now in her happy ending is the discomfort of realizing that our childhood heroes were never perfect. It is the necessary discomfort of appreciating that feminism is far more complicated than glorious rebellion, and of acknowledging that the triumph of any one woman may come at the silent cost of many marginalized others.

But before I could come to all of that understanding, I needed to fall in love with Jane.

"There was no possibility of taking a walk that day."[3]

There literally was not: I was stuck with my younger sisters in our powder-blue Datsun hatchback, somewhere on the highway between Georgia and Michigan. The novel's opening sentence had me hooked.

It was a slow-going road trip, punctuated by bathroom breaks and our mother's naps. She had limited driving stamina and a proclivity for rousing narrative songs on which we could all chime in. "There was a desperado from the wild and wooly west . . ." and "Oh, the grandfather's clock was too large for the shelf, so it stood ninety years on the floor . . ." We liked "Down by the sea, where the watermelons grow . . ." because we could make up endless verses of our own, in between rounds of the alphabet game and the state-license-plate-collecting game and the invisible ink puzzle books we all had. And in between all of those, I read. Unlike my middle sister, I did not get carsick. And unlike the youngest, I was reading big, fat books that could last me a good long while. I had commandeered the tiny station wagon's "way-back," leaving the back seat to my sisters. The sun warmed my legs through the sloped window, and I reveled in a space I did not have to share, small though it was and situated between suitcases. I could not have been more primed to offer sympathy to Jane (ten, just like me!) as she pored over her *Bewick's History of British Birds*—both of us taking happy refuge from the world in a book.

Everything about Jane Eyre, the girl and the book, entranced me from the first page. My copy of her story was old and hardbound, and I have a vague recollection that it had belonged to a grown relative when she was a child, which I liked. I do not think I had ever encountered a book this big with a heroine this small and so like myself. I wore glasses, which, as far as I could figure, she did not. But I understood what it was to be impatient with senseless chattering when all a person wanted to do was read. And I could feel deep down the intense satisfaction that must surely come from shutting oneself up in a window seat behind red moreen curtains on a dreary winter day.

Red moreen curtains! Had any ten-year-old ever had a place more magnificent-sounding in which to hide and read? How I longed for a cushioned window seat of my own! And if it had had curtains to shut me away from the rest of the world? What bliss that would have been. Who knew what moreen was? Not me. But it was certainly something thick and warm, possibly glamorous, and obviously affording secrecy.

And so, I lay on my stomach and dove into Jane's story, forgetting the time and the miles and my sisters and the awkward lumps of metal, molded around the spare tire, that lay just under the thin carpet of the way-back. I was outraged at John Reed's imperiousness. (I surely did not know that word, but the visceral memory I carry of that reading tells me that I *felt* that is what he was, although I could not have named it as such.) I was horrified by the dual abuse of books and Jane as he threw the heavy *Bewick's* volume at her head—and drew blood. I cowered with her in the red bedroom, longed for Bessie to be kinder to her more often. And I was in absolute awe of the child who dared to stand up to injustice practiced by a grown-up. Jane's verbal defeat of the terrifying Aunt Reed, who slanderously told Brocklehurst that Jane was a liar, was the most glorious thing I had ever read—so much bolder than I could ever be, exactly as bold and eloquent as I would have longed to be if I were the heroine of my own story.

Jane was me and not-me all at once. She seemed like the kind of girl who could sit quietly, staring out a window and imagining for hours. The way she was misunderstood in the Reed house felt familiar, like my own quietness at school writ larger. She was awkward and ungainly. Brainy and dreaming. Her sufferings were, thankfully, nothing like my lot—but that only made me love her more. I felt I understood her mind and her desires, while at the same time her difficulties activated so much of my imagination. And her way out of them was simply extraordinary.

Jane and her story were like nothing I had ever met in a book before. Now I might posit that this is because prior to then, I had never read a book that was not explicitly written for child readers. Surely, one of the things that lent exuberance to the pens of all the Victorian and Edwardian authors whose books I had loved was that there was a clear place for complicated, imaginative writing in the newly defined children's market. But while I would not have put it in these terms on that seemingly endless summer drive, nothing on the good shelves was as morally complex as

*Jane Eyre*. The Bastable children were clever, and their adventures were fascinating and magical. But, like the siblings in the "Boxcar Children" books, they were shepherded by an older sister more motherly than child-like. Jo March was a marvel, and was going to be a writer, as I was sure I would be, but she had Marmee. Laura was bold and questioning, but Ma Ingalls was the orderly center of her world and kept her in check. And Mary Lennox? Well, she was not a child you could like, even as an orphan, until she was softened by gardening and the baked potatoes provided by Dickon's comfortable mother.[4]

The good shelves and their ilk had impressed upon me that in the world of books, *someone* was always caretaking, following rules, ensuring people ate and washed up and grew up. Even children who were left to their own devices ultimately needed benevolent uncles to resolve the bigger problems in their worlds. And those uncles always showed up. In *Jane Eyre*, breathtakingly, the adults in charge were bad at being in charge. They were cruel and capricious and snobby and ineffective and petty. They let children go hungry out of something called "false economy," and they defied the cardinal rule of all poverty-stricken-family books I had ever read: namely, that when you had nothing, kindness was somehow going to get you out of the worst of situations. They were never kind.

Obviously, the uncle, or at least his fortune, eventually appears like a fairy godmother's aid in *Jane Eyre* too, but my fascination with Jane on that first reading was far more focused on the fact that the vivid adults in her childhood world were the enemies of her well-being. The one exception, Miss Temple, was both a welcome relief and a character who seemed ephemeral, made mostly of seed cake and Jane's memories of her quiet compassion. Furthermore, for a very long time before she had Miss Temple, Jane had no one to rely on but herself. Compounding that, she fit none of the criteria of good-little-girlhood that my reading experience suggested were necessary to her success. Although she was impressively good at tidying and dusting, she found it neither rewarding nor her proper duty. *She*, one presumed, would not cheerfully forage for spoons in the local dump and scrub them with sand at the creek, and pretend to be camping in a found boxcar while eating the berries she picked; *she* would think scathingly about how unfair it was that she should have nothing to eat when her relatives had plenty, and finally she would get hungry enough to tell them so to their faces. This would be deeply satisfying, emotionally.

But nothing in the books I had read suggested it would actually solve her subsistence problems, because girls who won in the end were domestic nurturers, not outspoken proponents of justice.

Jane appealed to me, in short, because she resisted being a good little girl in ways that felt astonishing and liberating to a good little girl who had carefully internalized all the imperatives of goodness, littleness, and girlness. Jane may have been punished repeatedly for speaking up, but nowhere in the story was it implied that the adults were right to punish her or that she was supposed to regret what she had done in standing up for herself. Therein lay the marvel. That even while every precedent suggested Bessie and Abbot were correct to lament that Jane was not prettier and more guileless, because all of that proper femininity would enable her to go far in life, the novel sided with Jane in pooh-poohing those standards and thereby defying Aunt Reed. Even Jane's own remorse as she stood on the hearthrug was driven only by the sense that children could not defy their elders and get away with it, rather than that she had actually done anything objectively wrong. Jane showed me, in terms a child could understand, the power of claiming one's own voice as a girl.

Through giving voice to her frustrations, Jane helped me find my own feminism before I had the language to name it as such. Perhaps unsurprisingly, the chapters focused on Jane's early life made the deepest impression on me during that days-long car ride. When I witnessed bookish child-Jane staking a claim not to be mocked or misrepresented, I concluded that internal exhilaration and freedom were the logical result of speaking up. She continued to appeal to me as a studious teenager—when the popular girls with their expert makeup and layered, logo-adorned shirts were Georgianas to my Jane—because her vision transcended the limits of her own small sphere. Thus, when I read *Jane Eyre* in high school, I began to see her in terms that, although still more intuited than theorized, moved beyond herself. I began to perceive that anger at systems, rather than only at individuals, was sometimes warranted.

The bit of the novel I remember with the most clarity from my high school reading of *Jane Eyre* is the point where, aged eighteen, Jane positions herself on the parapet of Thornfield, looking out over the countryside, and proclaims,

> Anybody may blame me who likes, when I add further . . . that then I longed for a power of vision which might overpass that limit; which might reach the

> busy world, towns, regions full of life I had heard of but never seen: that then I desired more of practical experience than I possessed; more of intercourse with my kind, of acquaintance with variety of character, than was here within my reach. . . . It is in vain to say human beings ought to be satisfied with tranquility; they must have action; and they will make it if they cannot find it. Millions are condemned to a stiller doom than mine, and millions are in silent revolt against their lot. Nobody knows how many rebellions besides political rebellions ferment in the masses of life which people the earth. Women are supposed to be very calm generally: but women feel just as men feel; they need exercise for their faculties, and a field for their efforts as much as their brothers do; they suffer from too rigid a constraint, too absolute a stagnation, precisely as men would suffer; and it is narrow-minded in their more privileged fellow-creatures to say that they ought to confine themselves to making puddings and knitting stockings, to playing on the piano and embroidering bags. It is thoughtless to condemn them, or laugh at them, if they seek to do more or learn more than custom has pronounced necessary for their sex. (177–78; chap. 12)

Jane is here filled less with the pure rage of a child than with the articulate indignation of the near-woman. The standard reading of her is that, on the whole, she learns to moderate her anger thanks to Miss Temple and Helen Burns, that even here she is either confining her thoughts to a page or shouting them into the wind over a lonely estate rather than having a public outburst. But high-school-me read parapet-Jane as the teenage version of the same Jane who defiantly won the field by declaring her cousin Georgiana the liar in the house. I did not see her anger as diminished simply because her words were more sophisticated and carefully chosen. The eloquent claim that "women feel just as men feel" was, I thought then, controlled, but the defiance of "anybody may blame me who likes" was the corollary to standing up to Aunt Reed on the hearthrug.

Virginia Woolf explicitly mentions this passage when she argues that Charlotte Brontë's "indignation" got in the way of her "genius," that Brontë wrote "in a rage where she should write calmly."[5] Woolf seems to conflate Jane with Charlotte, as have readers for generations afterward when discussing this speech. I am not sure such conflation is wholly wrong, but for me this speech makes the novel internally coherent, while Woolf finds that Charlotte's anger at the patriarchy distractingly overtook Jane's voice. Yet, the idea that Brontë failed because she did not "write calmly" undermines her right to anger at all, and defines her ability to succeed as an author through an imperative to some version of feminine reasonableness. Woolf is hardly blind to the material and ideological conditions faced by the Brontë sisters, George Eliot, and other women authors of their moment; she writes witheringly of the dual pressures of poverty and respectability that bound them. And yet, in denying anger as a reasonable response to such limitations, Woolf seems to me to be judging this passage by an upper-middle-class model of English womanhood that presumes, for a start, that Brontë had a platform from which she would be heard if she spoke in more modulated tones.

To me as a teen, such modulation would have been far less moving than this speech, which captured Jane's anger, clear and bright, and felt wholly consistent with the child she had been. White-hot fury is not too strong a thing to aim at the "narrow-minded . . . more privileged fellow-creatures" who consign women to time-wasting occupations and then *laugh at them* for wanting more. Jane takes on all the sneering John Reeds of the world in the same breath that she defies all the Bessies who find pretty girls easier objects of sympathy and the Mrs. Fairfaxes who favor placid women who will not disrupt anyone's tranquility with ambition. "Anybody may blame me who likes" challenges the reader: acknowledge that women's minds carry the same flexible potential as men's, or know you are a thoughtless, narrow-minded consigner of half the human population to a life of still doom. As a reader, I felt, you could not take intense satisfaction in the success of Jane's enormous childhood outrage and then *not* align yourself with her later critique of patriarchal limits on women. You were either Jane or you were every "anybody" who blamed her.

To be sure, Jane's righteous anger over the idea that girls are not supposed to have minds was offset by the fact that she had to baldly admit her own limits. In high school, however, I did not see that those limits might also include speaking her mind with too much self-righteousness. What I saw was only her sense of social inferiority, epitomized in the chalk self-portrait that she heart-wrenchingly entitled "Portrait of a Governess, disconnected, poor, and plain" (237; chap. 16). In a way that felt painfully familiar, Jane seemed the embodiment of the principle that a girl cannot be both smart and pretty, that she must choose, over and over and over again, throughout her life, between feeding her mind and being understood as appealing.

Rochester, in breaking with stereotypes and finding her attractive *because* she has a mind of her own rather than in spite of it, struck me then as a most romantic kind of man. Reader, I sighed with satisfaction when she married him. It was years before I realized how heavy-handed the burning bed scene is, how disconcerting it is that Rochester is so willing to take advantage of his position of power over her. The sexual tension there is palpable, but only to someone old enough to recognize what sexual tension is. And the hierarchies that render Jane his subordinate in so many registers are ones that require a finer understanding of history than I had as a teenager. In that moment Rochester is not romantic, I figured out sometime in college, but manipulative, trying to cajole his young, inexperienced employee into his arms. It is a harbinger of the ways that he, throughout the novel, shows himself off-puttingly keen to exploit women. Rochester uses his class position, his imperial authority, his family name, and every form of privilege he possesses to get what he wants.

Jane's quiet refusal of his advances is even more jaw-dropping than her outburst at Aunt Reed, though I am sure it was not until I was in my twenties that I understood what it took for her to stand there in quiet comprehension and not only resist him but protect herself at the same time. For, of course, a man who later proves himself capable of threatening to rape her if she will not comply with his proposal to pretend to be married as they travel abroad ("Jane! Will you hear reason? . . . because, if you won't, I'll try violence") is not a man to be rejected easily at midnight as he stands there in a dripping wet nightgown (392; chap. 27).

There is a gap in my recollections of reading this novel, one that corresponds to a shift in my identifications with it. I cannot pinpoint when it happened, but somewhere in the decade between majoring in English and becoming an English professor who regularly teaches *Jane Eyre*, I stopped thinking of Jane as a book friend (and as a person who could have made other choices besides those Brontë wrote for her). Instead, I began to think how spectacular it would have been to know Charlotte Brontë.

As a child, Charlotte created an imaginary world with her sisters called Angria. *Angria!* Charlotte, I learned from an exhibit at the Morgan Library in Manhattan, had a tiny frame that she clothed in immaculate chintz dresses with sloped shoulders and the smallest shoes imaginable. Charlotte, with the overbearing, philandering, alcoholic brother who was both co-creator of Angria and, surely, prototype for some of the worst tendencies in all the men his sisters ever wrote about.[6] Charlotte, who was raised within the proprieties of good little girlhood and had the strength of pen to declare that this was not enough. Clearly, I assumed, she would be a fantastic woman to have at a dinner party or to count as a friend.

In conversations with students over the years, I have contextualized the power of Jane's invective against the narrowness of her lot within the frames of nineteenth-century domestic and class-based gender imperatives, the difficulties for women of becoming public figures in the literary marketplace, and Brontë's own famously intense reserve in public. (I learned eventually that she would *not* have been a perfect person to invite to a dinner party.)[7] I find that many students are primed to think of Brontë as an early feminist, given their generalized sense that women were oppressed in the Victorian period and the eloquence with which Jane Eyre identifies herself with the legions of women in "silent revolt" against a "stiller doom" even than her own. One of the complex pleasures of teaching the novel, then, has become the imperative to help students think through the limits of this feminist reading of the novel. For while Jane is an admirable advocate of her own personhood, she denies that personhood to Bertha Mason Rochester.

As exhilarating as it is to realize that nothing in the novel suggests Jane is wrong for standing up for herself, it is simultaneously essential to register that nothing in the novel offers to stand up for Bertha, that there is no acknowledgment of Bertha as a wronged woman. In the sociopolitical, interpersonal drama that unfolds, Jane—poor, insecure, outspoken, nontraditionally feminine Jane—is the victim left at the altar. The "creature" who makes Jane's marriage impossible is not simply given no agency; she is deprived even of the dignity of being seen as maltreated by this proposed bigamy. She is a "thing." Jane is a victim.

Presumably, some of the novel's original readers agreed with reviewer Elizabeth Rigby (later Lady Eastlake), who was deeply offended by Jane's outspokenness, by the prospect of a governess marrying her employer, by Jane's "anti-Christian" dissatisfaction with her position in life.[8] A scholarly understanding of the history of the novel's moment of production and its reception adds nuance to the more visceral gratification of its feminist position experienced by my younger self. But to the extent that reviews are an adequate judge of contemporary opinions, it seems Victorian readers did not think to consider, let alone be offended by, what was left out of Rochester's version of events.[9] It would not have occurred to them to note that the fortunes of the Rochesters—and "the passport of an old name"—were surely built upon colonial exploitations (401; chap. 27). None of Brontë's contemporaries asked what might motivate Rochester's representation of Bertha as a hypersexual creature who inherited all the worst excesses of her climate and family—because what motivated him were widely accepted cultural norms. And thus, none of those reviewers criticized Jane for not asking that question either.

For all these reasons, where I fell in love with *Jane Eyre* as a child because of the mind-blowing things it shouted from hearthrug and parapet, this novel remains one I return to again and again because it makes me grapple with the problems that lie in its silences.

Does *Jane Eyre* invite us to critique the quiet acceptance of colonial fortunes that are only possible at the expense of colonized bodies who are perceived to be disposable, silenceable, subhuman? Or does the novel merely replicate that disposal because its author could not see, any more than can its narrator, the multiple systemic oppressions on which Rochester's—and even Jane's—privilege is predicated? To put it another way, to what extent might its author and original readers be implicated in the novel's willful silences, or are we mistaken to assume that its apparent silences would have been invisible to a nineteenth-century reader?[10]

We read Jane as victim because, of course, she tells her own story of being profoundly deceived by a man who purports to respect her mind and yet in fact prizes her for the quiet, morally pure antidote she seems to provide to his philandering, dissatisfied, extravagant life. She represents for him a moral center that is deeply, conventionally feminine in Victorian terms—which is in itself a level of betrayal that Jane cannot ever confront.[11] Instead, she allows herself to be dramatically recharacterized in an instant. Where Rochester has long described her in preternatural terms such as "imp" and "fairy sprite," and valued her for her contrary nature and propensity to offer unvarnished criticism, he suddenly identifies her as a conventional "young girl, who stands so quiet and grave," with "clear eyes," in contrast to the "clothed hyena" and the "gambols of a demon" that form the dangerous femininity of the Creole Bertha.[12] Jane chooses to accept this revision of her self in part because it represents her having attained the respectable form of middle-class femininity that others have always presumed was inconceivable for the orphaned daughter of a disinherited mother.

But what does it tell us, to register that the unthinking acceptance of Bertha as the logical foil for Jane represents the nineteenth century's embrace of intersectional hierarchies of race, class, and gender? The most charitable reading of the silence that attends denying Bertha the very personhood that Jane loudly claims for herself is that it tells us something about the pose of autobiography within the novel. Because we see the whole story through Jane's eyes and voice, everyone in the novel plays a role in the crisis of self that characterizes Jane's youth and young womanhood. This is a reading that is both attentive to genre and psychologically appropriate to the obsessions and perspective of Jane's developmental ages throughout the novel. It is also as generous to the book as it is critical of its eponymous character. For it asks us to view Jane's complicit characterization of Bertha as an animal as a flaw in Jane herself, and thus it implies that the silence around Bertha's personhood and femininity is being criticized by the narrative.

But to read Charlotte Brontë as actively critiquing the vision of colonized women as even more disposable than white Englishwomen feels as if it is giving Brontë too much credit. The narrative impossibility that Bertha should be considered fully human by anyone seems more damningly to reflect Brontë's blasé sense that a Creole woman is not really a woman. There are reasons this novel was a darling of second-wave feminism, giving title to a groundbreaking book of 1970s feminist theory. The recovery work of that generation of feminists was prodigious and important. Yet the eponymous "madwoman in the attic" has her identity erased even as she gives that book its title: her name does not matter; her trope does.[13] And her trope is that of "dark double," which troublingly replicates the nineteenth-century reading of her as a foil for Jane's quiet integrity, rather than as a woman in her own right.

A feminist reading of *Jane Eyre* today must necessarily be a postcolonial one.[14] In rejecting Rochester's horrifying treatment of Jane as unjust, we highlight the fact that although she is an articulate woman who gets five hundred pages to tell her own story, she has nonetheless been wronged repeatedly by patriarchy. But we are obliged to be similarly indignant on behalf of the character who is his first wife and who is never allowed to speak for herself. Surely the woman who is cast aside, doomed to be driven slowly mad (or madder) through near-solitary confinement in a windowless room for a decade, deserves to be understood as wronged, at least as much as Jane has been wronged. We name and acknowledge Bertha Antoinetta Mason Rochester. And in doing so, we call out Rochester's and

Jane's identification of her as a "thing" for what it is: a mark of the blindness of their own privileges of race and colonial domination. This is not a victimization contest. It is, though, a call to think about what it means that Jane is a role model to a particular sort of introspective girl, but that the world of the novel posits that it is both possible and acceptable for that girl not to give Bertha a second thought.

Moreover, because the term "Creole" in the 1840s could have meant the Caribbean-born, white descendant of colonists or the mixed-race progeny of plantation owners and their enslaved laborers, any consideration of Bertha unavoidably raises important questions about her position within the system that produced her fortune. The novel's lack of clarity around her origins is yet another potent silence, one that invites us to recall the many silenced women throughout colonial history, who were positioned as chattel, objects of sexual conquest, or subjects of exchange between men. In light of the novel's assumptions about (or, perhaps, its lack of interest in considering seriously) Bertha as an individual, it becomes incumbent upon us as feminist readers in the twenty-first century to acknowledge that Jane's success is ultimately thanks to an inherited Caribbean fortune, earned through the production of Madeira wine. Imperialist exploitation frees white, now-middle-class Jane from dependence on any man, and it remains unquestioned.[15]

It feels uncomfortable to like Jane somewhat less, especially if we have spent long years thinking of Jane as ourselves. But it is necessary. It is also necessary to remember that while Jane is a fiction, she is a fiction born in a particular cultural moment, and that her success is predicated upon layers of assumptions we must question in part precisely because she does not. I will, I think, always take immense satisfaction in the hearthrug scene and be grateful to parapet-Jane for claiming the right of women to have ambitions. At the same time, Jane is not perfect, and neither was Charlotte Brontë.

The reason this book is my Victorian novel is that it bears rereading and scrutiny, challenging and critiquing, and still gives us something in return. Through the book's inability to deal well with Bertha, a careful reader who has been Jane's cheerleader in early chapters might do some introspective looking for her own blind spots, the silences around topics about which *she* might do better. She has an obligation, too, to listen to other readers, the scholars of history and culture who have helped frame our attention to the past both in terms of what it announced and what it had the luxury not to say. Such scholars provide wise interventions and serve as enlightening interlocutors who demonstrate the power of rereading.

Yet while both experience and theory have enabled me to revise my perceptions of this book—in ways that I hope have come to represent a more informed and nuanced understanding of the world of 1840s Britain—I am not sure my understanding of *Jane Eyre*'s significance would have become as rich had I not fallen uncritically in love with the book in the first case. For naïve readers are not simply unperceptive. Rather, they have alternate taxonomies of knowledge. To a nine-year-old bookworm, librarians are benevolent, all-knowing beings who want everyone to love to read; logically, they might easily choose to create *good shelves*. In the same way, young readers might value identification, and teen feminists might crave outspoken heroines, without having the tools to ask: who else might not be similarly allowed to speak? For whom is this model not accessible?

The value of rereading is not merely to replace one's first, uncritical encounter with a book with something more sophisticated. It is easy, but not especially productive, to condemn naïve reading. Instead, I posit, rereading allows us to consider both what produces emotional identification and what is missing from it. It enables us to formulate an understanding of a book within multiple frames of reference, and to reread not only texts and their histories, but also ourselves. It acknowledges that the power of the second encounter depends in part on the power of the first, and that subsequent readings, if they are thoughtful ones, will revise, refocus, correct, and expand but not wholly reject. Jane's, after all, is nothing short of a remarkable voice announcing the desire of women for "more than custom has pronounced necessary for their sex."

Rereading models the lesson we offer our students to avoid the trap of the "relatable," asking us to explain *why* we think a thing is so powerful, rather than just whether we find it so. But this does not negate the importance of what for so many readers is step one: identifying emotional power. It may not be a sufficient full reading, but it is often a precondition for analysis because it draws our attention to things that we intuit are worth analyzing even before we may have the language to assess them. Striving to be good teachers, we do not allow our students to stop at "relatable," any more than we allow ourselves to stop at our ten-year-old enthusiasm, or feminist politics to stop at second-wave recovery and celebration of the independence of some women without acknowledging the racial privileges inherent in that project. But in teaching *Jane Eyre* now, I secretly hope our initial conversations will include some unmitigated admiration for young Jane. Even if most of my students are not in the luxurious position of rereading the novel for my class, I want them to have the experience of engaging first with it on the level of championing her boldness in the face of potentially crushing gendered hierarchies—and so I assign the reading in sections that defer the spoiler as long as possible. Once they learn the secret of Thornfield's third story, they are eager to spend long discussions on what the novel takes for granted. They relish juxtaposing what Jane defies with what the novel accepts as the status quo—and their feminisms are far more intersectional than mine could have been at their age. They may only have fallen in love with Jane last Tuesday, but it is my hope that our conversations about *why* will help them re-envision her over the course of a couple of weeks in order to provide some sense of the power of layering new readings over prior ones.

In decades of experiencing this novel, I have come to the point where its silences feel its most potent part. The very best books, *Jane Eyre* has taught me, are ones that demand rereading and that encompass difficulties. They are books whose politics may be imperfect but whose complacencies have the power to make us uncomfortably aware of our own.

## NOTES

1. *Little House on the Prairie* is the third book in the well-known series by Laura Ingalls Wilder. Roald Dahl's most famous fantastical world is perhaps that of *Charlie and the Chocolate Factory*, whose sequel was *Charlie and the Great Glass Elevator*, although the adventure *James and the Giant Peach*, in which James flies across the ocean in a peach pulled by birds, to escape his cruel aunts, is spectacular. Noel Streatfeild's "Shoes" books center on the lives of different girls as they pursue their dreams; the books include *Ballet Shoes*, *Theater Shoes*, *Skating Shoes*, and *Dancing Shoes*. *The Story of the Treasure Seekers* has two sequels featuring the same family; these and *Five Children and It*, as well as dozens of other novels and children's story collections, are by E. Nesbit.

2. Anna Sewell, *Black Beauty*; Frances Hodgson Burnett, *A Little Princess*; E. Nesbit, *The Railway Children*; [Margaret] Marshall Saunders, *Beautiful Joe*; Gene Stratton-Porter, *A Girl of the Limberlost* and *Freckles*; Dinah Mulock Craik, *The Little Lame Prince and His Travelling Cloak*; James Otis, *Toby Tyler; or, Ten Weeks with a Circus*; George MacDonald, *The Complete Fairy Tales*; Wilson Rawls, *Where the Red Fern Grows*.

3. Charlotte Brontë, *Jane Eyre*, ed. Richard Nemesvari, 63; chap. 1. Further citations will be given parenthetically with both page numbers and chapter numbers, to facilitate references for those reading other editions of the novel.

4. The Bastable family is at the center of the "Treasure Seeker" novels (originally published 1899–1905) by E. Nesbit. The first books in the *Boxcar Children* series, by Gertrude Chandler Warner, came out in the 1920s. The Marches are in *Little Women* and its two sequels, by Louisa May Alcott (1868–1886). The Laura Ingalls Wilder "Little House" books were pitched for slightly younger readers and were based on her family's homesteading life in the 1870s, though published in the 1930s. Mary Lennox is the protagonist of *The Secret Garden*, by Frances Hodgson Burnett (1911), who also wrote *A Little Princess* (1905).

5. Virginia Woolf, *A Room of One's Own*, 69.

6. Branwell Brontë was alternately a brazen depleter of the family fortune and a sad penitent who literally tried to paint himself out of the picture: at one point, he painted a family portrait and then, dissatisfied, tried to paint himself out of it. However, he failed to erase himself. In the painting, the ghost of Branwell has over time risen to the surface from behind a column of gold, and in his sisters' literary skewerings, he lives on.

7. On Brontë's reserve, the dinner hosted in her honor by her literary hero, William Makepeace Thackeray (June 12, 1850), is a prime example; it was by all accounts a dismal failure thanks to her near-paralyzing shyness in public conversations, particularly where she was expected to play a central role. (See Eleanor Houghton's study of that evening, "Unravelling the Mystery," which includes everything from a consideration of Brontë's behavior to a fascinating archival discussion of her clothing.) Sarah Stickney Ellis wrote a series of conduct manuals detailing the attitudes women were duty bound to bring to their interactions, both familial and social—all bearing titles like *The Wives of England: Their Relative Duties, Domestic Influence, and Social Obligations*. Each book focuses on a different life stage, with ones for daughters, mothers, wives, and all women. Isabella Beeton's *The Book of Household Management* covered domestic duties and management of servants, and contained hundreds of recipes; it has been continuously in print since 1861. Recent useful work includes Margaret Homans, "*Jane Eyre*, *Incidents in the Life of a Slave Girl*, and the Varieties of Nineteenth-Century Feminism"; and Linda Peterson, *Becoming a Woman of Letters: Myths of Authorship and the Facts of the Victorian Market*.

8. Rigby famously reviewed the novel in conjunction with *Vanity Fair* and the work of the Governesses' Benevolent Institution. The review took Brontë to task for producing "preeminently an anti-Christian composition," by which Rigby seems to have meant that Jane ought to have accepted her lot. [Elizabeth Rigby], "*Vanity Fair*, *Jane Eyre*, and the Governesses' Benevolent Institution—Report for 1847," 173.

9. See John O'Hara, "From Myth to Materiality: Critical Reception of Charlotte Brontë's *Jane Eyre* from the 1840s to the 2010s," for a particularly useful reception study of the novel that covers its initial publication up to the 2010s.

10. Sue Thomas demonstrates convincingly that there were extensive public conversations around the 1823 and 1831 anti-slavery rebellions in the Caribbean, as well as the role of missionaries there vis-à-vis enslaved people, all of which were known to the Brontës. She contends that the imagery used to discuss these issues in the press appears repeatedly throughout the novel, which would have made it impossible for Brontë's original readers to miss her engagement with questions of race and colonial power. But merely gesturing toward the colonial contexts that underpin the novel may have made it easier for Brontë's contemporaries to take these contexts for granted—as Rochester does—rather than to critique them. Nonetheless, it is important to register that Brontë's original readers would have had the contemporary rhetoric associated with discussions of slavery and abolition in mind, while we are far removed from the resonance of many of those turns of phrase. Sue Thomas, "Christianity and the State of Slavery in *Jane Eyre*."

11. Indeed, Jane explicitly notes, "I would not say he had betrayed me" (384; chap. 26).

12. The "imp" and "sprite" language comes throughout the Thornfield section of the novel. The contrast of the "young girl" to the "clothed hyena" comes at the point when Rochester reveals the truth about his first wife to the clergyman and Jane after the aborted wedding (381; chap. 26).

13. Sandra M. Gilbert and Susan Gubar's field-changing *The Madwoman in the Attic: The Woman Writer and the Nineteenth-Century Literary Imagination* helped launch a wave of recovering nineteenth-century women writers from the obscurity into which they had fallen. Deanna K. Kreisel has written a nuanced and important update of this reading, "The Madwoman on the Third Story: Jane Eyre in Space."

14. See Gayatri Chakravorty Spivak, "Three Women's Texts and a Critique of Imperialism."

15. Both Alexandra Valint and April Pelt discuss the question of Jane's inheritance and its Caribbean origins. Jean Rhys imagined Bertha's backstory in her novel *Wide Sargasso Sea* (1966). Alexandra Valint, "Madeira and Jane Eyre's Colonial Inheritance"; April Pelt, "'Weary of Our Own Legacies': Rethinking Jane Eyre's Inheritance through Jamaica Kincaid's *The Autobiography of My Mother*."

## WORKS CITED

Alcott, Louisa May. *Little Women*. 2 vols. Boston: Roberts Brothers, 1868–1869.

Beeton, Isabella. *The Book of Household Management*. London: S. O. Beeton, 1861.

Brontë, Charlotte. *Jane Eyre*. 1847. Edited by Richard Nemesvari. Peterborough, ON: Broadview, 1999.

Burnett, Frances Hodgson. *A Little Princess*. New York: Charles Scribner's Sons, 1905.

———. *The Secret Garden*. New York: Frederick A. Stokes, 1911.

Craik, Dinah Mulock. *The Little Lame Prince and His Travelling Cloak*. London: Daldy Isbister, 1875.

Dahl, Roald. *Charlie and the Chocolate Factory*. London: Knopf, 1964.

———. *James and the Giant Peach*. London: Knopf, 1961.

Ellis, Sarah Stickney. *The Daughters of England: Their Society, Character, and Responsibilities*. London: Fisher, Son & Co., 1842.

———. *The Mothers of England: Their Influence and Responsibilities*. New York: D. Appleton, 1844.

———. *The Wives of England: Their Relative Duties, Domestic Influence, and Social Obligations*. New York: D. Appleton, 1843.

———. *The Women of England: Their Social Duties and Domestic Habits*. London: Fisher, Son & Co., 1839.

Gilbert, Sandra M., and Susan Gubar. *The Madwoman in the Attic: The Woman Writer and the Nineteenth-Century Literary Imagination*. New Haven: Yale University Press, 1979.

Hill, Cecily E. "'Words Could Not Vent Half Their Rage': School Stories and the Invention of *Jane Eyre*." *Women's Writing* 23.2 (May 2016): 176–92.

Homans, Margaret. "*Jane Eyre, Incidents in the Life of a Slave Girl*, and the Varieties of Nineteenth-Century Feminism." In *Literature and the Development of Feminist Theory*, edited by Robin Truth Goodman, 27–41. Cambridge: Cambridge University Press, 2015.

Houghton, Eleanor. "Unravelling the Mystery: Charlotte Brontë's 1850 'Thackeray Dress.'" *Costume* 50.2 (2016): 194–219.

Kreisel, Deanna K. "The Madwoman on the Third Story: Jane Eyre in Space." *PMLA* 131.1 (January 2016): 101–15.

MacDonald, George. *The Complete Fairy Tales*. New York: Penguin Classics, 1999.

Nesbit, E. *Five Children and It*. London: T. Fisher Unwin, 1902.

———. *The Railway Children*. London: Wells Gardner, Darton, 1906.

———. *The Story of the Treasure Seekers*. London: T. Fisher Unwin, 1899.

O'Hara, John. "From Myth to Materiality: Critical Reception of Charlotte Brontë's *Jane Eyre* from the 1840s to the 2010s." In *Jane Eyre*, edited by Katie R. Peel, 50–63. Hackensack, NJ: Salem Press, 2013.

Otis, James. *Toby Tyler; or, Ten Weeks with a Circus*. New York: Harper & Brothers, 1881.

Pelt, April. "'Weary of Our Own Legacies': Rethinking Jane Eyre's Inheritance through Jamaica Kincaid's *The Autobiography of My Mother*." *ARIEL: A Review of International English Literature* 41.3–4 (July 2010): 73–90.

Peterson, Linda. *Becoming a Woman of Letters: Myths of Authorship and the Facts of the Victorian Market*. Princeton: Princeton University Press, 2009.

Rawls, Wilson. *Where the Red Fern Grows*. New York: Doubleday, 1961.

Rhys, Jean. *Wide Sargasso Sea*. New York: W. W. Norton, 1966.

[Rigby, Elizabeth]. "*Vanity Fair, Jane Eyre*, and the Governesses' Benevolent Institution—Report for 1847." *Quarterly Review* 84.167 (December 1848): 153–85.

Saunders, [Margaret] Marshall. *Beautiful Joe: A Dog's Own Story*. Philadelphia: Griffith & Rowland, 1893.

Sewell, Anna. *Black Beauty*. London: Jarrold & Sons, 1877.

Spivak, Gayatri Chakravorty. "Three Women's Texts and a Critique of Imperialism." *Critical Inquiry* 12 (1985–1986): 243–61.

Stratton-Porter, Gene. *Freckles*. New York: Grosset & Dunlap, 1904.

———. *A Girl of the Limberlost*. New York: Grosset & Dunlap, 1909.

Streatfeild, Noel. *Ballet Shoes*. London: J. M. Dent & Sons, 1936.

———. *Curtain Up* [published as *Theater Shoes* in the United States]. London: J. M. Dent & Sons, 1944.

———. *White Boots* [published as *Skating Shoes* in the United States]. London: Collins, 1951.

———. *Wintle's Wonders* [published as *Dancing Shoes* in the United States]. London: Collins, 1957.

Thomas, Sue. "Christianity and the State of Slavery in *Jane Eyre*." *Victorian Literature and Culture* 35.1 (2007): 57–79.

Tytler, Graeme. "Physiognomy and the Treatment of Beauty in *Jane Eyre*." *Brontë Studies: The Journal of the Brontë Society* 41.4 (November 2016): 300–311.

Valint, Alexandra. "Madeira and Jane Eyre's Colonial Inheritance." *Victorian Literature and Culture* 45.2 (2017): 321–39.

Warner, Gertrude Chandler. *The Boxcar Children* series. New York: Rand McNally, 1924–1976.

Wilder, Laura Ingalls. *Little House on the Prairie*. New York: Harper & Brothers, 1935.

Woolf, Virginia. *A Room of One's Own*. New York: Harcourt Brace Jovanovich, 1981.

CHAPTER TWO

# Mourning Glencora

Deborah Denenholz Morse

## On *The Duke's Children* by Anthony Trollope

Rachel Brownstein's germinal study *Becoming a Heroine: Reading about Women in Novels* (1982) centers on the female reader's identification with the heroines of nineteenth-century English fiction. Brownstein writes about Austen's heroines and Charlotte Brontë's, about George Eliot's, Henry James's—and Virginia Woolf's early twentieth-century heroines. Brownstein does not discuss Anthony Trollope's vibrant, engaging female characters, but it is one of these, Glencora M'Cluskie Palliser, central heroine of the great Palliser chronicle, that has haunted my mind for forty years. The final Palliser novel, *The Duke's Children* (1880), opens with Glencora's death. Her sudden absence from the Palliser saga was a shock when I first read the novel, but it has become a settled mourning for a loved character whom I have come to know over five novels and several decades of her life—and more decades of my own. I grieve the woman with whom I not only sympathize and identify, but whom I have come to love. Losing this created female character felt—especially the first time I read of her death—like a wonderfully authentic, intimate friend had died. And it is the affective experience of coming to know Glencora and then of losing her that has remained with me, in a version of the reading experience that Rachel Ablow and other scholars discuss with a "renewed attention to feeling rather than knowing."[1] My memory of reading about Glencora and responding to her experiences while living my own life thus becomes a crucial part of my encounters with her each time I read and teach *The Duke's Children*.

Glencora is a living presence in my life, a person I know well—who, more mysteriously, has "known" me at different phases of my life, as I imagined and responded to her when I was a young woman and in my middle age and as I continue to be in a relationship with her in my sixties. My feeling of loss at Glencora's death was most jarring upon a first reading of *The Duke's Children* in the late 1970s, as I studied the novels in sequence in preparation to take my comprehensive exams and write the PhD dissertation that eventually became *Women in Trollope's Palliser Novels*. At the end of *The Prime Minister*, Glencora is not even ill, but her death is announced in the first line of the following novel, *The Duke's Children*. We expect a story of her middle age—this is, after all, the Palliser *series*—but that story is denied. Her death is reinforced with the complete erasure of her little girl Glencora, who is never mentioned in *The Duke's Children*—or by scholars of the Palliser saga.

My students of course experience the novel differently, as very few of them have read Trollope before my course and none have ever read any of the previous Palliser novels. Despite most students' buoyant focus upon the Duke's recovery from mourning Glencora through his love for his three grown children—and upon the successful love affairs of his daughter and elder son—the sense of loss has deepened for me each time I teach the novel, nearly every year for the past three decades. I find myself recalling Glencora from the earlier novels of the series, revivifying her each time I read passages from *Can You Forgive Her?* or *The Prime Minister* to evoke her character for my students—only to lose her again at the outset of *The Duke's Children*. I commonly now spend at least half of the first class teaching the novel's Palliser background, showing images of the previous novels' illustrations and screening film clips of the incomparable Susan Hampshire in the 1970s BBC adaptation, who embodies Glencora's liveliness, beauty, and frustration so perfectly that I have always thought Trollope himself would applaud her performance.

I also find myself projecting into the future, beyond the confines of *The Duke's Children*'s ending, to create an alternate history for this flamboyant, rebellious woman. In a variation on Barbara Hardy's *Dorothea's Daughter and Other Nineteenth-Century Postscripts* (2011), my reading past the ending of *The Duke's Children* begins with a desire to change the very beginning of the novel, to alter Trollope's opening line: "No one, probably, ever felt himself to be more alone in the world than our old friend, the Duke of Omnium, when the Duchess died."[2] I become, like Barbara Hardy, not only reader but author, imagining plot and character trajectories that are a mixture of extrapolation from Trollope's creation and my own, building a new narrative scaffolding. My reading of Trollope's novel has evolved over time into an encounter not only with the text he wrote in relation to the earlier novels of the series but also with alternative fictions I have imagined of what the novel *might* be if Trollope had allowed Glencora to live through the weddings of her children and into late middle age and even old age, the territory I will be entering only a decade or so from now.[3]

*The Duke's Children* concludes the magnificent Palliser saga, five novels—*The Eustace Diamonds* (1873) was not included in Trollope's conception of the series—and three thousand pages long. *Can You Forgive Her?* (1864), the first novel of the series, narrates Glencora's story of compelled marriage to one man, the staid Plantagenet Palliser, future Duke of Omnium, while loving another, the beautiful scapegrace Burgo Fitzgerald. While the Phineas novels, *Phineas Finn* (1869) and *Phineas Redux* (1874), center on the eponymous Irishman, Glencora's immersion in both motherhood and politics is also represented, and she becomes the Duchess of Omnium after the old duke dies and her husband becomes duke. In these novels she forms her closest female friendship, with the brilliant, beautiful Viennese widow Madame Max Goesler (later Mrs. Finn), and much of what we know about Glencora is related in dialogue with this most loving, moral, and intelligent woman. In between the Phineas novels Trollope published *The Eustace Diamonds*, centering upon the adventures of the devious Lizzie Eustace; Glencora figures chiefly as one of those in upper society who get a vicarious frisson from Lizzie's erotic, marital, and legal troubles. *The Prime Minister* (1876) tells of the Duke and Duchess in their glory and vexation as he heads a coalition government and she is his confidante and indiscreet, albeit influential, political hostess. The end of that great novel marks a quiet, affectionate moment in their marriage as the Duke is forced to leave office and Glencora must also relinquish the excitement of political influence for what she has only half jokingly called his ideal of "Darby and Joan."[4] About the Palliser series, Trollope wrote in *An Autobiography*:

> To carry out my scheme I have had to spread my picture over so wide a canvas that I cannot expect that any lover of such art should trouble himself to look at it as a whole. Who will read *Can You Forgive Her?*, *Phineas Finn*, *Phineas Redux*, and *The Prime Minister* consecutively, in order that they may understand the characters of the Duke of Omnium, of Plantagenet Palliser, and of Lady Glencora? Who will ever know that they should be so read?[5]

On the plan to add *The Duke's Children*, Trollope stated: "I have a plan that I will even yet once more have recourse to my political hero as a mainstay of another story."[6]

I am one of Trollope's hoped-for ideal readers, because I did read the Palliser novels in order, not once but several times. It was truly an immense saga that I lived in at intervals for months at a time, while also living my own intense life. I was in my later twenties and early thirties during the first three readings of the series as a whole, and that urgent time of early marriage, babies, and writing a dissertation is deep in the palimpsest of my mind as I read the novels once again, even though the emotional turbulence of that fervent and chaotic period is layered over with many more readings since. Only a few years older than Glencora when I first read *Can You Forgive Her?*, I identified with her longing for excitement, passion, and sexual satisfaction. At this time in my life, her loss of these elements struck me as tragic, and I could not imagine sufficient recompense. This was also a period of resurgent grieving for my wonderful pediatrician father, who had died when I was not yet sixteen—grief reanimated no doubt by the birth of the son and daughter my father would never know, never be able to care for as he had cared for my siblings and me and hundreds of other children. Mourning Glencora's losses was, from the first readings, imbricated with mourning my own, very different loss of a father who also died in middle age. When I read for the first time that Glencora was dead, I recollect thinking of this most terrible of deaths I had experienced, and of my father's child patients in rows at his funeral, especially the anguish of one boy, who threw himself sobbing on the casket.

Early on in *The Duke's Children*, we learn of Glencora's most devastating loss, the forced separation from her dashing wastrel lover, divinely handsome Burgo Fitzgerald, and marriage to a man she does not know, Plantagenet Palliser, heir to the old Duke of Omnium. As Trollope tells us in *An Autobiography*, "[I]t must ever be wrong to force a girl into a marriage with a man she does not love,—and certainly the more so, when there is another man she does love."[7] Soon we hear that in the months before her death, Glencora secretly condoned the engagement of her only daughter, Mary, to Francis Tregear, the Cambridge friend of Glencora's son, Silverbridge, and the brilliant, handsome younger son of a small Cornish squire. We discover that Mary's lover reminded Glencora of Burgo, "that other beautiful one she had known in her youth," although she also recognized that Tregear is cut from finer cloth, "altogether different in mind and character."[8]

Glencora's personal loss is now only a part of my focus upon dispossession in the novel as I teach *The Duke's Children*. I lecture about devastating losses in the British Empire, the oppressions and issues of Englishness and nationhood not represented in *The Duke's Children*—part of the "unnarrated hinterland" of the Victorian novel of which John Sutherland writes in *Lives of the Novelists* (2011)—which nevertheless very much centers on the English ruling classes. We discuss social class exclusions in the novel and marginalized characters such as the racing man Major Tifto and the lady's companion Miss Cassewary. We often hear echoes of Shakespearean tragedies and the darker elements of the history plays, which Trollope knew well and loved, copiously annotating his copies as well as editions of scores of other Elizabethan and Jacobean dramas. One student last year wrote upon *The Winter's Tale* and another on *Hamlet* in their *Duke's Children* papers, and I myself have written a brief section of a forthcoming essay on Major Tifto's Falstaffian loss in relation to *King Henry IV, Part II* and on Silverbridge's generosity to his former crony Tifto as a re-visioning of Henry V's disavowal of Falstaff. On a more personal note, having been married for forty-six years, I am now more deeply saddened by the Duke's trauma after his beloved wife's death, more vividly able to imagine that catastrophe—even though many years ago I had already lived through my own father's death, when my mother was only forty-four. Her eight years of intense grieving seemed endless then, I recall—whereas now it seems, in retrospect, simply what is due to great love of long duration. I fell in love with my husband Chas at twenty, when I was just a year older than Glencora was when she married the Duke. Like Susan Gubar, my senior by only a few years, I have found that "late-life love" seems even more precious in the diminishing time left to us.[9]

The new edition of *The Duke's Children* edited by Steve Amarnick and based upon Trollope's original manuscript centers more on the Duke's elder son and heir Lord Silverbridge's accession to manliness, his "gaining by degrees age and flavour."[10] However, the generous-hearted Silverbridge's possession of all good things in English society—including the American beauty Isabel Boncassen—cannot wholly countervail my vision of *The Duke's Children* as primarily a novel about loss. Although dispossession has been most discussed in relation to the Duke's bereavement, scholars have recognized Glencora's losses much less often. Most readers—including my students—decide that *The Duke's Children* is ultimately about the reconciliation and reconnection that culminates at the novel's close in two weddings, unions the Duke has opposed for his children but ultimately affirms in the process of resolving his grief for Glencora.[11] Thus, for most, the novel is about *his* traumatic mourning and *his* re-immersion in life.

I want to de-center the narrative from the Duke (and in the original manuscript, from Silverbridge) and position Glencora as the protagonist. I now think as much about how alone the *Duchess* must often have felt during her marriage to the Duke as about how isolated the Duke is after "the Duchess died." What disturbs me most is that Glencora was basically discontented—emotionally isolated and sexually unsatisfied—during all of her long marriage to Plantagenet Palliser, who "in manner was as dry as a stick."[12] Even though Glencora is the richest heiress in Scotland, she does not get to choose her husband. After she is compelled at age nineteen to give up the man she loves, her excitements lie in the thrill of power she has in relation to her husband's political life and in smoothing her daughter's path to true love, revising her own history through Mary's. Glencora makes accommodations and becomes good friends and partners with the Duke, and she even grows to love him, a tale narrated over many hundreds of pages. As Trollope tells us in *An Autobiography*, "The romance of her life is gone, but there is a rich reality of which she is fully able to taste the flavour."[13] But she does not feel passion for her husband, and this is what she wants for her beloved only daughter, Mary. Glencora dies before she can know that after much suffering, her daughter does wed Francis Tregear, the man she fervently desires, a marriage that takes place in the Priory ruins, where Glencora—strolling in the moonlight with her friend Alice Vavasor—confesses her love for Burgo during the early years of her marriage, narrated in *Can You Forgive Her?*, the first Palliser novel.

Reading figured generally as a voyage in another person's mind—both the mind of the writer and the minds of the characters—is a trope used perhaps most famously by Proust.[14] Reading fiction as a pleasurable experience has been much commented upon, from Roland Barthes's theoretical *The Pleasure of the Text* (1973) through Kate Flint's magisterial work on gendered reading, *The Woman Reader, 1837–1914* (1993). It is women's experience of reading with which Brownstein is concerned in *Becoming a Heroine*, in particular the female reader's identification with and empathetic immersion in a female character's fictional life. As Flint's work makes clear, certain reading materials were forbidden to Victorian and Edwardian girls and women because they contained sexual knowledge that was considered part of the male domain. Female novel reading could be interpreted as analogous not only to sexual indulgence but to consuming forbidden foods. Feminist scholarship—from Janice Radway's and Tania Modleski's books on women reading romance novels through Susan D. Bernstein's interpretations of women reading "dirty" sensation novels in the 1860s—analyzes women's rebellion against these reading sanctions.

I am a woman reader who was once an avid child reader. When I learned to read, I spent a few months doing nothing *but* reading, refusing to play except when compelled. The questions that frame my obsession with Glencora Palliser's life are somehow bound up with deep needs that I and other readers must fulfill by experiencing alternative lives—or reimagining our own lives—in the private world of reading novels. Even as a girl, I felt this reading space to be inviolate. When I was reading a book, I not only closed the doors—I locked them. I resented any interruption to the imagining of my world elsewhere. Reading in the conventional 1950s and early 1960s, I especially admired heroines who rebelled against authority and exhibited characteristics like bravery that were gendered male. My favorite early childhood readings included Alice Turner Curtis's "Little Maid" books such as *A Little Maid of Ticonderoga* and *A Little Maid of Bunker Hill*, in which I identified with the girls who courageously ran with messages behind the lines to save the fort; Laura Ingalls Wilder's *Little House on the Prairie* series, in which I imagined myself as Laura because I was aware Mary's goodness made us an improbable and undesired match and I feared her fate of blindness; Frances Hodgson Burnett's *The Secret Garden*, in which I was orphaned Mary Lennox, back from exotic India; all of the Nancy Drew, Judy Bolton, and Cherry Ames books, of which my favorite was *Cherry Ames, Army Nurse*, by Helen Wells, because my father had been a doctor in World War II. (Later, I wondered why Cherry did not want to be a doctor rather than to marry one.) The steamy historical fiction I read once I reached adolescence, especially Anya Seton's *Katherine*, the story of John of Gaunt's beautiful mistress Katherine Swynford, helped me imagine romance and sexuality. I recently read *Katherine* again and discovered a new perspective on the book: my identification with Katherine is now based on her maternity, her suffering, and her serious reflection more than on her stormy, illicit sex with her royal lover. Based upon my own reading encounters and what other readers tell me about theirs, the act of reading is an imaginative plunge that is very often a deep, all-consuming experience of empathy as well, altering as the reader goes through life—and reads many other books.

Why, then, to get back to Glencora Palliser, is the Duchess's story so absorbing for me? There are so many other frustrated—and even doomed—loves in the great Victorian novels. Our desire for consummated love and a happy ending for the novel's lovers is seldom realized in this fiction, as it is in Austen's novels. If a seemingly perfect marriage of minds and bodies occurs at last, it is achieved only through great suffering, as in *Jane Eyre* or *Middlemarch*. Brownstein writes about the way we live our lives more intensely through the stories of English literature's great heroines. As we read *Middlemarch*, perhaps the greatest of Victorian novels, we admire the beautiful idealism of Dorothea's yearning to "make life beautiful—I mean everybody's life."[15] We suffer with her through her first miserable, constrained marriage with the tyrannical pedant Casaubon and celebrate her fulfilled love with cosmopolitan, poetic Will Ladislaw. I love Dorothea, but I have suffered for many more years with that other great Victorian heroine, Glencora Palliser. I have never fully been able to rejoice with her. I long to read that my favorite heroine, the sparkling Glencora, experiences a marriage more like Dorothea's—more like my own. We yearn for our fictional characters' happiness as if they were our dearest friends—or indeed, our very selves.

In comparison to most famous Victorian novel heroines, Glencora might indeed seem lucky. In Emily Brontë's *Wuthering Heights*, Catherine finds union with Heathcliff only in *Liebestod*. Her sister Charlotte's Lucy Snowe, in *Villette*, loses her great love, Paul Emanuel, in a shipwreck. Courageous, dark Maggie Tulliver in George Eliot's *The Mill on the Floss* drowns with her brother at the novel's close, and Elizabeth Gaskell's self-sacrificing fallen woman, the eponymous Ruth, dies of a fever after nursing her seducer back to health. Almost any novel by Thomas Hardy focuses upon a doomed heroine, from the Romantic, queenly Eustacia Vye in *The Return of the Native* to the beautiful, sensitive peasant girl Tess Durbeyfield in *Tess of the D'Urbervilles*. Eustacia, bored with both her husband Clym and her lover Damon Wildeve, drowns herself in the weir. Tess does finally consummate her love for her husband, Angel Clare, but soon afterward she is hanged for murdering Alec, her seducer. Their loves end in tragedy, while Glencora presumably dies in her bed, surrounded by a loving husband, children, and best friend, Mrs. Finn. Why then does Trollope's Glencora in particular haunt me, when she was merely restless and unhappy?

The answer is, I think, that Glencora is a woman I can imagine *being*—someone who seems more like me and the kind of women I know than fiery, childish, poetic Catherine Earnshaw, repressed, passionate Lucy Snowe, or stoic, pious Ruth Hilton. Glencora's aristocratic experience is as far away from me as Tess Durbeyfield's peasant one, but Glencora discusses quotidian matters with her women friends and her husband much as I talk with my closest friends and my spouse. Her experiences seem less transcendent than Catherine's and less tragic than Tess's, and her open manner of speaking about her life feels contemporary. Certainly a part of Trollope's modernity comes from the sense of real, lived experience that he creates in his novels of manners, in which both dialogue and the representation of consciousness are crucial elements. Trollope's favorite novel at nineteen was *Pride and Prejudice*; like Jane Austen, Trollope respects and loves his women characters, aspects I would eventually term his feminism.[16] However, my emphasis on Glencora's life as a kind of "real" experience that continues to influence my own subjectivity in complicated emotional as well as ethical ways has been discouraged until recent interventions by Rachel Ablow and others.[17] I have never dismissed this kind of immersion and speculation in my teaching of the novel, even as we analyze it as a work of art. Students have avid responses not only to Glencora's life as it emerges in *The Duke's Children*'s allusions to past scenes and events before her death but also to the lives of the three young women characters—Mary, Mabel, and Isabel—who are about the students' age and who are struggling with their own relationships in complicated marriage plots.

As I read and reread Glencora's story during the course of my own marriage, I wondered continually about this character's inner life during her problematic union. After *Can You Forgive Her?*, we do not have a great deal of access to Glencora's interiority. In that novel, we know she strongly considers leaving her marriage to be with Burgo, that she waltzes madly with him at Lady Monk's ball with his elopement proposal in her pocket, and that she confesses her love for Burgo to her chagrined husband, who then magnanimously offers to take her on a European tour with her cousin and only close woman friend at that time, Alice Vavasor. She gets pregnant during this respite and gives birth to their first child, Silverbridge, an event that partly reconciles her to her marriage. After that first Palliser novel, however, Glencora rarely speaks of her former desires to a dear friend, except in *The Prime Minister*, when she confides in Mrs. Finn (Madame Max Goesler in the earlier Palliser novels). Toward the close of the second Palliser novel, *Phineas Finn*, Glencora becomes intimate with this wise, beautiful, rich Viennese widow, who refuses the old Duke of Omnium's marriage proposal and thus preserves the title for Glencora's little boy Silverbridge, fulfilling Glencora's passionate maternal desire. That close friendship between Glencora and Madame Max continues through *Phineas Redux* and *The Prime Minister*, but Glencora is older, resigned—and committed—to her marriage, and not quite so prone to confession as she was with Alice in *Can You Forgive Her?* We often do not know what she is thinking, despite her outspokenness and racy, modern language of rebellion, her use of slang in resistance to her husband's formal Latinate phrases.

Glencora's experience is malleable in my mind, if not in Trollope's novel—as I think our favorite heroines' lives become transformed by our reading of them and continue to change as we think about their experiences over time. We "know" these women, and they become real presences in our lives. We think about what they might say or do in particular circumstances, or imagine ourselves performing as they would perform, saying what they might say. This is not so very different than Trollope's own legendary daydreaming, in which he lived with his fictional characters for years, constructing his novelistic world, as he tells us in *An Autobiography*: "It was my study that these people, as they grew in years, should encounter the changes that come upon us all; and I think I have succeeded."[18] Thus I can reimagine Glencora's story even if Trollope did not write it except in the lives of the younger generation's women in *The Duke's Children*, in her steadfast daughter's passion for Tregear and the depth of love the quicksilver, intelligent American beauty Isabel Boncassen feels for Glencora's son, Silverbridge, and even in the discarded first love of Lady Mabel Grex, who discovers too late that she will always love Francis Tregear.

I have in fact imagined several scenarios for Glencora in which she is happier and more satisfied in her life. The first alternative life for Glencora I have written in my head is that she marries Burgo Fitzgerald rather than abandoning him. In this revision of Trollope, Glencora M'Cluskie and Burgo Fitzgerald, with their Scottish and Irish surnames, enact a national story of resistance to English hegemony; one might argue that colonial oppressions are evoked by Glencora M'Cluskie's Scottish heritage and Burgo Fitzgerald's Irishness, from his illustrious surname to his dark good looks and reckless abandon on horseback. In this imagined narrative, Glencora is influenced by my reading of Sir Walter Scott, becoming a heroine who is a cross between the brave, doggedly resilient Jeanie Deans from *The Heart of Midlothian* and her beautiful fallen sister Effie, for whom Jeanie walks across all of Scotland. Glencora, "the wayward heiress with the bright waving locks who had been most strongly minded to give herself and her wealth to Burgo Fitzgerald,"[19] looks very like a Scottish heroine. Her cousin Alice Vavasor thinks of Glencora:

> What a strange, weird creature she was, with her round blue eyes and wavy hair, looking sometimes like a child and sometimes almost like an old woman! . . . What things she said, and what terrible forebodings she uttered of stranger things she meant to say![20]

Alice's perception of Glencora as somehow both a child and an old woman, and of her words as incantations or omens, make Glencora seem almost otherworldly—or perhaps just Other, just a Scotswoman more in touch with her own turbulent interiority, her country's violent history, and her national folklore than the London-bred Englishwoman Alice Vavasor, with the Norman surname indicative of her conquering ancestors.

The story of Glencora's and Burgo's love would flout the conclave of relatives who, in *Can You Forgive Her?*, are appalled by Glencora's preference for the handsome ne'er-do-well Burgo:

> Burgo . . . had almost succeeded in obtaining the hand and wealth,—as people still said he had obtained the heart,—of the Lady Glencora M'Cluskie. But sundry mighty magnates, driven almost to despair at the prospect of such a sacrifice, had sagaciously put their heads together, and the result had been that the Lady Glencora had heard reason. She had listened,—with many haughty tossings of her proud little head, with many throbbings of her passionate young heart; but in the end, she listened and heard reason. She saw Burgo, for the last time, and told him that she was the promised bride of Plantagenet Palliser, the nephew and heir of the Duke of Omnium.[21]

What if Glencora had not listened to her mighty relatives, to her guardian, the Marquis of Auld Reekie (Trollope's joke), or to Lady Midlothian (surely Trollope's tribute to Sir Walter Scott)? Glencora and Burgo would have eloped to the Continent, and when the relatives became somewhat reconciled to the marriage—perhaps by the birth of a son—the newlyweds would have lived in Scotland, on one of Glencora's estates. She was the greatest heiress of the day, and one of the richest women in Britain. Glencora might have stood her ground and clung to her love for Burgo, despite the clamorings of her relatives and their dire prophecies of ruin, much as her daughter, Mary, later perseveres in her love for Tregear, making herself quite ill in her rebellion against the Duke when he refuses to let her see or even write to her lover. The marriage of the Scottish heiress M'Cluskie to the Irish scion Fitzgerald—a name associated with a long history of rebellion against English rule[22]—would have suggested a new line of resistance to English imperial-colonial policies. Burgo might have gone into Parliament, where he would have argued for Irish tenant rights, as the country doctor's son Phineas does in the second Palliser novel, *Phineas Finn*.

How could this rebellion have been effected? If Alice Vavasor had only allowed Glencora and Burgo to rendezvous at her home in Queen Anne Street (not a promising name for marital happiness), all might have been well with the lovers in *Can You Forgive Her?* They could have planned the elopement then, unchaperoned except by Alice. But Alice's scruples keep her from this gesture of friendship and resistance to the status quo that might have nurtured Burgo's and Glencora's love in a domestic space where they would not be policed. The rather stiff-necked Alice explains to Glencora that "she, an unmarried woman, who had hitherto not known her cousin, could not give such help as that! 'If you will not help me, I am helpless,' said the Lady Glencora."[23] Glencora kneels at her feet, promises to love Alice, and calls Alice "heartless," but Alice still does not support the lovers by providing a trysting place. She does allow Glencora to visit her every day, and the two become friendly—but Alice's principles mean more to her than Glencora's love. No wonder Alice is erased from the series after *Can You Forgive Her?* and replaced with the brilliant and empathetic Madame Max.

Readers of *Can You Forgive Her?* might with good reason complain that this story ignores Burgo's sweet but profligate character. They might recall Trollope's almost mythic description of Burgo Fitzgerald, a man with nearly divine beauty, whom Trollope's narrator later praises as having "a glorious mouth, such as the old sculptors gave to their marble gods."[24] But Burgo has an ordinary soul:

> No more handsome man than Burgo Fitzgerald lived in his days; and this merit at any rate was his,—that he thought nothing of his own beauty. But he lived ever without conscience, without purpose,—with no idea that it behooved him as a man to do anything but eat and drink,—or ride well to hounds till some poor brute, much nobler than himself, perished beneath him.[25]

This portrayal of Burgo is difficult to overcome, but I will counter that he could change if the violent Lord Chiltern in *Phineas Finn* can do so, when that red-headed peer finally gains his childhood beloved Violet Effingham. Chiltern becomes a pattern Master of Hounds—and could not Burgo do so as well? While it is true that some tradesmen are out of pocket through Burgo's spendthrift ways, Chiltern's great debt causes his sister's self-sacrificing and disastrous marriage to the religious madman Kennedy, when she could otherwise have chosen her beloved Phineas Finn. Surely Chiltern is more culpable—and yet Trollope provides him with his true love, a healthy baby not long afterward, and work to which he is perfectly suited. Perhaps Burgo could be reclaimed as well. His sweet nature seems more malleable than Chiltern's unruly one. This sweetness is evidenced by his kindness to the prostitute on the street not once but twice, first when she is starving and he feeds her, and again when he gives her a shilling and a kiss on their second encounter, after she accosts him on Bond Street. On neither occasion does Burgo try to make the encounter sexual, nor does he even treat her condescendingly.

Perhaps the most satisfying story—and the most true to Trollope's novel—would be a tale in which Plantagenet Palliser learned to be more passionate within his marriage. He is a man who is unemotional in his demeanor, although we know there is deep feeling within him. He is not simply the public servant who longs to be chancellor of the Exchequer more than he wants to be prime minister, and certainly more than he desires a dukedom. He is also the intensely private man left bereft at his wife's death. Early on in the novel, we learn that "in spite of her faults, her name was so holy to him that it had never once passed his lips since her death, except in low whispers to himself—low whispers made in the perfect, double-guarded seclusion of his own chamber. 'Cora, Cora,' he had murmured, so that the sense of the sound and not the sound itself had come to him from his own lips."[26] The Duke is the father who learns to express his love for his three children as well, after a lifetime of reticence. No reader of *The Duke's Children* can fail to be moved, for instance, by this scene in his son's London club, the Beargarden, when Silverbridge makes clear his love and respect for his distinguished, reserved father:

> "I should be glad to see you marry early," said the Duke, speaking in a low voice, almost solemnly, but in his quietest, sweetest tone of voice. . . . "There is so much which I should only be too ready to give up to you!"
>
> "I can't bear to hear you talking of giving up anything," said Silverbridge energetically.
>
> Then the father looked round the room furtively, and seeing that the door was shut, and that they were assuredly alone, he put out his hand and gently stroked the young man's hair. It was almost a caress,—as though he would have said to himself, "Were he my daughter, I would kiss him."[27]

Perhaps, then, the story I want in place of *The Duke's Children* is not so much *The Duchess's Children* but *The Duke and Duchess's Children*—a story about how *both* the Duke and Glencora coped with Silverbridge, Gerald, and Mary's coming of age, and perhaps how their children's loves reignite their own. Rather than a story of grief and healing, it would be a tale of great love realized at last, in mature age. To change this narrative from one of the Duke's revelation that his wife had remained dissatisfied to one of their mutual discovery of passion, the Duke would have to manifest some of the tender love he expresses to Silverbridge in this scene—and that he is rarely able to exhibit throughout the series. In the first novel of the Palliser series, there is hope that the Duke might become a tender lover when Glencora finally tells him of her love for Burgo. In the remarkable chapter "The Pallisers at Breakfast" in *Can You Forgive Her?*, Glencora declares her continuing passion for Burgo while admitting her misery in her marriage: "I do love Burgo Fitzgerald! I do! I do! I do! How can I help loving him? Have I not loved him from the first, before I had seen you? Did you not know that it was so?" Glencora has not been able to become pregnant with Plantagenet's child, and she admits that she has thought of drowning herself instead of running away with Burgo "so that you might marry again, and have a child. . . . I'd die—I'd die willingly. How I wish I could die! Plantagenet, I would kill myself if I dared."[28] Trollope's scene of reconciliation is, to my mind, one of the most powerful in all his fiction:

> Softly, slowly, very gradually, as though he were afraid of what he was doing, he put his arm around her waist. "You are wrong in one thing," he said. "I do love you."
>
> She shook her head, touching his breast with her hair as she did so. . . .
>
> ". . . I do love you. If you cannot love me, it is a great misfortune to us both. But we need not therefore be disgraced. As for that other thing of which you spoke,—of our having, as yet, no child"—and in saying this he pressed her somewhat closer with his arm—"you allow yourself to think too much of it;—much more of it than I do. . . . I would rather have you for my wife, childless—if you will try to love me—than any other woman, though another might give me an heir. Will you try to love me?"[29]

In the immediate aftermath of this speech, Palliser gives up his long-coveted appointment as chancellor of the Exchequer, while Glencora agrees to go abroad with him and Alice Vavasor. Trollope shows that the acknowledgment of both husband's and wife's desires and the mutual sacrifice they make for each other is rewarded when they conceive their first child, Lord Silverbridge, during their travels.

However, even deep into the penultimate Palliser novel, *The Prime Minister*, it is evident that although Glencora loves her husband, she is still not in love with him. He has clearly not been able to sustain his sexual passion and lover's role in the marriage. Glencora recalls Burgo to Madame Max when that wise friend speaks to her of the Duke's devotion:

> "You ought to love him."
>
> "I do—but what's the use of it? He is a god, but I am not a goddess; and then, though he is a god, he is a dry, silent, uncongenial and uncomfortable god. It would have suited me much better to have married a sinner. But then the sinner that I would have married was so irredeemable a scapegrace."
>
> "I do not believe in a woman marrying a bad man in the hope of making him good."[30]

Trollope would agree with Madame Max—and yet there is that case of wild Lord Chiltern taming himself in order to gain Violet's hand in marriage.

There is also the instance in *Phineas Redux* of Gerard Maule, another sexy man of an entirely different character than Chiltern, a lackadaisical gentleman who attracts the energetic Adelaide Palliser—whereupon both of them are made happy by Madame Max's windfall, her renounced inheritance of £20,000 from the Duke of Omnium. It is Glencora, significantly, who wants to make this love match possible and who suggests that the inheritance be given to Adelaide so that she can marry the man she loves, unimpressive as he is, rather than the solid farmer Mr. Spooner, her other, unfavored suitor.

Rather than imagining a more passionate marriage for Glencora, Trollope decides instead to revise her narrative in the stories of her daughter, Mary, her future daughter-in-law, Isabel Boncassen, and Lady Mabel Grex, as I argued years ago in *Women in Trollope's Palliser Novels*. Trollope understood women's desire, and he understood the frustration of that desire in a society that often restricted women but that was also increasingly promising change. Between 1864 and 1880, the span in which Trollope published the Palliser novels, he formed the most special friendship of his life, with the American feminist lecturer, actress, and journalist Kate Field. Field is most likely the beautiful, vibrant original of Isabel in *The Duke's Children*. Trollope met Field at his brother Tom's in Florence in 1860 and visited her on his trip to America in 1861–1862. They had a lifelong, intimate friendship and correspondence that lasted until Trollope's death in 1882. In *An Autobiography*, Trollope famously states:

> There is an American woman, of whom not to speak in a work purporting to be a memoir of my own life would be to omit all allusion to one of the chief pleasures which has graced my later years. In the last fifteen years she has been, out of my own family, my most chosen friend. She is a ray of light to me, from which I can always raise a spark by thinking of her.[31]

For my students, Isabel in particular is a hopeful character, and she is indeed one of Trollope's great creations. She is intelligent, witty—and exasperated with the immaturity and witlessness of most of the young men she meets in London. One of the most humorous scenes in the novel depicts the languid Adolphus (Dolly) Longstaff proposing to Isabel at her "river-party." Dolly speaks first:

> "Miss Boncassen."
>
> "Mr. Longstaff! If you sigh like that you'll burst yourself."
>
> "I'll—what?"
>
> "Burst yourself!" and she nodded her head at him.
>
> Then he clapped his hands together, and turned his head away from her towards the little temple. "I wonder whether she knows what love is . . ."
>
> "No, she don't," said Miss Boncassen.
>
> "But I do," he shouted, turning back towards her. "I do. If any man were ever absolutely, actually, really in love, I am the man."
>
> "Are you indeed, Mr. Longstaff? Isn't it pleasant?"
>
> "Pleasant—pleasant? Oh, it could be so pleasant."
>
> "But who is the lady? Perhaps you don't mean to tell me that."
>
> "You mean to say you don't know?"
>
> "Haven't the least idea in life."
>
> "Let me tell you then that it could be one person. It never was but one person. It never could have been but one person. It is you." Then he put his hand well on his heart.
>
> "Me!" said Miss Boncassen, choosing to be ungrammatical in order that he might be more absurd.[32]

This wonderful comic scene ends with Dolly trying to explain his position in English society to Isabel, who replies, serious at last, "Mr. Longstaff, I rather fancy that wherever I may be I can make a position for myself. At any rate I shall not marry with the view of getting one. If my husband were an English Duke I should think myself nothing, unless I was something as Isabel Boncassen."[33]

When Isabel marries Lord Silverbridge, she has made it clear that she desires him, stating that "from the sole of your foot to the crown of your head I love you as I think a man would wish to be loved by the girl he loves."[34] Isabel marries Silverbridge after making her vision of their marriage on "terms of equality" as clear as her longing for her future husband. In earlier heroines such as Lily Dale in *The Small House at Allington* and Lucy Robarts in *Framley Parsonage*, Trollope gives us desiring women. Lily tells her mother after her fiancé Adolphus Crosbie has jilted her that, nevertheless, "when he kissed me I kissed him again, and I longed for his kisses. I seemed to live only that he might caress me." The Shakespearean Lucy sounds like Rosalind in *As You Like It* when she jokes about her desire for Lord Lufton, " Oh, Fanny, is it his legs, think you, or is it his title?"[35] Trollope's fullest evocation of this ideal, however, is in the heroine he created in the late 1870s, during the fierce struggle for women's rights, just as the 1882 Married Women's Property Act was about to become law.[36] In *The Duke's Children*, Trollope portrays Isabel Boncassen as a woman who possesses not only the right to desire, but also the right to choose a marriage that promises both erotic fulfillment and equality.

My solace in reading *The Duke's Children* is that Trollope revises the possibilities of love in the late Victorian era in the passionate marriage of brilliant, lovely Isabel to generous, loving Silverbridge. We know that Glencora would have sanctioned this union because we realize that she wanted her children to marry for love. If marrying the granddaughter of an American dockworker may not seem rebellious, Silverbridge does resist the blandishments of both the Duke and Lady Mabel in order to marry the woman he loves "better than my life."[37] I now interpret both Silverbridge and Isabel as Glencora's heirs in love—and it is their union that embodies all that Glencora desired but could not experience. Perhaps I am finally ready to accept Trollope's decision to write the end of Glencora's story in the happiness of Isabel Boncassen with Silverbridge—the beloved son whose loving, generous nature is so much like Glencora's own, and whose birth reconciled Glencora to her husband in *Can You Forgive Her?* This displacement of fruition onto the next generation of both sexes accompanies Trollope's other dislocations of the marriage plot, including his intense focus upon the long, only partially satisfying marriage of Glencora to the Duke. At the end of my *Women in Trollope's Palliser Novels*, I wrote that Glencora's "dissatisfied ghost broods over the weddings of her children."[38] Now at last I may have finished mourning Glencora, as I realize that the full consummation of her story in the love of her son for a remarkable woman of great strength of character might indeed have been not only Trollope's desire, but her own.

## NOTES

1. Rachel Ablow, ed., *The Feeling of Reading: Affective Experience and Victorian Literature*, 2.

2. Anthony Trollope, *The Duke's Children*, ed. Dinah Birch, 1. Further references in notes are from this edition.

3. Steve Amarnick's edition of *The Duke's Children* based upon Trollope's original uncut manuscript suggests that Trollope may have been considering a further installment in the Palliser series, but this book was not written, possibly because Trollope died in 1882, two years after *The Duke's Children* was published (although Trollope originally wrote the novel in 1876).

4. Anthony Trollope, *The Prime Minister*, 1:169.

5. Anthony Trollope, *An Autobiography*, 184.

6. Trollope, *Autobiography*, 361–62.

7. Trollope, *Autobiography*, 182.

8. Trollope, *Duke's Children*, 17.

9. John Sutherland, *Lives of the Novelists: A History of Fiction in 294 Lives*, 342; Susan Gubar, *Late-Life Love: A Memoir*.

10. Trollope, *Duke's Children*, 272.

11. Christopher Herbert, in "Trollope and the Fixity of the Self," notably demurs from this view, arguing that the Duke has no "conversion." It is worth remarking here that in the original manuscript version, the Duke is more reconciled to Tregear as husband to his daughter, Mary, and more clearly admires his new son-in-law.

12. Trollope, *Prime Minister*, 2:153.

13. Trollope, *Autobiography*, 183.

14. There are many quotations from Proust's *In Search of Lost Time* that refer to experiencing art as the only real voyage of discovery. One from *Time Regained*: "Through art alone are we able to emerge from ourselves, to know what another person sees of a universe which is not the same as our own and of which, without art, the landscapes would remain as unknown to us as those that may exist on the moon. Thanks to art, instead of seeing one world only, our own, we see that world multiply itself and we have at our disposal as many worlds as there are original artists, worlds more different one from the other than those which revolve in infinite space" (299).

15. George Eliot, *Middlemarch*, chap. 22.

16. See "Trollope the Feminist" in *The Routledge Research Companion to Anthony Trollope* (London: Routledge, 2016).

17. Ablow, *Feeling of Reading*; Rachel Ablow, *The Marriage of Minds: Reading Sympathy in the Victorian Marriage Plot*.

18. Trollope, *Autobiography*, 184.

19. Anthony Trollope, *Can You Forgive Her?*, 189.

20. Trollope, *Can You Forgive Her?*, 232.

21. Trollope, *Can You Forgive Her?*, 188.

22. Trollope uses the name Fitzgerald in his Irish Famine novel *Castle Richmond*.

23. Trollope, *Can You Forgive Her?*, 189–90.

24. Trollope, *Can You Forgive Her?*, 93.

25. Trollope, *Can You Forgive Her?*, 188.

26. Trollope, *Duke's Children*, 95–96.
27. Trollope, *Duke's Children*, 167–68.
28. Trollope, *Can You Forgive Her?*, 189–90.
29. Trollope, *Can You Forgive Her?*, 190.
30. Trollope, *Prime Minister*, 2:154.
31. Trollope, *Autobiography*, 316.
32. Trollope, *Duke's Children*, 204–5.
33. Trollope, *Duke's Children*, 206.
34. Trollope, *Duke's Children*, 334.
35. Anthony Trollope, *The Small House at Allington*, 630; Anthony Trollope, *Framley Parsonage*, 319.
36. In my *Reforming Trollope: Race, Gender, and Englishness in the Novels of Anthony Trollope* (Farnham, UK: Ashgate, 2013), I discuss a number of Trollope's novels in relation to the agitation for women's rights.
37. Trollope, *Duke's Children*, 449.
38. Deborah Denenholz Morse, *Women in Trollope's Palliser Novels* (1991), 139.

## WORKS CITED


Ablow, Rachel, ed. *The Feeling of Reading: Affective Experience and Victorian Literature*. Ann Arbor: University of Michigan Press, 2010.

———. *The Marriage of Minds: Reading Sympathy in the Victorian Marriage Plot*. Stanford: Stanford University Press, 2007.

Barthes, Roland. *The Pleasure of the Text*. 1973. Translated by Richard Miller. New York: Hill & Wang, 1975.

Bernstein, Susan D. "Dirty Reading: Sensation Fiction, Women, and Primitivism." *Criticism* 36.2 (1994): 213–41.

Brownstein, Rachel. *Becoming a Heroine: Reading about Women in Novels*. 1982. New York: Columbia University Press, 1994.

Burnett, Frances Hodgson. *The Secret Garden*. New York: Harper Collins, 2010.

Curtis, Alice Turner. *A Little Maid of Bunker Hill*. New York: Knopf, 1952.

———. *A Little Maid of Ticonderoga*. Carlisle, MA: Applewood, 1997.

Eliot, George. *Middlemarch: A Study of Provincial Life*. Edited by Gregory Maertz. Peterborough, ON: Broadview, 2004.

Flint, Kate. *The Woman Reader, 1837–1914*. 1993. Oxford: Clarendon, 1995.

Gubar, Susan. *Late-Life Love: A Memoir*. New York: Norton, 2018.

Hardy, Barbara. *Dorothea's Daughter and Other Nineteenth-Century Postscripts*. Brighton, UK: Victorian Secrets, 2011.

Herbert, Christopher. "Trollope and the Fixity of the Self." *PMLA* 93.2 (March 1978): 228–39.

Modleski, Tania. *Loving with a Vengeance: Mass-Produced Fantasies for Women*. London: Routledge, 2007.

Morse, Deborah Denenholz. *Women in Trollope's Palliser Novels*. Ann Arbor: University of Michigan Research Press, 1987. Reprint, London: Boydell & Brewer, 1991.

Proust, Marcel. *Time Regained*. Vol. 6 of *In Search of Lost Time*. Translated by Andreas Mayor and Terence Kilmartin. Revised by D. J. Enright. New York: Random House, 1993.

Radway, Janice. *Reading the Romance: Women, Patriarchy, and Popular Literature*. Chapel Hill: University of North Carolina Press, 1991.

Seton, Anya. *Katherine*. New York: Houghton Mifflin, 1954.

Sutherland, John. *Lives of the Novelists: A History of Fiction in 294 Lives*. 2011. New Haven: Yale University Press, 2012.

Trollope, Anthony. *An Autobiography*. Edited by Michael Sadleir and Frederick Page. Introduction and notes by P. D. Edwards. Oxford: Oxford University Press, 2008.

———. *Can You Forgive Her?* Edited by Andrew Swarbrick. Introduction by Kate Flint. Oxford: Oxford University Press, 1999.

———. *The Duke's Children*. Edited with an introduction and notes by Dinah Birch. London: Penguin, 1995.

———. *The Duke's Children*. Reconstructed and edited by Steve Amarnick. Introduction by Max Egremont. New York: Knopf, 2017.

———. *Framley Parsonage*. Edited by David Skilton and Peter Miles. London: Penguin, 2004.

———. *Phineas Finn*. Edited with an introduction and notes by Simon Dentith. Oxford: Oxford University Press, 2011.

———. *The Prime Minister*. Edited by Jennifer Uglow. Introduction by John McCormick. Oxford: Oxford University Press, 1985.

———. *The Small House at Allington*. Edited with an introduction and notes by Julian Thompson. London: Penguin, 2005.

Wells, Helen. *Cherry Ames, Army Nurse*. New York: Grosset & Dunlop, 1944.

Wilder, Laura Ingalls. *Little House on the Prairie*. 1935. New York: Harper Collins, 2007.

CHAPTER THREE

# A Skeptical Education

Terrance Riley

## On *The Adventures of Sherlock Holmes* by Arthur Conan Doyle

I would have been twelve or thirteen years old and newly aware that books are complicated things when I purchased my first hardcover: the Doubleday one-volume *Complete Sherlock Holmes*, first published in 1927 and reprinted at irregular intervals since. It might have been eight dollars (this was the early 1960s). I've acquired other editions in the intervening years, but the Doubleday, somewhat faded by time and familiarity, still occupies an eye-level position on my shelf alongside Arthur Conan Doyle's neglected historical romances, just down from Lewis Carroll's *Complete Works*. The purchase was not accidental or speculative: I knew what I was in search of and had every reason to believe I'd find it in this book. As it happened, this purchase paid off in unexpected but richer ways than I'd foreseen. I was to learn that the character Sherlock Holmes was not merely the protagonist of some passable adventures but an organized array of possibilities and options. He embodied values I saw nowhere around me in the factory town of Flint, Michigan, but values that I recognized at once as compelling. He had motives and objectives that helped me understand my own half-formed dispositions. Holmes's lessons were often cryptic, but they were literally, for this reader, unforgettable.

My acquaintance with Holmes did not begin with Conan Doyle's nineteenth-century texts, but with filmed adaptations—then as now a common experience. In my case, it was the fourteen films starring Basil Rathbone, produced first by 20th Century–Fox and then by Universal Studios between 1939 and 1946. In my youth, before cable and satellite television, local television stations had long periods of time to fill on weekday afternoons and on weekends, when the three major networks provided no programming. These could be filled with local news and features, but a cheap and frequent alternative was to lease packages of old black-and-white films from distributors. I was almost guaranteed an opportunity to see the whole Sherlock Holmes series every year or two. I took advantage of that opportunity often enough to learn which of the films were fully satisfying and which scenes to watch for, and the disappointing ones that did not reward repeated viewings. The films are uncomplicated, but for a young mind, becoming a fan was a healthy exercise in critical discrimination. Twelve of the fourteen are poorly conceived and executed; occasional brilliant sequences are buried in mediocre exposition. This Holmes and Watson may have been the worst-matched couple in cinematic history: the polished, authoritative Rathbone, considered by many to be the best Holmes on film, paired with the buffoonish Nigel Bruce, a prosecutable slander against Conan Doyle's Watson. As I experienced them on television, out of order and without commentary or analysis, the films were wildly uneven in purpose and in quality. Two of them—the first two to be produced, I learned later—were set in the Victorian period: one an able and faithful version of *The Hound of the Baskervilles* (1939), the other *The Adventures of Sherlock Holmes* (1939), which pitted Holmes against Moriarty's attempt on the Crown Jewels. In both of these, Watson is of near-average IQ. The remaining twelve films are set in the 1940s, World War II either foregrounded in stories of Holmes fighting the Nazis or backgrounded as a setting for a patriotic scouring of criminals from the green and pleasant land. In all of these, Watson appears capable of losing the war single-handedly.

The only consistently appealing feature of the film series is Rathbone's Holmes, who remains throughout aristocratic, articulate, witty, steady in the face of the unknown, and independent in moral judgments: "I interfere wherever and whenever I like," he says in *The Adventures of Sherlock Holmes*.[1] He was not young—Rathbone was forty-seven when the first film came out—but he was energetic and self-assured. Like many who have lived a long connection to Sherlock Holmes, I can recall being drawn early on to a character whose chief virtues were also the characteristics of a bookish child: curiosity, skepticism, an inclination toward science, and a fascination with the perversities of the adult world, along with his renowned powers of observation and logic. One could find these several traits scattered about in popular accounts of detectives, lawyers, and doctors, both real and fictional, but never, in my experience then, collected in a single character. More to the point, I could see no one who reminded me of Holmes, even partially, anywhere around me. His qualities were not prized in the culture I grew up in. Careful observation and reasoning were not, and still are not, highly valued in America, except in certain contexts: law courts, laboratories and clinics, some classrooms and lecture halls. So Holmes came to represent for me options and alternatives to Flint, as well as aspirations I could try or test. It might constitute an improvement in my life if I could be smarter, I thought, more articulate or more observant, even a bit more aristocratic, or simply confident, in manner.

Such ambitions took shape slowly, along with my understanding that the movies were lacking in the kind of artistic judgment Holmes deserved. Much of the problem was the intellectual dead weight of Bruce's Watson, but also dialogue, plotting, and character development were often clumsy or insufficient. I wanted more Holmes, more and better than I was getting from the films. So when I spotted the book in a local department store, displaying Holmes in profile wearing the familiar deerstalker on the spine, I knew this had to be the stuff I was looking for, pure and abundant.

It almost was. Conan Doyle's narratives enriched with detail and motive most of my favorite elements in the films: foggy streets at night, gaslit salons, coded messages, clues and false leads, all navigated confidently by Holmes, using a sharp eye and the scientific method. The dialogue was animated and smart; villains and victims alike were recognizably complex persons; it was a great relief to find that the "real" Watson was not mentally impaired. I was satisfied, knowing that I was in the presence of the more refined set of options and attitudes that I had suspected lurked within the films.

I remember no disappointment in discovering that the Holmes in print is very different from the Holmes on celluloid. Rathbone's Holmes is sociable, friendly, occasionally charming (he smiles often). Conan Doyle's Holmes is scornful, cold, and humorless, except when, often with a "chuckle," he is pointing out the failures and discomforts of others. The author is at pains to assemble a cluster of unpleasant characteristics in the opening scene of "A Scandal in Bohemia," the first of the twelve short stories that were published as *The Adventures of Sherlock Holmes* in 1892: "All emotions [and particularly love] were abhorrent to his cold, precise but admirably balanced mind. . . . He never spoke of the softer passions, save with a gibe and a sneer"; he alternated, Watson says, "from week to week between cocaine and ambition, the drowsiness of the drug, and the fierce energy of his own keen nature." When Watson visited him after an absence of some months, "his manner was not effusive. It seldom was." He "loathed every form of society" and had no friends.[2] "Except yourself," he added to Watson in a later story published in the *Adventures*, "The Five Orange Pips."[3]

Thus I found a different kind of "real thing" in the texts than I could have predicted, and a different appeal. This Holmes is still the boyish skeptic, scientific and "deeply attracted by the study of crime."[4] But he is also absorbed in his own projects to the exclusion of human contact, a deliberate loner who feels no craving for acceptance or companionship, not the conventional hero (as I could see now) portrayed by Rathbone but an anti-hero in the mold of Heathcliff (as impersonated by Laurence Olivier in William Wyler's 1939 *Wuthering Heights*, another film of my acquaintance in those days). This Holmes, then, turned out to be quite agreeable to an isolated eighth grader. Staying off by yourself could signify superior priorities.

Holmes is a kind of perennial schoolboy, but not the sort of role model welcome on school premises: he is not a team player and has too many defiant attitudes. Indeed, there is something delightfully scandalous about Holmes's irreverence toward education. In the second chapter of *A Study in Scarlet* (Holmes's first appearance in print), Watson puzzles over Holmes, whose "ignorance was as remarkable as his knowledge," for he "would acquire no knowledge which did not bear upon his object." Watson catalogs his friend's attainments:

1. Knowledge of Literature.—Nil.
2. " " Philosophy.—Nil.
3. " " Astronomy.—Nil.
4. " " Politics.—Feeble.
5. " " Botany.—Variable. . . .
6. Knowledge of Geology.—Practical, but limited. . . .
7. Knowledge of Chemistry.—Profound.
8. " " Anatomy.—Accurate, but unsystematic.
9. " " Sensational Literature.—Immense. . . .[5]

I was aware of showing disrespect just by picking the book up. I shouldn't have been wasting my afternoons on Sherlock Holmes. Good literature is difficult; it has profound and carefully concealed themes about the hardships of life and the loneliness of the universe; above all, it is morally elevating. And I shouldn't have been going back and forth between movies and books—that felt like cheating, somehow. These things I was pretty sure of, but none of the objections were powerful enough to send me back to diagramming sentences or multiplying decimals. There were too many attractions in this subversive stranger.

I have vivid, living memories of my preferred reading in those days: John Carter of Mars; Tarzan; Doc Savage; anything by Agatha Christie; my mother's old *Ellery Queen Mystery Magazines* from the 1940s, with their lurid cover art; and stories by Dashiell Hammett, Margery Allingham, and Cornell Woolrich. By contrast, I have no interesting memories of school reading whatsoever. There were novels, I think, though I remember only two. The first, *A Lantern in Her Hand*, by Bess Streeter Aldrich, is still in print (I have just discovered). The Amazon synopsis is revealing:

> Abbie Mackenzie dreamed of becoming a fine lady like her aristocratic grandmother, devoting herself to music and art. But at eighteen Abbie found a different dream, turning away from the promise of a comfortable life as a doctor's wife to marry handsome, quiet Will Deal. Together, they eagerly accepted the challenge of homesteading in Nebraska territory, where the prairies stretched as far as the eye could see, and only the strongest survived for long.[6]

School, as I recall it, was in the business of cultivating low expectations of life, preferably free of any of this musical or artistic nonsense; resignation and compliance were encouraged. It was therefore not a liberating but rather a hugely ironic experience to be assigned, in my first year of high school, *The Catcher in the Rye*, whose protagonist has adopted a pretense of cynicism calculated to hide his yearning to join the normative mainstream. It was easy to feel superior to Holden Caulfield after my exposure to a more sophisticated iconoclast and phony-spotter. After Holmes helps to free the king of Bohemia from the multitalented blackmailer Irene Adler, the king remarks, "Would she not have made an admirable queen? Is it not a pity that she was not on my level?" Holmes replies "coldly" and sarcastically, "From what I have seen of the lady, she seems, indeed, to be on a very different level to your Majesty."[7] Had *Catcher in the Rye* not already been among the most notorious of banned books, I would have forgotten it immediately.

Toward the end of these early years with Holmes, I began just to glimpse a final complication of my passage from the films to the texts: the recognition that the character is inextricable from the fictional London from which he is made to arise. On screen (as re-created on the Fox and Universal backlots), Rathbone's London is a maze of boulevards and dark alleys, big houses, broad sidewalks, and brownstones. Carriages clip-clop by, pedestrians move along briskly. Stock long shots of the city at dusk capture the Thames and Westminster Palace and St. Paul's. These settings and locations appear in the texts as well, but when overlaid with plot details—last-minute journeys, secret meetings, and desperate pursuits—this "London" becomes a moral as well as a geographical environment, alive with purpose and intelligence. The existing state of affairs is people about their business, obeying the codes of civility and fair play as naturally as they follow the traffic patterns. Crime disrupts the patterns. It is an environment to which Holmes is perfectly suited. "It is a hobby of mine to have an exact knowledge of London," he says in "The Red-Headed League."[8] He monitors the city. A crime in London disturbs his sense of order. That neither the character nor his environment ever existed as Conan Doyle drew them was lucky for me: instead of mourning their passing, I could move directly on to reimagining their values for my own purposes. One of those purposes was imagining a set of circumstances—some parallel to this fictional London—in which Holmes's eccentricities could be regarded as virtues.

I never felt that I had left Holmes behind. I had been sufficiently immersed long enough to permanently absorb both his peculiarities and his London by the time I moved on, sometime in the mid-1960s. And there were always reminders, mostly in the form of new film and television adaptations every three or four years, as the cultural industry of borrowing Holmes and Watson for new stories and new settings was beginning to take off. But I had other books to read and other subjects to look into, and you don't make time, in your twenties, to reread childhood favorites. But luck was on my side again when I unexpectedly ran into Holmes years later, in graduate school—not as a pastime now, but as an object of study in a class on the Victorian novel. In this class, surprisingly egalitarian even for the 1970s, such revered classics as Thomas Hardy's *The Mayor of Casterbridge* and *Jude the Obscure* were read on an equal footing with works of middlebrow reputation, such as Robert Louis Stevenson's

*The Master of Ballantrae* and *Strange Case of Dr. Jekyll and Mr. Hyde*. This effacing of the distinction between the serious and the popular was strengthened for me by my final project in the class. The assignment was to choose a Victorian periodical and characterize its contributions to the literature of the day. In another stroke of luck, I happened upon a bound set of *The Strand* magazines on my first visit to the library. *The Strand* began publication late in 1890. Early in 1891, the publisher contracted with Arthur Conan Doyle for twelve Sherlock Holmes stories, the first of which appeared in July 1891. I would have come back to Holmes at some point, I think, because of my eventual interest in Victorian fantasy and mystery, but that was still years away. Had I not taken this course and had I not chanced upon the brightly embossed cover of *The Strand*, I would have missed altogether a deeply memorable intellectual engagement at about the age of twenty-seven.

The first Holmes works, the novels *A Study in Scarlet* and *The Sign of Four*, were published in 1886 and 1890, to generally positive reviews. For *The Strand*, Conan Doyle perfected both a method of back-design composition and a narrative structure that would allow him to turn out one tightly organized story a month for the next two years. In the most familiar pattern he used, we initially find our main characters at home. Watson inadvertently provides the occasion for Holmes to show off his superior deductive power, which often takes the form of a life history of that stranger across the street, or this queer object left at the door. The exposition continues with the arrival at 221B Baker Street of a client, whose responsibility it is to provide a sketch of a mystery, guided by Holmes's questions. Rising action finds Holmes and Watson surveying the crime scene and meeting the principals; the climax identifies the evildoer; and a falling action takes place back at the flat, with Holmes clearing up a minor point or two. The first twelve of these demonstrations, collected in *The Adventures of Sherlock Holmes* (1892), brought Holmes an enthusiastic audience in the tens of thousands, demanding more. The next twelve, which would become *The Memoirs of Sherlock Holmes* (1893), left Conan Doyle miserable, burdened with a golden goose that prevented him from pursuing the historical fiction he felt was his best work.

Reading the critical and biographical backgrounds of stories that had meant so much to me as a teenager, while also studying them in their original context (including Sidney Paget's indispensable illustrations in their original size and placement in the text), was an extraordinary and absorbing experience, like disassembling the mechanism of a favorite toy. The most interesting discovery of all was aesthetic. The stories are not great—they are barely good. As a group, they are remarkably, almost embarrassingly, uniform in structure and affect. Those pleasures that drew me in as a teenager—the dramatization of reason, justice, and independence—are very nearly obliterated by reading several of these routine performances in a row, and you can understand why Conan Doyle grew weary of them. Watson's estimate of Holmes as "the most perfect reasoning and observing machine that the world has seen" is pitifully unsupported. His reasoning often consists in unjustified leaps, such as deducing from an observation of a man's "right cuff so very shiny for five inches" that the man "has done a considerable amount of writing lately." Like many of the detective writers who imitated him, Conan Doyle skimps on crucial details (Watson observes the "discoloured" silk lining of a hat in "The Adventure of the Blue Carbuncle," whereas Holmes identifies it as a formerly "excellent" lining—a fact Watson should have noticed but of which the reader could not be aware).[9] As for the bright conversation I thought I remembered, much of it is stilted and implausible, with unaccountable echoes of the eighteenth-century essay. Here is Holmes delivering Watson a backhanded compliment for avoiding sensationalism in his accounts of their adventures:

> "To the man who loves art for its own sake . . . it is frequently in its least important and lowliest manifestations that the keenest pleasure is to be derived. It is pleasant to me to observe, Watson, that you have so far grasped this truth that in these little records of our cases which you have been good enough to draw up, and, I am bound to say, occasionally to embellish, you have given prominence not so much to the many *causes célèbres* and sensational trials in which I have figured but rather to those incidents which may have been trivial in themselves, but which have given room for those faculties of deduction and of logical synthesis which I have made my special province."[10]

And despite his protestations that "the status of my client is a matter of less moment to me than the interest of his case,"[11] Holmes develops the annoying habit of mentioning his assistance to the rich and powerful:

the king of Bohemia (in "A Case of Identity" and "The Adventure of the Copper Beeches"), the royal family of Holland (in "A Scandal in Bohemia" and "A Case of Identity"), and the pope (in *The Hound of the Baskervilles*).

But I also began to see that missteps and inconsistency can be expected given the experiment in character Conan Doyle had set himself. Holmes is no mere cynic or heart-of-gold curmudgeon. As Conan Doyle attempts to draw him, he is deeply misanthropic, untouched by the precious emotional certainties of his fellow humans. "My life is spent in one long effort to escape from the commonplaces of existence," he complains in "The Red-Headed League," and his escape would appear to be entirely successful.[12] He never displays love for any other person; he never mentions his childhood or parents at all, and well into their acquaintance, in the twenty-first story, Watson is surprised to hear that Holmes has a brother. Money, status, fear, shame, hatred, compassion—the familiar motivations are absent. This is, as I said, how Conan Doyle attempted to draw the character, "as deficient in human sympathy as he was pre-eminent in intelligence."[13] The stray emotion does pop up, such as the pride of association noted above, and there are a few, rare expressions of affection toward Watson. But it is clear, especially in the early stories in the *Adventures*, that Conan Doyle was attempting to answer a difficult question: what would a person be like who was really a hardened skeptic, who accepted nothing on faith but brought science and reason to bear on every new situation, on every social phenomenon, and on every single person he met?

Conan Doyle was aware that other writers were experimenting along similar lines, and for the same reasons. Two centuries of scientific progress culminating in Darwin had made scientific materialism a respectable viewpoint, at least among the freethinkers, and many writers were turning toward naturalism, the often grim depiction of human beings in a world without transcendent values. This perspective can be found in the works of some of the most influential novelists of the late nineteenth century: Gustave Flaubert and Émile Zola in France, Stephen Crane and Frank Norris in America, and George Eliot, Thomas Hardy, Robert Louis Stevenson, and George Gissing in England. Conan Doyle was probably the first writer to create a heroic (as opposed to a defeated or cynical) materialist, one whose intellectual independence is proof against the confusion and tragedy that befall the protagonists of most naturalist fiction, such as Hardy's Jude Fawley and Theodore Dreiser's Caroline Meeber. The novelists were joined by philosophers in developing nineteenth-century naturalism into twentieth-century humanism: Herbert Spencer in Britain, William James and Charles Sanders Peirce in America, Auguste Comte in France, and, notoriously, Friedrich Nietzsche in Germany. In *Thus Spoke Zarathustra* (1883), Nietzsche described what he called the Übermensch, or Over-human: individuals who can live in a universe without gods or God, who reject inherited systems of belief and instead nurture their own visions, and who are able to live in peace with their fellow creatures without fear or envy.[14] Such a human being is Holmes. He attends no church, expects nothing from Providence, and scorns the supernatural. He tolerates his own kind but never speaks of their "softer passions, save with a gibe and a sneer." He labors for peace and order, but does so in his own way, interfering "wherever and whenever I like."[15]

Holmes's decisions to interfere are systematic; gradually, over the course of the first two novels and especially in the stories, in which Conan Doyle seems to have nailed down his own positions on current philosophical issues, we can see the fictional enactment of a new set of values. Or a recovered set: the values most apparent in the Holmes stories had already been laid out a number of times in the previous century, most famously by John Stuart Mill, himself a philosopher of Nietzschean stripe, though less flamboyantly so. In *On Liberty* (1859) Mill proposes his fundamental maxim of civil freedom:

> [T]he only purpose for which power can be rightfully exercised over any member of a civilised community, against his will, is to prevent harm to others. His own good, either physical or moral, is not a sufficient warrant. He cannot rightfully be compelled to do or forbear because it will be better for him to do so, because it will make him happier, because, in the opinions of others, to do so would be wise, or even right.[16]

On the subject of individual differences and nonconformities, Mill argues that "the free development of individuality is one of the leading essentials of well-being; . . . it is not only a co-ordinate element with all that is designated by the terms civilisation, instruction, education, culture, but is itself a necessary part and condition of all those things."[17]

Mill is not describing the England he knew. He is offering a utilitarian vision of the future, of social and psychological conditions he hoped would come to prevail. But he *is* describing the London I could see dimly in the early films, a setting first fully articulated in the stories: free individuals locating their own interests, investigating options, making decisions, and occasionally causing harm to others and thus attracting the attention of London's monitor and his acquaintances at Scotland Yard. It is an ethically purposive and dynamic society bearing strong traces of Conan Doyle's own open-minded politics. And it is an idealistic vision, for equality and respect for individual differences were hardly the norm in 1890. But the class system, institutionalized poverty, the legal subordination of women, and the empire itself were under attack, and in retreat, by the last decade of the century. In Holmes and in Holmes's London, Conan Doyle animates equality of worth and welcoming of difference, and he blends these experimental qualities freely with what he probably saw, to judge by those historical novels of his, as the true English virtues: hospitality, common sense, hope for the future, and freedom in a secular society, all of it unimpeded by ideology, dogma, or tradition. My report on Conan Doyle's stories in *The Strand* for my graduate seminar on the Victorian novel was not as organized or wide-ranging as it would be now, but all the components were there.

By the time the first wave of contemporary Holmes adaptations and metafictions in the 1980s and 1990s crested in Jeremy Brett's ten-year run as Sherlock Holmes for ITV/Granada, I had become a teacher of serious literature. When I thought about Holmes at all, which was not often, it was to remember him as an early mentor permanently lodged in my ways of thinking about social class and equality, about received wisdom versus free thought, about artistic merit and aesthetic pleasure—and about the search for explanations and solutions. I wouldn't have thought that there was much more to be gotten out of him, but there was to be a third, somewhat chastening learning experience. After twenty years of teaching Wordsworth, Dickens, the Shelleys, the Brontës, and the Brownings in a rather old-fashioned way, as texts for analysis, it finally occurred to me to ask my English majors about their reading outside of class, what they had read as children and what kind of books they enjoyed currently. Their answers were predictable, in retrospect. They learned to read on J. K. Rowling's Harry Potter books and Lemony Snicket's *A Series of Unfortunate Events*. Later they added J. R. R. Tolkien, H. P. Lovecraft, and other fantasists I'd never heard of. I read the Harry Potter series then myself (and became a fan) and some other books my students recommended. However, I was still proceeding on an unexamined assumption that I fear is common among English professors: that I was helping my students move on from their modest intellectual origins toward more refined judgments and more complex levels of literacy. And if they celebrated the chance to reread *The Fellowship of the Ring* over Christmas break—some of them for the third or fourth time—that simply meant that they were tuckered out after a semester of great books. I even harbored the delusion that the challenges of Jane Eyre and Elizabeth Bennet were supplanting the less demanding Frodo and Hermione. I should have realized years before that the literate teenagers who populated my classes were walking the same paths that I had, escaping the prison house of school-sponsored reading, with its tests and papers and moral elevation, to pursue imaginative possibilities in the texts that had already become part of their life histories.

It was that recognition that took me back once more to Holmes, but this time also to Alice and Doc Savage and John Carter, and then to the European intrigues of Eric Ambler and the noir California of Hammett and Raymond Chandler. I found much that I remembered clearly from twenty or forty years earlier, and much that I realized I only now understood. My experience recalls the opening sentences of *The Sign of Four*, a powerful and haunting image of the outsider:

> Sherlock Holmes took his bottle from the corner of the mantelpiece, and his hypodermic syringe from its neat morocco case. With his long, white, nervous fingers he adjusted the delicate needle and rolled back his left shirtcuff. For some little time his eyes rested thoughtfully upon the sinewy forearm and wrist, all dotted and scarred with innumerable puncture-marks. Finally he thrust the sharp point home, pressed down the tiny piston, and sank back into the velvet-lined armchair with a long sigh of satisfaction.[18]

And a few of the pleasures of reading the Sherlock Holmes stories had remained largely unchanged. Age has little impact on the pure fun of breaking rules.

> "By the way, Doctor, I shall want your cooperation."
> "I shall be delighted."
> "You don't mind breaking the law?"
> "Not in the least."
> "Nor running a chance of arrest?"
> "Not in a good cause."

"Oh, the cause is excellent!"

"Then I am your man."[19]

These stories may not be great literature, but they are engaging, especially when they cheerfully flout ethical conventions.

Did reading Sherlock Holmes have any effect on my mature character? This on-and-off reading of the Holmes canon, with all its renewals and reconsiderations, its massive, 120-year-long fandom of spin-offs and adaptations, and my occasional treks into the critical and cultural commentary that has grown up around the character and the canon—did it make a difference? Most assuredly. First, Holmes normalized for me the questioning of traditional authority and received opinion. As an "evidence only" thinker, he brought the scientific method out of the classroom and into the streets and drawing rooms of London. I might have found this inclination toward systematic thought elsewhere as a child, if I'd known where to look. But, in the event, I did not. The adults I grew up around were uniformly reverent toward the church and deferential, or at least obedient, toward the agents of the state. This included the science teachers I knew. Basil Rathbone's Holmes was the only adult I could imagine setting up a chemistry experiment on the dining room table, and I admired him for that. The Holmes of Conan Doyle's stories was equally adept at dressing down a police inspector, exchanging witticisms with the most dangerous man in England, or comforting a frightened young serving girl. He was not the kind of role model you are offered in school, but more's the pity for that.

Holmes was my entry point into nineteenth-century British literature, which was to shape my scholarly career, and he was the first of a long series of utterly fictional British gentlemen I met with in that literature. I learned from him that fairness is more important than winning, judgment superior to action, and a love of learning—as distinct from schooling—the highest virtue of all. And it was from Holmes and his descendants that I picked up the King's English. No one in my intellectual circles today can wield phrases like "most assuredly," "more's the pity," and "I shall be delighted." No one uses the word "shall."

Have Sherlock Holmes and his London made any contribution to the classically liberal social views I came to adopt or to my humanist outlook? Yes, for my encounters with the character and the world Conan Doyle built to house the character provided models and images and a sort of rhetoric to think through the citizen's responsibilities toward and protections from her fellow citizens. I stumbled into this line of ethical inquiry in many of my favorite books, mysteries especially, long before I knew the meaning of "liberal" or "humanist," longer still before encountering Bentham or Mill or William James. Conan Doyle created a place, a kind of refuge, where I could entertain all those images and observations that had not yet acquired the clarity of ideas, and inspect and question the ideas when they did materialize.

It bears stressing that this refuge is not attractive because it is reassuring. Customary platitudes of right and wrong are rare; human goodness is visibly an effort; most people are just trying to get by and get along; there is always work to do ("Give me problems, give me work," Holmes exclaims in *The Sign of Four*).[20] The philosophy is pragmatism, the faith is trust in reason. The stories are altogether worldly, and our main character is largely morally neutral, save for the clear if unexpressed endorsement of property rights (which Holmes frequently extends to the property and persons of the weak and disempowered). The word "love" occurs only eighteen times in the twelve stories that make up the *Adventures*, and some of these uses are idiomatic, unromantic, unaligned with Christian virtues. "I know, my dear Watson, that you share my love of all that is bizarre and outside the conventions and humdrum routine of everyday life," says Holmes at one point. Sometimes the word is used diagnostically: "This fellow is madly, insanely, in love."[21] The word "happy" occurs exactly eighteen times in the *Adventures*.

The word "friend," by contrast, occurs sixty-nine times. Holmes and Watson are loyal to each other in the manner of brothers or soldiers—thrown together by accident, kept together by devotion to the "excellent cause" of putting clear thinking in the service of improving society, and if they occasionally actually enjoy each other's company, that camaraderie may be among the few best pleasures we have in life. The stories are optimistic about human prospects, if guardedly so. They are confident, but watchful. It is at least these ethical qualities that keep the stories popular, and now more than ever, for that swelling of spin-offs and retellings that began in the 1960s has grown beyond anything that could have been predicted: hundreds of new novels and stories in the last forty years, dozens of film and television adaptations, and new editions of Conan Doyle's originals published year after year. A guarded optimism is merited.

## NOTES

1. *The Adventures of Sherlock Holmes*, directed by Alfred L. Werker.
2. Arthur Conan Doyle, "A Scandal in Bohemia," in *Sherlock Holmes: The Complete Novels and Stories* (2003), 239, 240. All subsequent Conan Doyle citations in notes are from this edition.
3. Arthur Conan Doyle, "The Five Orange Pips," 332.
4. Conan Doyle, "Scandal in Bohemia," 239.
5. Arthur Conan Doyle, *A Study in Scarlet*, 13.
6. Bess Streeter Aldrich, *A Lantern in Her Hand* (Puffin, 1997), synopsis at https://www.amazon.com.
7. Conan Doyle, "Scandal in Bohemia," 262.
8. Arthur Conan Doyle, "The Red-Headed League," 278.
9. Conan Doyle, "Red-Headed League," 265; Arthur Conan Doyle, "The Adventure of the Blue Carbuncle," 378, 379.
10. Arthur Conan Doyle, "The Adventure of the Copper Beeches," 492.
11. Arthur Conan Doyle, "The Adventure of the Noble Bachelor," 445.
12. Conan Doyle, "Red-Headed League," 287.
13. Arthur Conan Doyle, "The Greek Interpreter," 682.
14. Friedrich Nietzsche, *Thus Spoke Zarathustra: A Book for Everyone and Nobody*, ed. Graham Parkes, 11–15, 125.
15. Conan Doyle, "Scandal in Bohemia," 239; *The Adventures of Sherlock Holmes* (1939 film).
16. John Stuart Mill, *On Liberty*, 10.
17. Mill, *On Liberty*, 59.
18. Arthur Conan Doyle, *The Sign of Four*, 123.
19. Conan Doyle, "Scandal in Bohemia," 253.
20. Conan Doyle, *Sign of Four*, 124.
21. Conan Doyle, "Red-Headed League," 263; Arthur Conan Doyle, "The Boscombe Valley Mystery," 319.

## WORKS CITED

Conan Doyle, Arthur. *Sherlock Holmes: The Complete Novels and Stories*. Vol. 1. New York: Bantam, 2003.

Mill, John Stuart. *On Liberty*. In *The Basic Writings of John Stuart Mill: "On Liberty," "The Subjection of Women" and "Utilitarianism,"* edited by J. B. Schneewind. New York: Modern Library, 2010.

Nietzsche, Friedrich. *Thus Spoke Zarathustra: A Book for Everyone and Nobody*. Edited by Graham Parkes. New York: Oxford University Press, 2005.

Werker, Alfred L., dir. *The Adventures of Sherlock Holmes*. Los Angeles: 20th Century–Fox, 1939.

CHAPTER FOUR

# Victorian Fable-Lands

So Young Park

## On *The Newcomes* by William Makepeace Thackeray

How many brothers did Colonel Newcome have? What was the name of the Anglo-Indian bank that went bust, causing the plot of the 1,009-page narrative to unravel? And who was the first nobleman to jilt Ethel Newcome? These are just a few of the many questions that compel me to reread William Makepeace Thackeray's *The Newcomes* (1855)—perhaps the least-read, greatest, most sprawling novel of the long nineteenth century.

*The Newcomes* was published serially over the course of twenty-three months from 1853 to 1855, as Thackeray tells readers near the end of the book.[1] The author was forty-two years old and six years out from the phenomenal success of *Vanity Fair*, the fast-paced story of the adventuress Becky Sharp and her spectacular social rise and fall in Regency England. *The Newcomes* in comparison is desultory and expansive, indeed a classic example of Henry James's beloved "large loose baggy monsters" of the 1800s.[2] *The Newcomes* features two key aspects that, for me, define great Victorian novels like *Middlemarch* and *Our Mutual Friend*. The first is an encyclopedic range, the second an uncanny coherence that keeps the novel from becoming formless. *The Newcomes* offers disparate microworlds spinning perfectly on their individual axes, all kept in dynamic rotational rhythm by the finesse of a stylish narrative voice.

I cannot put this novel down once I begin reading it. For one thing, its multiple plotlines spread out and converge in unexpected ways: one extended family's genealogy merges with various domestic and financial plots encompassing London, Paris, and parts of British India. Thackeray's exploration of the Victorian marriage market brings his readers into the bedrooms of the aristocracy and then all the way down the social hierarchy to the public streets, where grooms gossip about the fashionable people they drive in their carriages. Then there is the wealth of detail from the Victorian world: watercolor paints called "gamboge" and "lake," vehicles such as the *britzka* (a small carriage), and blue-dragon Chinese jars. And last but not least, Thackeray's satirical, always ironical voice guiding readers through the maze of complexities that was Victorian England.

Perhaps for these reasons, *The Newcomes* is the Victorian novel I reach for in times of stress. I give in to its mesmeric narrative pull, and in return it takes me away to a whole new world. What I remember the most about the novel is reading it beginning on the night of 9/11, when the world seemed to have turned upside down. On that night, my hands instinctively reached for Thackeray's tome, and without a second thought I began to read his lively prose. Just one chapter per night, I told myself, and let's see how many I can read before the world ends.

I first read *The Newcomes: Memoirs of a Most Respectable Family* in a CUNY graduate seminar on Victorian studies. High up, on the fortieth floor of a midtown high-rise, I sat week after week, behind on the reading, hoping my professor would mistake my silence for profound thought. We went through Carlyle, Tennyson, the Spasmodics, and then through behemoths like *The Bertrams*, by Anthony Trollope, and finally Thackeray's story about a large Victorian family on the rise.

*The Newcomes* follows the story of Colonel Thomas Newcome, his artist son, Clive, and his aristocratic niece, Ethel, against the backdrop of a Victorian society flush with cash. Colonel Newcome makes his fortune in India, and on his return to London, he spends it lavishly on his only child, Clive. To help Clive get on in society, the Colonel reacquaints himself with his extended family, the Newcomes, particularly his twin half-brothers, Hobson and Sir Brian. The latter's daughter is Ethel, a beauty, and Clive soon falls in love with her—as does the Colonel. Ethel reminds the Colonel of his first love, and so begins his dream of seeing his son and Ethel married, which lasts for the remaining sixty-five chapters of the novel. But Ethel is under the strict guardianship of her grandmother, Lady Kew, who is on the watch to marry her off to Lord Frank Kew, her favorite grandson. Barnes, Ethel's selfish and cruel brother, hates Clive for his total lack of deference toward him. Barnes and Lady Kew impede Ethel's friendships with the Colonel and Clive.

Ethel at seventeen is very intelligent and strong-willed. The narrator calls her a "severe Diana," the most beautiful and feared among the "May Fair nymphs" (308). Ethel is well aware that she is a commodity on the marriage market, and she sarcastically tells her grandmother that she might as well put a price tag on her when she takes her into society. Lady Kew, however, pushes Ethel to accept Lord Kew. Meanwhile, Clive decides to become an artist and embarks on a bohemian life. While traveling in Europe, Clive runs into Ethel and her family, and accompanies them to Baden, where the Newcomes have gathered to marry Barnes to Lady Clara Pulleyn. Clara has been coerced by her family to give up her love, Jack Belsize, who has no money. When Jack arrives in Baden to win Clara back, ugly scenes ensue between him and her family. These family ruptures over money and Jack's self-destructive behavior make Clive see the dangers of his own pursuit of Ethel. He leaves Baden, simply defeated by the Newcome family's desire for money and status.

And here is where the plot gets all mixed up in my mind: was I confusing the bohemian bits of Clive's life with that of Pendennis, detailed in another Thackerayan novel titled *The History of Pendennis*? There is a subplot involving a Miss Higg from Manchester, or was it a Miss Clack, an evangelical from London? And Lord Kew's former lover slanders him in Baden, causing a break with Ethel. (Here I may be interpolating scenes from *Daniel Deronda*'s Lydia Glasher and Grandcourt.) Later, Clive despairs of Ethel's supposed indifference toward him and marries the quiet Rosey. (Or was it the doll-like Dora?)

And I remember a long episode in a Paris garden where Clive meets Ethel after her break from Lord Kew. It's told in the form of a play, with dialogue only: Clive is angered by her new pursuit of Lord Farintosh, the richest (and possibly the most foolish) man in England. Ethel tells Clive that she must marry Farintosh in order to financially support her many siblings. Then Ethel and Clive, with time on their hands, wander into the Salon des Refusés. Afterward, they head to Le Havre, crossing the river on an old ferry to Bennecourt. They have some food, two bottles of wine, and then go hiking, after which Clive paints a portrait of Ethel, which is selected for the next year's Salon, and he meets his friend Pierre Sandoz . . . no, this is Zola! His *The Masterpiece*.

On my first reading of the novel, I was overwhelmed by the profusion of details and the complicated plotlines. I read the book during meals, during office hours as a TA, and while waiting for my commuter train at Penn Station in midtown Manhattan. While my fellow New York straphangers read the Bible, the Koran, or the *National Enquirer*, I delved into my *Newcomes*.

But the book required me to slow down my reading. Furthermore, the story evaded efficient note-taking on the computer. To remember, I had to take detailed notes by hand on paper: Clive and Ethel part in Paris, Ethel to follow Farintosh, Clive to pursue his career as a painter. In the meantime, the Colonel returns to India, where he invests in the Bundelcund Banking Company, a firm that deals in everything from Chinese opium and Australian wool to copper mines, yielding dividends of 12.25 percent. Back in London, the Colonel invites his wide circle of friends to invest in the company. Worried about Clive's obsession with Ethel, the Colonel decides to give Clive £60,000 outright, substantially increasing his son's yearly income, enabling him to marry Ethel. But Barnes and Lady Kew scoff at the offer: Farintosh has £15,000 a year! In anger, the Colonel thrashes Barnes, thus beginning a family feud. There is one bit of good news for Ethel, though: Lady Kew dies happy, leaving Ethel a huge inheritance that gives her power.

The novel so far has been narrated by Arthur Pendennis, who is also a character in the story. Lawyer-turned-novelist and erstwhile country gentleman, Pendennis acts as confidant to both Clive and the Colonel. Around the midpoint of the story, Pendennis marries Laura, who becomes close friends with Ethel, and by virtue of her closeness to both Pendennis and Ethel, Laura becomes a co-narrator of sorts. In the denouement, Pendennis reports what Laura tells him about Ethel's feelings: that Ethel loves Clive, that she is worried about Barnes's abusive treatment of Lady Clara. Pendennis is shocked to learn that Jack Belsize, now Lord Highgate, plans to run away with Clara. Things come to a head when Jack pulls Barnes off his high horse (literally). The narrator cuts to the ensuing divorce case that ends in money for Barnes (£20,000 in damages), and in unhappiness for Jack and Clara, who flee to Europe as nomads.

Jack and Clara's scandal serves as a cautionary tale for Ethel, as it did for Clive in Baden. Against Farintosh's protests, Ethel breaks off the engagement with great relief, giving Farintosh permission to say he jilted her. Laura writes to the Colonel in hopes of uniting Ethel and Clive, but it's too late, the Colonel has married Clive to the pretty Rosey Mackenzie, the niece of a dear friend. On hearing the news, Ethel is silent.

My first reading of *The Newcomes* was a humiliating failure. The novel seemed to play tricks on me, making me forget characters, their social networks, their subplots. I had prided myself on my reading memory; it was the one thing I could rely on to get me through graduate school. I could visually recall certain passages in Victorian novels by where they fell on the page: *Middlemarch*, squirrel's heartbeat, upper left quadrant, chapter 20. What was exasperating was that *The Newcomes* made me not only forget things but also misremember details. I was especially flustered by the amounts of money that passed between characters, so I kept pages of notes just on Thackeray's money: Rosey's dowry is £17,000, which Clive gives to the Colonel to invest in the Bundelcund Banking Company. Clive settles only £3,300 on her, much to the shock of Pendennis. Rosey's mother, Mrs. Mack, invests her entire savings of £1,500 in the Bundelcund. The Colonel racks up debts of over £3,000 when he opposes Barnes for his seat in Parliament. As Clive and Pendennis expected, the Bundelcund goes bankrupt when its founder, Rummun Loll, dies of cholera in Calcutta, leaving only 800 rupees in the company treasury. After this "complicated, enormous, outrageous swindle" (901), the company's debts of £500,000 are partly met by the good Colonel, who refuses to the end to cash out his shares, going into voluntary exile in Boulogne, where Rosey delivers a stillborn son and Clive gives art lessons. Pendennis laments that Clive has only £140 to support a family of five. Before the crash, the Colonel had assets estimated to be around £85,000. The novel's deus ex machina comes in the form of money: Ethel anonymously bequeaths £6,000 to Clive when she discovers an unpaid legacy from her grandmother. It enables him to pay his remaining debts and to support his son Tommy.

The reading problem I was encountering was one of sheer cognitive difficulty. In *Arguing with the Past*, Gillian Beer brilliantly explains the difficulty of Victorian novels as arising from their complexity. Beer maintains that Victorian fiction is hard to remember because of its intricate, "arboreal form," a form that promotes "copiousness and hyperproductivity." In addition to their amplitude, long Victorian novels, according to Beer, are difficult because of their "insistence on the moral duty to recall and connect," which poses a problem in thinking and feeling for readers and writers alike.[3]

At eighty chapters and over a thousand pages, *The Newcomes* is a multiverse, containing myriad plots and personalities. Thackeray's novel further scuppered my total recall by presenting multiple temporalities. For instance, in chapter 28, set in Baden, the narrator critiques the Victorian marriage of convenience as a social sham, a polite front for the selling of daughters. We see Lady Kew tearing a green ticket from Ethel's dress, placed there as a joke on Ethel's part to mock her grandmother's mercenary marriage schemes. This domestic scene, however, takes place the "previous May" in London, we are told (360). In chapter 30, the novel jumps back in time to the 1790s, when Lady Kew, as a young woman, entertains the Duke d'Ivry in exile from revolutionary France. Chapter 34 ends with the shocking news of Lord Kew's injury in a duel, but we don't find out what happened until chapter 37. Chapter 35 jumps forward three months to Clive in Rome and leaves him there for four chapters, while the rest of the narrative set in Baden catches up timewise. And finally, in chapter 39, Clive is dispatched from Pompeii to Marseilles and then to Ethel in London.

Thackeray's copious use of prolepsis and analepsis seems a child's game in our current digital era of time-traveling Dr. Who's and the time eraser that is the internet. But back in the analogue 1990s, Thackeray's sliding of narrative time confused and challenged me. To be fair, early in the novel, the narrator explains that he will go where the "Muse leadeth him," "break[ing] the promise of a former page" and the sense of a clear, linear narrative (135). The risk to the reader of misremembering, then, is embedded throughout the novel. On the other hand, this keeps the narrative fresh and unpredictable, making me want to return to it. Sometimes the jumps in the story's timeline draw attention to how emotions and trauma work: for instance, when Pendennis hears of the Bundelcund Banking Company's collapse and the Colonel's financial ruin, he abjures describing what happened next. There is a lacuna in the text, circumventing the pain of public shame. The narrator simply ends the chapter by asking, "Where are you, dear Clive, gallant young friend of my youth?" (903). It's only in flashback in a later chapter that the narrator retreads that night of Clive's flight from London and the bailiffs.

Thackeray's scrambling of linear narrative time expanded my capacity to understand and experience the Victorian world. But I agreed with Beer: some Victorian novels were very difficult to remember and to connect with. I skimmed the rest of the novel. After my course ended, I put *The Newcomes* aside.

I ran from my car into the office building, late for my appointment with the doctor. When I walked into the reception area, something felt off. The radio was on. People sat apart, but they seemed focused on the same thing.

I apologized to the receptionist for being late.

"It's terrible!" the receptionist said.

"I'm so sorry, I know the doctor is busy. I can reschedule."

She shook her head. "A small plane crashed into the Twin Towers just now. It's just awful!"

I saw in my mind's eye a small propeller plane crashing into the antenna on top of one of the towers.

"I hope the pilot's okay," I randomly said as I sat down next to a middle-aged woman.

"No, honey," she said. "I think it crashed into the building. The building's burning."

Just two days before, I had driven past the Twin Towers. My dad had picked me up from Newark Airport as I returned from Manchester, England, from my first-ever literature conference. We had taken the Battery Park Tunnel on the south end of Manhattan. I had swerved my head up to catch the Twin Towers rising above me as we emerged from underground.

"Have you ever been to the top?" I asked my father.

"Of course. I never took you up there? You should go."

"Too busy," I said. And they were always going to be there.

The receptionist called my name.

When I saw the doctor, he was solemn. "I remember when Kennedy was shot. You're going to remember today. It's your generation's Kennedy moment."

By the time I left the doctor's office, all planes flying in US airspace had been grounded. People gathered in the lobby and the parking lot. They said that more planes had been reported falling from the sky.

I tried to get on the expressway, but all traffic was diverted to the frontage road. Hundreds of cars were inching along. I could see Interstate 495, the Long Island Expressway, to my left through the trees and brush. I heard siren after siren as police cars and fire trucks sped toward the city.

I had lived on Long Island for many years, and the 495 had never closed down before. Several drivers gave up and parked their cars along the side of the road.

Nothing on the radio made any sense. I looked to my right. The driver in the next car stared at me with the same look of confusion that was on my face. In my mind's eye I still saw a tiny plane just brushing the top of a radio tower. I couldn't see the magnitude of what was happening.

By taking back roads, I finally made it to a major turnpike before running out of gas. It was a beautiful day, balmy weather for September. I got out of the car and looked in the direction of the city. Even though I was thirty miles away I saw a thick plume of smoke on the horizon. I started to go numb.

My friends and family were safe. It was my day off from teaching, so I hadn't been in the city. Like millions of people, I sat in disbelief, looking at the images on TV. That night, I couldn't get to sleep. The crickets were very loud. How could nature go on when this catastrophe was happening? I looked at the stack of books piled next to my bed. My hands reached for the thickest book, *The Newcomes*. It was at the bottom of the pile, which toppled over when I dislodged it.

I picked up the book from the floor and began to read. I made myself stop after the first chapter, telling myself, one chapter, one day, before the world ends. And each night, I read one chapter as if my world depended on it. Thackeray's plush Victorian world seemed to absorb the jagged sounds and smells and images of post-9/11 New York City. The noise of Bohemia and London dining clubs frequented by Clive and Pendennis drowned out, if for a brief while, the piercing silence on the subway the week following 9/11, when no one spoke. The smell of the Colonel's cheroot pipe and Aunt Honeyman's cooking covered the acrid smell of smoke coming from Ground Zero, where the towers continued to burn for months. The sudden jolt and panic that I, like everyone, experienced when hearing a loud noise during that fraught time, I erased by thinking of holding the soft, frayed pages of this heavy book in my hands, reading it slowly, on my own time.

Strangely, the world of *The Newcomes* felt more real than my life in New York City. My city became dreamlike, surreal: fighter planes flying along the FDR Drive, Penn Station guarded by soldiers with machine guns standing in front of the hot dog stand where I used to buy popcorn before getting on the train. Some of the soldiers looked as young as my first-year students. Military vehicles lurched out of the Park Avenue Armory on the Upper East Side. I had nightmares of walking out of Penn Station and looking up to see a brilliant Magritte sky and the Empire State Building, burning.

I reached for Thackeray's novel because it was the longest, the most complex story I had in my possession. I wanted to get lost in it, because I was scared that the world I knew might never return. Years later, looking back, it seems that perhaps another compelling reason was that I knew *The Newcomes* and I had nothing in common and I needed to make a connection with Victorian literature, my future, my career. In the nervous days and weeks that followed 9/11, my friends and I talked about what to do with our lives in the face of this national trauma. What was the point of studying literature at such a time? The conversations in graduate seminars and coffee hangouts around campus centered on this question. Some felt that we had entered a new world order in which geopolitics, terrorism, and security issues would drown out everything else. Others felt that we were in exactly the right place: teaching, researching, and continuing our ordinary lives.

The cataclysm of 9/11 made me question my place in the academy. On my long subway rides to campus, I began to have severe doubts. I had been a happy English major in college, and was making steady progress in my PhD program. I loved reading Victorian novels, but four friends of Asian descent had left the program, more if I counted acquaintances. They left for various reasons, but I felt as if I didn't belong. I had never been taught by an Asian American woman professor, not in the humanities. I had never needed a role model before, because I had had excellent mentors throughout my studies. But now I wanted proof that people who looked like me could succeed in academia. The placement officer warned us about the long haul: one to two years to write the dissertation, then an average of three years on the job market, plus six years to tenure, if you're lucky.

As I was reading *The Newcomes*, I was testing Thackeray's book and the Victorian novel form to see if we could go on together: would we continue to keep each other interested for the long haul? Would the study of literature be worth the things I gave up to try to finish my doctorate? Although my family would never say it, I had been alienating everyone by spending so much time in my Victorian otherworld.

The Korean word my family used to describe what I did all day was *gongbu*, a generic term meaning "study," as in "*Gongbu hae-yo. . . .* She's studying." Is she coming to Grandma's birthday party? No, *gongbu hae-yo*. Can your daughter translate this insurance form for us? No, *gongbu hae-yo*. Can you ask her to read over my son's college essay? No, *gongbu hae-yo*. I had cordoned myself off from my large extended family because I was tired of code-switching from Korean to English, from millennial US culture to the Confucianist value systems espoused by my family. In my effort to be efficient, I rigorously separated my family from my study of literature. Part of this was by default: except for the younger generation, no one in my family knew English well enough to read Victorian literature. As I specialized more in my studies, I fell into the habit of clinically dissecting texts, absorbing difficult literary theories, and being unwilling to discuss literature with nonspecialists.

And yet my family was the main reason I was able to continue with my studies. My sister cheered me up when I despaired of ever finishing my thesis; she took me to lavish sushi dinners and on shopping sprees in downtown Manhattan. Aunts encouraged me by saying they were rooting for me, the first woman scholar in our family. When my mother thought I would abandon the PhD, my father, who never praised or blamed, told her, "If she can't finish it, no one can." My family trusted my judgment in pursuing an academic career, but I didn't. No one in my family was ever going to read *The Newcomes* or *Middlemarch* or any of the chronicles of Barset. My problem was connecting my lived world with my working life.

In retrospect, I see that this was a hopelessly naïve, solipsistic response to a violent historical event. But at the time, I needed to answer these questions to continue to live in my small quadrant of the world. I needed not only to recall *The Newcomes*, but also, to borrow Beer's words, to answer the moral call to connect.

Robert Douglas-Fairhurst, in *Victorian Afterlives*, points out that the social or moral significance of Dickens's novels is built into "the sprawling connections made by his plots, between types of subject-matter and people which many of his contemporaries struggled to keep at a distance from one another."[4] *The Newcomes*, too, is a complex representation of the circulation and flow of people, ideas, and money. In a way, New York City after 9/11 felt like a living text built on the multiple connections people made with one another. People were kinder. That was one of the changes

I noticed after the initial shock of 9/11 began to lessen. People looked out for each other, helping each other up subway stairs, starting conversations, opening doors. Once, I was at a restaurant with communal tables, and a couple offered their appetizers for me to try. That had never happened to me before. Familiar walls and boundaries collapsed; the city appeared to me alive and ready for new connections.

Why was I holding myself back from making connections between the Victorian world and my own? Although I knew intellectually that the Victorian novel was multiform, multiplotted, polyvocal, and multitemporal, I had lost the sense of it as a vibrant social form, filled to the brim with ideas and conflicts about life, death, love, jobs, children, money, success, and failure. But my own daily life resonated with these concerns: my life was a variegated, hybrid mess with family, friends, and colleagues speaking a myriad of languages and espousing a host of cultural and philosophical beliefs. Why shouldn't I mix Korean with English, Victorian London with twenty-first-century New York?

Lady Kew came to mind. She says it's love for Ethel that makes her scheme on her behalf in the marriage market. Unlike my cousins and college friends who worked in law, medicine, or finance, I had neither a husband, a mortgage, nor a car to my name, a fact that distressed my grandmother. She was the opposite of Lady Kew, but she nonetheless asked her church friends for blind dates for me (without telling me first). She belonged to a huge church in Brooklyn: it was like Facebook for Koreans before the internet. If you wanted to locate a long-lost Korean relative or a friend in the diaspora, you would go to this church and ask around. It was also a paradise for grandmothers with unmarried grandchildren. Soon I began to receive query emails from the female relatives of eligible men, mostly from Los Angeles, which has the largest Korean population in the United States. When I politely refused requests for my photograph, I mortified my grandmother, who asked if I was ever going to get married. "Yes, probably. After I finish my dissertation."

"And how long will that take?" she asked. She had had her first child by the time she was nineteen.

My aunts hadn't married and had a rich social life centered on their church. I listened now to them talking about internecine political battles within the church. My aunts always spoke kindly, but I let my imagination run. A new pastor, whom the elders wanted to rout, sounded like a Mr. Slope, a parvenu from a seminary in Georgia, or like Charles Honeyman, the opportunistic clerical man-about-town bailed out time and again by Colonel Newcome. When my aunts spoke of rich deaconesses, somewhat reluctant to let unmarried women into their ranks, I thought of Miss Clack from *The Moonstone*, Aunt Norris from *Mansfield Park*, and Mrs. Proudie from Trollope. My aunts didn't need to read the chronicles of Barset, they were all over it.

Some of my friends specializing in Shakespeare or modernism couldn't stand the moralizing tone of Victorian authors. I wondered why I could tolerate it. Then I realized it was because I had heard it all my life, from distant relatives, my parents' friends, and random adults in the Korean American community. Perhaps because my parents never lectured me, others thought fit to take me aside and say things like, "A woman is incomplete without a husband. . . . Study is good, but don't become one of those unmarried women: sorry and stale! . . . Why aren't you in law school? Don't waste an Ivy League education to become a teacher!" I thought these comments and words of advice, kindly meant, were patently untrue. Compared to these voices, I found the didacticism of Victorian writers to be rather mild.

Then there was Colonel Newcome: he stayed in India to make money for his son, Clive, and sent the boy to England. They were separated for years during a crucial time in the child's life. Like Colonel Newcome, my dad didn't see my sister and me for many years after he left for the United States, and we stayed in Korea while he obtained his green card. He sent us money and presents from New York. I had forgotten what my dad did for us. Reading *The Newcomes* reminded me.

In a letter to Dorothy Wellesley, W. B. Yeats says he could hear it when a poem became whole and complete: "A poem comes right with a click like a closing box."[5]

Things clicked for me. My separate worlds merged.

The night I reached the end of Thackeray's thousand-page novel, I felt a sense of elation. The novel ended, but, thank goodness, the world I lived in didn't. Even though the towers were still smoldering, the city began to return to its familiar, frantic rhythm, but with a somberness that I don't think has gone away.

Across eighty chapters and eighty days, the long novel had cocooned me in another world. Thackeray's novel contained within its pages time itself: nearly three months of linear time, spooled in its story world. I emerged with a host of connections I hadn't made before I reread *The Newcomes*. Edward Mendelson describes this kind of happening between readers, writers, and literary works in terms of intimacy, but of a "special kind." In particular, Mendelson draws attention to the unique connection between reader and writer that is created without the two ever meeting "face to face." He reminds us of Virginia Woolf's pragmatic advice to writers of modern fiction: give readers something recognizable that sparks their imagination and so engages them in what Woolf calls "the difficult business of intimacy."[6]

Something like what Woolf and Mendelson describe had occurred during my second reading of *The Newcomes*. Thackeray's novel became a point of contact from which I could make connections to disparate parts of my life. Lest I go overboard and make *The Newcomes* the Rosebud of my autobiography, I was also mindful of Thackeray's ironical voice: early in *The Newcomes*, he says that in his story, "events follow each other without necessarily having a connexion" (296). Referring to Roman historians (and Herodotus in another chapter), Pendennis states that a writer must make things up, including the connections: "You tell your tales as you can, and state the facts as you think they must have been" (297).

In short, the narrative connections will always be tenuous and artificial. The arboreal multiplots that spread out like a network of capillaries are artificially created by the writer. Though they appear organic, they are in the end fabricated. But what isn't made up is the palpable feeling of social relationships and their complexity and intimacy conveyed in *The Newcomes*. This is the kind of connection that matters. The Victorian novel is that arboreal-artificial structure that can speak to readers across time and space as Thackeray's novel had spoken to me.

As with many Victorian novels, *The Newcomes* ends with new life enabled by death. It ends with three deaths. The Colonel, Rosey, and her stillborn son are dispatched to Kensal Green Cemetery.[7] Thackeray plays with readers' expectations by refusing to tie up loose ends. Instead, he leaves us with fragments that point to possible happiness. Clive is traveling abroad with his wife. Could it be Ethel? The famous artist J. J. Ridley has painted a portrait of Mrs. Clive Newcome. The lady has dark hair in the portrait. Could it be Ethel? The novel ends with surmises about Ethel, Clive, and their host of friends.

Over the next twenty years, on days when things didn't go well at work or at home, I would try to drift off to sleep, and instead of counting sheep, I would tell myself the story of Ethel and Clive and the Colonel: The story begins when Thomas Newcome, a weaver from the north, marries Sophia Alethea Hobson, an heiress to cloth factors from Clapham, London. He has a young son, Thomas, whom Sophia dislikes. He runs away to India after reading Orme's *History of India*. . . . As Lord Kew convalesces in Kehl from a bullet wound received during a duel, his mother, Lady Walham, reads *Oliver Twist* to him. Barnes Newcome dies in a railway station, distracted by reading *The Pickwick Papers*. . . . The Colonel's twin brothers, Hobson and Sir Brian, leave their fortunes to distant relations, twins named Diavolo and Angelica, alias the Heavenly Twins. . . . The Colonel works for the East India Company as a young man. He meets John Herncastle, who steals a huge diamond called the Moonstone. The Colonel despises Herncastle and steals the Moonstone and gives it to Ethel, who falls in love with Franklin Blake, who is already married to Lady Audley, who has a secret . . .

Perhaps it's an occupational hazard, but it seems to me now that the nineteenth century is one long, complicated Victorian novel. The serpentine plots, the thousands of characters minor and major, and the millions of words of love, hate, fear, and joy inscribed in Victorian fiction merge in my imagination. Occasionally, Clive and Ethel and the Colonel and Lord Kew populate a mash-up of plotlines from Dickens, Dostoevsky, and George Eliot. In a battle royale between Lady Kew and Svidrigailov, who would win? Is Ethel's ideal partner not Clive at all, but rather Darcy or Ladislaw? If Merton Densher were to narrate *The Newcomes*, would it be as loose and baggy a novel? Did Arthur Clennam's father and the Colonel cross paths in the East? And what about the novel that Thackeray left unwritten—a young-adult novel based on the adventures of Lord Kew, Lord Highgate, and Lord Dorking (alias "Rooster") as teenagers?

In the aftermath of 9/11, I saw the true gift of Thackeray's parting words, now intensified, to the reader: "But for you, dear friend, it is as you like. You may settle your fable-land in your own fashion" (1009). To Fable-Land I went. By gesturing toward possible futures and refusing to tie down the story to a definite plot, Thackeray opened a new landscape of imagination into the Victorian world. True to his narratorial disclosures throughout *The Newcomes*, Thackeray ended his novel by inviting new configurations and plotlines from readers. Whenever I look at my copy of *The Newcomes* I am reminded of the time when it took me to another world, when the present was full of extreme turbulence and uncertainty. *The Newcomes* was the novel that invited me to Fable-Land, and the novel that inspired me to continue my study of Victorian novels. Though worth only £6.99 in 1990s currency, it has steadily accrued in value since then. It's my Victorian novel, and it's priceless.

## NOTES

1. William M. Thackeray, *The Newcomes: Memoirs of a Most Respectable Family*, ed. Andrew Sanders, 1007. Further references will be given parenthetically.
2. Henry James, preface to *The Tragic Muse*, x. James lists three novels as key examples of "large loose baggy monsters": *The Newcomes*, *The Three Musketeers*, and *War and Peace*.
3. Gillian Beer, *Arguing with the Past: Essays in Narrative from Woolf to Sidney*, 14, 15.
4. Robert Douglas-Fairhurst, *Victorian Afterlives: The Shaping of Influence in Nineteenth-Century Literature*, 92.
5. W. B. Yeats to Dorothy Wellesley, September 8, 1935, in *Letters on Poetry from W. B. Yeats to Dorothy Wellesley*, 22. Yeats contrasts the process of correcting nonfictional prose, which he says is "endless," and revising poetry, which ends when he hears a click.
6. Edward Mendelson, "Authorship, Intimacy, and an Editorial Question about Auden," 277; Virginia Woolf, "Mr. Bennett and Mrs. Brown," 20.
7. When Thackeray died in 1863, he was buried at Kensal Green Cemetery.

## WORKS CITED

Beer, Gillian. *Arguing with the Past: Essays in Narrative from Woolf to Sidney*. London: Routledge, 1989.

Douglas-Fairhurst, Robert. *Victorian Afterlives: The Shaping of Influence in Nineteenth-Century Literature*. New York: Oxford University Press, 2002.

James, Henry. Preface to *The Tragic Muse*. Vol. 1 of *The Novels and Tales of Henry James*. New York: Charles Scribner's Sons, 1908.

Mendelson, Edward. "Authorship, Intimacy, and an Editorial Question about Auden." *Essays in Criticism* 68.3 (July 2018): 273–82.

Thackeray, William Makepeace. *The Newcomes: Memoirs of a Most Respectable Family*. Edited by Andrew Sanders. New York: Oxford University Press, 1995.

Woolf, Virginia. "Mr. Bennett and Mrs. Brown." In *The Hogarth Essays*, 3–29. New York: Doubleday, Doran, 1928.
Yeats, W. B. *Letters on Poetry from W. B. Yeats to Dorothy Wellesley*. New York: Oxford University Press, 1964.

CHAPTER FIVE

# "What do I think of glory?"

Beverley Park Rilett

## On *Middlemarch* by George Eliot

"What do I think of *Middlemarch*? What do I think of glory?"[1] This is the famous reply Emily Dickinson wrote to her bookish cousins in 1873 after her first reading of George Eliot's novel. Dickinson's sentiments were also my own when I completed my first reading of *Middlemarch* (1871–1872), about thirty-five years ago. *Middlemarch* is the book that made me realize literature could be more than a source of entertainment, that it could be Art with a capital A. Here was a text with fascinating and seemingly limitless possibilities for interpretation that would continue to reward scrutiny. Of course, I didn't come up with that assessment entirely on my own. Since its publication, *Middlemarch* has ranked among the world's most popular and highly acclaimed literary works. It was one of the staples of Victorian literature courses and was essential reading for English majors at Queen's University in Canada, where I completed two undergraduate degrees. Even before I learned that "George Eliot" was the pseudonym of a female writer, Mary Ann Evans, I'd been conditioned to recognize her name as part of the canon of Great Authors, a list dominated by male writers such as Homer, Chaucer, Shakespeare, Conrad, and Joyce. I still meet people all the time who have heard of *Middlemarch* as one of the world's best-loved novels and know George Eliot is the author but don't know she was a woman, let alone the most successful woman writer of the Victorian era. Knowing a book is on the "should read" list and actually reading it are two entirely different things, and I must confess I never did make it all the way through Tolstoy's *War and Peace*. Reading *Middlemarch*, however, turned out to be life-changing, igniting my passion for Victorian literature and for George Eliot in particular.

What I hope to convey here is how and why this Victorian novel and its author continue to inspire me.

The virtues of *Middlemarch* aren't easy to summarize. The novel is so comprehensive that it contains something for everyone: layers of narrative wit and wisdom about history, sociology, science, mythology, religion, philosophy, economics, and art have kept critics excavating and theorizing for nearly 150 years. *Middlemarch* is also rhetorically rich, full of striking metaphors and allusions, and delivered in a characteristically precise diction tuned to intentionally complicated connotations, all of which encourages readers to attend to the novel's subtle nuances of language. There is always something fresh to notice, a new thread one can follow through the labyrinth of potential meanings. Eliot's long, meticulously careful sentences, which I will be quoting liberally, make her writing endlessly rewarding to decode over successive readings.

As suggested by the novel's subtitle, *A Study of Provincial Life*, Eliot demonstrates a sociologist's understanding of how communities of people function. Her *Middlemarch* characters are concerned about their little community in provincial England in the 1830s, yet their personalities and problems are recognizably timeless. This acuity for the nuances of human motivation distinguishes Eliot as a gifted psychologist as well. She is able to depict not only how her characters behave but why they behave the way they do, exposing the pressures and constraints that motivate secrets, misunderstandings, and disastrous choices. She often explores how difficult it is for any of us to really know another person, how many of our decisions are made on too little information in relation to too much hope. For example, *Middlemarch*'s narrator comments that without our illusions and "liberal allowance of conclusions" about other people, marriage could never take place: "Has any one ever pinched into its pilulous smallness the cobweb of pre-matrimonial acquaintanceship?" she asks, as she dramatizes the monumental consequences to individual characters who make the commonest of mistakes.[2] Eliot's novels remain relevant precisely because the human foibles she writes about *are* common—any one of us could fall into tragedy despite our best intentions. Her novels open our hearts and minds to ways other people experience the world and show us that their problems aren't so different from our own. In short, Eliot's novels teach us to become more sympathetic human beings.

*Middlemarch* came to mean more to me than any other book, but in my early readings of it I was only partially attuned to several intersections between the novel and my own life that seem more obvious in retrospect. I was an idealistic if naïve young woman about the same age as Miss Dorothea Brooke the first time I read *Middlemarch*. We were both eldest daughters determined to do something important in life. I sympathized with Dorothea's lack of reliable parental guidance, especially the way she had to figure out how to reach her goals primarily on her own. I was a good student, proud to have been accepted into my college's honors program in a challenging track toward concurrent bachelor's degrees in arts and education, in addition to earning a position on the varsity synchronized swimming team. I'd moved over four hundred miles from home, escaping parents whose marriage after twenty-five years had begun to implode. My parents' divorce had been a long time in the making before they finally accepted the inevitable, taking so long probably because no one on either side of our extended families had ever officially split up. Being so far away from home when it finally happened made their breakup seem somehow unreal to me; throwing myself into the physical labor of swim practice and the intellectual labor of coursework deferred the grief and conflicted emotions I couldn't immediately process. In hindsight, preoccupation with my parents' dysfunctional marriage prepared me to recognize in *Middlemarch* what I still consider the novel's paramount concern: the disaster of incompatible marriage caused by incomplete knowledge of self and other. As I confront my twenty-year-old self, I'm amazed at my eagerness to start my own career and family—to try to have it all and do it all successfully. Like Dorothea, I was short-sighted and in a tremendous hurry to grow up. Though I can't recall with certainty, I may even have imagined that Dorothea's headlong rush to the altar was perfectly reasonable.

Now, as an older and potentially wiser woman, I've become more like *Middlemarch*'s narrator, looking back on Dorothea with sympathetic head-shaking, knowing what difficulties lie ahead of her and wishing she didn't have to actually live through those life lessons. I also have grown to respect Dorothea's more practical sister, Celia, who unabashedly wants and seeks pleasure in her life and doubts that female self-sacrifice is necessarily a virtue. I judge Dorothea's choices differently now. As the old saying goes, one cannot step into the same river twice; similarly, with every reading, I am a new person with a slightly different perspective on the issues and problems that affect the Middlemarch residents and community. Eliot's presentation of her major characters' thought processes is nuanced; she offers readers multiple ways of understanding their behavior not only in relation to their individual temperaments but also in relation to the social web that connects and affects them all. We care about what happens to them; as the narrator recognizes, "the fragment of a life, however typical, is not the sample of an even web: promises may not be kept, and an ardent outset may be followed by declension; latent powers may find their long-waited opportunity; a past error may urge a grand retrieval" (3.Finale:455). While many of the characters in *Middlemarch* continue to fascinate me, it's Dorothea's story with its mixed elements of tragedy and triumph that remains the most compelling.

*Middlemarch* opens by introducing its heroine, Dorothea Brooke, an earnest, sincere, ambitious, and stubborn nineteen-year-old on the cusp of life. With a yearning for social justice and a genuine desire to help the less fortunate, Dorothea has not yet worked out any specific vocational path. She has dedicated a great deal of time to designing new, more practical cottages she believes will make life easier for the tenant farmers residing on her Uncle Brooke's property, but without proper training as an architect, she can't be sure whether she has designed "incompatible stairs and fireplaces" (1.1:19). The narrator of *Middlemarch* conveys Dorothea's yearning to be a force for good in life larger than what was allotted to women:

> For a long while she had been oppressed by the indefiniteness which hung in her mind, like a thick summer haze, over all her desire to make her life greatly effective. What could she do, what ought she to do?—she, hardly more than a budding woman, but yet with an active conscience and a great mental need, not to be satisfied by a girlish instruction comparable to the nibblings and judgments of a discursive mouse. (1.3:39)

In 1830s England, social obstacles are most obviously in Dorothea's way. Women were not yet admitted to colleges, and professional careers were still the exclusive purview of men. Restricted from producing a great work of her own, Dorothea covets "masculine knowledge" and begins to imagine that she can achieve a meaningful life through a particular kind of marriage, wherein she could "learn to see the truth by the same light as great men have seen it by" (1.3:40). She fantasizes about marrying a fatherly mentor figure whose manuscript she can help produce, a promising scholar whose "odd habits it would be glorious piety to endure" (1.3:12). Though Dorothea's hopes and dreams didn't seem so preposterous to me a generation ago, my students see through her deluded foolishness. They're able to recognize the irony of Dorothea's grandiose idea of enduring miserable years for the sake of "glorious piety," and they protest against the unjust social conditions that prevented women like Dorothea from achieving success independently, which are at least partly responsible for her disastrous choice to marry Edward Casaubon.

How did the patriarchal pre-feminist setting of Dorothea's story relate to my own Canadian middle-class university experience of the 1980s? While Dorothea was prevented from pouring her intellect and creativity into a self-actualizing vocation, I was embarking on an independent life, discovering the ever-expanding world of history, philosophy, and literature and learning about the great writers and thinkers of the Western literary canon. *Middlemarch* helped open my eyes to both the persistence of gender inequality and the hard-won advances women had already achieved since Dorothea's day. The English department at Queen's University in the 1980s was dominated by male professors who assigned mostly male-authored texts; I was elated that my required class in Victorian literature was not only taught by a woman but included more than 50 percent women writers on the syllabus. Dr. Cathy Harland started each class with a pithy quotation and then lectured for a full hour, though it felt too brief to me. Dr. Harland inspired my lifelong devotion to the works she loved, including *Pride and Prejudice*, *Jane Eyre*, *Wuthering Heights*, *Aurora Leigh*, and *Middlemarch*. As destiny would have it, at least two women in that class—myself and Lisa Surridge—went on to become professors of Victorian literature. An observation by the narrator of *Middlemarch* explains such serendipity beautifully:

> But any one watching keenly the stealthy convergence of human lots, sees a slow preparation of effects from one life on another, which tells like a calculated irony on the indifference or the frozen stare with which we look at our unintroduced neighbour. Destiny stands by sarcastic with our dramatis personae folded in her hand. (1.11:142)

We never know when the stranger sitting next to us will end up playing a significant role in the rest of our lives.

My appreciation for *Middlemarch* was instilled, in part, by the passion of Dr. Harland, but I also remember being captivated by the wisdom, wit, and generous nature of the story's narrator, who self-consciously considers how to make her art meaningful. In the following passage, for example, she specifically calls attention to her intent and process using the first-person pronoun: "I at least have so much to do in unraveling certain human lots, and seeing how they were woven and interwoven, that all the light I can command must be concentrated on this particular web, and not dispersed over that tempting range of relevancies called the universe" (1.15:214). The narrator positions herself usually as a knowing watcher or transcriber who is interested in conveying the experiences of a "particular web" of characters. This is what makes the novel endlessly readable, in my opinion, because the generous narrator is able to reveal minute details and psychological insights in a measured, understanding tone that seems to me, after having read all nine volumes of the author's letters, to be the voice of the gentle genius who called herself George Eliot. Her philosophy, which she states repeatedly throughout her writing, is that art should generate a sense of sympathy with our fellow erring humans. In *Middlemarch*, she writes, "What do we live for, if it is not to make life less difficult to each other?" (3.72:308).

Eliot contended that tragedy not only happens to the great and powerful but occurs every day in the ordinary, private lives of common people. It is a concept represented in her description of *Middlemarch* as a "home epic." In one of the novel's most famous passages, the narrator refers to the secret pain of failure taking place all around us, but specifically to Dorothea, who after only six weeks of marriage realizes she has gravely misjudged her husband's character:

> That element of tragedy which lies in the very fact of frequency, has not yet wrought itself into the coarse emotion of mankind; and perhaps our frames could hardly bear much of it. If we had a keen vision and feeling of all ordinary human life, it would be like hearing the grass grow and the squirrel's heart beat, and we should die of that roar which lies on the other side of silence. As it is, the quickest of us walk about well wadded with stupidity.
>
> However, Dorothea was crying . . . (1.20:297–98)

Beginning with the distant view, wherein tragedy and heartbreak are so common they have become imperceptible, Eliot zooms in with "keen vision and feeling" on a particular individual's suffering, directing the reader to witness Dorothea's personal tragedy, a moment of painful recognition "which lies on the other side of silence" and might otherwise go unnoticed. Excusing the reader's inability to take into account the unbearable enormity of all human misery, the narrator leads the reader to recognize, along with the heroine herself, a moment of epiphany—that she made an irrevocable error of judgment in marrying Casaubon.

The fact that Dorothea might be culpable for ignoring the warnings of family members and friends necessarily complicates the way readers judge her tragic choice. After all, Dorothea stubbornly charged into a lifelong commitment with a clerical scholar nearly thirty years her senior whom she barely knew, believing he was the next Pascal, Hooker, or Locke. She insisted that she was the only person in town who could understand Casaubon and recognize his "great soul." Dorothea knowingly flouts the whole community, including her uncle and sister, cognizant that "all the world round Tipton would be out of sympathy with this marriage" (1.5:71). Part of her tendency toward martyrdom includes the idea that she would be scorned by the majority but ultimately rewarded for having a more capacious faith and vision. To what extent should the reader blame Dorothea for her bullheaded but ultimately tragic choice? Wasn't her insistence on autonomy the very impulse that allows heroic individuals to succeed where others fail? In my early readings of the novel, I completely sympathized with Dorothea's defiance instead of judging it.

The narrator admires her enterprising protagonist and would never call her stupid, but the humor and irony in her depiction of Dorothea's "self-mortification" tendencies became apparent to me only in later readings. Dorothea embraces this description because it matches the way she likes to think about herself, but when Celia adds that her sister "likes giving up," Dorothea corrects her with, "If that were true, Celia, my giving-up would be self-indulgence, not self-mortification. But there may be good reasons for choosing not to do what is very agreeable" (1.2:24). This is the same scene in which Dorothea determines to stop horseback riding, which she loves but has "always looked forward to renouncing" because "she felt that she enjoyed it in a pagan, sensuous way" (1.2:11–12). Celia responds to her sister's peculiarities with knowing acceptance but not total admiration, which seems to match the narrator's perspective. Before marriage, Dorothea's choice of Casaubon over Chettam implicitly indicates that she was willing to renounce sexual fulfillment in exchange for learning.

The neighborhood gossip, Mrs. Cadwallader, throws up her hands at Dorothea's decision, "wish[ing] her joy of her hair shirt" (1.6:88). Our heroine's martyr complex is both funny and a little ominous, which seems to me now what Eliot must have intended. After all, Eliot was a devotee of Shakespeare, whose tragic scenes are typically juxtaposed with comic ones. He knew how to break the tension through laughter that helped the audience achieve a more balanced perspective on the drama. Though the first-time reader may not notice, the narrator of *Middlemarch*, with knowingness that comes from sexual maturity, appears to be using subtle irony to balance our impression of Dorothea's saintliness.

My interpretation of Dorothea and Casaubon's miserable marriage, particularly my judgments about Dorothea's relative responsibility, evolved over years. In my early readings of the novel, it never occurred to me that Dorothea could be blamed for choosing an incompatible spouse, though the narrator regularly throws subtle jabs by describing her, for example, as "enamored of intensity and greatness, and rash in embracing what seemed to her to have these aspects" (1.1:9). For all her love of "giving up," Dorothea had not prepared herself to be shut out of Casaubon's intellectual endeavor after their marriage, which was her real motivation for marrying him. It took me years to sympathize even a little with Casaubon's self-absorbed fears of failure in his lifelong scholarly project, his imposter complex, or the intense jealousy he felt toward Will Ladislaw, his attractive young cousin. What conception could I have had of the fears of an aging scholar? Then, I could only bristle at Casaubon's businesslike letter of proposal and resent his intention to limit Dorothea's role to that of a secretarial assistant who would prove useful in saving his eyes from excessive strain (1.5:60–62). It is a testament to Eliot's writing that I experienced Dorothea's unrequited love and her missed opportunities as if they could have happened to me. Dorothea's enthusiastic acceptance of a role that demanded complete subjugation was disastrous, of course, but surely, I assumed, not caused by her own immaturity or myopia, even though Dorothea admits to being, literally, "rather short-sighted" (1.3:42). Instead, I blamed Casaubon for expecting unquestioning worship from a woman as intelligent and idealistic as Dorothea, for figuratively slamming and locking the door of her prison after she has become enmeshed in the patriarchal fantasy of what a wife should be. I either missed or chose to ignore the narrator's interpretive guidance to consider both sides. It took rereading years later to appreciate how Eliot points a gentle finger at society, at Casaubon, and at Dorothea, whose ignorance and lack of healthy self-preservation prove to be dangerous, and avoidable.

Although the narrative generates sympathy for Dorothea by explaining her feelings and showing the pain caused by her husband's lack of interest or affection, at the same time the narrator builds a case for sympathizing with Casaubon. In chapter 29, the narrator famously switches gears as she is about to launch into a new paragraph about Dorothea's feelings. She stops herself and interjects, "—but why always Dorothea? Was her point of view the only possible one with regard to this marriage?" (2.29:9). "Poor Casaubon" has discovered on his honeymoon that his "stream of affection" has turned out to be "an exceedingly shallow rill" (1.7:91). He is humiliated and disillusioned by the marriage too, but he is a man of the cloth and no doubt believes in the authority of the biblical injunction "What therefore God hath joined together, let not man put asunder" (Mark 10:9). In any case, before England's Matrimonial Causes Act of 1857, marriages were virtually impossible to escape legally. Throughout history, unhappy marriages have been difficult for many people, especially women, to leave, whether for religious, legal, economic, or other reasons. There is nothing for Casaubon and Dorothea to do other than endure in silence, hiding their misery even from the servants. Though other characters disparage Casaubon throughout the novel, even after he is known to be gravely ill, the narrator never articulates negative judgment: "For my part," she says, "I am very sorry for him" (2.29:12). The narrator's rhetoric doesn't seem to match the realities of the relationship described, a distancing that invites readers to weigh behavior against intention. As coercive and cruel as Casaubon proves to be, the narrator who witnesses and describes his conduct doesn't explicitly condemn him. Like those of a parent who loves two children who hurt one another, or a child who loves both quarreling parents, the narrator's sympathies shift back and forth, but she refuses to settle the blame on either side. There is no villain in this novel—only different ways of interpreting behavior. Without being prescriptive, the narrator models the kind of generous attitude she wants to encourage in the reader.

I conceptualize the relationship between Dorothea and Casaubon differently with every reading, and with age and experience have become somewhat more sympathetic to Casaubon's case. By contemplating Casaubon's wasted years, his missing out on love, friendship, and community as he toils alone in dim libraries in search of "the Key to all Mythologies," I recognize the trade-offs and sacrifices inherent in pursuing an academic career and share some of Casaubon's fears about the value of my scholarly labor. I've also known the dread of waiting nervously for biopsy results and can imagine Casaubon's anxious fear as he confronts his own mortality shortly before he succumbs, appropriately, to his degenerated heart. Even though Casaubon rejects pity, the narrator asks readers to consider the man's sensitivity and desperation. Eliot never lets the reader forget that we are witnesses to a failed but feeling human being. Eliot's ability to develop fully realistic individuals across the usual lines of gender and class is extraordinary in itself, but to produce both contempt and pathos in the same reader for a single character is an astonishing and rare achievement in fiction.

Throughout *Middlemarch*, characters misunderstand the signs that seem to indicate the motivations of others; they act on false assumptions and learn to face the consequences of their mistakes. Only the narrator can read minds—everyone else, as in life, is only guessing. Differentiating between reality and delusion is as difficult for the characters involved as it is for the readers to decipher. Judgment is left to the reader, and one of the pleasures I find in rereading *Middlemarch* is the surprise of discovering a new detail that alters my previous assumption or conclusion. I had focused until now on Dorothea and her marriage to Casaubon because that was what initially drew me into the novel. To more fully explain how my initial connections with *Middlemarch* have shifted over subsequent readings, I want to consider two other relationships in the novel that I've been rethinking recently: the marriage of Lydgate and Rosamond and the friendship between Lydgate and Dorothea. Obviously, my personal experiences have influenced my sense of what details matter during a particular rereading, which may be further evidence that interpretations are at least partially dependent on the reader's evolving priorities and values.

Eliot's novel started as two separate projects, both variations on the theme of incompatibility in married life. Although the "Miss Brooke" section ultimately was placed at the front of the novel and tends to dominate discussions of *Middlemarch*, Eliot's first inclination was to narrate the experience of a handsome young doctor, Tertius Lydgate, whose "plan of the future [is] to do good small work for Middlemarch, and great work for the world" (1.15:225). Lydgate's story of moving to Middlemarch, meeting his future bride, and then capitulating to pressures of financial insecurity that gradually ruin his marriage and career are events that run parallel to but separate from the Dorothea-Casaubon story for most of the novel's first half. These two narrative strands are brought into conversation when Lydgate becomes Casaubon's physician and, deeply moved by Dorothea's wifely devotion, learns to appreciate her value. In his intellectual passion and his aspiration to "do good," Lydgate resembles Dorothea. They seem temperamentally well suited.

When I first read the novel, I recall hoping, like many readers, that Lydgate and Dorothea would fall in love, but Eliot never considered this option. Now I believe the novel is far better for developing the relationship between these two as a bond of sympathetic friendship that rehabilitates Lydgate's character. An analysis of Lydgate's development throughout the novel helps to demonstrate Eliot's extraordinary rendering of the complexities of human psychology—the aspect of the novel that has always interested me most. Lydgate is arguably Eliot's greatest achievement in characterization, the most complicated individual she ever created. Noticing not only his altruism but also the darker side of his nature is key to appreciating his wholeness.

Lydgate is attracted to the beautiful but dangerous femme fatale type, exemplified by his first love, Madame Laure, the French actress who murders her husband to escape the constraints of marriage. Lydgate's romantic history is relevant because his infatuation with the fragile-looking but fiercely determined Rosamond Vincy shows he remains attracted by the same sort of woman. He has no time for "plain women," whom he initially "regarded as he did the other severe facts of life, to be faced with philosophy and investigated by science" (1.11:140). Rosamond is the town beauty, a gorgeous blonde, the highly accomplished "flower" of Mrs. Lemon's finishing school, who knows exactly the kind of life she wants to lead—comfortable, respected, and far from Middlemarch (1.11:143). Although the narrator suggests that "[a] woman dictates before marriage in order that she may have an appetite for submission afterwards" (1.9:107), the notion of submitting after marriage never strikes Rosamond as necessary. Her rebellion takes the form of passive resistance to her husband's attempts to direct and manage her behavior. The narrator sums up Rosamond as "mild in her temper, inflexible in her judgment, disposed to admonish her husband, and able to frustrate him by stratagem" (3.87:460). Although Rosamond is not blameless, certainly, and seems cruelly selfish in her reluctance to sympathize or compromise with her husband in the early days of their financial distress, I recognize now that she is not evil, that mistakes were made on both sides, and that Rosamond's willfulness can be read as a strategy of self-preservation. The narrator interjects, "Poor Lydgate! or shall I say, Poor Rosamond! Each lived in a world of which the other knew nothing" (1.16:251). The unknowability of other people, even in marriage, is at fault, perhaps, rather than Rosamond or Lydgate themselves.

The women Lydgate is drawn to are completely opposite to Dorothea in temperament and in their responses to their husbands. Neither the selfish Rosamond nor the selfless Dorothea achieves a happy first marriage. Dorothea seems more admirable and Rosamond seems more repugnant to most readers, a response that may be related to social conditioning of people to see submissive women as good, long-suffering, and heroic, whereas powerful women who resist domination are seen as bad. Recently, I have noticed striking parallels in Dorothea's and Rosamond's dysfunctional marriages and have argued that these are related case studies showing opposite responses to controlling husbands that culminate in nearly identical results. Too much selflessness is as debilitating to the partnership as too much selfishness.

*Middlemarch*'s narrator assesses Lydgate's positive and negative qualities in an interesting passage that acknowledges both his aspirations and potential goodness as well as his deficiencies:

> Lydgate's spots of commonness lay in the complexion of his prejudices, which, in spite of noble intention and sympathy, were half of them such as are found in ordinary men of the world: that distinction of mind which belonged to his intellectual ardor did not penetrate his feeling and judgment about furniture, or women, or the desirability of its being known (without his telling) that he was better born than other country surgeons. (1.15:227)

In my early readings of the novel, I attended to Lydgate's "noble intention and sympathy" and failed to notice that the narrator also offered specific criticism. Lydgate's "spots of commonness" didn't matter to me in my early reading as much as his appealing "intellectual ardor." His large hands and powerful body were similarly alluring, especially in contrast with descriptions of Casaubon's unhealthy appearance—his sallow skin, hairy facial moles, and skinny legs. In the same passage above in which the narrator praises Lydgate's "distinction of mind" and his "noble intention and sympathy," we find mention of his social pride and his "prejudices" in which his "feeling and judgment about furniture, or women" are lumped together (1.15:227). Lydgate's objectification of women rankles me today more than it did years ago when I was new to feminist criticism; to the Victorians, I suspect, it would have been so common as to be unnoticeable. Nevertheless, Lydgate's disrespectful attitude about what a wife should be clearly contributes to the failure of his marriage. "[G]uided by a single conversation," Lydgate had determined that Dorothea "did not look at things from the proper feminine angle" and that the "society of such women was about as relaxing as going from your work to teach the second form, instead of reclining in a paradise with sweet laughs for bird-notes, and blue eyes for a heaven" (1.11:141). Rosamond flirts and projects feminine helplessness to attract Lydgate, but it is his arrogance and willful blindness that cause him to view her as that sweetly singing bird who would give him nothing but pleasure as he reclines in a marital paradise.

After I began to compare Lydgate to Casaubon, noticing their similar egotistical behavior and the way they both dominate their wives, for example, I became far less sympathetic to Lydgate's disappointments in his marriage. More attuned to issues of social justice and better informed about the warning signs of domestic abuse than I used to be, I noticed the clues the narrator was also leaving regarding Lydgate's narcissism. In the following passage, for example, the narrator comments casually on Lydgate's claim of superiority and expectation of deference from those he views as his inferiors: "Lydgate's conceit was of the arrogant sort, never simpering, never impertinent, but massive in its claims and benevolently contemptuous. He would do a great deal for noodles, being sorry for them, and feeling quite sure that they could have no power over him" (1.15:226–27). Lydgate is clearly concerned about maintaining the balance of power in his own favor, not only in his relations with the lowly townsfolk who become his patients but also in his expectations of the deference a husband is due. What first attracts Lydgate to Dorothea, in fact, is her wifely submission and devotion to her husband, a whole-hearted self-sacrifice that, according to Dorothea, is motivated by a combination of duty and feeling.

Lydgate's young bride refuses to submit when she feels she is right, even to her husband. Sometimes she *is* right, sometimes not, but her instinct is to dig in and resist Lydgate's attempts to control her behavior. Lydgate's muscular body and his barely contained rage are threatening to Rosamond, who uses silence and passive-aggressive tactics to deflect her husband's potential violence and to assert her equal status in running the household. When Rosamond offers to ask her father for money or suggests that Lydgate should write to his wealthy family members for a loan, he forcefully shuts her down. Later, when he believes the idea originated with him, Lydgate decides to try these same options, but he is too late. His assertive wife has taken the matter into her own hands and has already investigated these alternatives. If Rosamond's attempts to rectify the problem had succeeded instead of falling flat, she wouldn't be condemned for disobeying her husband and going behind his back; instead, she would be appreciated as resourceful. As Rosamond's husband, Lydgate is shown at his worst—an incommunicative, condescending, and threateningly angry husband, whose "outbursts of indignation either ironical or remonstrant" were considered a "kind of violence" and "totally unwarranted" by his coolly calm wife (3.69:259). Regardless of what kind of wife Rosamond is, Lydgate has all the hallmarks of an emotionally abusive husband. Although he does restrain himself from physical violence, his hot temper is terrifying. He stops short of hitting his wife, but the implication is that he is so frustrated with her that he is barely maintaining control. Rosamond's refusal to engage with his tantrums leaves him "bruised and shattered" and entirely dumbfounded that he cannot win the battle for power in the relationship (3.69:259). The power dynamics depicted in the Lydgates' marriage further demonstrate the depth and insight with which Eliot dissects the psychology of human relationships, especially dysfunctional domestic partnerships.

Although I have been interpreting Lydgate as an abusive husband, he is certainly not a villain. Throughout the novel, he is a consistently positive influence on others, and though he makes his wife miserable behind closed doors, Lydgate is shown to improve and learn from his mistakes. Consider the development of his friendship with Dorothea. The novel brings Lydgate and Dorothea together in three scenes that demonstrate their increasing emotional understanding and trust in one another. These scenes of friendship used to convince me that Eliot meant us to read Lydgate as a victim of a cruel spouse, perhaps even as much as Dorothea is, but as I reread the novel over time, my views changed again. Even more than Casaubon, Lydgate is realistically multifaceted; he can be an angry, controlling bully in his private relations with his wife, while showing great sympathy and love for others outside his marriage.

The extent to which Lydgate develops as a character can be traced in his changing responses to Dorothea. The two meet at a dinner party held in honor of her engagement, where Dorothea exhausts his patience by "talking cottages and hospitals with him" while "nothing could seem much less important to Lydgate than the turn of Miss Brooke's mind" (1.10:136). Throughout their encounter, Lydgate is comparing Dorothea unfavorably with Rosamond, whom he regards as not only "strikingly different from Miss Brooke" but also "what a woman ought to be" (1.10:141). They are two inexperienced, short-sighted young people confident in their mistaken first impressions and not yet subjected to the rude awakening in store for them both. After this inauspicious meeting, Lydgate next encounters Dorothea in a professional context. He is the physician who diagnoses Casaubon's first heart attack and breaks the news to both patient and caregiver regarding the precariousness of the older man's health. Dorothea's sobbed response is both surprising and deeply affecting:

> "Advise me. Think what I can do. He has been laboring all his life and looking forward. He minds about nothing else. And I mind about nothing else—"
>
> For years after Lydgate remembered the impression produced in him of this involuntary appeal—this cry from soul to soul, without other consciousness than their moving with kindred natures in the same embroiled medium, the same troublous fitfully illuminated life. (2.30:27)

Lydgate is so struck by this second, counterbalancing meeting with Dorothea that "for years after" he remembers it as a heartfelt moment of illumination of their "kindred natures" (2.30:27). He believes they are experiencing "the same" troubles in their private lives and imagines they both are victims, which is surely how Lydgate feels, even though, objectively, this conclusion is debatable. Although Lydgate seems to be deluding himself into believing he bears no responsibility for his marital breakdown, at least his feelings of suffering allow him to recognize and respond to Dorothea's with genuine compassion.

The third scene between Lydgate and Dorothea is even more intimate and adds to the emotional sympathy that has begun to develop between the two. Lydgate, who is called after Casaubon suffers a second heart attack, arrives to find he has two patients to care for: the unconscious Casaubon, who is approaching death, and Dorothea, who is emotionally shattered. The previous day, Casaubon had asked his wife to give her word that she would complete his life's work, his "Key to all Mythologies," if he should die before its publication. After deliberating all night, fully understanding the futility of the project and the many years of labor it would take to complete, Dorothea had prepared herself to make that disastrous vow to her husband. She had been on her way to tell him when she found him unconscious. She urges Lydgate to convey to Casaubon that she is ready to give her life over to completing his work. Dorothea may be rambling, but she has definitely decided and urgently wants Casaubon to know her answer. The narrator reports that Dorothea knows Lydgate "and call[s] him by his name" and that she appears to think it right that she should explain everything to him, and again and again begs him to explain everything to her husband. "'Tell him I shall go to him soon; I am ready to promise. . . . Go and tell him.' But the silence in her husband's ear was never more to be broken" (3.48:318). Dorothea is saved from having to promise by the author's decision to end Casaubon's life before he can hear her vow. Although many critics view this plot device as unfittingly melodramatic in a realistic novel, I see this authorial rescue as a brilliantly appropriate way for Eliot to maintain the characters' psychological consistency. Lydgate had been moved by Dorothea's wifely devotion after her husband's first attack, but in this scene, the narrator doesn't explain Lydgate's response to Dorothea's resolute martyrdom, leaving the reader to assemble disparate clues.

A detail I had previously overlooked, and other readers seem not to have discussed, strikes me as noteworthy, if not hugely significant: that Lydgate appears to play a crucial role in rescuing Dorothea from her own self-sacrificing generosity. There is never any doubting Dorothea's sincerity, though she recognizes her husband's work as futile: "Bound by a pledge given from the depths of her pity," the narrator explains, "she would have been capable of undertaking a toil which her judgment whispered was vain for all uses except consecration of faithfulness which is a supreme use" (2.50:335). At this point, however, Dorothea is still unaware of something Lydgate detects, that Casaubon's request had been made out of "hidden alienation, of secrecy and suspicion" (2.50:335). Lydgate's intuition and insight into the Casaubons' marriage, the narrator proposes, "had enabled him to form some true conclusions concerning the trials of [Dorothea's] life" (2.50:332). Because he recognizes Dorothea as a person of integrity who will keep her vows, Lydgate perceives Casaubon's request as a particularly cruel attempt "to keep his cold grasp on Dorothea's life" (2.50:335). As Lydgate attends at the bedsides of both Dorothea and Casaubon on the night Casaubon passes, Dorothea feels the urgent need to confess and "explain everything" to the sympathetic doctor. He feels deeply for her plight and understands the nature of her distress. If Lydgate had relayed Dorothea's insistent message to her husband that she was "ready to promise," she wouldn't have had to beg him "again and again" to go to her husband and "tell him" (2.48:318). Lydgate either does not deliver Dorothea's message or does not deliver it in time. Whether or not his failure to act is intentional, no further comment about it seems to be made by any character or by the narrator. Nevertheless, Lydgate's lack of response to Dorothea's request may have helped prevent her from sabotaging her future. Because the narrator reports on the scene of Casaubon's last night without revealing Lydgate's thoughts, the reader is seemingly invited to speculate on what motivates the doctor's apparent reluctance to act on the foolish entreaties of a woman he has grown to care about. Did Lydgate insist Dorothea stay in her own bed that night as her husband languished in another room? The narrator won't implicate him in any assertion whatsoever—he is described merely as a witness. How we interpret this scene, I think, reveals more about our own values than it does about the text itself. It is one of those intriguing little gaps in the narrative that keep readers invested in returning to *Middlemarch*. There is always the possibility that substantiating clues may be hidden in plain sight in another part of the novel, but that isn't as important as acknowledging that my new reading must be exposing a new interpretive bias I have brought to the novel this time that I didn't bring to previous readings. *Middlemarch*, remarkably, can sustain them all.

Along with his possible role in preventing Dorothea's capitulation to Casaubon's final request—one that would have conscripted the next fifteen years of her life—Lydgate's sympathetic understanding of Dorothea's miserable marriage redeems his character. There is one more scene of connection between Lydgate and Dorothea demonstrating his compassionate nature I find fascinating. After hearing that Lydgate plans to leave Middlemarch, Dorothea summons him to her home to inquire how her inheritance could benefit the hospital. As she waits for Lydgate, she thinks back on her own marital troubles and on what she has divined about his. She has also heard rumors that Lydgate accepted a large loan from Mr. Bulstrode, the banker, as blackmail. That backstory isn't relevant to my point about Lydgate's character and his relationship to Dorothea. What matters is Dorothea's response to this rumor; she states matter-of-factly,

"You would not do anything dishonorable," which was "the first assurance of belief in him that had fallen on Lydgate's ears" (3.76:351). Dorothea does not know Lydgate well, but they share two significant emotional moments and she trusts her instincts that his integrity matches her own. In response,

> . . . he gave himself up, for the first time in his life, to the exquisite sense of leaning entirely on a generous sympathy, without any check of proud reserve. And he told her everything. . . .
>
> "Why should I not tell you?—you know what sort of bond marriage is. You will understand everything." (3.76:353–57)

One of the reasons Lydgate's marriage had broken down was his unwillingness to communicate with his wife about their financial difficulties and about the stress it caused him. He had resorted to making prescriptive statements without listening to her or trying to work out a compromise together. It was apparently too late to resurrect Rosamond's love for him, but when Lydgate responds to Dorothea's implicit trust in him by telling her that he can't stand to see Rosamond miserable, he is signaling a momentous breakthrough in which he prioritizes his wife's feelings instead of his own. Lydgate confesses, "She married me without knowing what she was going into, and it might have been better for her if she had not married me" (3.76:357). It is the admission of a man who seems ready to change. The long conversation between Lydgate and Dorothea in this scene and the sympathetic moments of emotional connection they experienced in their previous interactions leads not to a romantic attachment but to a "fountain of friendship" in which Lydgate learns that "a man can make a friend of her" (3.76:362). He has come a long way from his initial objectification of women.

From alluring intellectual to abusive husband to compassionate friend, my readings of Lydgate have emphasized different aspects of his complex character depending, in part, on what was relevant in my own experience. And when I return to the novel, I will be a different person again, ready to discover different stratums and gradations in the temperaments and relationships of the characters and other aspects of George Eliot's masterpiece.

As I peruse my various editions of *Middlemarch*, I find I'm most attached to my old Norton, edited by Bert G. Hornback, too broken now to use but too precious to discard. Faded yellow highlighting and underlining along with notes in pencil and at least three different inks remind me of the physical and emotional spaces I inhabited as I read. These pages also bring back some of the layered associations I was making, usually subconsciously, with some of the novel's settings, circumstances, and characters. For example, in Dorothea there was some of my own enthusiastic shortsightedness; in Mary Garth, my daughter's studious sensibility; in Fred Vincy, my son's carefree optimism; and in Camden Farebrother, my husband's willingness to put others' recognition ahead of his own. *Middlemarch*, for me, includes all of this and still holds the promise of more because it invites readers to consider the important, always open-ended questions in life. How do people understand themselves? What motivates them? Why do they make the mistakes they do? And most of all, what can we learn from their stories? I am fortunate to have discovered "my Victorian novel," *Middlemarch*, a brilliant work of art that continues to surprise, delight, and teach me, and no doubt will reward the scrutiny of another thirty-five years or so. It's that glorious.

## NOTES

1. Emily Dickinson, *The Letters of Emily Dickinson*, ed. Thomas H. Johnson and Theodora Ward, letter number 389.

2. George Eliot, *Middlemarch: A Study of Provincial Life*, vol. 1, chap. 2, p. 30. I cite here the standard version for citations, the Cabinet edition, which represents Eliot's final corrections to Blackwood's 1871–1872 edition. Further references to volume, chapter, and page number will be given parenthetically. This edition is available online at the *George Eliot Archive*: https://georgeeliotarchive.org/.

## WORKS CITED

Dickinson, Emily. *The Letters of Emily Dickinson*. Edited by Thomas H. Johnson and Theodora Ward. 3 vols. Cambridge: Harvard University Press, 1958.

Eliot, George. *Middlemarch: A Study of Provincial Life*. 1871–1872. Cabinet ed. Edinburgh and London: William Blackwood & Sons, 1876. Accessed at https://georgeeliotarchive.org/items/show/13.

CHAPTER SIX

# Unhinged

Ellen Rosenman

## On *Daniel Deronda* by George Eliot

Partway through my probationary period as an assistant professor, I realized I hadn't read a novel for pleasure in over a year. I was thrilled to have a tenure-track job. In graduate school, my friends and I had decided during our job search that we would be satisfied with a request for a writing sample. When that arrived, we upped our hopes: just a Modern Language Association Conference interview, then maybe an on-campus interview, then any kind of offer (this was in 1979, reputed to be the worst academic market year in history; some things don't change much). Now I was close to grabbing the gold ring of tenure, with a book under contract, a shaky teaching record improved, a solid place among faculty I respected and, in most cases, actually liked. I was a much better scholar than I had been in graduate school, more able to see patterns of language and structure, to identify themes, to tease out broader implications, to apply apt theoretical approaches. I had become a critic, but what had happened to me as a reader?

Like most English professors, I had devoured books from an early age, curled up on my parents' hideous brown couch for hours, drawn in by the strangeness of fictional worlds and their gorgeous, evocative language. These worlds were real but unreal, richer and more marvelous than anything in my own ordinary suburban childhood, often beyond my understanding in their complexity and depth. This was the pleasure of reading: the feeling that a whole other dimension of experience was held out to me that just eluded my grasp. I read three volumes of Anthony Powell's *A Dance to the Music of Time* and, when I finished, thought, "I wonder what that was all about." I couldn't have given the most rudimentary plot summary, but what an amazing world of words! When I grow up,

I thought, then I'll be able to fully enter these worlds, to be as wise as their authors. But I wasn't nearly there. Especially when I moved on to college and graduate school, it seemed that everyone else had a more analytic bent than I did. It took serious retraining to tame my unruly associative mind and develop a critical faculty, and I still feared that I hadn't quite succeeded. But be careful what you wish for. With the most important professional milestone awaiting me in the near future, I wondered whether the trade-off had been worth it. Should I quit my job and become a piano tuner so I can read for pleasure again? This seemed like a drastic solution. Instead, I chose a less self-destructive path: I changed my scholarly focus from the modernists to the Victorians. I had been fascinated by the experiments of modernist literature, but nothing gave me pleasure like reading Victorian novels. Reading *Jane Eyre* in bed late one night for class, I thought that I might be doing the same thing if I were on vacation. (As an assistant professor, you don't take very glamorous vacations.) But though the process was more enjoyable, I couldn't shake the feeling that I wasn't making meaning fast enough, hard enough. My aim was still to transform my inchoate reactions into analysis and conclusions.

And then I read George Eliot's astonishing *Daniel Deronda* (1876), that Niagara Falls of a novel: grand, powerful, overwhelming. When people ask me what my favorite novel is, I don't hesitate, this is the one. Both realistic and fantastic, it seemed to me unlike anything I'd ever read. Eliot the moralist, who wrote *Adam Bede* to teach us to be kind to our ugly, irritating neighbors, had gone far beyond the reaches of such a straightforward aim. Like Beethoven's late quartets and Shakespeare's late romances, *Daniel Deronda* relinquished the beauty of coherence for dissonance and mystery. I could not get a handle on anything but the tiniest corner of this 800-page behemoth, so I did what critics do: I decided to analyze it. I read and reread it, wrote about it in three articles, and taught it repeatedly, struggling to get to the bottom of it. Happily, I never succeeded. I have never fully comprehended *Daniel Deronda*, in the sense both of understanding and of fathoming, encompassing. It exceeds me. I finally stopped trying to write about it because I was embarrassed by my attempts to translate its strangeness into an argument. But I continue to teach it, partly because I want to introduce it to new readers and partly because I want to hear new responses to it—not to arrive at a comprehensive interpretation (whatever that would be) but to collect in my mind the many ways of holding the novel up to the light to trace its thrilling, confounding effects.

For readers who are unfamiliar with *Daniel Deronda*, let me quickly summarize the plot (or plots). Two intertwined modes make up the novel's DNA. The most recognizable is the story of Gwendolen Harleth, a vain, superficial young woman who imagines her good looks will win her a tractable aristocratic husband but who is driven into marriage with the sadistic Henleigh Mallinger Grandcourt instead. This is the familiar Victorian world of clothing, conversation, status, and money. The other mode is harder to label but is governed by prophecy and destiny rather than social conventions and forms of power. In this thread, Daniel Deronda, presumed to be the illegitimate son of the very English Sir Hugo Mallinger, discovers that he is the legitimate son of a larger-than-life Jewish opera star who repudiated both him and Judaism. Highly moral but somewhat aimless, Deronda is thrilled by this discovery for several reasons: he has found his lost mother (though this discovery is more fraught than he imagined, as I'll discuss shortly); he can marry Mirah, the deeply religious Jewess he has saved from drowning; and he has found his purpose in life, to fulfill his grandfather's desire to found a Jewish state in Palestine. An indefinable gravitational pull between Gwendolen and Deronda draws these threads together, while divergences in tone and plot tug them apart.

In this multi-plot novel, Eliot engages themes and formal experiments as wide-ranging as any critic could wish for; the interpretive possibilities are deep and nearly endless. But what really interests me are intense and inscrutable moments in the novel, small-scale depth charges that unsettle my ability, and even my desire, to make meaning. They are powerful precisely because they aren't woven into the flow of the narrative. One scene in particular epitomizes the aura of my first encounter with *Daniel Deronda*. Early in the novel Gwendolen Harleth—beautiful, supremely self-possessed, selfish, and naïve—arrives with her family to their new home, Offendene. The narrator remarks on the family's precarious social position, the "border territory of [their] rank," and gives us a detailed picture of the house ("rigidly rectangular"), its surroundings ("the long thatched roofs of the distant village, the church towers, the scattered homesteads"), and its interior ("all dark oak and worn red satin damask, with a copy of worrying, snarling dogs from Snyders [a seventeenth-century painter] over the sideboard and a Christ breaking bread over the mantel-piece").[1] We are squarely in the realm of "classical realism," a genre in which, according to Elaine Freedgood, the "aspiration to reference" a coherent reality produces the "stability of its representational world."[2] (Freedgood argues that this genre is actually a critical invention that oversimplifies Victorian fiction, and *Daniel Deronda* certainly bears out this claim.) Gwendolen has a wholly conventional reaction to the house, imagining it as "a romantic place" and "a good background for anything"—especially for herself. There is an organ in the drawing room, and she poses beside it in the character of St. Cecilia, imagining herself as the subject of a painting (54). (St. Cecilia, patron saint of music, was killed in her own house, a detail that seems to have eluded Gwendolen.) At that moment, her sister accidentally opens a panel in the wainscoting, which reveals "the picture of an upturned dead face, from which an obscure figure seemed to be fleeing with outstretched arms." Gwendolen's body registers her fright: she "shudder[s] silently," chastises her sister in "her angriest tone," "snatch[es]" the panel, closes it "hastily," and flushes deeply (56).

The descriptions of the house and of Gwendolen's reaction are detailed and precise, in contrast to the vague one of the image on the panel—two unidentified bodies, one dead, one fleeing. The image is unnerving. It needs explanation, an interpretation that will contain its disturbing effect. What does it mean? Critics have asserted that the figures in the panel foreshadow Grandcourt's death, or that it is a vision of Gwendolen's future as she flees from spiritual death, or that it represents her unconscious and reveals the hidden terrors of even the most apparently superficial people. But the image gives us very little to analyze. It is as if the details attributed to "classical realism"—the solidity of the house and Gwendolen's precisely detailed movements—are revealed as a cover-up for a vague menace, like the panel itself, which appears to be part of an elegant wall. This sense is intensified when, shortly after her panic, Gwendolen performs the role of the young lady to perfection for her aunt and uncle in an attempt to bury her fear. Springing open the panel, Eliot drops us into a different realm defined by a *lack* of detail with a representation that is all the more powerful for being so shadowy, like a cinematic monster we glimpse but never see. Classical realism has briefly opened into . . . what? A horror story? An existential abyss? What exactly are we looking at? Though a master of narration and description, Eliot is reticent. Attempting to map or describe this realm would tame it. The panel erupts into the everyday and then returns, unintegrated, into its own strange universe. The motif of opening and closing suggests that another realm of experience, whatever it is, always lies in wait beneath the attractive décor of a house and skillfully performed social roles. It is all the more shocking because it is *framed* by the conventions of classical realism. The "stability of [the] representational world" is momentarily undone as we are thrust into something scarier, more enigmatic, with an accidental turn of a hinge.

I refuse to interpret this panel. To me, the panel is powerful, terrifying, unfathomable. That's enough. The metaphor of "fathoming" is apt here since the image lies behind the panel of the wall, but once we penetrate the surface, what we have is not "the answer" but a feeling of dread that eludes understanding. My initial response to the image—the reductive "what does it mean?"—felt paltry next to the somatic and psychological energies it stirred in me. Rita Felski's definition of shock, one of the reading responses she discusses in *Uses of Literature*, approaches my reaction. Shock is "a sudden collision, an abrupt, even violent encounter" that "rupture[es] familiar frames of reference," Felski says. "The essence of shock is to be jarring," she concludes.[3] The passage jarred me the first time I read it as much as the fictional experience jarred Gwendolen. I inhaled sharply, put my finger in the book to mark the page, and burrowed into the feelings of dread and confusion. And I stayed there for a while, not thinking but feeling.

Of course, criticism and understanding have their own rewards. One reason my reinvention as a Victorianist "took" was the simultaneous emergence of feminist criticism, especially Sandra M. Gilbert and Susan Gubar's groundbreaking work *The Madwoman in the Attic* (1979). Focusing on nineteenth-century women writers, it established themes and tropes that I suddenly saw everywhere: madness, anger, speech vs. silence, rebellious subtexts, subversion, demonic doubles, the politics of space. I no longer felt as lost in my immediate responses; I had something to say after I read a novel. What an enormous relief! Nothing was more satisfying than teaching my beloved *Jane Eyre*, the centerpiece of Gilbert and Gubar's argument. I felt like a magician, pulling Bertha-as-Jane's-angry-double out of a hat. I don't mean to denigrate *The Madwoman in the Attic* as a kind of recipe book, with simple instructions about how to read all women writers, nor to represent my hard-fought attempts to make sense of literature as the application of simple formulas. One of my early articles, which I'm still proud of, interprets Virginia Woolf's *A Room of One's Own* as a dialogue between text and subtext, narrated by a woman writer who attempts to both suppress and express her anger.[4] Seeing *A Room of One's Own* through a feminist lens was a eureka moment, one of the most satisfying of my career. It was exhilarating to be able to make meaning, especially meaning I cared about. A lifelong feminist, I could finally unify my politics and my work.

But, again, my obsession with *Daniel Deronda* derailed my critical aspirations. The figure that perplexed me most was Alcharisi, the self-named, and brilliant, singer who reveals herself as Deronda's mother. In some ways, she was a perfect example of Gilbert and Gubar's thesis, a passionate woman who abandons her family to pursue a career as an artist, only to lose her voice at the height of her powers and capitulate to her hated father's wish for her to act as a "makeshift link" in a patriarchal genealogy (694). Anger, self-expression and silence, subversion and containment. In my younger, pre-maternal days, I thought, "Good for her! And how tragic that the patriarchy catches up with her!" In fact, I wrote an article about speech and silence in the novel with Alcharisi as a central figure, one of those too-simple interpretations I look back on with some embarrassment.[5] Now, as a mother, I recall George Eliot's conscientious parenting of George Henry Lewes's children, and I know she had something more complex in mind. But, again, what? Like the panel in the wall, Alcharisi refuses interpretation, demonstrating a kind of radical neutrality about her relationship with Deronda in the face of his desperate attempts to connect with her. "Mother!" begs her son, "take us all into your heart—the living and the dead. Forgive everything that hurts you in the past. Take my affection." Alcharisi coolly replies, "I reject nothing, but I have nothing to give" (697). She cannot even give him a reason for having summoned him after so long a separation: "Oh—the reasons for our actions," she says casually (691). For the reader, as well as for Deronda, her motives are unfathomable.

As if to underscore Alcharisi's inscrutability, her placement in the narrative is like the mysterious panel in the wall at Offendene. She emerges out of the blue, a strange figure whose presence is far in excess of her plot function, which is to reveal Deronda's Jewish identity. With her intense emotions and almost supernatural experiences—the failing voice, the loss of memory, and the sense of diminished selfhood that befalls her after her father's death—she seems to enter from another world. Moreover, her conversation with Deronda is split by a chapter focusing on a letter from his friend Hans, a correlate to the details of classical realism. Her magisterial speech stands in striking contrast to the jaunty tone and quotidian details of Hans's letter. Like the panel, her character opens up another dimension of human experience, one that cannot be integrated into the everyday, the domestic, the social. She arrests our attention only to disappear as abruptly and completely as she arrived. She refuses the reader's desire for intimacy and understanding just as she does her son's. Over the years, I have struggled to find a feminist paradigm that does justice to this character. But perhaps the most radical characterization Eliot could create was of a woman, and especially of a mother, who remains a cipher. In her radical otherness, she cannot be reduced to an idea, a function, a role. Alcharisi is beyond judgment.

I do not want to overstate the distinction between the intellect, the emotions, and the body, but I have found that the more analytical I am, the further away I become from other registers of response. The experience of reading disappears in the rearview mirror of analytical reconstruction. Our discipline "espouses *vigilance*," Felski argues, training us to "stand back from the pleasure of reading to encourage critical reflection."[6] When I sought more conscious understanding, I had legitimate intellectual aspirations, but I also wanted to find a position of mastery. To feel smart is the abiding desire of both the child and the professor. When you finish three novels by Anthony Powell and think "What was that all about?" what have you accomplished? I have seen the tension between analysis and immediate response in the graduate students I have taught over the years, as they struggle to cultivate a critical mind, as I once did. I remember in particular one class in which we discussed Victorian essays condemning novel reading. Immersing oneself in fiction would encourage readers to live in a world of fantasy, where they might imitate the actions of fictional characters, turning to crime or adultery because those things looked exciting, these writers maintained; novel reading would overheat the imagination and disable reason by making fictional worlds as real as, and more compelling than, ordinary life. At first my students laughed at these overheated responses. Didn't these zealous moralists know that readers could tell fiction from reality? But then one student recounted her experience reading *Wuthering Heights* during a violent thunderstorm and being absolutely terrified when Lockwood rakes ghost-Catherine's wrist over the broken glass of the casement window. At a particularly bleak time in my life, I experienced my own midnight terrors with Cormac McCarthy's *The Road*, which I read straight through three times until I could cope with the subterranean panic it unearthed in me. As an adult, I felt disoriented to be flooded with emotions I had no desire to feel. Yet don't we want to respond to literature with intense feeling and engagement? I doubt that any amount of literary analysis could have produced the minor therapeutic miracle of my reading-induced catharsis.

For many people, I'm sure, analysis and psychological intensity aren't in conflict, but for me, they often are. I found that writing about popular fiction was a good way out because overall it isn't as layered and complex as canonical fiction, so I didn't feel as bad about "explaining" what it said and how it worked. I don't mean that popular fiction is less interesting or less significant, but I don't think it's interesting or significant in the same way as a novel by George Eliot. Others, I'm sure, will disagree. But for me, because the experience of being both a reader and a critic is especially vexed, I had to find a way to bridge the two.

More than any other novel, *Daniel Deronda* returns me to my readerly past, the mystery of reading, and the excitement of entering a realm of experience that is thrillingly complex to navigate. Iris Murdoch has suggested that the nineteenth-century novel possesses "a great consoling power . . . a deep relaxing of tension, however alarming or horrible the events which are narrated, because of a sense of the strength of society, and of politics as a natural and ordinary part of the human scene."[7] *Daniel Deronda* doesn't console me in this way. Just the opposite, it reassures me by unnerving me, granting me vicarious experiences and emotions more vivid than those of the everyday. Though I have read the panel opening in a very specific (nonspecific) way, it has come to stand for the feeling I used to get when I read any novel as a young adult. My real life felt classically realist, stuffed with things, roles, and social forms: hideous brown couches, Villager sweaters with their grosgrain plackets and white buttons, trips to the local A&P in our turquoise DeSoto, family dinners consisting invariably of a meat, a starch, a vegetable, and a smattering of small talk, and what seemed to me a wholly inexplicable investment in the merits of various household products on the part of my mother and aunts. When I wanted more than this outward life, books were my mysterious panel.

## NOTES

1. George Eliot, *Daniel Deronda*, 51, 51, 52, 55. Further references will be given parenthetically.
2. Elaine Freedgood, *Worlds Enough: The Invention of Realism in the Victorian Novel*, ix, xi.
3. Rita Felski, *Uses of Literature*, 113.

4. Ellen Rosenman, "Sexual Identity in *A Room of One's Own*."
5. Ellen Rosenman, "Women's Speech and the Roles of the Sexes in *Daniel Deronda*."
6. Felski, *Uses of Literature*, 12.
7. Iris Murdoch, "Existentialists and Mystics," 222.

## WORKS CITED

Eliot, George. *Daniel Deronda*. 1876. London: Penguin, 1996.

Felski, Rita. *Uses of Literature*. Malden, MA: Blackwell, 2008.

Freedgood, Elaine. *Worlds Enough: The Invention of Realism in the Victorian Novel*. Princeton: Princeton University Press, 2019.

Murdoch, Iris. "Existentialists and Mystics." 1970. In *Existentialists and Mystics*, edited by Peter Conradi, 221–34. New York: Penguin, 1997.

Rosenman, Ellen. "Sexual Identity in *A Room of One's Own*: 'Secret Economies' in Virginia Woolf's Feminist Discourse." *Signs: Journal of Women in Culture and Society* 14 (1989): 634–50.

———. "Women's Speech and the Roles of the Sexes in *Daniel Deronda*." *Texas Studies in Literature and Language* 31 (1989): 237–56.

CHAPTER SEVEN

# Words Like Violence

Sara Malton

## On *The Return of the Native* by Thomas Hardy

> "In God's mercy don't talk so, Eustacia."
>
> Clym Yeobright in *The Return of the Native*

> This is a record of hate far more than of love.
>
> Graham Greene, *The End of the Affair*

"How could there be any good in a woman that everybody spoke ill of?"[1] With this, Clym Yeobright's chilling question of his wife, Eustacia, I commenced my inquiry into Thomas Hardy's *The Return of the Native* (1878) two decades ago, and it is with this interrogative, which has never left my memory, that I shall here yet again begin.[2] When considering this strange and evocative novel, it seems that one cannot ever really escape Clym's accusation, for the way that individuals communicate in *The Return of the Native* is at the root of the novel's tragedy. Critics have frequently observed the extent to which classical drama dictates much of the novel's narrative structure, but it also, I would suggest, influences much of the novel's linguistic structure.[3] That is to say—as in those classical dramas that the novel invokes, such as *Oedipus Rex* and *King Lear*—in *The Return of the Native*, saying the right words and accurately interpreting signs become matters of survival. The inability to do so has devastating consequences: the entire physical environment turns upon the doomed character, and death results, be it, in Hardy, by snake bite or by drowning.

Thus, the interpretative failures that plague the characters in *The Return of the Native* are not merely a function of human failure but are also a result, at least in part, of the oblivion of Egdon Heath itself, where so often "the obscurity in the air and the obscurity in the land closed together in a black fraternization" (47). Egdon, David Sweeney Coombs observes, "is defined by gloom not as a mood of despondency but as a state of darkness."[4] Seemingly everything happens in the dark and under the cover of night, which is only occasionally illumined by scores of violent shades of fiery red. The "particular glory" of the heath, we are told, transcends mere visual perception, for it "could best be felt when it could not clearly be seen" (47). Only occasionally do we see the light of day; the action of the novel largely takes place in obscurity, beneath the moon or under the latter's eclipse. The "vast dark surface" of the heath itself seems to obscure the vision and interpretive capacities of its dwellers (12). This most overtly emerges in Clym's literal and figurative blindness, yet it seems to affect even the precision of the narrator's vision: of the old man whom we first encounter at the beginning of chapter 2, "[o]ne would have said that he had been, in his day, a naval officer of some sort or other" (51).

My 2000 essay on *The Return of the Native*, "'The Woman Shall Bear Her Iniquity': Death as Social Discipline in Thomas Hardy's *The Return of the Native*," offered a Foucauldian reading of the novel, focusing on what I saw—and what I still in many ways see—as Hardy's depiction of a culture's transition from primitive (physical punishment, torture) to more modern methods of social discipline (surveillance, regulation). Hardy's novel had much to teach me then, as a young scholar, and still has much to teach now—about the violent silencing of women, about the hemming in of women by convention, about the dangers of marital entanglements that involve an unhealthy intimacy between middle-aged mothers and their sons, and about the disastrous nature of social isolation. *The Return of the Native* has much to say about Hardy's ongoing focus on contingency and the problematics of supposed individual choice and agency in a hostile environment.

Pervaded by obscurity, darkness, and the absence of generative communication, *The Return of the Native* largely concerns the use and misuse of signs, literal and figurative, and the disaster inherent in their misinterpretation. Yet, like earlier dynastic tragedies, it also foregrounds the significance of strategy, alliance, and betrayal in the context of both public and personal relationships. As I shall show, in Hardy's novel, familial and romantic relationships are predicated on the tactical, competitive use (and, indeed, often the misuse) of language. Thirty-five years on, then, Patricia Meyer Spacks's important study, *Gossip*, offers crucial insight into the often destructive function of language that a text such as *The Return of the Native* dramatizes. In examining the ways in which "gossip impels plots," Spacks observes the intimate connection between covert communication and destruction: "The idea of talking in secret . . . about someone recalls old conceptions of words as dangerous weapons."[5] If anything, words are combative on Egdon Heath. Mrs. Yeobright's ability to indict Eustacia as a "hussy" largely derives from her access to the rumors in circulation about the "young witch-lady," rumors that are generally the speculation of lower-class heath-dwellers (165, 153). The destruction resulting from the appropriation of these stories by such figures as Mrs. Yeobright and, later, Clym demonstrates how gossip can supply a "powerful weapon" and "can effect incalculable harm, . . . sowing insinuations which generate tragedy."[6]

The reddleman, Diggory Venn, is particularly instrumental in Mrs. Yeobright's communicative plotting, and he carries out a significant amount of his own. When Venn tells Mrs. Yeobright of Wildeve's prior involvement with Eustacia, Mrs. Yeobright "thank[s] God for the *weapon* which the reddleman [has] put in her hands" (88, emphasis added). Mrs. Yeobright's efforts to regulate others' behavior through language renders her, like Venn, a figure of destructive intervention. Here, she becomes yet another exercise in Hardyean irony, for although her identity as protective *mother* thoroughly defines her character and role in the narrative, she is yet intimately bound up with an annihilative impulse that pervades the novel and, indeed, much of Hardy's work. So frequently in Hardy it is an event that *fails* to happen or one that is abruptly, even violently halted that sets the tragic wheel in motion: in the poem "Hap" (1866) hope but "*un*blooms"; the story "The Son's Veto" (1891) centers on the barring of a marriage; and, pervaded by failed unions and false starts, *Jude the Obscure* (1895) is framed by literal and figurative abortion, commencing with a pregnancy that may have been ended by Arabella's recourse to Vilbert's "female pills" (22) and concluding with the annihilation of Sue and Jude's children at the novel's harrowing climax. Likewise, aborted plans and events dominate *The Return of the Native*: the novel commences with a wedding that has failed to happen, Wildeve has been trained as an engineer but soon gives that over, Clym leaves his successful work in the diamond industry behind, and so on. When forced, as a result of his blindness, to turn to physical labor as a furze-cutter, Clym's very work, though apparently intimately connected to the heath, evokes the sense of destruction, dismemberment, and annihilation that elsewhere pervades the text.

We first learn of Mrs. Yeobright's oppositional tendencies from the heath-dwellers, who reveal how she attempted to put a stop to Wildeve and Thomasin's desire to marry by going so far as to stand and oppose the banns in church. Thus she is figured early on as a powerful force of destruction, an antagonist to generative human union. We know little to nothing of the circumstances of her own marriage, apart from the fact that "though her husband had been a small farmer she herself was a curate's daughter, who had once," like Eustacia, "dreamt of doing better things" (32). Mrs. Yeobright's narrative, then, is itself informed by defiance, disappointment, and loss. Her excessive interference in both the marriage of her niece, Thomasin, and that of her son, Clym, underscores Hardy's sense of the prophetic danger of antagonistic speech. Although she ultimately relents and gives the marriage of Thomasin and Wildeve her blessing, her initial objection to the marriage haunts the plot, manifesting itself again in their botched attempt to wed at Anglebury and, later, in Wildeve's failed escape with Eustacia, with whom he had intended to go at least as far as Budmouth and perhaps even as far as Paris. Likewise, in appropriating the witch stories that swirl about Eustacia, tales that she first rejects out of hand as mere superstitious nonsense, Mrs. Yeobright invests such discourse with a dangerous amount of authority and seems capable of bringing her words into being, even at her own peril. As it has frequently been observed, the horrific image on the Quiet Woman Inn sign of a woman carrying her head under her arm anticipates the violent fate likely to befall a defiant, outspoken woman on Egdon Heath.[7]

Eustacia Vye's narrative illustrates this all too well. Subject to Egdon's "surrounding tongues" (314), her public identity effectively rises up from the narrative lore of the heath, which hearkens back to the pagan superstition that informs the bonfire rituals, for instance, and the characterization of Eustacia as a witch.[8] The heath-dwellers' talk exemplifies Spacks's sense of the way gossip can "solidify a group's sense of itself by heightening consciousness of 'outside' (inhabited by those talked about) and 'inside' (the temporarily secure territory of the talkers)."[9] Spacks's implicit allusions to concepts linked to dwelling ("inhabited"), defense ("secure"), and proprietorship ("territory") have particular resonance for the intricate relationship between orality, land, and social exclusion on the heath. Gossip and conjecture marginalize Eustacia, positioning her as a threatening competitor in the eyes of the women of Egdon. Susan

Nunsuch chiefly identifies Eustacia as a menacing figure, and Mrs. Yeobright comes to adopt a similar attitude. Men, in contrast, are more light-hearted about the matter, intrigued as they are by the "well-favoured maid" (30). Timothy doubts that he "ever . . . should call a fine young woman such a name" as witch (47), and Grandfer Cantle would "be very glad to ask her in wedlock, if she'd hae [him], as take the risk of her wild dark eyes ill-wishing [him]" (47).

While, thus, at least two competing narratives about Eustacia make their way into circulation—destructive witch or captivating beauty—Eustacia herself does much to complicate matters, cultivating her image as a woman to be reckoned with by invoking the heath-dwellers' narrative mythology. Marjorie Garson rightly suggests that Eustacia initially "participates enthusiastically in her own encoding," referring to herself, for example, as the "Witch of Endor."[10] Yet her simultaneous resistance to her surroundings renders her generally incapable of understanding the heath, which "has a language of its own which requires learning for full comprehension."[11] Comprising contradictory impulses, Eustacia paradoxically exhibits an intimate connection to the landscape she so decries.[12] The novel thus portrays the dangers inherent in a bifurcated identity and the ease with which one can be absorbed into an environment, however foreign. The heath brushes her hair, and her very sigh forms part of its "wild rhetoric" as she waits upon it: "The bluffs had broken silence, . . . the heather-bells had broken silence; at last, so did the woman; and her articulation was but as another phrase of the same discourse as theirs" (61, 50–51). Although she desires escape from Egdon, her "jail," her form "was so much like an organic part of the entire motionless structure, that to see it move would have impressed the mind as a strange phenomenon" (15). Thus, Eustacia's end, whereby she is absorbed into the landscape, seems inevitable even in the early stages of the novel.

I will return to those particular circumstances that make certain Eustacia's imprisonment, but before doing so it is worth pointing out how her plot likewise emphasizes that oral report, speculation, argument, and gossip are hardly the only destructive verbal activities operative in *The Return of the Native*: silence proves equally damaging to relationships and identity. Eustacia's frequent recourse to signs and silence, rather than verbal communication, is, as Jennifer Gribble observes, a manifestation of her "urge for love, sexual need, boredom, and [frustration]."[13] Yet in seeking to fulfill such urges, she operates in dangerous and subversive ways—moving across the heath at night, mumming, communicating through signals and signs, and carrying out clandestine meetings. Eustacia's isolation from her community initially marks her as a figure of disruptive power, as well as an enigmatic object of fascination and desire. She will not engage with the usual community rituals, whether building bonfires or attending church. Her "instincts toward social non-conformity" lead her to resist involvement in such activities such "that she may be unoppressed with a sense of doing her duty" (65). Her self-imposed solitude both incriminates and dehumanizes her, and those around her detect, in the words of Garson, "something sinister in the mendacious way Eustacia appropriates and distorts nature's language."[14] Her approach to the elements, too, is one of exploitation; in her hands fire and water are but instruments in the calls of a siren, that "lonesome dark-eyed creature that some say is a witch" (47). And her willingness to trivialize and divest traditional rituals of their "communal significance" ("[f]or mummers and mumming [she] had the greatest contempt" [107]) marks out her dangerous inability to read the language of the heath. A kind of interpretive myopia also informs her relationship with Clym, who shares a deep affinity with the Egdon landscape. Her unwillingness to interact—socially, linguistically, and otherwise—with the Egdon community positions Eustacia as a figure of both extreme suspicion and vulnerability.

The highly competitive model that informs many of the relationships on Egdon is thus shown to have its primary basis in the manipulation of language and signs. When Wildeve appears in response to Eustacia's signal flame, for example, she asserts, "I determined you should come; and you have come. I have shown my power" (59–60). Indeed, "[s]he seldom schemed, but when she did scheme, her plans showed rather the comprehensive strategy of a general than the small arts called womanish, though she could utter oracles of Delphian ambiguity when she did not choose to be direct" (66). So much of the novel involves ongoing strategic maneuvering—one move, followed by a countermove, and so on—that the text's frequent references to Napoleon and the period of the Napoleonic wars, "the year four," as Grandfer Cantle would have it, are indeed fitting. They also register Hardy's ongoing fascination with the Napoleonic era and its legacy, something that he would return to in his next novel, *The Trumpet-Major* (1880), which is set during a time when this part of England was under perpetual threat of an attack by Napoleon. *The Trumpet-Major* more thoroughly engages with this context, yet the sense of a possible incursion by a looming alien invader reverberates throughout *The Return of the Native* as well.[15] Mirroring such a shadowy, menacing figure in the distance, Eustacia represents a particularly potent combination of feminine subtlety and masculine authority. She makes frequent use of men in her communicative strategies: Johnny, her "little slave," sets her bonfire alight, Venn delivers her letter of rejection to Wildeve, and, sensitive to "the power of this girl's face and form," Charley offers up his mumming costume, including his "sword and staff," in exchange for holding her hand (55, 133, 109, 111). Eustacia is, for much of the novel, a woman to be reckoned with.

Apparently signifying the extent of her potency, Eustacia's well-known performance as the Turkish Knight during the mumming sequence concentrates in a single event those activities that dominate the novel as a whole: surveillance, stealth, and calculated silence. This, her initial encounter with Clym, is aptly framed in terms of combat, which emphasizes the aggressive, strategic function of Eustacia's role as a mummer and characterizes her covert activities generally. Like Bathsheba in the erotically charged sword scene in *Far from the Madding Crowd* (1874), the female figure here is conceived of as an enemy on the battlefield. But Bathsheba, of course, serves as the passive object of Troy's sword exercise. In contrast, as the title of the chapter, "The Two Stand Face to Face," suggests, Eustacia's mumming performance identifies her as a far more nearly equal adversary, at least initially. Before long, though, her disguise gets the better of her. In costume, Eustacia soon finds "the power of her face all lost, the charm of her motions all disguised, . . . nothing but a voice left to her: she had the sense of the doom of Echo" (125). We learn at this moment that Eustacia's voice, like so many women's voices, will not finally be enough for her to win the day, but will simply fade, in time, into nothingness. Her very destruction is prophesied by her own claim about the heath: "'Tis my cross, my misery, and will be my death" (78). Later, the very form of her death, by drowning—in a "boiling cauldron"—fulfills Mrs. Yeobright's earlier warning that she is "on the edge of a precipice" (307, 206). Conjecture, time and again, becomes truth.

Eustacia's reference to "the cross" here turns us toward another crucial encounter between her and Clym—to a scene that rather more subtly reveals much about both the limits of Eustacia's voice and, furthermore, the vulnerability inherent in her silence. The chapter's title, "The First Act in a Timeworn Drama," tells us that this scene also notably involves a "precipice" overlooking water below, and while it thus may look forward to the manner of Eustacia's death, it also, I would suggest, takes us back nearly two centuries. I am referring here to Eustacia's encounter with Clym at her grandfather's well, a moment that only in my recent rereading of the novel have I seen as a clear invocation of that scene in the Gospel of John in which Christ, having opted to pass through Samaria on his way back to Galilee, encounters the Samaritan woman at Jacob's well (John 4:4–42). It is resonant moments like these that, I think, my earlier commitment to a Foucauldian lens prevented me from fully seeing and appreciating. In Hardy's narrative, Sam has explained to Clym and Mrs. Yeobright that the "captain's bucket has dropped into the well, and they are in want of water," and so Clym offers to assist with the rescue of the bucket (153). After several failed attempts, the men who had joined in the effort go home, and Clym alone attempts to retrieve a little water for Eustacia with a pail. This effort fails as well and leaves Eustacia, who had attempted to assist him by holding on to the rope, wounded:

> She opened her hands. The rope had dragged off the skin. Eustacia wrapped it in her handkerchief.
>
> "You should have let go," said Yeobright. "Why didn't you?"
>
> "You said I was to hold on. . . . This is the second time I have been wounded to-day." (158–59)

The first wound occurred when, presuming Eustacia is a witch, Susan Nunsuch stabbed her "with a long stocking-needle" in church (151). The subsequent identification of Eustacia with the Woman at the Well and her apparent stigmata seemingly offers a renunciation of Susan's superstitious actions and their potential implications. Yet I would suggest that Hardy's ironic revision of the gospel story nonetheless bodes ill for Eustacia. In John's gospel, the Samaritan woman initially accosts Christ for being without a bucket to retrieve any water, to which he responds that "no one who drinks the water that I shall give him will ever be thirsty again," but will instead have eternal life (John 4:13–14). Following this, the woman goes on to identify Christ as the Messiah, and thereafter "[m]any Samaritans of the town *believed in him on the strength of her testimony*" (John 4:39, emphasis added). The Woman at the Well narrative is a story of evangelization and the redemptive power inherent in a woman's speech and testimony. These biblical allusions that I formerly overlooked strike me as greatly ironic now. For in the New Testament story, it is notably through the faith and the speech of this fallen woman (a woman who has had five husbands and is now living with a man who is not her husband) that the community will be redeemed. Yet as we come to find in the fallen world of *The Return of the Native*, and undoubtedly so often our own, a woman's refusal to refute the charges laid at her feet will frequently be met with verbal and even physical violence. Furthermore, whereas Christ and the Samaritan woman recognize each other completely, the scene involving Clym and Eustacia, like the mumming scene prior, is predicated entirely on *misrecognition*. Although Eustacia insists that she finds the heath but "a cruel taskmaster," by the scene's conclusion Clym is convinced that "a beautiful woman had been intertwined" with his plans to commence an education scheme on the heath (160). "Now, I am ready to begin," he tells himself (160). Such words seem an ominous, brutal parody of Tess Durbeyfield's admission, "I am ready," as she arises from her slumber and submits to her fate.[16] This moment, then, marks for me the crucial turning point when a potential story of love rushes inevitably onward to death and tragedy, becoming, in the end, to quote Graham Greene, but "a record of hate."

"Record" is indeed the apposite word here: the association of silencing with violence and misrecognition emerges most sharply in the latter stages of the text, when Clym devotes himself to what develops as a criminal investigation of Eustacia's behavior. He turns to the containment available in a highly regulated, taxonomic form of orality—the language of the legal realm.[17] Relying on increasingly narrow, definitive explanations, Clym pieces together a range of incriminating evidence, both oral and written. He conducts interviews ("Attend, and speak the truth!" he demands of Johnny Nunsuch [267]), examines various objects "as a means of gleaning new particulars," and surveys evidence, such as Eustacia's letters, that are related to his investigation (266).[18] The result of this trial is summary judgment and punishment: "You shut the door—you looked out the window upon her—you had a man in the house with you—you sent her away to die. The inhumanity—the treachery—I will not touch you—stand away from me—and confess every word!" (271). The disjointed nature of Clym's diction reveals the intensity of his anger and also illustrates the cumulative process of his piecemeal narrative construction. Yet, crucially, Eustacia will not confess, refusing to "enter into [her] defence," for, she asserts, "it is not worth doing" (273). Such silence, Karin Koehler aptly claims, "constitutes a revolt against her husband's legal right to penetrate her inner life," but such a strategy time and again proves deadly.[19] For Clym fills in the silence with his own assumptions: now deemed by her husband "a well-finished and full-blown adept in a certain trade," Eustacia is exiled from their home, bearing the label of murderess and prostitute (272). The great irony of course lies in the fact that despite his recourse to the authority of legal method and taxonomies, Clym's very indictment of Eustacia is thoroughly informed by the oral gossip that had relentlessly pursued her: "How bewitched I was! How could there be any good in a woman everybody spoke ill of?" (273).

Clym may feel he has his story straight now, but as we proceed toward the narrative's tragic conclusion, Hardy forcefully resists and thus critiques such a tendency toward historical certitude. The novel's relentless ambiguity thoroughly informs its tragic climax, which leaves the events of Eustacia's final moments the text's greatest uncertainty. In saying as much I make a sharp turn from the certainty I expressed when claiming in my earlier essay that Eustacia's death was unequivocally a suicide. I would rescind that claim now—not entirely ruling it out as a narrative possibility, but, rather, observing that Hardy's depiction of the ambiguity of the nature of her death, his insistence on a lack of narrative closure, is more to the point, and more consistent with his aesthetic concerns. Eustacia's death occurs off-stage, as a private exchange between the heroine and the environment she despised:

> . . . heading out into the wild weather, Eustacia opened her umbrella and went out from the enclosure by the steps over the bank, after which she was beyond all danger of being perceived. Skirting the pool she followed the path towards Rainbarrow, occasionally stumbling over twisted furze-roots, tufts of rushes, or oozing lumps of fleshy fungi, which at this season lay scattered about the heath like the rotten liver and lungs of some colossal animal. (293)

Her steps, like her plot, are vulnerable and bound to the environment that has possessed her in life and that will, like a colossal beast, consume her in death.

We can contrast this with the suicidal impulses of other of Hardy's characters, such as Father Time and Mr. Boldwood. When a character is determined upon self-destruction, Hardy tends to make it clear. In the end, for Mrs. Yeobright's death and for Eustacia's likewise, there is in fact neither one individual nor one particular action to blame. Such is universally the case in Hardy, whose novels tend to strongly resist their culture's most insistent desires, which, as Jill Matus argues, are intimately "[b]ound up with the idea of responsibility." Such resistance contrasts with many prominent narratives of the period, especially those that grapple with emerging understandings of trauma, shock, and the workings of the unconscious, which, as Matus observes, tend to be "less concerned with *victimhood* than they are with accountability." Exposing, particularly in the novel's concluding sequences, the very limits of blame and certitude, *The Return of the Native* is marked, in contrast, by what Matus identifies as "a strong . . . interest beyond the attribution of blame."[20] Hardy's works largely show the futility of that aim, even as we read on, addictively, compulsively, trying to solve a puzzle, to unwind what can never be unfurled. Clym momentarily seems to realize that human entanglements are far more complex than a straightforward whodunit, as he tells Venn plainly following Eustacia's death: "[Y]ou don't know all the circumstances" (313). But that is short lived, for in finally insisting, inwardly even, that his mother is blameless he adheres to a narrow model of accountability regarding victim and guilty party.

*The Return of the Native* thus points us toward Hardy's sense of the limits of realism. At this stage of his career, Hardy's realism paradoxically inheres in obscurity, in what is not known, not documented. We do not ultimately know whether Eustacia fell into the water or jumped to her death; we do not know whether she intended to live as Wildeve's mistress, we do not know whether he intended to stay with her in Budmouth and then go onward with her to Paris or to leave her there. We become, like the heath-dwellers, possessed of rather uncertain knowledge about the history of events, although we are perhaps far less comfortable with this ambiguity than they.

As in *The Trumpet-Major*, where the sailors' wives fascinate the heroine, Ann Garland, because they possess knowledge that cannot merely "be got from books," it would seem, finally, that at this point in Hardy's narrative oeuvre, orality trumps textuality—a fluid, shifting, and often dangerous orality is, ironically, the realism central to Hardy's written word in *The Return of the Native*.[21] Histories are but obscured, subject to ongoing mediation and translation by speech, report, and the tragic repression that so frequently characterizes spoken interactions. By the time we reach *Jude the Obscure* the menace of language in Hardy will have shifted nearly entirely to text, in a world where less the tongue but more so "the letter killeth."[22]

And if the letter, the text, the printed word—associated as it will increasingly be in Hardy with modernity and the "modern vice of unrest"[23]—becomes in his vision the source of so much death and destruction, speech remains somehow potentially generative in *The Return of the Native*, at least among the heath-dwellers, among those who seemingly *belong* and thus survive. In many ways, as I turned the early pages of the novel in my latest reading, I was struck by all the joy, the tenderness—in Hardy's treatment of the denizens of the heath, for instance—that I didn't fully perceive in my earlier engagements with this novel. Furthermore, and perhaps most importantly, I find it deeply ironic that I once so painstakingly mapped Foucault's finite model onto a novel that unequivocally refuses to be contained. That very refusal—concentrated in Eustacia's own recourse to silence—is perhaps in the end the source of so much of the novel's chilling brilliance. While thinking about the vexed relationship between silence and power in our own context I was struck by the parallels between Hardy's novel and the Depeche Mode song "Enjoy the Silence," from which I saw fit to draw my title for this essay. There, "[w]ords like violence" become but a source of pain as they "[p]ierce right through me."[24] As on the heath, words pierce, they wound, like weapons. Recourse to silence may offer a measure of protection from such violence, yet may also bring about additional, and sometimes equally devastating, consequences. This gives us much to consider in an era dominated by a culture of insistent disclosure, where borders between public and private life have all but evanesced, and yet where, paradoxically, a woman's demand for justice and the unveiling of truth remains all too often met with shaming and disavowal. It is interesting for me to consider why I would have, at an earlier time of my life, come to admire so deeply a novel that is indeed in many ways "a record of hate," a novel that articulates the pain of social isolation and of a woman who finds herself nowhere believed or understood. The answers are ones perhaps that I must myself continue to ponder, and to return to, in time.

## NOTES

I wish to thank Shyloe Beals for her thoughtful, intelligent assistance with my research for this essay; Lisa Surridge, under whose guidance I first encountered Thomas Hardy; Keith Wilson for his ongoing support of my work on Hardy; and Ulrich vom Hagen for alerting me to the relevance of the lyrics of Depeche Mode's "Enjoy the Silence" for my thinking about such issues as silence and destructive language in Hardy's works. I am also very grateful to my students of English 4555 at Saint Mary's University, who made my return to this novel in the fall of 2018 such a fruitful one.

1. Thomas Hardy, *The Return of the Native*, ed. Phillip Mallett, 273. Further references will be given parenthetically.

2. Sara Malton, "'The Woman Shall Bear Her Iniquity': Death as Social Discipline in Thomas Hardy's *The Return of the Native*."

3. See Penny Boumelha, *Thomas Hardy and Women: Sexual Ideology and Narrative Form*, 49–52. See also Jakob Lothe, "Variants on Genre: *The Return of the Native, The Mayor of Casterbridge, The Hand of Ethelberta*."

4. David Sweeney Coombs, "Reading in the Dark: Sensory Perception and Agency in *The Return of the Native*," 950.

5. Patricia Meyer Spacks, *Gossip*, 7, 11.

6. Spacks, *Gossip*, 4.

7. Jennifer Gribble examines this particular issue at length in her article "The Quiet Women of Egdon Heath."

8. See Ruth A. Firor, *Folkways in Thomas Hardy*, 89–91, and Jacqueline Dillion, *Thomas Hardy: Folklore and Resistance*, 34–70, for discussions of the origins of the witchcraft motifs found in *The Return of the Native*. See also Malton, "'Woman Shall Bear,'" 154–56.

9. Spacks, *Gossip*, 5.

10. Marjorie Garson, *Hardy's Fables of Integrity: Woman, Body, Text*, 70.

11. Simon Gatrell, *Thomas Hardy and the Proper Study of Mankind*, 44.

12. See Boumelha, *Hardy and Women*, 54–55, on the "critical commonplace" of Eustacia as a divided figure.

13. Gribble, "Quiet Women," 240.

14. Garson, *Hardy's Fables*, 67.

15. Trish Ferguson likewise considers the novel in terms of its political contexts, but she is concerned with rising fears about radical violence in the more recent 1840s. According to Ferguson, a "division between political and economic

radicalism is figured in the distinction between the alienated romantic heroine Eustacia Vye's association with bonfire burning and Paris and the Egdon labourers whose bonfire burning is an age-old symbolic act of rebellion that is also associated with contemporary economic radicalism." "Bonfire Night in Thomas Hardy's *The Return of the Native*," 88–89.

16. Thomas Hardy, *Tess of the D'Urbervilles*, ed. Tim Dolin, 396.

17. On Hardy's intensive engagement with legal issues during the 1880s, see William A. Davis, *Hardy and the Law: Legal Presences in Hardy's Life and Fiction*.

18. Karin Koehler rightly observes this instance as one of many that underscore the "conceptual link between letter writing and sexuality" in Hardy's works and in nineteenth-century culture more generally. *Thomas Hardy and Victorian Communication: Letters, Telegrams and Postal Systems*, 55.

19. Koehler, *Hardy and Victorian Communication*, 56.

20. Jill Matus, *Shock, Memory and the Unconscious in Victorian Fiction*, 186–87.

21. Thomas Hardy, *The Trumpet-Major*, ed. Linda M. Shires, 60.

22. Thomas Hardy, *Jude the Obscure*, ed. Patricia Ingham, epigraph.

23. Hardy, *Jude the Obscure*, 79.

24. "Enjoy the Silence," track 6 on Depeche Mode, *Violator*, Mute Records, 1990.

## WORKS CITED

Boumelha, Penny. *Thomas Hardy and Women: Sexual Ideology and Narrative Form*. Brighton, UK: Harvester, 1982.

Coombs, David Sweeney. "Reading in the Dark: Sensory Perception and Agency in *The Return of the Native*." *ELH* 78.4 (2011): 943–66.

Davis, William A. *Hardy and the Law: Legal Presences in Hardy's Life and Fiction*. Newark: University of Delaware Press, 2003.

Dillion, Jacqueline. *Thomas Hardy: Folklore and Resistance*. London: Palgrave Macmillan, 2016.

Ferguson, Trish. "Bonfire Night in Thomas Hardy's *The Return of the Native*." *Nineteenth-Century Literature* 67.1 (June 2012): 87–107.

Firor, Ruth A. *Folkways in Thomas Hardy*. 1931. New York: Russell & Russell, 1968.

Garson, Marjorie. *Hardy's Fables of Integrity: Woman, Body, Text*. Oxford: Oxford University Press, 1991.

Gatrell, Simon. *Thomas Hardy and the Proper Study of Mankind*. Charlottesville: University of Virginia Press, 1993.

Greene, Graham. *The End of the Affair*. 1951. With an introduction by Monica Ali. London: Vintage, 2004.

Gribble, Jennifer. "The Quiet Women of Egdon Heath." *Essays in Criticism* 46.3 (July 1996): 234–57.

Hardy, Thomas. *Far from the Madding Crowd*. 1874. Edited by Suzanne B. Falck-Yi and with an introduction by Linda M. Shires. New ed., Oxford: Oxford University Press, 2008.

———. "Hap." 1866. In *Thomas Hardy: The Complete Poems*, edited by James Gibson, 9. London: Macmillan, 2001.

———. *Jude the Obscure*. 1895. Edited with an introduction by Patricia Ingham. Rev. ed. Oxford: Oxford University Press, 2002.

———. *The Return of the Native*. 1878. Edited by Phillip Mallett. 2nd ed. New York: W. W. Norton, 2006.

———. "The Son's Veto." In *Life's Little Ironies* (1891), edited by Alan Manford with an introduction by Norman Page, 33–48. Oxford: Oxford University Press, 2008.

———. *Tess of the D'Urbervilles*. 1891. Edited with notes by Tim Dolin and an introduction by Margaret R. Higonnet. London: Penguin, 1998.

———. *The Trumpet-Major*. 1880. Edited with an introduction by Linda M. Shires. London: Penguin, 1997.

Homans, Margaret. *Bearing the Word: Language and Female Experience in Nineteenth-Century Women's Writing*. Chicago: University of Chicago Press, 1986.

Koehler, Karin. *Thomas Hardy and Victorian Communication: Letters, Telegrams and Postal Systems*. London: Palgrave MacMillan, 2016.

Lothe, Jakob. "Variants on Genre: *The Return of the Native, The Mayor of Casterbridge, The Hand of Ethelberta*." In *The Cambridge Companion to Thomas Hardy*, edited by Dale Kramer, 112–29. Cambridge: Cambridge University Press, 1999.

Malton, Sara. "'The Woman Shall Bear Her Iniquity': Death as Social Discipline in Thomas Hardy's *The Return of the Native*." *Studies in the Novel* 32.2 (Summer 2000): 147–64.

Matus, Jill. *Shock, Memory and the Unconscious in Victorian Fiction*. Cambridge: Cambridge University Press, 2009.

Spacks, Patricia Meyer. *Gossip*. New York: Alfred A. Knopf, 1985.

CHAPTER EIGHT

# Stock Exchanges

Jonathan Farina

## On *Vanity Fair* by William Makepeace Thackeray

> **Who was the blundering idiot who said that "fine words butter no parsnips"? Half the parsnips of society are served and rendered palatable with no other sauce.**
>
> William Makepeace Thackeray, *Vanity Fair*

No doubt every novel we reread becomes more about our history with it than about itself. Thackeray's *Vanity Fair* (1848) feels exceptionally resonant of my history as a reader, and it seems to me to document how academic reading, like all professions, threatens to alienate that personal history and its affective connections. Fredric Jameson has written that what we read is "always-already-read," apprehended through "sedimented layers of previous interpretations," and my Norton Critical Edition of *Vanity Fair*, with its stray, interleaved and annotated boarding passes (Newark to Toronto, Nashville to Newark) and its layered marginalia, physically testifies to his point.[1] My clustered marginal notes archive a kind of personal and professional development, with personal remarks ("ha!" "Amazing!") awkwardly overwritten by professional juvenilia ("empire," "fetishistic disavowal") and maturing into dismally bureaucratic lists of cross-references and signposts for teaching ("narrative irony," "George dead"). My Norton *Vanity Fair*, the very copy I bought as an undergraduate, has physically accompanied me through this profession. I read it for my PhD exam list and carried it to my job talks; I have taught it in undergraduate and graduate courses at three different universities; and it bears accordingly the traces of all the modes of interpretation I have learned and critical trends that have passed. I have been "Jones" reading along as if at my club, pencil in hand, rendering my aesthetic pleasure into work.

Here I want to undo that rendering by writing an essay on my aesthetic investment in this novel that, for all its alienations, nevertheless uncannily resonates with me and my home. Sons alienated from fathers, lovers alienated from partners, families alienated from their property, characters alienated by commodities, a nation alienated from the colonies and battlefields that sustain it, even a narrator cynically alienated from his narrative: *Vanity Fair* seems to be a catalog of emotional distances. But some of our greatest affections and intimacies transpire over distance. The frisson *Vanity Fair* generates between the preoccupations of its characters and the rich background noise of the Stock Exchange, the Peninsular War, India, and London animates for me the way people and things touch us from afar—and also how apparently estranging idioms, such as professional jargon and foreign words, foster intimacy within family life.

To be sure, the background noise of *Vanity Fair* comes very close to home for me, for the background noise of my childhood was a peculiar patois of Wall Street and nostalgic English. My father (and my uncle, several cousins, and my brother and my brother-in-law, for a while) was a stockbroker. My mother grew up in England. We were fortunate to be safe from bankruptcy, and war fronts, and (most of) the dysfunctions of the Sedley, Osborne, and Crawley families, but our domestic idiom blended Wall Street slang with British colloquialisms. Reading *Vanity Fair*, which figuratively represents the modern world as a stock exchange and particularly a market for conventional language, brings back for me the background noise of growing up. For children, parents' talk of work and of other lives led in places far away and in the past conjures attachment over distance. The nostalgia of such attachments is a payoff for investing in *Vanity Fair*.

Elizabeth Rigby's contemporary review of *Vanity Fair* describes a "remarkable novel" as "a kind of common friend, about whom people can speak the truth without fear of being compromised, and confess their emotions without being ashamed."[2] Critics have often taken Rigby to imply that novels thus function as surrogate confidantes—repositories of the reader's interiority, cultivated in solitary hours with their books—but she seems to me rather to suggest that novels serve as social intermediaries, neutral acquaintances about whom people can engage in small talk together without disclosing anything intimate. These "common"—which is to say shared, public, and ordinary—friends facilitate sociable gossip. The English "are a particularly shy and reserved people," Rigby explains,

> and set about nothing so awkwardly as the simple art of getting really acquainted with each other. We meet over and over again in what is conventionally called "easy society," with the tacit understanding to go so far and no farther; to be as polite as we ought to be, and as intellectual as we can, but mutually and honourably to forbear lifting those veils which each spreads over his inner sentiments and sympathies.[3]

With its sustained satire, *Vanity Fair* might affect to lift such veils and breach decorum in behalf of compromising and shaming people, but in a variety of ways it actually renders the mutual reserve of "easy society" into motifs. It is, as C. L. R. James observes, marked by "restraint," by what goes unsaid.[4] Mr. Osborne, for one obvious example, cannot manage to forgive or admit his love for his son George: "His English habit, pride, awkwardness perhaps, had prevented him from saying more."[5] Osborne also harbors extraordinary resentment and selfishness, but who among us articulates every feeling he feels? Who doesn't have regrettable restraint? Certainly my father and brother and I have communicated far more in shared silences together than in talk.

Almost as a matter of course, Rigby implies that English readers ought to be less awkward and less guarded than they are, but she nevertheless appreciates the ease afforded by fiction in general, and *Vanity Fair* in particular, as a common investment that hedges against the risk of private commitments and leaves much unsaid, if only by saying something else agreeable instead. "A host of devices have been contrived by which all the forms of friendship may be gone through, without committing ourselves to one spark of the spirit," she points out, as if to suggest that we ought to prefer the spirit to the mere forms. "We fly with eagerness to some common ground in which each can take the liveliest interest, without taking the slightest in the world in his companion." She further disparages "various fashionable manias" for charity, science, and so on as "only so many clever contrivances for keeping our neighbour at arm's length." And yet Rigby frets that people discuss novels with the "deliberate and malicious object" of exposing the "real feelings" of our neighbors without being known by them in return. However much she appreciates the extraordinary intimacy and interiority of *Jane Eyre*, she seems equally taken by the "average . . . game of life" depicted by *Vanity Fair*, which incorporates an array of formal features that keep characters "at arm's length" and variously represents the pleasurable distances that conventions maintain between us.[6]

*Vanity Fair* reproduces the small talk, the stock exchanges of an "easy society" that trades in conventions, perhaps because it regrets the superficiality and reserve of that society, but more so because, like Rigby, it tacitly appreciates the affective touch of such exchanges, which do not bear the discomfiting "open secret," as D. A. Miller famously put it, of maintaining secret subjectivity.[7] Though satire ostentatiously proffers an aesthetic of disclosure, with its histrionic raising of the curtain, the principal allure of *Vanity Fair* is, for me, its masterful reproduction of the stock exchanges by which people interact and enjoy a kind of intimacy—"at arm's length"—with each other and the world.

Nicholas Dames describes Thackeray's narrator as "simply *phatic*: attempting to find social contact, any contact, to somehow escape the trap of self-enclosure or opacity that is the fate of any of his momentarily absorbed characters."[8] But for me the contact extends beyond the narrator into these stock exchanges, even though these exchanges often appear to be symptoms of estrangement. I say "stock exchanges" partly because the novel is awash with literal references to the stock exchange and a commercial idiom. Mr. Osborne's chief clerk, Chopper, is "an old file and knows Change as well as any man in London"; he reports that Sedley has "been dabbling on his own account" (134). Jos's "property had been muddled away in speculations, and was represented by valueless shares in different bubble companies" (687). But *Vanity Fair* also consistently portrays the world, in all its manifestations, as a market for transacting stock characters, trite sayings, conventional gifts, objects, emotions, and ideas. The preface acknowledges "a great quantity of eating and drinking, making love and jilting, laughing and the contrary, smoking, cheating, fighting, dancing, and fiddling," as if life were to be appreciated by volumetric measure rather than quality (xv). The opening chapter famously concludes with Becky tossing Dr. Johnson's dictionary, the standard impersonal gift for graduates of Miss Pinkerton's school, out the coach window (7). The novel refers to and appropriates "genteel jargon," among other stock discourses, and makes genealogical, racial reference to "a gentleman's family—good old

English stock" (289). Dobbin attends Dr. Swishtail's Academy on "mutual principles," "the representative of so many pounds of tea, candles, sugar, mottled-soap, plums . . . and other commodities" (148, 38). This reduction of Dobbin to his father's wares appears to be critical, but to me it evokes how much emotional resonance resides in the objects and products that accompany our everyday lives, the brands of soap and toothpaste and foods our grandparents and parents kept in stock.

Throughout *Vanity Fair*, characters hoard reserves of wine, jewelry, money, food, clothing, and small talk as securities to protect against an uncertain world. Even "the sculptors of those days," Thackeray says, "had stocks of such funeral emblems on hand; as you may see still on the walls of St. Paul's, which are covered with hundreds of these braggart heathen allegories" (354). Likewise, the rituals through which the world customarily recognizes the sacred are mocked as pro forma customs: Sir Pitt's funeral, as a case in point, transpires in "the most becoming manner," with "the neighbouring gentry's carriages at three miles an hour, empty, and in profound affliction; the parson speaking out the formula about 'our dear brother departed,'" and other "humbug and ceremonies," including a tombstone "written all over with lies" (420). The novel encourages us to disparage the global trade in conventions, but conventions, like genres, accumulate because they store and transact emotion efficiently.

Of course, Mr. Sedley—"John Sedley, Esquire, of Russell Square, and the Stock Exchange"—is a stockbroker bankrupted and broken by the stock exchange, which Thackeray leverages into a discussion of realism as a genre, that is, stock forms of fiction writing (29). "I know that the tune I am piping is a very mild one (although there are some terrific chapters coming presently)," he writes wryly with hackneyed realist humility, "and must beg the good-natured reader to remember that we are only discoursing at present about a stockbroker's family in Russell Square, who are taking walks, or luncheon, or dinner, or talking and making love as people do in common life, and without a single passionate and wonderful incident to mark the progress of their loves" (49). By turns apologetic and facetious, Thackeray's narrator here performs perhaps the signature convention of realism: an apology for stylistic restraint and a disavowal of incident that paradoxically legitimates the credibility of the fiction by subordinating the originality of its contents to that of the novels of sentimental or sensational Newgate and romantic alternatives, which prove just as generic as novels of common life. With Byronic irony, Thackeray affects to denigrate his own prose as a modest "middle course," less thrilling than the alternatives about which he speculates, as if he were an investor in fictional forms: "We might have treated this subject in the genteel, or in the romantic, or in the facetious manner," he opines, in the optative mood. "Suppose we had laid the scene in Grosvenor Square, with the very same adventures—would not some people have listened?" (53, 49).

*Vanity Fair* indulges a few pages of speculative generic alternatives, whose parody ably demonstrates Thackeray's capacity to write in the style of Edward Bulwer-Lytton's *Paul Clifford*—"The night was dark and wild—the clouds black—black—ink-black"—and in the "the genteel rose-water style" of sentimental romance (50). But Thackeray punctuates these speculations—the term is appropriate for a novel partly about speculation on the stock exchange—with an acknowledgment, almost redolent of Wordsworth's spots of time, that all of us have chapters in our lives "that seem to be nothing and yet affect all the rest of the history" (52). Against the inclinations of many of my students, who show up to class with a penchant for plot and for "relatable" characters, I confess my own taste for the affecting "nothing" to which Thackeray refers, the various feelings and interactions that amount to little individually but that collectively generate the very feeling of history, the background noise that affords affective depth to memory. How much of our lives consists of digressive conjectures? Idle conjectures: but such idleness constitutes a substantial portion of life, as *Vanity Fair* recognizes. And how terribly human Mr. Sedley is to me, not despite but *because of* the way he inhabits the stock idiom of the Exchange that Thackeray uses to dehumanize him.

Thackeray's passages of speculative alternative fiction are among many passages and figures in the novel that present ordinary events—what actually happens in the novel—in terms of opportunity cost, to stick with the idiom of finance.[9] Thackeray regularly acknowledges what he could have written, or what his characters might have otherwise done, were circumstances different. Such moves add interest to what does happen in the text by gesturing outward to other kinds of writing and other possibilities, written and unwritten. Such moves therefore reproduce the logic of investment: to invest in stocks is to pay to participate in the risks, the rewards and costs, of work done elsewhere by others. *Vanity Fair* teems with these stock exchanges that operate accordingly, generating interest by referring to value made elsewhere by others without committing to them in the present. More than just portraying the stock market, then, *Vanity Fair* internalizes a value system by which characters and even the narrator consistently invest in distant repositories of value, including alternative generic possibilities like those fictions with (ostensibly) exceptional heroes and incidents; and stock expressions and opinions, which are idioms or discourses owned collectively by the classes that speak or share them in lieu of creating their own thoughts; and distant events, places, objects, and people that variously inscribe the present from afar, such as the Napoleonic War, India, and the goings-on at different houses where the narrative is not presently focalized.

Jos, for instance, the caricatured "nabob," personifies a stock characterological investment abroad, as his persona is almost altogether limited to the food, clothing, language, and habits he has acquired in India. His father mocks this overseas investment. "'Order Mr. Jos's elephant, Sambo,'" he says, teasing Jos about his imperial appetite, size, affectation, and lassitude and prodding him to chaperone Amelia and Becky to Vauxhall Gardens. But Sedley's mockery itself manifests his investment in 'Change over and above the domestic, familial relations that presumably ought to obtain for him at home: "'Send to Exeter 'Change, Sambo,'" he says, "—but seeing Jos ready almost to cry with vexation, the old joker stopped his laughter, and said, holding out his hand to his son, 'It's all fair on the Stock Exchange, Jos—and, Sambo, never mind the elephant, but give me and Mr. Jos a glass of Champagne. Boney himself hasn't got such in his cellar, my boy!'" (27). Ever the stockbroker, unable or unwilling to differentiate "his mysterious operations in the City" from life at his "opulent cheery comfortable home" with the admirable alacrity of Wemmick in *Great Expectations*, Mr. Sedley compensates Jos for his offense not with some articulate apology but with a bottle of champagne from his stock (120). As it happens, "Boney himself"—Napoleon Bonaparte—returns to haunt the novel from the periphery, precipitating Sedley's financial ruin and the battle that kills his son-in-law.

Given our humanistic penchant to denigrate capitalism and finance and given, too, Thackeray's pervasive cynicism, we might be as inclined to frown upon this system of value as we are to register Rigby's disappointment in our general reticence to get to know each other. But if Becky Sharp coarsely manifests this "stock exchange" sentiment in her greed—"'Heigho! I wish I could exchange my position in society, and all my relations for a snug sum in the Three Per Cent. Consols'; for so it was that Becky felt the Vanity of human affairs, and it was in those securities that she would have liked to cast anchor"—the novel intimates that material investments and genuine affections share an analogous form (423). Such exchanges include Thackeray's summation of the ethic of the novel through the figure of roast beef: "It is all vanity to be sure," he acknowledges,

> but who will not own to liking a little of it? I should like to know what well-constituted mind, merely because it is transitory, dislikes roast-beef? That is a vanity; but may every man who reads this, have a wholesome portion of it through life, I beg. . . . Sit down, gentlemen, and fall to, with a good hearty appetite; the fat, the lean, the gravy, the horse-radish as you like it—don't spare it. (501)

Echoing Dickens's analogy in *Oliver Twist* between streaky bacon and life's vicissitudes, goading us to appreciate the ambivalence—the fat and the lean—of his novel and our existence, Thackeray rebuts the moral hypocrisy of sanctimoniously disparaging material pleasures that people clearly enjoy.

The ephemerality of eating that Thackeray registers as a conventional drawback to savoring our roast beef and its temporal correlatives elsewhere aligns with writing, whose pleasurable intensity corresponds proportionately to its contingency. Amelia's misplaced love for George Osborne, for example, comes out in copied, redundant language: "[S]he wrote whole pages out of poetry-books without the least pity," Thackeray says, and "she underlined words and passages with quite a frantic emphasis; and, in fine, gave the usual tokens of her condition. She wasn't a heroine. Her letters were full of repetition" (123). And yet Thackeray admits, perhaps with his tongue in his cheek, that this contingency is real and therefore all right—that originality and permanence would not comport with his realist novel, as contingent and replaceable as the next:

> Vows, love, promises, confidences, gratitude, how queerly they read after a while! There ought to be a law in Vanity Fair ordering the destruction of every written document (except receipted tradesmen's bills) after a certain brief and proper interval. Those quacks and misanthropes who advertise indelible Japan ink should be made to perish along with their wicked

> discoveries. The best ink for Vanity Fair use would be one that faded utterly in a couple of days, and left the paper clean and blank, so that you might write on it to somebody else. (192)

If there is self-consciousness here in the prose of a serial periodical contributor, there is also a sense that it is sometimes all right to "write in" somebody or something else. Inflexible commitments are incommensurable with liberal individuality, and indeed most readers presumably want Amelia to turn her heart to Dobbin. And who hasn't made unoriginal effusions that might be embarrassing after the fact, but that in their moment mean as much as any original metaphors might have done? Most communication probably is generic and yet works and moves all the same.

In a compelling interpretation of *Vanity Fair*, Andrew H. Miller claims that Thackeray, in his parody and mimicry of conventional, commercialized forms of writing, "instead of enjoying the form and then revealing its hollowness . . . accidentally inverts this process: he asserts the emptiness of the form—and the moral claims that form makes for its heroes and heroines—only then to discover, shamefacedly, its pleasures." Miller suggests that "the literary experience," for Thackeray, "is identical to the fetishistic experience of commodities: a process of attraction and repulsion, of authenticity and falsehood." Thus, for him, reading Thackeray feels like looking through a plate-glass window at objects one cannot buy, "able to see the objects we desire but unable to possess them."[10] The logic of the argument feels right because we want to decry commoditization and because Miller so neatly ties the novel together, but I daresay *Vanity Fair* defies the pleasures of possession and exhibits how attached we can become to those things, worthy and unworthy, that we cannot own, or grasp, or keep.

Mary Poovey observes how mid-nineteenth-century Literary writers, however personally active in commercial activity, generally wrote fictions opposed to the capitalist credit economy by posing the Literary as "a moralizing antidote to the attitudes and behaviors normalized by economic writing." Thackeray certainly belongs in this group, given Sedley's bankruptcy and Osborne's disloyalty. For Poovey, this critical posture was enabled by "distancing conventions," including literary allusions, obtrusive narrators, animated objects, dehumanized characters, and translations of financial, military, and political conflicts into romance plots—conventions that reinforced "the boundary that identified the textual world as *not* real, *non*referential, that is, as art."[11] Perhaps because I grew up in a stockbroker's house, perhaps because Poovey was my teacher, perhaps just because I love *Vanity Fair* and refuse to reduce it to a commodity, I think about *Vanity Fair* as an aesthetic investment rather than a commodity self-consciously critical of commodities. Readers, after all, are not mere buyers behind the glass but investors, at a remove from the text but rewarded with interest for our sustained commitments to it. *Vanity Fair* masterfully depicts how it feels to live with, but at a distance from, history, incidents, and alternative lives. This distance affords independence, ease, and interest, above all, as much as it alienates. To me, the novel also resonates because of how it shows that genuine personal attachments rely on conventions.

Platitudes abound in *Vanity Fair* as mediums for filling silences, keeping in touch, and getting along, among friends and enemies alike. Lady Jane and Becky, for example, "my-loved and my-deared each other assiduously, but kept apart generally," Thackeray says (455). These are stock exchanges not only because my-loving and my-dearing is a conventional practice of employing terms of endearment but because the hypocrisy of these two characters, between whom no love is lost, is common. Everyone in the novel and plenty of readers, too, bite their lip and maintain pleasant terms with Becky. "It is very strange that the reader has a sort of liking for her in spite of his knowledge," admits G. H. Lewes, for one, in the *Athanæum*. Lewes cannily registers that this affinity occurs because Thackeray "has contrived in a surprising way to represent not only Becky's *mind* but her *manner*."[12] Anthony Trollope felt similarly; "we forgive it all," he says of Becky and the novel's cynicism, "because of the telling."[13] This manner of telling enables Becky to fill in awkward silences that discomfit other characters: "[I]t was mortifying to remain silent," the narrator explains, "still more mortifying to know that you had nothing to say, and hear that little audacious Mrs. Rawdon dashing on from subject to subject, with a word for every man. And a joke always pat" (454). Thus Thackeray relishes mundane topics "of general interest such as the Opera, the Prince's last ball at Carlton House, or the weather—that blessing to society," all the small change of conversation that shows people have an investment in general life, whether or not they have private stakes in any given subject (117). For Bronisław Malinowski, these "phatic" expressions prioritize the willingness to communicate or one's mood of sociability over the need to communicate information.[14] And such expressions draw me to Thackeray:

I am interested not like an antiquarian in the references themselves (the historical weather or opera, say, or the tactics of Osborne's regiment) but in the mood and the linguistic play they enact.

Thackeray defends small talk accordingly as a source of contact even when characters wield it with ulterior motives. Consider when obsequious Mrs. Bute Crawley, angling for the Crawley inheritance, encourages Miss Crawley's maid to keep her informed of her lady's secrets and inclinations by offering a steady stream of stock affections. Mrs. Bute, Thackeray says, "had secured the latter's good-will by a number of those attentions and promises, which cost so little in the making, and are yet so valuable and agreeable to the recipient" (187). Just when the narrator seems poised to ridicule her for serving, and the maid for savoring, these empty promises and flatteries, however, he proceeds to defend them not as the base currency of a degraded and unabashedly deceitful social economy but as a kind of nonstick spray lubricating a society otherwise prone to friction. "Indeed," he writes,

> every good economist and manager of a household must know how cheap and yet how amiable these professions are, and what a flavour they give to the most homely dish in life. . . . As the immortal Alexis Soyer can make more delicious soup for a half-penny than an ignorant cook can concoct with pounds of vegetables and meat, so a skilful artist will make a few simple and pleasing phrases go farther than ever so much substantial benefit-stock in the hands of a mere bungler. Nay, we know that substantial benefits often sicken some stomachs; whereas, most will digest any amount of fine words, and be always eager for more of the same food. Mrs. Bute had told Briggs and Firkin so often of the depth of her affection for them; and what she would do, if she had Miss Crawley's fortune, for friends so excellent and attached, that the ladies in question had the deepest regard for her; and felt as much gratitude and confidence as if Mrs. Bute had loaded them with the most expensive favours. (187)

Here stock expressions explicitly substitute for "benefit-stock," as they constitute an investment in a relationship that may pay off dividends in knowledge, monetary returns, social ease, or advancement of other kinds. A kind of dressing, these small words—white lies, cheap praise, and the like—butter life insofar as they both flavor it and keep it from sticking. In their comic recycling, in ironic situations, in excess, in puns, and in combination with food and money, pathos and sarcasm, these stock exchanges sustain interest without asking a reader to relate to or respect or care for any of the characters involved, just as any decent human must cope with, treat well, and hopefully enjoy the company of all sorts of people with whom he or she cannot relate, or even much like.

Small talk and the idiom of 'Change stream through the novel as the ticker tapes of stock prices scroll across television screens and as the background chatter of uptown and downtown, hedges and puts, bearish sentiment, net-net, all the language of Wall Street flows through the kitchen at my parents' home. Audrey Jaffe argues that nineteenth-century writing portrays "members of stock-exchange or stock market-societies, whether actor investors or not" as "'in' the market," part of the game; and, Jaffe adds, this market society depends on the image of the stock market graph, in various modes, as "an image in which the emotional and economic life of the individual are tied together in a trajectory that also figures the individual's assimilation to the group." Thackeray does not explicitly depict the graph, though he does embrace average characters and average life and he does regularly recur to the "continuing emotional drama" reified and measured by stock market movement, which in this novel indexes Bonaparte's actions and Britain's collective happiness and success.[15] The Sedley family ascribes the movement of Mr. Sedley's moods to the market, just as the characters in *Bleak House* ascribe John Jarndyce's moods to the East wind: "I suppose the funds are falling," they say, when Mr. Sedley closes himself in his study or goes sour, as if nothing immediate or personal could matter to or affect him (131). Likewise, because of their greed, Thackeray's characters are always interested in Miss Crawley's movements, her health, her relative attachment to Rawdon, Bute, and the rest of the family. His characters are persistently invested in the goings-on at other houses—"the doings at the Hall," for example, "were the great food for conversation at the Rectory" (101).

But the grammar of the novel also strongly ties the affective life of the novel's present to the market or other distant affective indices, such as the war. Throughout the novel, Thackeray uses zeugma to yoke emotions to commodities, as when war news "was agitating all the hearts and all the Stocks of Europe" (120), or when Rawdon sends Rebecca and family a "profusion of blind love and unbounded credit" (162) along with a piano, gloves, shawls, stockings, perfume, and jewelry, or when Thackeray writes of "eating prawns, and devouring the Times for breakfast" (218), or when he says the men will "come back to the Major's wife, the ladies and the baggage," to acknowledge how the soldiers treat their wives as accessory accompaniments and encumbrances (293).

The grammar of *Vanity Fair* also reinforces the sense that the narrator only tells us what we already know, stock information. Demonstrative pronouns ("that," "those") and a colloquial classificatory idiom ("sort," "kind") further represent the world as both recognizable or familiar and fungible. Amelia and Becky share "that impetuosity which distinguishes the behaviour of young ladies towards each other," as if we all knew *that* impetuosity (145). Dobbin likewise "showed those signs of disquietude, and practised those desperate attempts at amusement, which men are accustomed to employ when very anxious, and expectant, and perturbed in mind," as if we men were all accustomed to behaving predictably in *those* ways (215). Similarly Miss Crawley asks whether George is "a presentable sort of person," as if people came in two styles, presentable and unpresentable, and that were all that mattered (146). Even the "best people," about whom Thackeray writes for a page, turn out to be not so much a class unto themselves as commensurate with the social class that epitomizes the average: "They talked about each others' houses, and characters, and families: just as the Joneses do about the Smiths" (503). An ordinary language philosopher *avant la lettre*, Thackeray uses these expressions sarcastically with an irony that allows him implicitly to critique their assumptions even as he recirculates them. The irony further allows him to address both types of readers (those who use those expressions and those who know better), but my point is how these modes of expression also gesture at a distant source of meaning, the fiction of the knowing reader who gets it all already and reads along not for knowledge but for idle sociability on a par with eating prawns or devouring the *Times*. Or, still closer to home, the knowing reader whose own family talk resembles that of the Joneses and Smiths.

Even superlative, extraordinary, ineffable qualities are rendered familiar so that ineffability itself is rightfully reduced to a phatic mannerism rather than a referential signifier. Thackeray thus concludes a list of attributes with "all which simplicity and sweetness are quite impossible to describe in print," only to then ask, "But who has not beheld these among women, and recognised the presence of all sorts of qualities in them, even though they say no more to you than that they are engaged to dance the next quadrille, or that it is very hot weather?" (266). The novel here concomitantly mocks and appreciates our ability to register common speech and stock manners as indices of inexpressible individuality. Such ambivalence dominates the novel. Defending Dobbin's delusional image of Amelia, the narrator quips, "But what man in love, of us, is better informed?—or is he much happier when he sees and owns his delusion?" (435). Either we are all complicit, all at fault, or all experienced already with what he says: "Who has not admired the artifices and delicate approaches with which women 'prepare' their friends for bad news?" he writes, as he describes the "apparatus of mystery" with which Briggs and Mrs. Bute report on Sir Pitt Crawley's proposal to Becky. "What need to particularise?" he asks about Sedley's bankruptcy. "If success is rare and slow, everybody knows how quick and easy ruin is" (178). And, describing the mendacity and meanness of those in financial distress, he adds, "Who has not remarked the readiness with which the closest of friends and honestest of men suspect and accuse each other of cheating when they fall out on money matters? Everybody does it. Everybody is right, I suppose, and the world is a rogue" (181). This rhetorical inclusivity allows Thackeray effectively to excuse Becky, for all her grossness, with the blasé rhetorical question "She has her enemies. Who has not?" (689).

*Vanity Fair* consistently and casually treats the reader as being "in the know," not about the intimate details of characters—indeed, even the narrator often disavows knowledge of characters' motives and secrets—but about sundry matters of allegedly common knowledge. Twenty times in the novel Thackeray says "as they say" to announce his deference to the generic and yield the voice of the prose to some general but absent collective "they," without a referent, never mind an antecedent. The same deference of voice occurs through the conceit of "little Tom Eaves, who knows everybody's affairs [and] is ready to account. . . . (the reader must bear in mind that it is always Tom Eaves who speaks)" (465). Eaves personifies not just the eavesdropping world of servants—"the Vehmgericht of the servants' hall"—but "all the world," a favorite nineteenth-century abstraction, indulgently employed by Austen and Trollope alike to denominate everybody without naming anybody in particular: "All the world knows that Lord Steyne's town palace stands in Gaunt Square" (467, 445, 464).

But Tapeworm, the Secretary of Legation, also fulfills this function: "He knew everything and a great deal besides, about all the world—in a word, he made the most astounding revelations to the simple-hearted Major"(667), and so does the infamous Mrs. Grundy:

> "I" is here introduced to personify the world in general—the Mrs. Grundy of each respected reader's private circle—every one of whom can point to some families of his acquaintance who live nobody knows how. Many a glass of wine have we all of us drunk, I have very little doubt, hob-and-nobbing with the hospitable giver and wondering how the deuce he paid for it. (362)

The epitome of moral probity, Mrs. Grundy here suggests we are all replaceable, because all of our private social circles have one of her as well as one of those people who mysteriously live on who-knows-what. Mrs. Grundy, moreover, originates in Thomas Morton's 1798 play *Speed the Plough*, which refers to her repeatedly without ever putting her on stage. She thus aptly personifies how Thackeray's stock exchanges work, investing in value offstage so that they can enjoy the present without morals or meanings getting in the way.

Putting morals out of the way nicely describes *Vanity Fair* because the novel seems to treat morality as obvious, which is to say, etymologically "in the way." Obviously, Becky is terrible. Obviously, George and his father and his sister and Rawdon and Mrs. Bute and Miss Crawley and Sir Pitt, the whole roster of characters, behave by turns selfishly, greedily, stupidly, meanly, immorally. Even "honest Dobbin" only becomes interesting when love for Amelia transforms him into "hypocritical Dobbin," as I suggested ten years ago during a teaching demonstration for my present job, which coincided with my teaching *Vanity Fair* at Vanderbilt University in a Victorian novel course. *Vanity Fair* naturalizes formal hypocrisy as a prerequisite of realistic characterization. The irony cultivated by mismatched intentions or emotions and externalized expressions or actions produces the interest that critics from at least Henry James onward have tacitly recognized as psychological realism.

Putting morality aside came closer to the fore, though, in my first pedagogical encounter with the novel in graduate school at New York University, where I led a discussion session of a course on the nineteenth-century novel just a few years after 9/11. Mr. Osborne's trip to Waterloo and Quatre Bras to tour the battlefield where his son George died and where "peasants and relic-hunters about the place were screaming round the pair, as the soldier told his story, offering for sale all sorts of mementoes of the fight, crosses, and epaulets, and shattered cuirasses, and eagles" resonated strongly with my students, just blocks north of Ground Zero, the periphery of which had become a market for cheap patriotic paraphernalia and memorabilia (355). The commercialization of war, terrorism, and tragedy is obviously gross and vulgar, but the interesting thing that emerged from the discussion that day was how everyday interests and exchanges, small talk and meals and work, enable us to act as though we were not perpetually at risk, as if momentous, significant events were not always ongoing somewhere in the background of everyday life. *Vanity Fair* evokes the feeling of average life as a sustained series of stock exchanges conducted a world apart from incidents, whether they be other genres, or other mysterious lives led by our families and friends when we are not around, or historical events and systemic ideologies and apparatuses—war, finance, imperial politics—that underwrite that life (as if) from afar. The novel keeps touching me from such a distance, uncannily satirizing a dark alternative version of what my life could have been.

As Trollope observes, many readers questioned whether *Vanity Fair* really was a novel, given its overriding cynicism and Thackeray's determination "to run counter to the recognized taste of novel readers." The cynicism of satire consistently resists interpretation precisely because its referents—almost allegorical—seem to dramatize their own disclosure, leaving critical readers, bent on interpretation that requires discovering something hidden, with a sense of belatedness as if the exposure had already happened. Trollope defends the morality of *Vanity Fair* despite his attraction to Becky, because "[t]here may be details of evil painted so as to disgust—painted almost too plainly—but none painted so as to allure," but his ultimate commendation comes in terms of investment return: upon finishing the novel, the reader "will unconsciously have found that every page he has read will have been interesting to him."[16] Investment in the novel pays "interest."

Trollope presumes that Becky is the interest of everyone reading the novel: "When we speak of *Vanity Fair*, it is always to Becky that our thoughts recur" because "the absurd, the ludicrous, and even the evil, leave more impression behind them than the grand, the beautiful, or the good."[17] I hate to disagree with him, and surely Becky preoccupies many readers, but the interest that accrues to me comes in the multitude of passing exchanges whose puns and idioms gesture at distant networks of meaning and years of accumulated associations, personal and professional. These phrases seem to acquire poignancy in proportion to their divergence or distance from the plot or themes of the novel. Late in *Vanity Fair*, after ten years of absence from home, even the selfish reprobate Jos thinks fondly about "home and early ties" because, as Thackeray says, "[d]istance sanctifies both" (590). I cannot but feel that the same works in some cases with rereading. I am hardly so bad as Jos, I hope, but all the same, "distance sanctifies" not just the obvious—"home and early ties"—but also the most trivial background accompaniments to life: after-dinner chatter about Dad's work, the mysterious operations of the city that I didn't understand but that I have for some reason almost loved. The virtual Britain conjured by my mother's and grandmother's English idiom and English food. My uneventful but moving memories of a shadow stockbroker life, my memories of my first trip to England and of my study abroad there. The background noise of my life turns up in Thackeray's novel, which as Dames suggests imagines novel reading itself "as a background process, a kind of agreeable mental noise, that in its very refusal to insist upon strict attention . . . allows interior reverie to blossom."[18] When Thackeray jokes, for instance, "If I had time and dared to enter into digressions, I would write a chapter about that first pint of porter drunk upon English ground," I cannot but recall my first porter drunk upon English ground and indeed my first weekend upon English ground (577). Thackeray's play, his investment in stock language and sociability and materialism, however gross, yields real personal and affecting interest. We are all stockbrokers in our libraries and reading nooks: trucking investments in value produced or deposited elsewhere, in these texts whose dividends we gather from afar. To boot, academic readers like me compulsively translate their feelings into a professional jargon as foreign from reality as Sedley's 'Change, but the feelings are there in both cases all the same. *Vanity Fair* is my most affecting literary investment.

## NOTES

1. Fredric Jameson, *The Political Unconscious: Narrative as a Socially Symbolic Act*, 9.
2. [Elizabeth Rigby], "*Vanity Fair*, *Jane Eyre*, and the Governesses' Benevolent Institution—Report for 1847," 153.
3. [Rigby], "*Vanity Fair*," 153.

4. C. L. R. James, *Beyond a Boundary*, 51.

5. William Makepeace Thackeray, *Vanity Fair: A Novel without a Hero*, ed. Peter L. Shillingsburg, 353. Further references will be given parenthetically.

6. [Rigby], "*Vanity Fair*," 153, 154, 154, 155.

7. D. A. Miller, *The Novel and the Police*, 192–220.

8. Nicholas Dames, *The Physiology of the Novel: Reading, Neural Science, and the Form of Victorian Fiction*, 94.

9. Consider, for another example: "If Rawdon Crawley had been then and there present, instead of being at the club nervously drinking claret, the pair might have gone down on their knees before the old spinster, avowed all, and been forgiven in a twinkling. But that good chance was denied to the young couple, doubtless in order that this story might be written, in which numbers of their wonderful adventures are narrated—adventures which could never have occurred to them if they had been housed and sheltered under the comfortable uninteresting forgiveness of Miss Crawley" (163).

10. Andrew H. Miller, *Novels behind Glass: Commodity Culture and Victorian Narrative*, 46, 49.

11. Mary Poovey, *Genres of the Credit Economy: Mediating Value in Eighteenth- and Nineteenth-Century Britain*, 373, 374.

12. [G. H. Lewes], review of *Vanity Fair*, in Thackeray, *Vanity Fair*, 756, emphasis in original.

13. Anthony Trollope, *W. M. Thackeray*, 94–95.

14. Bronisław Malinowski, "The Problem of Meaning in Primitive Languages," 296.

15. Audrey Jaffe, *The Affective Life of the Average Man: The Victorian Novel and the Stock-Market Graph*, 42.

16. Trollope, *Thackeray*, 91–92.

17. Trollope, *Thackeray*, 105, 97.

18. Dames, *Physiology of the Novel*, 110.

## WORKS CITED

Dames, Nicholas. *The Physiology of the Novel: Reading, Neural Science, and the Form of Victorian Fiction*. New York: Oxford University Press, 2007.

Jaffe, Audrey. *The Affective Life of the Average Man: The Victorian Novel and the Stock-Market Graph*. Columbus: The Ohio State University Press, 2010.

James, C. L. R. *Beyond a Boundary*. London: Yellow Jersey Press, 2005.

Jameson, Fredric. *The Political Unconscious: Narrative as a Socially Symbolic Act*. Ithaca: Cornell University Press, 1981.

Malinowski, Bronisław. "The Problem of Meaning in Primitive Languages." In *The Meaning of Meaning: A Study of the Influence of Language upon Thought and of the Science of Symbolism*, edited by C. K. Ogden and I. A. Richards, 296–336. London: K. Paul, Trend, Trubner, 1923.

Miller, Andrew H. *Novels behind Glass: Commodity Culture and Victorian Narrative*. Cambridge: Cambridge University Press, 1995.

Miller, D. A. *The Novel and the Police*. Berkeley: University of California Press, 1988.

Poovey, Mary. *Genres of the Credit Economy: Mediating Value in Eighteenth- and Nineteenth-Century Britain*. Chicago: University of Chicago Press, 2008.

[Rigby, Elizabeth]. "*Vanity Fair*, *Jane Eyre*, and the Governesses' Benevolent Institution—Report for 1847." *Quarterly Review* 84.167 (December 1848): 153–85.

Thackeray, William Makepeace. *Vanity Fair: A Novel without a Hero*. Edited by Peter L. Shillingsburg. New York: W. W. Norton, 1994.

Trollope, Anthony. *W. M. Thackeray*. English Men of Letters Series. New York: Harper Brothers, 1887.

CHAPTER NINE

# An Ethics of Place

Mary-Catherine Harrison

## On *North and South* by Elizabeth Gaskell

> "Yo're not to think we'd ha' letten 'em clem, for all we're a bit pressed oursel'; if neighbours doesn't see after neighbours, I dunno who will."
>
> Bessy Higgins in *North and South*

When I was a third of the way through my doctoral program, I had a crisis that was both existential and professional. As a Quaker I was raised to be a social-justice warrior, albeit a pacifist one. But I could no longer ignore the reality that writing about literature makes nothing happen. Not quite the remove of the Lady of Shalott, but graduate school did feel more ivory tower than trenches. I had a clearer sense of the purpose and vocation of teaching, but at the time I was teaching in an elite public university where the majority of students came from the top quintile of family income. Increasingly, higher education appeared to consolidate privilege rather than build a more just and equitable society. What kind of vocation was that?

At the same time, I was struck by the conviction of Victorian social-problem authors that literature can and should effect social change. In the "Hungry Forties" and 1850s, Elizabeth Gaskell, Elizabeth Barrett Browning, Charles Dickens, Benjamin Disraeli, Charles Kingsley, Charlotte Elizabeth Tonna, Frances Trollope, and others turned to fiction and poetry to expose conditions of poverty and prevail upon middle-class readers to intervene. Suffused in their writing is the idea that novels and poems can and should have a tangible impact on the emotional and ethical convictions of readers, and through them, transform society. What if, as critics, we took these aspirations seriously? I became interested in the mechanisms of narrative ethics—the strategies employed by Victorian authors to help shape readers' beliefs and behaviors as well as current social scientific research that illuminates what happens when we read.

Ironically, it is literary critics who are often most skeptical of literature's ethical impact. If social-problem authors aspired to "bridge the gulf" between rich and poor, critics steeped in the hermeneutics of suspicion have seen their attempts as well-meaning but futile or accused them of reifying class difference in their attempts to overcome it. In "Industrial Culture and the Victorian Novel," for example, Joseph Childers acknowledges that social-problem novels attempted to "bridge [the] divide" between rich and poor but concludes that these novels "acted as a sort of *cordon sanitaire* insulating the middle classes, defining and broadening the gap between the two nations."[1] Raymond Williams's account of Gaskell and other "industrial" novelists in *Culture and Society* typifies the view that the objectives of Victorian writers—sympathetic imagination, ethical intervention—would not be realized: "Recognition of evil was balanced by fear of getting involved. Sympathy was transformed not into action, but into withdrawal."[2]

For those of us trained in critical reading, the "folk ideology of [our] learned profession," the aspirations of social-problem literature seem terribly naïve.[3] But when I read Elizabeth Gaskell's novels, and later her letters, I was struck by the disconnect between what I found in their pages and what I encountered through criticism. It is true that she was committed to melioration and social reform, but her Christian ethics are more radical than conciliatory. And rather than hold a Pollyannaish view of the power of literature to prompt sympathy and social change, Gaskell and many of her fellow writers were acutely aware that readers' emotional responses toward fictional characters might *not* result in ethical interventions in the real world, an anxious awareness that contributed to the new critical premium on verisimilitude and the rise of realism in the mid-nineteenth century.[4]

Ironically, while Gaskell is widely considered the most "sympathetic" of the social-problem novelists, I think she was especially cognizant of the obstacles to cross-class imagining. As a Unitarian minister's wife, Gaskell visited poor and working-class families in their homes—and invited them to hers; taught their children in the Lower Mosley Street Sunday School; and cared for sick and struggling members of her husband's congregation and the broader Manchester community. Moreover, her visits and advocacy were not limited to the so-called deserving poor. She was inspired by the prison reformer and ironworker Thomas Wright to include prisoners in her ministry, and some of her most passionate advocacy—in life and in fiction—was on behalf of "fallen" women. It was this kind of contact, she claims in the preface to her first novel, *Mary Barton: A Tale of Manchester Life* (1848), that allowed her to capture the "state of feeling" among Manchester's workers.[5]

The high stakes of cross-class empathy are fundamental to both of Gaskell's "industrial" novels, *Mary Barton* and *North and South* (1854–1855), and so too is its difficulty. In *Mary Barton*, Gaskell speaks directly to middle- and upper-class readers, asking them to interrogate their own affective, ethical, and political responsibilities to their poor and working-class contemporaries. The novel employs a self-conscious treatment of narrative empathy, acknowledging that class limits one's point of view while simultaneously guiding middle-class readers through increasingly difficult perspective-taking. Gaskell repeatedly flags her own middle-class identity—and that of her narrator—to model the moral imperative of imagining suffering that is not one's own.[6] Even when her working-class hero, John Barton, is desperate enough to kill a factory owner's son, Gaskell asks readers to empathize with his anger and despair. Unsurprisingly, the novel provoked angry pushback from wealthy Mancunians—including members of her husband's congregation—who felt that *Mary Barton* was unfair to industrialists.

For a number of modern critics, *North and South* does not live up to expectations set by Gaskell's earlier novel because its heroine, Margaret Hale, is a middle-class woman. Arnold Kettle, for example, locates the power of *Mary Barton* in its ability to "transcend the limitations of [Gaskell's] conscious outlook"; *North and South* does not compete because it "presents its picture of English life entirely from a middle-class point of view."[7] I was initially in this camp myself. Like Gaskell, Margaret moves as a young woman from her rural hometown to one of the new industrial cities of "modern" Britain. The novel traces Margaret's growing sympathetic identification with her poor and working-class neighbors in Milton, a fictionalized Manchester, as she serves as de facto mediator between John Thornton, a self-made millowner, and Nicholas Higgins, a weaver and union representative, and his daughter Bessy, who is dying from byssinosis as a result of inhaling cotton dust. The novel is not exactly conciliatory—when Thornton defends basic tenets of capitalism, Margaret retorts that they are not "chivalric," or, as her minister father corrects her, "Christian" (303). But since the book focuses on the ethical development of Margaret Hale, rather than centering the lives of working-class families, it felt to me like Gaskell was beating a retreat.

As so often happens, however, my feelings changed when I encountered the novel from a different perspective, this time as a new faculty member working in Detroit, the most impoverished large city in America, and the most racially segregated.[8] In 2018, 37.9% of Detroit's residents lived in poverty; the median household income was $27,838.[9] Working to combat economic and educational inequality has become a core part of my vocation—both as a faculty member and administrator and, more recently, as director of a literacy initiative that works to expand access to literature for children, regardless of their zip code or family income. In each of these roles, I have defined my work in terms of justice and equity. At the same time, I have grappled with my conscience about working in Detroit and living forty-five minutes away in Ann Arbor, where my children live and go to school in a highly resourced neighborhood. Based on my own experience, I suspect that Gaskell's divided life in Manchester—living in the suburbs, working with those struggling "on the margins"—made her acutely conscious of the incongruence between her ethical principles and her failure to bring them to fruition. When I reread *North and South*, I saw Gaskell's focus on Margaret Hale not as a retreat but as a symptom of her own anxious recognition that where we choose to live and work can foster—and impede—emotional and ethical engagement across social divides. Thus John Barton's insistence, in *Mary Barton*, that "[i]t's the poor and the poor only, as does such things for the poor,"[10] or Bessy Higgins's observation, in *North and South*, that "if neighbours doesn't see after neighbours, I dunno who will."[11]

Like Gaskell, I was raised a "Dissenter," and the core tenets of my Quaker upbringing, like those of Gaskell's Unitarianism, stipulate one's ethical obligations to neighbors "in the good-Samaritan sense of the word."[12] In both Unitarian and Quaker traditions, loving one's neighbor is not merely an affective state; it places immediate demands on the ethical—and political—commitments of believers. But as the Parable of the Good Samaritan (Luke 10:25–37) makes clear, the category of "neighbor" has been used to exclude as often as embrace. The lawyer in the parable recites the two central precepts to gain eternal life: love God with all your heart and love your neighbor as yourself. But as if to delimit his affective and ethical obligations, the lawyer queries Jesus, "And who is my neighbor?" (Luke 10:29). The story Jesus tells in response emphasizes that love of one's neighbor must be concretized in the form of compassionate care, and it argues for the most radically inclusive interpretation of "neighbor." The Samaritans were not only foreigners, they were reviled by the Jews; they were untouchable and impure. And yet it is the enemy of the Jews who exemplifies the commandment to love others as we would love ourselves. At the same time, the parable reveals the significant hurdles to loving one's neighbor, even among those who consider themselves people of God. Before the Samaritan stops to bind the wounds of the stripped and beaten man, the priest and the Levite cross the road to avoid him.

Despite her own deep faith, Gaskell understood, I think, that biblical injunctions do little in the face of very real sociological obstacles to "loving thy neighbor." In Detroit, as in Manchester, underlying economic structures mean that rich and poor are rarely neighbors in the literal sense. Rather than seeing in Gaskell a naïve proponent of the novel as an agent for social change, I began to recognize her as a keen social critic exploring the impact of the twin gulfs of social difference and geographic distance. And I began to see her self-conscious approach to perspective-taking as a narrative strategy designed to push middle-class readers into a particular affective and ethical stance.

As I became more interested in the complex interplay between geography and justice in Detroit and its surrounding communities, I also came to see how *North and South* anticipates and illuminates contemporary research on social geography—the movement and distribution of groups of people in geographic space.[13] Much of the research on social geography—in the nineteenth century and our own—has focused on causes, examining the "economic, cultural, and political processes" that shape the distribution of populations.[14] But more recent research has also examined the perceptual, behavioral, and political *effects* of the social spaces in which we live and move. As social scientist Ryan Enos puts it, "Geographic space structures social cognition—that is, how people think about other people—and this, in turn, structures our politics."[15]

Enos's research has shown that rapidly shifting social geography—specifically, widespread social segregation accompanied by proximity and large group size—leads to a sharp escalation in stereotyping and outgroup bias and the rise of political ideology rooted in exclusion and fear. His research focuses on racial segregation in the contemporary American context, but I think it has equally powerful implications for social geography in the mid-nineteenth century, when industrialization and urbanization led to wealthy Britons' living near and yet segregated from mass populations of poor and working-class people.[16] During Gaskell's lifetime the percentage of the British populace living in cities soared—from 19.2 percent to 39.6 percent in the first half of the century.[17] The population of Manchester quadrupled. But as thousands of laborers moved in, middle-class families moved out to garden suburbs that pushed farther and farther away from the city center.

Gaskell was just a few years older than Margaret Hale when she moved to Manchester on her twenty-second birthday, Michaelmas, 1832. She settled with her new husband, Rev. William Gaskell, at 1 Dover Street (now 14), off of Oxford Street.[18] Ten years later Friedrich Engels moved in only a few blocks away when he arrived, also at the age of twenty-two, to work for his father's business and conduct the research that became *The Condition of the Working-Class in England*. Coming from Knutsford, a "little, clean, kindly country town," Gaskell must have found her move to the third largest—and fastest-growing—city in England disorienting.[19] Her new home was walkable to city center and the Cross Street Chapel, where William served as assistant minister, but the middle-class suburb where they lived was a world away from the factories and slums of Manchester. "For Manchester," she reported to William Turner soon after they were settled, their neighborhood was "very countrified."[20] Even years later, as Manchester continued to expand, she could write to Mary and William Howitt, "[M]y lot is now to live in or rather on the borders of a great manufacturing town."[21]

The Gaskells were certainly not unique in removing themselves from city center. In an 1832 letter Richard Cobden describes how his middle-class neighbors moved away from Mosley Street to the outer suburbs of Manchester, and their homes were turned into warehouses. The wealthiest families, including Unitarians, built mansions in the countryside.[22]

The enormous disparities between wealthy and poor neighborhoods—and the palpable impact on the bodies and souls that lived there—would have appeared in especially stark relief on Gaskell's arrival in Manchester in the midst of the 1832 cholera epidemic. Before her wedding that August she had written to her friend Harriet Carr about "this fearful Cholera"; although she had heard about the advance of the disease she was not overly worried about its arrival in rural Knutsford.[23] But the disease *had* struck Manchester, where the couple would move after their honeymoon in North Wales. According to Henry Gaulter's *The Origin and Progress of the Malignant Cholera in Manchester*, published the following year, 1,325 of the city's inhabitants contracted the disease from May until December; over half of those, 674 men, women, and children, died.[24] As in most cities, the impact of cholera was felt disproportionately in Manchester's poor neighborhoods: early reports emphasized that it was "confined to the shacks and hovels of the new industrial districts" and that "better-class districts were not affected."[25] Although fears of the contagion surely would have affected any new arrival to Manchester, Elizabeth Gaskell did not merely hear vague reports of the disease. Her new brother-in-law, Sam Gaskell, was starting his first medical appointment that year at Swan Street Hospital, an emergency cholera hospital in Ancoats, where thousands of working-class Mancunians were employed in the spinning mills that would later appear in *North and South*.

I feel certain that the disconnect between Gaskell's life of privilege in Manchester's suburbs and the suffering she and her husband and brother-in-law encountered in the city heightened her cognizance of the ethical hazards of social segregation. In Manchester, Engels observes the near erasure of working-class and poor homes: "One is seldom in a position to catch from the street a glimpse of the real labouring districts." He is merciless as he describes the unofficial policy of lining Manchester's streets with shops in order to "hid[e] from the eyes of wealthy ladies and gentlemen of strong stomach and weak nerves the misery and squalor which forms the complement of their wealth." Slums, meanwhile, form a "separate territory," where poverty is "removed from the sight of the happier classes" to "struggle along as it can." Engels names the Gaskells' neighborhood as one of those outside the "girdle" of "unmixed working-people's quarters," where wealthier inhabitants enjoy "free, wholesome country air, in fine, comfortable homes."[26]

William Cooke Taylor's *Notes of a Tour in the Manufacturing Districts of Lancashire* (1842) also emphasizes "the geographical limits of non-intercourse established in Manchester," calling them "the greatest of the special evils connected with that town."[27] He makes special note of the relationship between Ardwick, one of the suburbs where the Gaskells lived, and Ancoats, home to some of the poorest Mancunians:

> The isolation of classes in England has gone far to divide us into nations as distinct as the Normans and the Saxons: in our wisdom we have improved on the proverb, "One half of the world does not know how the other half lives," changing it into "One half of the world *does not care* how the other half lives." Ardwick knows less about Ancoats than it does about China, and feels more interested in the condition of New Zealand than of Little Ireland.[28]

The social geography of Manchester, Engels and Taylor suggest, is not merely a symptom of class alienation; it is its cause.

Like all of us, Gaskell was not immune to the effects of social geography. In her attitudes about class she gravitates toward sympathy rather than solidarity, and like many social-problem authors, her novels betray her fear of unions and working-class mobs.[29] But at the same time, Gaskell's fiction offers keen insight into the structural obstacles to cross-class relationships that were built into the new urban and industrial landscape.

In *North and South* the critical role geography plays in human relationships is invoked by the novel's title and highlighted further by Nicholas Higgins's use of "North and South" as a metonym to describe his family's nascent friendship with Margaret Hale: "Yo' see," Higgins says of their unlikely connection, "North and South has both met and made kind o' friends in this big smoky place" (73). But Gaskell also emphasizes that the social geography of Milton is more likely to preclude cross-class friendship than to foster it. Before she meets Nicholas, the main point of contact between Margaret and working-class Mancunians is when she is "unfortunate" enough to be on the street during shift changes; as "streams" of men and women pour out of the factories, Margaret is frightened by the "disorderly tumult" (71, 72). But much like Louisa Gradgrind's in Dickens's *Hard Times* (which was serialized in *Household Words* immediately preceding the publication of *North and South*), Margaret's dehumanizing perception of "the masses" is transformed through personal contact with Nicholas Higgins and his daughters, Bessy and Mary.[30] After several chance encounters, Margaret shares a smile with the poor weaver and says, "I think we must be neighbours, we meet so often on this road" (73). The scene reminds me of Gaskell's preface to *Mary Barton*, in which she describes her own growing concern for the "care-worn men" who "elbowed me daily in the busy streets of the town in which I resided."[31] From this point forward, Margaret becomes more "at home" in Milton and more aware of the human cost of capitalism. And after she visits the Higgins family in *their* home, her view of the city streets is transformed through the simple act of "having learnt to care for a dweller in them" (100).

As the burgeoning relationship between the Hale and Higgins families suggests, the ethical stakes of "loving thy neighbor" are central to the novel's plot. But in point of fact Margaret Hale and Nicholas Higgins are *not* neighbors, which Gaskell emphasizes when Margaret and her father go "house-hunting" (60). Despite their newly straitened circumstances, the Hales have a family budget of thirty pounds a year, putting them in a different rental bracket than Nicholas and Bessy Higgins, and the Hales rent an apartment in Crampton, "by far the most healthy suburb in the neighbourhood of Milton" (64). Thus, the dividing line between the new "neighbors" is not merely regional—North and South—but within Milton—suburb and city—a barrier that extends to their respective social networks and impacts every aspect of their life experiences.

Moreover, segregation is built into Milton's social fabric. While Margaret might arrive unannounced at the homes of her poor neighbors in rural Helstone (in part because of her role as minister's daughter), when she moves to the urban north, where her father is no longer a minister, there is no comparable social arrangement. In fact, when she suggests visiting, Nicholas Higgins is initially surprised and even offended by her impertinence (73). Gaskell makes it clear that the intimacy established between the Hale and Higgins families is not at all characteristic of the new industrial model, which discourages cross-class relationships in favor of the "deep selfishness of competition" (408). As Margaret puts it, there is no "equality of friendship" in Milton because "every man has had to stand in an unchristian and isolated position, apart from and jealous of his brother-man" (122). Perhaps it is not surprising, then, that Higgins describes their newfound connection as making "*kind o'* friends" (73, emphasis added).

Only one behavior has been demonstrated to have a significant impact in mitigating the perceptual impact of social segregation: getting to know and understand other people as individuals rather than as members of stigmatized social groups. Since Gordon Allport's work on social contact theory in 1954, researchers investigating a broad range of intergroup dynamics have found that positive effects on attitudes and behavior accrue as a result of interpersonal contact in optimal conditions, especially in contexts where personal relationships and intergroup friendships are formed.[32] Given this finding, it is all the more striking that Gaskell's Christian ethics highlight the moral imperative of human connection, especially across the "great gulf" between rich and poor. In *North and South* Gaskell does not represent a reconciliation of "the classes" per se; instead, she reveals how a connection between two individuals can help broker a friendship and understanding between their respective social groups. Higgins introduces Margaret to his daughters and another factory worker's family, the Bouchers; Margaret introduces Higgins to her father and the factory owner, Thornton; Thornton in turn meets other workers who are friends of Higgins's. The personal expands into the social, as Thornton's "friendship with one" evolves to an "acquaint[ance] with many" (420).

The real political potential of personal contact is seen in the relationship between Thornton and Higgins, which is formed as a result of Margaret's relationship with each of them. As a factory owner, Thornton has "no general benevolence,—no universal philanthropy" (211). He is an unfeeling master who can coolly calculate the costs and benefits of economic principles and talk of the ruin of men as if it were an "entirely logical" consequence of economic law (151). Once he meets Nicholas Higgins, however, Thornton begins "cultivating some intercourse with the hands beyond the mere 'cash nexus'" (420). As Margaret puts it, the two men need to "speak out together as man to man"; once they are "brought face to face," Thornton is able to see his workers not as "hands" but as men, and Higgins, in turn, is able to see Thornton as "a man, not a measter [*sic*]" (302, 331). Both men begin to recognize, as Wordsworth put it, "we have all of us one human heart" (419).

Concomitant to their nascent relationship are Thornton's "experiments" (431) with progressive management and the workers' willingness to look at things from their master's point of view. This kind of relationship building, Gaskell implies, is the only hope for class reconciliation. Gaskell has the reformed Thornton articulate her own doctrine of personal contact, his very reformation evidence of its power: "I have arrived at the conviction that no mere institutions . . . can attach class to class as they should be attached, unless the working out of such institutions bring the individuals and the different classes into actual personal contact. Such intercourse is the very breath of life" (421). Notably, Thornton's signature "experiment" (354) facilitates collective action on the part of his workers at the same time it creates a new social space for cross-class interaction. Thornton invests in a dining hall so that his employees can pool their resources to purchase wholesale meat and produce and share the cost of a hired cook. The workers, in turn, invite their employer to join them for the occasional meal. Here we have Gaskell's ethics realized within the modern industrial workplace, as capital and labor partake in the deeply symbolic Christian act of breaking bread together.

Gaskell's analysis of the destructive consequences of class segregation—and the transformative impact of personal relationships—is also evident in her depiction of women with social and economic privilege. Margaret's wealthy aunt, Mrs. Shaw, lives a life of ease and luxury, content enough that she "forgets to love the absent" and forgets to care for the suffering that she does not see (349). Not having been poor for twenty years, she has "forgotten all grievances" except the frivolous trials she suffers herself (16). Mrs. Shaw's daughter, Edith, lives a life even less troubled; it is, "like the deep vault of blue sky above her, free—utterly free from fleck or cloud" (67). Without "clouds" of her own, Edith is insensible to those of others. Gaskell's view of Margaret's aunt and cousin suggests that privilege itself undermines the capacity to love one's neighbor, *especially* if that neighbor is not in one's own social sphere. Notably, both mother and daughter are loath to leave their affluent neighborhood. Mrs. Shaw insists that a footman accompany the cousins "if they [go] beyond Harley Street or the immediate neighbourhood," and later in the novel, when Mrs. Shaw travels to Milton, she chooses not to accompany her niece to say her goodbyes to Nicholas Higgins, only warning Margaret to "be careful of herself, and not to catch any fever, such as [is] always lurking in such places" (70, 367). Later in the novel when Margaret begins to work in London's poor neighborhoods, her cousin Edith is horrified by the "wretched places" that Margaret "pokes herself into," proclaiming, "I should never dare to go down some of those streets without a servant" as they are "not fit for ladies" (427).

After the death of her parents, Margaret moves from Milton to her aunt's home in London and its life of "plentiful luxury" and "untroubled ease" (67). Ensconced in the fashionable neighborhood, Margaret struggles even to detect the suffering of others: "She found herself at once an inmate of a luxurious house, where the bare knowledge of the existence of every trouble or care seemed scarcely to have penetrated" (373). Rather than perceive her aunt's home as a refuge from outside cares, however,

Margaret sees it as a prison in which she is an "inmate." She is not relieved by its walls but stifled, afraid "lest she should even become sleepily deadened into forgetfulness of anything beyond the life . . . lapping her round with luxury" (373). If the house is a prison, then luxury itself is a kind of drug, one that does not alleviate her suffering but threatens to inure her to others'. Having witnessed true poverty in Milton, she is acutely aware of its invisibility in her new life: "There might be toilers and moilers there in London, but she never saw them; the very servants lived in an underground world of their own" (373). In Mrs. Shaw and Edith, Gaskell diagnoses not only the isolation and segregation between classes, but also the apathy that emerges from it. Wealth, she suggests, is inherently selfish, an idea reinforced by an allusion to the parable of the rich man and Lazarus (Luke 16:19–31). Contemplating the life of "household plenty and comfort" that Margaret would gain by marrying her son, Thornton's mother invokes the "purple and fine linen" that is associated with Dives, who ignores the beggar at his gates and is rewarded with damnation (210). The implication on Gaskell's part is that with Thornton's earthly goods would come too his negligence and lack of compassion.

Margaret, however, because of the friendships she has formed in Milton, does not succumb to the callousness bred by luxury. Instead she is left with a "strange unsatisfied vacuum in [her] heart and mode of life" and begins to pursue the charitable impulses that baffle her aunt and cousin (373). Even after inheriting a fortune, Margaret can hear the "still small voice" of conscience (Kings 19:12).[33] She resolves to pursue "her own ideas of duty" (417)—first through hands-on philanthropy and then through business—underwriting Thornton's benevolent management of her newly purchased mill. Unlike Carson, the heartless factory owner in *Mary Barton* who lives two miles out in the country, Thornton and Margaret will live, as a newly married couple, immediately next door to their factory.[34]

I think the reason *North and South* resonates so much with me is that I see in it a real-time working out of Gaskell's Christian ethics in the context of her own divided life in Manchester. Like her husband's sermons, Gaskell's novels "speak truth to power" about the high price—both physical and spiritual—of wealthy Britons' inaction. But Gaskell also ran a busy middle-class household, holding dinners, hosting houseguests, and caring for her growing family. She loved beautiful things—art, clothing, gardens, parties—and traveled as often as possible for welcome respite from "dear old dull ugly smoky grim grey Manchester."[35] Like many of us, Gaskell, I think, recognized that she did not live up to her own ethical standards, and she grappled with the implications. In one of my favorite of her letters—because it is so *human*—she acknowledges her internal struggle: "This is all a muddle, but I am trying in my heart to arrange how I can do my duty (i.e. stop at home this eveng [*sic*] for a class of Sunday School girls) & have my pleasure (i.e. go and dine at the Schwabes with the Scotts, Mrs. Fanny Kemble)—& I find I 'cannot serve two masters.'"[36] I often recognize myself in Gaskell's letters. Conscience can only coexist with comfort in uneasy tension; none of us can serve two masters.

By the time *North and South* began to appear in *Household Words* in 1854, the Gaskells had moved with their four daughters to 42 Plymouth Grove (now 84), a spacious neoclassical villa—with a greenhouse and private gardens—in an even more affluent suburb than their earlier homes. In a letter written soon after they moved to the Plymouth Grove house, Gaskell couches her ambivalence as a war of divided selves. Although her "social self" appreciates the beauty of the house and the creature comforts of domestic life, she admits that to take full pleasure in it she would need to "drown myself, (my *first* self)," the self who is "a true Christian—(only people call her socialist and communist)."[37] Uneasy about her privilege in a world of privations and unable to quiet her own "still small voice" of conscience, she asks her friend Eliza "Tottie" Fox to reassure her that "it is right to spend so much ourselves on *so* purely selfish a thing as a house is, while so many are wanting," saying, "thats [*sic*] the haunting thought to me."[38]

Gaskell dramatizes a similar cognitive dissonance in Margaret Hale after she visits the Higgins family during the strike and overhears Boucher, a desperate father, talk about his beloved son, who "lies clemming" at home (154). Margaret is utterly shaken. "How was she ever to go away into comfort and forget that man's voice," she wonders (156). Her feelings of guilt are exacerbated by the contrast between the elegant dinner she will attend that evening and the starvation the strikers and their families are experiencing at the same time, asking her mother, "[H]ow am I to dress up in my finery, and go off and away to smart parties, after the sorrow I have seen to-day?" (157).

This scene closely recalls an experience that Gaskell attributed as one of the "strong impulses" that led her to write her first novel, *Mary Barton*. While Gaskell was visiting a laborer's cottage, "trying hard to speak comfort, and to allay those bitter feelings against the rich which were so common with the poor," the father of the family grasped her arm tightly and said, with tears in his eyes, "Ay, ma'am, but have ye ever seen a child clemmed to death?"[39] In *Mary Barton*, the question is voiced by Gaskell's working-class hero, John Barton, whose son dies "for want of better food than [he] could give him." Responding to the ostensible privations of the masters in a down-turned market, Barton asks, his voice deep with emotion, "Han they ever seen a child o' their'n die for want o' food?"[40]

This question marks the limit of narrative empathy. Grieving the death of her own beloved son, Gaskell also recognized that all loss is not the same. Starvation is the bodily manifestation of poverty; as such, it is a societal disease. Neither Gaskell nor her middle-class readers would experience it themselves. Nor would their children. Both a physical and a phenomenological state, starvation is beyond imagination. Even the word used to signify starvation, "clemming," would be foreign to many of Gaskell's wealthy and southern readers, a fact she calls attention to by adding an author's note on the word's meaning in the Lancashire dialect.[41] I think Gaskell was haunted by this question because she knew that words on a page could never be adequate to relate the horror of the parent in this situation. Gaskell turned to fiction to "bring home" the suffering of neighbors that would otherwise remain unseen, unheard, and unfelt. But she was not confident that her novels could open doors wide enough for transformative change.

*North and South* is a novel about the moral necessity of loving our neighbors despite, or perhaps because of, the impediments inherent in social geography. Like Margaret Hale, Gaskell's readers enter the homes of the Higgins and Boucher families, and we are asked to love the neighbors we encounter there. We cannot know how many middle- and upper-class readers were inspired by Gaskell's fiction to pursue real-world relationships with their poor and working-class neighbors, or even to increase their charitable giving. But modern research in media studies, communications, and psychology suggests another mechanism through which her novels could have a transformative impact on readers' beliefs and behaviors. Research on parasocial relationships indicates that the positive social benefits of interpersonal contact extend to readers' relationships with fictional characters.[42] In other words, novel reading itself can help counteract the negative consequences of social segregation, resulting in positive belief change including reduced prejudice, stereotyping, and fear.

I still worry that my work as a literary critic makes nothing happen. But I am reassured that novels like *North and South*, the object of my life's work, can play a tangible role in social, ethical, and political change.

## NOTES

1. Joseph Childers, "Industrial Culture and the Victorian Novel," 79.
2. Raymond Williams, *Culture and Society*, 109.
3. Michael Warner, "Uncritical Reading," 14.
4. I discuss this further in "The Paradox of Fiction and the Ethics of Empathy: Reconceiving Dickens's Realism."
5. Elizabeth Gaskell, *Mary Barton: A Tale of Manchester Life*, 4.
6. See my discussion of these narrative dynamics in "How Narrative Relationships Overcome Empathic Bias: Elizabeth Gaskell's Empathy across Social Difference."
7. Arnold Kettle, "The Early Victorian Social-Problem Novel," 175.
8. John R. Logan and Brian Stults, "The Persistence of Segregation in the Metropolis: New Findings from the 2010 Census."
9. "QuickFacts Detroit city, Michigan," 2018 Data, US Census Bureau, https://www.census.gov/quickfacts/fact/table/detroitcitymichigan,MI/PST045218.
10. Gaskell, *Mary Barton*, 11.
11. Elizabeth Gaskell, *North and South*, ed. Angus Easson, 156. Further references will be given parenthetically.
12. Gaskell, *Mary Barton*, 72.
13. I discuss the intersections of geography and justice in greater depth in "Rx for Reading Detroit: Place-Based Social Justice Pedagogy."
14. Richard Dennis, *English Industrial Cities of the Nineteenth Century: A Social Geography*, 1.
15. Ryan Enos, *The Space Between Us: Social Geography and Politics*, 5.
16. See Asa Briggs, *Victorian Cities*, for more on the social demographics of Victorian cities.
17. See Paul Bairoch and Gary Goertz, "Factors of Urbanization in the Nineteenth Century Developed Countries: A Descriptive and Econometric Analysis."
18. Mrs. Ellis H. Chadwick, *Mrs. Gaskell: Haunts, Homes, and Stories*, 130.
19. Elizabeth Gaskell to William and Mary Howitt, May 1838, in *The Letters of Mrs Gaskell*, ed. John Chapple and Arthur Pollard, 15.
20. Elizabeth Gaskell to William Turner, October 6, 1832, in *Further Letters of Mrs Gaskell*, ed. John Chapple and Alan Shelston, 21.
21. Gaskell to William and Mary Howitt, May 1838, in *Letters*, 14.
22. Cobden's letter is recounted in John Chapple, *Elizabeth Gaskell: The Early Years*, 408.

23. Elizabeth Gaskell to Harriet Carr, August 8, 1832, in *Further Letters*, 20.

24. Henry Gaulter, *The Origin and Progress of the Malignant Cholera in Manchester* [. . .], 156.

25. E. Ashworth Underwood, "The History of Cholera in Great Britain," 166.

26. Friedrich Engels, *The Condition of the Working-Class in England in 1844*, 47, 26, 46.

27. William Cooke Taylor, *Notes of a Tour in the Manufacturing Districts of Lancashire*, 164.

28. Taylor, *Notes of a Tour*, 164.

29. See my "'The Great Sum of Universal Anguish': Statistical Empathy in Victorian Social-Problem Literature."

30. See my "'The Great Sum.'"

31. Gaskell, *Mary Barton*, 3.

32. For recent research on intergroup contact theory see John F. Dovidio, Angelika Love, Fabian M. H. Schellhaas, and Miles Hewstone, "Reducing Intergroup Bias through Intergroup Contact: Twenty Years of Progress and Future Directions"; and Thomas F. Pettigrew and Linda R. Tropp, "A Meta-Analytic Test of Intergroup Contact Theory."

33. Gaskell cites this passage in *Mary Barton*, 162.

34. Gaskell, *Mary Barton*, 65.

35. Elizabeth Gaskell to Charles Eliot Norton, December 7, 1857, in *Letters*, 489.

36. Elizabeth Gaskell to Mary Green, January 25, 1853, in *Further Letters*, 80.

37. Gaskell to Mary Green, January 25, 1853, in *Further Letters*, 80.

38. Elizabeth Gaskell to Eliza Fox, April 1850, in *Letters*, 108.

39. Mat Hompes, "Mrs. Gaskell," 130, 131.

40. Gaskell, *Mary Barton*, 10, 64.

41. In *Mary Barton*, Gaskell offers this footnote: "'Clem,' to starve with hunger. 'Hard is the choice, when the valiant must eat their arms or clem.'—Ben Jonson" (35n1).

42. See Edward Schiappa, Peter B. Gregg, and Dean E. Hewes, "The Parasocial Contact Hypothesis."

## WORKS CITED

Allport, Gordon. *The Nature of Prejudice*. Reading, MA: Addison Wesley, 1954.

Bairoch, Paul, and Gary Goertz. "Factors of Urbanization in the Nineteenth Century Developed Countries: A Descriptive and Econometric Analysis." *Urban Studies* 23 (1986): 285–305.

Briggs, Asa. *Victorian Cities*. New York: Harper & Row, 1965.

Chadwick, Mrs. Ellis H. *Mrs. Gaskell: Haunts, Homes, and Stories*. London: Sir Isaac Pitman & Sons, 1913.

Chapple, John. *Elizabeth Gaskell: The Early Years*. Manchester: Manchester University Press, 1997.

Childers, Joseph. "Industrial Culture and the Victorian Novel." In *The Cambridge Companion to the Victorian Novel*, edited by Deirdre David, 77–96. Cambridge: Cambridge University Press, 2001.

Dennis, Richard. *English Industrial Cities of the Nineteenth Century: A Social Geography*. Cambridge: Cambridge University Press, 1986.

Dickens, Charles. *Hard Times*. New York: W. W. Norton, 1990.

Dovidio, John F., Angelika Love, Fabian M. H. Schellhaas, and Miles Hewstone. "Reducing Intergroup Bias through Intergroup Contact: Twenty Years of Progress and Future Directions." *Group Processes & Intergroup Relations* 20.5 (2017): 606–20.

Engels, Friedrich. *The Condition of the Working-Class in England in 1844*. London: George Allen & Unwin, 1953.

Enos, Ryan. *The Space Between Us: Social Geography and Politics*. Cambridge: Cambridge University Press, 2017.

Gaskell, Elizabeth. *Further Letters of Mrs Gaskell*. Edited by John Chapple and Alan Shelston. Manchester: Manchester University Press, 2003.

———. *The Letters of Mrs Gaskell*. Edited by John Chapple and Arthur Pollard. Manchester: Manchester University Press, 1997.

———. *Mary Barton: A Tale of Manchester Life*. 1848. Oxford: Oxford University Press, 2006.

———. *North and South*. 1854–1855. Edited by Angus Easson. Oxford: Oxford University Press, 1973.

Gaulter, Henry. *The Origin and Progress of the Malignant Cholera in Manchester, Considered Chiefly in Their Bearing on the Contagiousness and the Secondary Causes of the Disease*. London: Longman, Rees, Orme, Brown, Green, & Longman, 1833.

Harrison, Mary-Catherine. "'The Great Sum of Universal Anguish': Statistical Empathy in Victorian Social-Problem Literature." In *Rethinking Empathy through Literature*, edited by Meghan Marie Hammond and Sue Kim, 135–49. London: Routledge, 2014.

———. "How Narrative Relationships Overcome Empathic Bias: Elizabeth Gaskell's Empathy across Social Difference." *Poetics Today* 32.2 (2011): 255–88.

———. "The Paradox of Fiction and the Ethics of Empathy: Reconceiving Dickens's Realism." *Narrative* 16.3 (2008): 256–78.

———. "Rx for Reading Detroit: Place-Based Social Justice Pedagogy." *Michigan Journal of Community Service Learning* 23.2 (2017): 117–30.

Hompes, Mat. "Mrs. Gaskell." *The Gentleman's Quarterly* 279 (July–December 1895): 124–38.

Kettle, Arnold. "The Early Victorian Social-Problem Novel." In *From Dickens to Hardy*, vol. 6 of *The New Pelican Guide to English Literature*, edited by Boris Ford, 164–81. Harmondsworth, UK: Penguin, 1982.

Logan, John R., and Brian Stults. "The Persistence of Segregation in the Metropolis: New Findings from the 2010 Census." *City & Community* 12.2 (2013): 160–68.

Pettigrew, Thomas F., and Linda R. Tropp. "A Meta-Analytic Test of Intergroup Contact Theory." *Journal of Personality and Social Psychology* 90.5 (2006): 751–83.

Schiappa, Edward, Peter B. Gregg, and Dean E. Hewes. "The Parasocial Contact Hypothesis." *Communication Monographs* 72.1 (2005): 92–115.

Taylor, William Cooke. *Notes of a Tour in the Manufacturing Districts of Lancashire: In a Series of Letters to His Grace the Archbishop of Dublin*. 2nd ed. London: Duncan & Malcolm, 1842.

Underwood, E. Ashworth. "The History of Cholera in Great Britain." *Proceedings of the Royal Society of Medicine* 41.3 (March 1948): 165–73.

Warner, Michael. "Uncritical Reading." In *Polemic: Critical or Uncritical*, edited by Jane Gallop, 13–38. London: Routledge, 2004.

Williams, Raymond. *Culture and Society*. New York: Columbia University Press, 1983.

CHAPTER TEN

# What Esther Thinks about Sex

Catherine Robson

## On *Bleak House* by Charles Dickens

I usually think that *Bleak House* (1853) is not, and never will be, "my Victorian novel"—if, that is, we take this volume's title to indicate the novel that lies closest to each contributor's heart. Let's imagine that all long works of literary fiction produced between 1837 and 1901 suddenly find themselves threatened by spontaneous combustion and I'm told that I can rescue only one text. I would not pluck *Bleak House* from the imminent flames and set it in a place of safety. On most days I'd risk my fingers for *Wuthering Heights* or *Great Expectations* (well, its first fourteen chapters or so), but then again, it might be *Tess of the d'Urbervilles* or *The Woodlanders* or *Far from the Madding Crowd*, or even, if I were feeling sufficiently high-minded, *Middlemarch*. But never, never *Bleak House*. While I'm aghast at colleagues and friends who'd reach for *Jane Eyre* or *Villette* (I'll qualify that a bit: I actually enjoy hating the second Mrs. Rochester and everything that she writes, but I'm genuinely sickened by Miss Snowe), I'm simply puzzled by those who profess to love above all others a novel that contains both Esther Summerson and an interminable chapter on Lords Boodle, Coodle, Doodle, Foodle, etc., etc., etc. More broadly, though, what can you do with a book that divides its story between two vastly different tellers and then refuses to say what the relation between those two narrators might be?

And yet, and yet, and yet . . . when I was approached about contributing to this volume, my mind went straight to *Bleak House*. An earlier version of this essay was written for delivery to a gathering of the Dickens Project's summer conference, an event known as the "Dickens Universe" and hosted each summer in the idyllic setting of the University of California's Santa Cruz campus, high above Monterey Bay. I thought of

Dickens's ninth novel again because what I wrote about it back then goes directly to some of the questions with which this collection is centrally concerned. Which is to say: what might Victorianists think or say about the novels from the period of their academic specialty when they are neither reading as, nor writing for, academic specialists, and how might this differ from what they produce in their day jobs? As it happens, the Dickens Universe audience is composed of roughly equal numbers of academics and members of the general public, so lecturers in Santa Cruz are always required to bridge the divide between "professional" and "lay" reading. The common denominator is simply a desire to talk about a given Dickens novel, and willfully obfuscatory academic prose is Just Not Tolerated. But the discussion below not only takes wide interest in *Bleak House* as the necessary ground of its existence. It also makes the relationship between the novel and different kinds of readers, both in the present moment and over time, a primary concern.

And *Bleak House*, it turns out, is "my Victorian novel" for yet another important reason. That snagging issue of the text's perplexing formal arrangement catches deep within. Trying to make sense of it, I am led toward topics and types of thinking that are more personally affecting than those with which I habitually engage in my scholarship, which usually has a historicist turn and addresses broad questions about childhood, class, memory, and war. Spoiler alert: this essay ultimately considers erotic relations and individual experience, and it reaches for assistance from such writers as the philosopher Galen Strawson and the psychoanalyst Adam Phillips. My attempt to understand what *Bleak House* thinks about sex and life, it will transpire, is closely connected to my attempt to understand what I (and others) think about sex and life.

To approach these intimate matters, however, I'll begin quite sedately with that formal issue of two-part divisions, and I'll bring an old saw into play. The world is divided into two sorts of people—those who think the world is divided into two sorts of people, and those who do not. I am definitely in the first camp. I firmly believe that the world consists of cat people and dog people (and that cat people are superior), and of Emily Brontë people and Charlotte Brontë people (I've indicated already that I find Emily people superior). It's a move that Charles Dickens himself likes: in chapter 8 of *Bleak House*, for instance, Mr. Jarndyce remarks that "there were two classes of charitable people; one, the people who did a little and made a great deal of noise; the other, the people who did a great deal and made no noise at all."[1] As I've already indicated, the two-part division that concerns me most here is that which falls between academic and nonacademic readers.

The problematic nature of my comments so far is obvious. I have been merrily lumping together all sorts of two-part divisions and acting as if they were all the same, when this is clearly not the case. Sometimes there are true divisions: you have either read *Bleak House*, or you have not. Some take the form of a Venn diagram: some of us are cat people, some are dog people, some are both, and some aren't in the diagram at all. Some are differences of degree rather than kind. Even more invidiously, I have been inserting little value judgments here and there—suggesting that one position in the binary is superior to the other, that Emily people are better than Charlotte people. I want to behave more responsibly in my discussion of that matter of the differences between academic and nonacademic readers—I will not say, for instance, that the former group read for work and the latter for fun, because such a statement is clearly specious inasmuch as it acknowledges neither the pleasure experienced by, say, a graduate student when she reads an assigned text for class nor the serious attention that is part of, for example, a nurse's engagement with a novel when he puts his feet up at home. But I do think it is true to say that there are some ways of talking about a work that are more likely to occur in an academic site, whether it be a seminar room or a scholarly lecture, and others that are more associated with the discourse in a book group or a conversation between friends.

When it comes to novels, there is a particular zone in which the differences between these community-specific modes of address are assumed to be especially apparent—a zone that is subject to an agreed-upon convention in one location but that operates with markedly less policing in the other. This zone is the discussion of characters. Simply stated, it is the received wisdom that lay readers are prone to talking about them as if they were real people, whereas academics implicitly or, on occasion, explicitly insist that they be treated as the textual constructs that they actually are. It is also assumed (at least by most academics) that the academic approach to characters is the superior one, the only intellectually defensible position. I contend that there is considerable bad faith in this article of our profession's code, and that it might be productive if we were to acknowledge that all of us, wherever and whenever we read novels, cannot help but perform the miraculous act of breathing life into the various assemblages of inked marks that are scattered around a text under the organizing rubric of a series of proper names. I believe that all of us—admittedly to greater or lesser degrees, depending on what kind of readers we are and what kind of novel we're reading—make flesh-and-blood people out of the words we find on the page. To paraphrase an observation made by the critic James Wood, we take the thin crescent moon of character provided by the author and flood it with our own knowledge of humanity until it becomes full.[2]

The second paragraph of *Great Expectations* sets before us a vignette of this process when Pip records how his younger self, left with no visual representations of his dead parents, foolishly yet touchingly constructed mental pictures of Philip and Georgiana Pirrip out of the only material evidence left to him, the shapes of the letters on their tombstone.[3] But whether or not we are the kind of readers who create a distinct image in our heads of the physical appearance of say, Mrs. Snagsby, and whether or not this vision is aided or abetted by depictions of Mrs. Snagsby that we have seen in illustrations or in film and television adaptations of *Bleak House*, we all to some degree bring something of our own to those parts of the text in which Dickens gives us something of Mrs. Snagsby, and we all therefore make both a Mrs. Snagsby who exceeds the print on the page, and a Mrs. Snagsby who is slightly, or considerably, different from any other reader's Mrs. Snagsby. My Mrs. Snagsby, for example, may take the form she does because Dickens's representations of her remind me of a certain prying and suspicious neighbor I had in my youth, and your Mrs. Snagsby may be the way she is because she is invigorated by your knowledge of a certain annoying aunt. If you and I are talking about Mrs. Snagsby in an academic setting, we will most likely keep my neighbor and your aunt out of the discussion and refer instead to the textual ground that is common to us both, but this does not negate what we do while we are reading and thinking about Mrs. Snagsby. On the contrary, we know that one of the great pleasures of literature inheres within this very experience, the experience of being co-creator with the author. "O Lady!" as Coleridge said, "we receive but what we give."[4]

Now, if you are happy to agree that "filling in" or "filling out" the character is an important part of the enjoyment of reading a novel, I'd like to make a new move: to start to think about how we might investigate the development of this process over time. "The character" has been an integral feature of various genres in all sorts of places for many centuries, but for the purposes of this discussion, I will limit my attention to characters in the Novel with a capital N and I'll refer to some recent work on the history of this literary form. Catherine Gallagher has argued that toward the end of the first half of the eighteenth century, readers started to receive a training in the curious enterprise of accepting the fictionality of an invented character. Consumers of the new genre of the novel stopped needing to believe that a "real person" existed behind the proper name of the individual whose experiences they were reading about, and they came instead to see that the nonreferentiality of the fictional character should be understood as having what Gallagher calls "a greater referentiality." Thus, whereas Daniel Defoe insisted in 1719 that Robinson Crusoe was actually a genuine, flesh-and-blood individual, by 1742 Henry Fielding was making it clear in *Joseph Andrews* that his novel set forth "not men, but manners; not an individual, but a species." Any given character, he asserted, was based not on "one pitiful wretch" but on a whole class of individuals. Thanks to texts informed by such thinking, successive generations of readers became increasingly adept at recognizing that their job was not to try and identify characters' real-life referents but to respond to a character as a plausible invention—plausible, because the novelist had drawn on his or her knowledge of what that sort of person is like in the real world, a knowledge that the reader then draws on to validate and thereby to enlarge his or her conception of the invented entity. Or, more precisely—and here I reach toward terms generated by E. M. Forster and deployed in Alex Woloch's work on what he calls "the character system"—to follow the author's lead in giving the key personages in the novel fuller, "rounded" human status and letting others stay relatively "flat" in the background.[5]

Such theorizations of novelistic character have encouraged a welcome revival of interest in the topic. But in attempts to discover how character-function has altered over time, attention has usually been given to the textual side of the equation only. This is hardly surprising. Copies of novels from the past three centuries are readily available, but how can we hope to gain access to the multitude of minds of those who read them at any given point in this period? Yet surely what is most of interest here is that continuous back-and-forth process whereby consumers of literature both give and receive—give, inasmuch as they fill out the characters in the novel they are reading by infusing them with what they know of human consciousness and behavior, and receive, because that very novel is at that moment providing them with further ways of thinking about human consciousness and behavior, ways that they may well take with them into their lives and toward any subsequent experience with a printed text. But how can we analyze this feedback loop in action?

I'll take a first tentative step toward the flesh-and-blood side of the loop via an idea put forward by Galen Strawson, a British analytic philosopher whose work has attracted the attention of narratologists, those who study the construction and constitution of narrative in the broadest and narrowest of terms. Strawson posits that people can be divided, surprise surprise, into two rough groups. The first camp is occupied by what he calls "Diachronics," individuals who understand themselves as being continuous selves over time: the self for these people is "something that was there in the (further) past, and will be there in the (further) future." In the other camp are the "Episodics." An individual in this camp sees the self as discontinuous over time: "[O]ne does not figure oneself . . . as something that was there in the (further) past and will be there in the (further) future," though such a person does recognize that these different selves are all part of one human being who has persisted over time. Strawson views these dispositions not as binary but as existing along a spectrum, and he is especially concerned to attack what he sees as the implicit moral coding of the two positions—the assumption that Diachronics are likely to be "better" people than Episodics.[6]

Strawson's formulation is of help in this context because of the strong, but not, he says, inevitable, linkage between those who understand their existence diachronically and those who see the connected moments of their existence as having some sort of story shape—in other words, those prone to seeing all, or part of, the temporal arcs of their lives as a narrative or narratives. I am going to stick with those people who experience their lives diachronically and narratively so that I can start to look *not* into the huge issue of all the different possible structures in the world from which they might take models for their stories, and *not* the even larger issue of how we might describe where different people in different times and places have been taking models for their stories, but instead a smaller question, a question pertinent to those of us who read and study the novel. And this is it: over the years, how have the precise arrangements of *fictional* representations of Diachronic selves affected the ways in which *flesh-and-blood* Diachronic, Narrative selves experience their existence? In other words, if generations of people have taken from their reading matter ideas of what constitutes a person, what kinds of effects have been created, both in the world and on the level of the individual, by the internalization of a textual model?

From what I have said so far, I hope you will agree that it is reasonable to assume that autobiography has a special status in this discussion. Distinguishing between the autobiographies of real persons and invented characters is not especially important to me. I'm happy to follow a critical consensus that maintains that the two kinds are structurally identical, given that both create a narrative that is not actually there, to be found in the real world—but here I am thinking specifically about the fictional variety. Novels in which a first-person narrator tells the story of his or her life have an extremely important founding, and continuing, presence in the history of the genre, and much has been written about their connections to such associated forms as the chronicle, the narrative of spiritual progress, the picaresque, the epistolary fiction, and so forth. I will make a cavalier leap over the first hundred and thirty or so years of development to concentrate on the state of play around the middle decades of the nineteenth century. This period saw the publication in Britain of a number of remarkable fictional autobiographies that staged the relation between the writing-self and the character-self in a very particular temporal manner. These novels present a narrative situation in which the writing-self is the identity that the character-self has achieved by the end of the book: that achieved self looks back in time to tell the story of his or her younger self in more or less chronological order, from childhood to adulthood, or, more precisely, to the point at which he or she will tell his or her history. These storytellers are then essentially Diachronic selves, selves who understand the relation between who they are now and who they were at all the earlier moments as points along a narrative arc that has a fixed end point, the scene of writing.

From this description, you will not be surprised to learn that the first-person narrators I have in mind are Charlotte Brontë's Jane Eyre (loathe her though I may, she is impossible to keep out) and Dickens's three examples of the genre: Esther Summerson, David Copperfield, and Pip. *Bleak House* seems to me to offer the most extraordinary opportunities to explore the issues I have been setting out, because of Dickens's decision to make the first-person portion of this novel tell only *half* of the story and because of his decision to split the narration between two radically different modes—the first, that unlocated, unidentifiable, diffuse, and omniscient voice that speaks, for the most part, in the present tense, and the second, Esther's retrospective, past-tense account of her life and times up to the point of writing.

So why on earth does Dickens decide to tell the story in these two incommensurate modes and why does he decline to supply us with any clear explanation of the connection between them? These two ultimately unanswerable questions could be, and have been, addressed in various ways, but I here take the possibly rash decision to consider their relationship to sex as my way through—as my way to make both a particular argument about the constitution of *Bleak House* and ultimately a broader suggestion about this novel's contribution to widespread modes of constituting the self in relation to time. Now, just in case you're saying to yourself, "But there is no sex in *Bleak House*, because the topic simply could not be addressed, given the mores of the mainstream publication forums of Dickens's day," let me come right back at you with this: I proceed from the assumption that sex is always in the Victorian novel, just as it is always in the world, because it is the vital connection that produces each and every one of the bodies that teem onto the pages of the former and the streets of the latter. What we need to consider is the manner in which it appears in this novel, especially the manner in which it relates to the sharply differentiated temporal arrangements of the two narratives of *Bleak House*.

Let's now start to get close to the text, at long last, via the writings of the Dickensian critic John Jordan. Jordan's fine book *Supposing "Bleak House"* has encouraged me to think about the retrospective nature of Esther's storytelling, to consider what it might mean to take full cognizance of the fact that the narrator of the first-person portion of *Bleak House* is not Esther Summerson, but Esther Woodcourt. Or rather, to reinscribe Jordan's defining lines of that achieved identity: the woman who is telling us the story of her life tells it from the position of one who has *already* uncovered the mystery of her birth and the identity of her mother, from the position of one who more than seven years earlier found the body of that mother lying "cold and dead" outside the graveyard (915). The reading that this awareness enables brings together four key terms—"mother," "child," "birth," and "death"—terms that guide Jordan's movement through Esther's narrative of her life, from her first awareness of being to the time of writing, giving him an alert ear and eye for the echoes and shadows of those things that Esther will learn only at *later* points in her journey toward that position of writing, and endowing him with an acute sensitivity to both the textual traces and the textual omissions that these knowledges create.[7]

The move I will now make follows this insistence that we notice that someone called Mrs. Woodcourt is telling this tale, but it puts the emphasis in a different place—one, I think, that is not ultimately as important to the primary emotional registers of Esther's story as Jordan's reading—but in a place that lets me address the issue that concerns me here. For the Mrs. Woodcourt on whom I wish to concentrate is not so much the woman who knows what happened at the scene of her birth, and who knows how her mother died, but a woman who has been Allan Woodcourt's wife for those past seven years, and who has two daughters. In other words, I am thinking about a woman who at the most conservative of estimates must be imagined to have had intercourse at least twice, but probably, and however much it may go against the grain for us to think this, a great many more times than that. So, it is the idea of Esther the sexually experienced adult that I wish to bring to bear upon my study of her narrative, or rather, in the interests of focus, upon just five sentences abstracted from chapter 51.

Entitled "Enlightened," the chapter as a whole presents Esther's account of the day on which she learned that Richard Carstone and Ada Clare had been married in secret some two months earlier. After this revelation, Ada remains with her husband in Symond's Inn and Esther heads off alone to Mr. Jarndyce's London lodgings. Yet she cannot keep away from her "darling" (789). Two or three hours later, Esther ventures out "at dusk" with her maid, Charley (789). Here are the five sentences:

> It was dark when we came to the new strange home of my dear girl, and there was a light behind the yellow blinds. It was very solitary and very dull, and I did not doubt that I might safely steal up-stairs. I left Charley below, and went up with a light foot, not distressed by any glare from the feeble oil lanterns on the way. I listened for a few moments; and in the musty rotting silence of the house, believed that I could hear the murmur of their young voices. I put my lips to the hearse-like panel of the door, as a kiss for my dear, and came quietly down again, thinking that one of these days I would confess to the visit. (789–90)

What exactly does Esther hear when she listens to "the murmur of their young voices" within that sepulchral apartment? Are they just talking, or is there something more going on? At this point in the narrative, we are in a position where we might speculate about the opening up of that gap between Esther Summerson and Esther Woodcourt, for it seems fair to assume that Esther's writing self knows things that her unmarried self perhaps only suspected. But whatever Esther thought she heard at the time, and however her married self might now better understand what it was she heard, both Esthers know well enough that she is, and was, fully outside the couple's intimacy. She may kiss the unresponsive boards of that deathly door, but she has no part in this portion of the life of these two lovers.

I suggest that there is heuristic value in seeing this moment of division between the self-narrating individual and the intercourse of others as an emblematic image for the novel as a whole. In other words, focusing on this spatial representation of Esther's exclusion from Richard and Ada's embrace can help us to understand both *Bleak House*'s driving concerns and its peculiar system of narrative organization. When our first-person narrator is separated from the two wards of Jarndyce, she is cut off from lovers of around her own age. This arrangement, I want to argue, figures as a temporal flattening of the novel's central mystery, the simultaneous connection and disconnection between the lovemaking of Captain Hawdon and Honoria Barbary, and the existence of their child, Esther. Dickens thus creates in *Bleak House* a dramatic instantiation of what is in fact a simple truth about reproduction and thus about the human condition: there is no necessary link between the desire and ability to have heterosexual intercourse and the desire and ability to be a fit parent to a child. In consequence, there is an ever-present possibility that a tragic gap will be fused between the satisfaction of immediate, short-term wants and the production of potentially long-lived, needy individuals. One of the astounding features of *Bleak House* is that it grants us a vision of that gap in unusually distinct terms, both on the level of plot and on the level of form.

To justify the move I have just made from Richard and Ada to Hawdon and Honoria, I could spend some time establishing connections between Esther's Symond's Inn experience and others she has told us about at earlier junctures—moments that on rereading stand out as key vista points in the charged emotional tourism of her narrative: the two occasions that she registers her encounter with the twice-repeated "dark door" of her father's room in Krook's house, that "sad and desolate place," that "gloomy, sorrowful place" that gave her "a strange sensation of mournfulness and even dread" (75, 232, 232); her walking beneath the one "lighted window" of the room at Chesney Wold that she believes contains the woman she has just learnt is her mother, and her admission that, once back in London, she patrolled her mother's dwelling, that she "passed and repassed the door of her house in town, loving it, but afraid to look at it" (586, 669). Further, to support my claim that chapter 51 offers a staging of the perplexing connect and disconnect between sex and offspring, I could look to the events related by the other narrator that are absolutely synchronous with this joyless day on which Esther was "enlightened." I could note that Jo, the text's prime example of a child without parental care, dies in the same afternoon that she learns that Richard and Ada have become one flesh—that the evening when their two bodies could conceivably be making one more scrap of humanity is the same evening in which the novel locates its most extreme example of a woman's passionate act, Hortense's murder of Tulkinghorn. But while I think it's important to notice the relentlessly negative nature of both what is in, and what connects to, the chamber in Symond's Inn, I am going to leave these matters of content as simple sketches so that I can approach instead the knotty question of *Bleak House*'s relationship to two different temporal arrangements.

I'll make a wild cast first, and then reel things back in. What if we used the gap between sex, an activity, and its product, an individuated being, as one way of understanding the relationship between that unequal pair of narrative modes in the novel? To put this another way, what might we see if we think of the juxtaposition of an endlessly fecund, unlocated present-tense voice and the retrospective telling of a single person's story as a bodying forth of the bonds and divisions between what Mr. Jarndyce ruefully calls the "indifferent parent" of the universe, existing in the moment-to-moment intercourse of everyday life, and its child, recounting one particular life lived (93)? I acknowledge that this is a reductive point of view, and one that requires a fair amount of slippage to make its argument—reductive, because to consider the omniscient narrator's voice only in terms of its tense is to ignore the myriad of other things it is and does; slippery, because to see that present-tenseness as a signifier for sex is to slide rather too blithely toward a perception of intercourse as a prime instance of that which happens in the moment; and both reductive and slippery at the same time, because the reading comes to rest on a rather glib conjunction of the essential copula "to be" and copulation *tout court*. But, to be honest, I don't really need you to be convinced by this, because

I have constructed this vision primarily for a strategic purpose. We now have a vantage point from which we can better perceive a particular oddity in the design of *Bleak House*, an oddity that shows us something important about that primary oddity, its division of the narrative between two voices in two tenses. If we focus our minds on sex, I am suggesting, we put ourselves in a good place to identify a marked bias in our novelist's handling of the various temporal dispositions adopted by different types of human beings. Briefly stated: Dickens gives himself the opportunity to present positive and negative versions of the relationships to time encoded in his two narrative modes—but he doesn't follow through on all parts of the deal.

The position from which sex is perceived in Esther's retrospective story is of course my larger concern, and it's the topic to which I'll return at the end of this essay. But I want to register here that Dickens provides both a highly valorized instance of a Diachronic self and a highly criticized one. He gives us Esther, someone whose goodness is intrinsically related to the discipline she enjoins upon herself to attend directly to the present *with the longer view in mind*, to organize her behavior in the moment in such a way that it will connect honorably with her past and future selves. But he also gives us Richard Carstone, a young man whose relationship to the present is ruined because he is "always looking forward to the termination of the suit," that seemingly unsolvable complexity of last wills and testaments, the contradictory words from the past mired in the hopeless stasis of Chancery (600). As Richard himself says, "There's no now for us suitors" (594). If Mrs. Jellyby is the model of the wrong way to direct one's energies in a spatial sense, Richard is her temporal equivalent: "Everything postponed to that imaginary time!" observes Esther in despair. "Everything held in confusion and indecision until then!" (599).

Some kind of balance, then, is achieved in Dickens's depiction of lives arranged in relation to an extended temporal arc, but what about life lived in, and for, the moment? Both voices of *Bleak House* explore these concepts, but neither, I maintain, gives them any degree of positive coding. I'll turn in a moment to Esther's portion, but let's focus on the other narrative first to see what kind of treatment it allots to "the now." If someone told you that you were about to read a text written in the present tense, you might reasonably assume that the author had chosen this mode at least in part because of the opportunities it affords for the representation of the preciousness of a fleeting minute, the capture of the transitory joy of existence, the registering of a pleasure that does not withstand the passage of time but is nevertheless a vital part of human experience. It might occur to you that the formal disposition of the long narrative does not as readily lend itself to the celebration of evanescent ecstasy as do artworks with more obvious alignments to the temporality of the moment, such as the painting, the sculpture, the short poem or piece of music—but even so, you'd probably be able to bring to mind scenes in novels in which the narrator switches from his or her habitual past tense into the present, the better to create the immediacy of an instant of bliss. Yet does Dickens avail himself of this, one of the clear benefits of present-tense writing, within the thirty-seven chapters of *Bleak House* that take this form, within what will turn out to be his career's most extended relationship with this temporal mode? He does not. He does, I grant you, make splendid use of its inherent advantages in rendering shock, horror, humor, and, once Bucket takes charge, speed—all quintessentially experiences of the moment—but joy? I don't think so.

No. For at least the first two-thirds of the text, the present-tense speaker mostly holds up its hands in dismay, and gives us a world in which presentness is dispiriting, to put it mildly: continual activity without progress, unceasing additions of particularities without order, a terrifying welter of motion without purpose. Jo, Guster, and Phil Squod are the true children of this present tense, produced by the momentary interaction of sex but radically without connection to an extended temporality of parental care, individuals thereby condemned to lives of meaningless movement, fractured consciousness, and relentless injury. Our last vision of Phil glimpses him putting the best possible spin, or rather, shine, on his lot, polishing away in a solitary "life of friction" in the stable yards of Chesney Wold (983). In other places, other art forms, other genres, other fictions, a moment of friction, even, dare I say it, the friction of one body with another, might be a cause for joy, might be captured in a rapturous textual evocation. But not here. Despite the potential offered by its formal allegiance to the moment, the present-tense narration finds nothing good to say about momentary pleasure.

And Esther? I could go on at length about the many different ways in which her narrative makes the case that it is morally reprehensible to experience moments without due cognizance of their necessary relationship to the past and the future, but to save space I'll just say "Skimpole." This novel's prime representative of a self-proclaiming Episodic is also its prime example of a deep-dyed hypocritical villain—and certainly the person that Esther hates above all others. Yet to offer just one other tiny illustration of the manner in which her text mounts its case against the pleasures of the moment, let us consider what it has to say about dancing, the activity that in certain circumstances can be a vertical expression of what is (usually) a horizontal activity. The sensuality of the dance, its bringing together of bodies in physical union, has offered artists of many kinds, in many times and places, the opportunity to represent sex by other means. It's an opportunity that even the generally hard-bitten present-tense narrator takes—although admittedly for the briefest of seconds, and only near the end of the text, and in retrospect to boot—the moment when that strapping sample of masculinity, Mr. George, "lies down in the state-bed of his brother's house" and is stirred to delicious confusion by "the images of his nieces (awful all the evening in their floating muslins), waltzing, after the German manner, over his counterpane" (954). But in Esther's text? Could there be a more anti-erotic, funny-but-pathetic site of dancing than Mr. Turveydrop's Academy? What does Caddy get when she runs away and marries for love but a ridiculous father figure, a parade of forlorn apprentices, a husband worn down to lameness, and, just to put the tin hat on it, a poor deaf-and-dumb baby? The only terms in which Esther can bring herself to redeem Caddy's life in the world of the dance are revealing: no appreciation for the sudden swirl of a sensuous skirt here, just sober praise for her long-term commitment to selfless labor, to her "course of industry and perseverance" (611).

Why does *Bleak House* find so many different ways to repudiate transitory joy? Psychoanalyst Adam Phillips maintains that the family, as currently understood, is basically about just two things, "bringing up children and regulating sexual relations." Yet these two aims, he argues, are opposed: "[I]n our erotic lives, we abandon our children, and in our familial lives, we abandon our desire."[8] In Dickens's career-long valorization of the idea of individuals being nurtured within a family, we witness the novelist's decision to put the weight on the child-minding side of the wheel. Of course, this is a commitment generally more represented in the breach than in the observance, but it is perhaps nowhere more apparent than in John Jarndyce's willed effort to make Bleak House into a home for Richard, Ada, and Esther. Yet taking the part of the child has catastrophic effects for eros. Let's return to that general truth about sex—its lack of interest in offspring (I am assuming, for the sake of argument, that "let's make a baby" is a fairly rare impetus for intercourse). It is this indifference, this carelessness about its possible result, a care-requiring being, that makes sex appear the way it does at the deep center of the novel: erotic abandon (which is to say, Hawdon and Honoria's coupling) is made absolutely identical to abandoning a child (which is to say, leaving Esther to a life without parents). The love between man and woman that *Bleak House* honors is not love in the moment but love that persists over time, love that issues, as Ada says, "from one unchanging heart" (608). In other words, it honors enduring, faithful, and responsible love, the kind of love, so the story goes, that creates a good environment for the supported development of an individual within a family home. But why should I be surprised that Dickens rigs the table the way he does? After all, he makes it clear from the very beginning, from the title he fixes over the entrance, that the House was always going to win. *Bleak House* is a novel that insists upon the primary importance of getting that house and its contents in order—spatially, on the level of the domestic and the nation, and temporally, in the moment and for the future. It is for this reason that sex is put behind a closed door and made monstrous, castigated for being the act that has created all the world's children, young and old alike, without thought for their necessary care.

That's the end of what I have to say about the internal constitution of *Bleak House*, but before I finish, I want to make three quick points to connect my ideas about the precise arrangements of Esther's "portion" to the question I was asking earlier. To recap: in what ways might novels that represent characters' consciousness of the temporal relation between the moments in their lives have affected how flesh-and-blood individuals have come to understand their own selves? I think Esther Woodcourt's narrative has an important presence in this process, but perhaps you'll object—the vast majority of people, you might say, are unlikely to go through the highly idiosyncratic travails of Esther's existence (laid aside for dead at birth, brought up by an unbending Calvinist aunt and an unfeeling nursemaid, etc., etc., etc.) and so how can the story of this life have the power to influence how others experience theirs? My three points are essentially defenses of my position, support for the idea that what might initially appear to be pathological, singular, and exceptional about Esther's narrative are actually, or have come to be, normative, representative, and exemplary characteristics.

In the first place, I counter the idea that Esther is a damaged peculiarity by noting that she is remarkably good at organizing not just herself but everything around her. Interestingly enough, it is Skimpole who nails her talents with the greatest nicety: "When I see you, my dear Miss Summerson," he comments, "intent upon the perfect working of the whole orderly system of which you are the centre, I feel inclined to say to myself—that's responsibility" (603). "Here is Miss Summerson," he declares on a subsequent occasion, "with a fine administrative capacity, and a knowledge of details perfectly surprising" (608). Behind the modesty-garment of her repeated and wearying self-deprecation, Esther conceals the shapely form of an extremely effective individual. It is not an identity that can be achieved without constant care and the full functioning of all her faculties—this is one of the points that I take Dickens to be making in those remarkable paragraphs in which Esther describes how her illness destroyed her ability to keep the chronology of her life in order—but if you put in the work and follow Esther's blueprint, you too could be the successful executive manager of not just yourself and your household but most likely of a sizable corporation as well.

While we are waiting for *The Esther Woodcourt Guide to Time Management* to appear on Amazon, we can move to my second point, and console ourselves with the fact that a text called something like *What Esther Thinks about Sex* has already enjoyed remarkably broad circulation. When we stood outside that door with our heroine earlier in this essay and listened to the sound of a couple within, I pointedly didn't say something that you may well have been thinking. Yet what is this scene, after all, but Freud's primal scene, a scene in which a child witnesses the lovemaking of its parents from a position of exclusion, experiences it as a frightening act of rejection and betrayal? As I mentioned earlier, Esther lives this moment twice over—first, as Esther Summerson, the self-in-formation, and second, as her achieved self, the grown-up Esther Woodcourt, a woman who has had full marital relations but who nevertheless still views sex from exactly the same position, the child's position. The theory that Freud got all his best ideas from his favorite novelist is not news. Dickensians have long suspected that the great man knew that something called "the Copperfield Complex" wouldn't quite cut it, so he opted instead to make strategic raids on those cultural heavyweights Sophocles and Shakespeare, but the connections between the Summerson Syndrome and Freud's concepts of normative psychological development are worth pondering.

Recognizing the novelistic ancestry of a widespread and powerfully influential model of the self helps us get closer to a turn in the feedback loop, a moment when a textual construction made its way into the domain of flesh and blood, and to wonder: at what costs have we received a version of adult individuality that views sex from the position of a child?

My third and final point consists largely of a quotation, a quotation from one of those foundational fictional autobiographies over which I casually jumped a good few pages back.

> I wish either my father or my mother, or indeed both of them, as they were in duty both equally bound to it, had minded what they were about when they begot me: had they duly consider'd how much depended upon what they were then doing;—that not only the production of a rational Being was concerned in it, but that possibly the happy formation and temperature of his body, perhaps his genius, and the very cast of his mind;—and, for aught they knew to the contrary, even the fortunes of his whole house might take their turn from the humours and dispositions which were then uppermost;—Had they duly weighed and considered all this, and proceeded accordingly,—I am verily persuaded I should have made quite a different figure in the world, from that in which the reader is likely to see me.[9]

In these, the opening words of *Tristram Shandy* (published in 1759), Sterne's eponymous hero begins his life story with one extreme version of the child's position, the individual's impossible desire for his parents to have been thinking precisely about *him* during the act that brought him into being. I bring Tristram into the picture to suggest that far from offering an exceptional case, Esther takes on the paradigm of all first-person narrators in her reaction to her own conception, a moment that was at once all about her and not about her at all. I found one of my starting points for this piece in Woloch's observation that childhood in *Bleak House*, *David Copperfield*, and *Great Expectations* "always begins with the narrating protagonist's troubled contemplation of his or her origin, highlighting the belated relationship each character has to a world that both has given rise to *and* only exists in-and-through his or her consciousness."[10] This remark reminds me of what my own children used to say when they were little when my husband or I referred to any incident that had happened to the two of us before they were born. "But what was I doing then?" they would ask indignantly. "Where was I?" I cite their comments not because I am a fondly doting mother who finds her children exceptional but because I think they voiced the common, the default response. Children—and first-person narrators—are understandably resistant to anything that precedes their own existence. "I begin the world," they say, and we answer, "Yes, the world began with you." Like any statements worth holding onto in this life, these words are absolutely true, and absolutely false, at the very same time. So perhaps *Bleak House* does turn out to be my Victorian novel after all. How could it not, when it has helped me to look into these matters, to think about the condition of being a child, an adult, a parent, and a wife; to speculate about my experiences of sex, time, and narrative? And if I've found anything worthwhile here, then perhaps the next time I read it, I will discover still more—even supposing—.

## NOTES

1. Charles Dickens, *Bleak House*, ed. Nicola Bradbury, 124. Further references will be given parenthetically.
2. James Wood, *How Fiction Works*, 113.
3. Charles Dickens, *Great Expectations*, 35.
4. Samuel Taylor Coleridge, "Dejection: An Ode," line 47.
5. Catherine Gallagher, "The Rise of Fictionality," 342; Daniel Defoe, *Robinson Crusoe*; Henry Fielding, *Joseph Andrews*, 189; Alex Woloch, *The One vs. the Many: Minor Characters and the Space of the Protagonist in the Novel.*
6. Galen Strawson, "Against Narrativity," 190.
7. John Jordan, *Supposing "Bleak House,"* chap. 1.
8. Adam Phillips, *Side Effects*, 72–73.
9. Laurence Sterne, *The Life and Opinions of Tristram Shandy, Gentleman*, 5.
10. Woloch, *One vs. the Many*, 190, emphasis in original.

## WORKS CITED

Coleridge, Samuel Taylor. "Dejection: An Ode." In *The Complete Poems*, edited by William Keach, 307–11. Harmondsworth, UK: Penguin, 1997.

Defoe, Daniel. *Robinson Crusoe*. Harmondsworth, UK: Penguin, 2004.

Dickens, Charles. *Bleak House*. Edited with an introduction by Nicola Bradbury. Preface by Terry Eagleton. Harmondsworth, UK: Penguin, 2003.

———. *Great Expectations*. Harmondsworth, UK: Penguin, 2004.

Fielding, Henry. *Joseph Andrews*. Harmondsworth, UK: Penguin, 1999.

Forster, E. M. *Aspects of the Novel*. Harmondsworth, UK: Penguin, 2000.

Gallagher, Catherine. "The Rise of Fictionality." In *The Novel*, edited by Franco Moretti, 1:336–63. Princeton: Princeton University Press, 2006.

Jordan, John. *Supposing "Bleak House."* Charlottesville: University of Virginia Press, 2013.

Phillips, Adam. *Side Effects*. New York: Harper Perennial, 2006.

Sterne, Laurence. *The Life and Opinions of Tristram Shandy, Gentleman*. Harmondsworth, UK: Penguin, 2003.

Strawson, Galen. "Against Narrativity." In *Real Materialism and Other Essays*, 189–208. Oxford: Clarendon Press, 2008.

Woloch, Alex. *The One vs. the Many: Minor Characters and the Space of the Protagonist in the Novel*. Princeton: Princeton University Press, 2003.

Wood, James. *How Fiction Works*. New York: Farrar, Straus & Giroux, 2008.

CHAPTER ELEVEN

# Liking *David Copperfield*

Michael J. Flynn

## On *David Copperfield* by Charles Dickens

> I do not find it easy to get sufficiently far away from this Book, in the first sensations of having finished it, to refer to it with the composure which this formal heading would seem to require. My interest in it, is so recent and strong; and my mind is so divided between pleasure and regret—pleasure in the achievement of a long design, regret in the separation from many companions—that I am in danger of wearying the reader whom I love, with personal confidences, and private emotions. . . .
> . . . Yet, I have nothing else to tell; unless, indeed, I were to confess (which might be of less moment still) that no one can ever believe this Narrative, in the reading, more than I have believed it in the writing.
>
> Charles Dickens, Preface to *David Copperfield*

My first experience with *David Copperfield* (1850) came in January 1995. A junior at a small liberal arts college in western Illinois, I'd more or less completed a history major by the end of my sophomore year and had started taking English classes mostly because there weren't many history courses left in the catalog. In winter term, I'd enrolled in a Victorian literature class taught by a professor I remembered fondly from an introductory liberal arts course a couple of years earlier. I certainly didn't sign up because of the content, which I didn't know much about. I have a vague recollection of having read in grade school what must have been an edited-for-children and heavily illustrated version of *Great Expectations*; its depiction of Miss Havisham's decaying room and single shoe sticks with me, though not much else does. I'd been assigned *Hard Times* in high school and hated it, because my school felt an awful lot like the Gradgrind-M'Choakumchild system of education, and the novel offered little hope of escaping that kind of environment. (To be fair, I did not try joining a circus.) And I'd seen the 1938 film version of *A Christmas Carol* so many times—Chicago's WGN ran it religiously on *Family Classics* during the holidays—that to this day I associate the story line with such off-putting sentimentality that I've never been tempted to read any of Dickens's Christmas books. That was the extent of my experience with Victorian literature.

So if I went into the class with any expectation at all, it was that I probably wasn't going to like *David Copperfield*, which was scheduled for early in the semester. It came as a shock, then, that I found myself enraptured from the very first page. I loved the heft of the book, which seemed to convey Dickens's confidence that he could draw me in and keep me in for the duration. I loved the sprawling cast of Dickensian grotesques who would reappear like old friends after long absences. I loved the humor, and the narrator's willingness to laugh even when the joke was on him. (My single favorite phrase in the entire Dickens canon comes in the second monthly installment, when the friendly waiter claims that he's heard of a student just like David, who's died in London at a school just like David's, and to David's query about how the boy died, responds, "With whopping."[1] Motiveless malignancy has never been funnier.) Most of all I loved the narrator's voice, which combined what I would later come to recognize as the richly rhetorical nature of Dickens's third-person style with a deeply felt first-person perspective. That voice made the novel infinitely more vibrant than the legal and political documents I'd been working with in my history classes; it rang in my head in a way that only Marlow's voice in *Heart of Darkness* (another novel whose plot is intimately connected with the traumas of its author's biography) has ever come close to doing. The best way I can put it is to echo Dickens's preface: the tangibility of that voice made me believe the narrative.

But the formative moment, the one that made me a Victorianist and has indelibly shaped the way I see the field, came halfway through the book, at the end of the tenth monthly number, when Steerforth eloped with Em'ly. I was totally unprepared for it. I shouldn't have been, if for no other reason than that I'd read *Hard Times* and seen Harthouse's attempted seduction of Louisa; I knew that that plot development was in Dickens's repertoire. But I was—unprepared, and absolutely devastated. I think I had an idea that Steerforth's lack of direction made him a problematic model for David, but I am sure I had no more suspicion of Steerforth brutally betraying his trust than David himself did. It came like a physical punch in the gut. We were reading the entire novel in just a week (I shudder at the thought of asking my own students to do that now), so I must have had a hundred and fifty pages to get through that night, but I was forced to put the book down, get up from my chair in the library, and take a walk. And though it may not be to my credit, I have to admit that when I came back and picked the book up again, I found some solace in the fact that David felt about the betrayal much the way I did—that the "greater loss" of chapter 31 was not Em'ly but Steerforth, and that "I never had loved Steerforth better than when the ties that bound me to him were broken" (380, 388). I felt personally betrayed, as David did, but was, like David, less angry than sad, because the betrayal meant that one of my favorite characters was not going to reappear in those pages for a very long time.

The physical characteristics of my copy of *Copperfield* reinforced the rupture at the center of the book. We'd been assigned the old Penguin English Library edition (readers of my generation and the one before will remember the series' distinctive orange spines), and whether my individual copy was getting old or the glue holding those cheaply constructed books together was, as a general rule, better suited to titles the length of *The Warden* than to *Copperfield*, I don't know. But the cover detached itself from the rest of the book before I'd gotten very far into the novel, and without that card stock to reinforce the spine, the thing split in two as I was reading it. The point at which it split was bound to be the point of greatest physical stress, the halfway point of the book—which, in the case of *Copperfield*, coincides with the moment of greatest emotional stress, the revelation of Steerforth's betrayal at the end of the tenth number. That revelation had literally torn my book in half.

It was the emotional power of that moment that made me add English as a second major, and then go to graduate school in literature rather than in history. I'd enjoyed my history classes, but I'd never had a moment in them where, to paraphrase Dickens's preface once again, I'd found it hard to get sufficiently far away from a book to refer to it with composure. It was the emotional power of Steerforth's betrayal that made me a Victorianist; as I took classes in other periods of literature, I came to understand that not every era was as interested in making me believe a narrative as the Victorian period was.

I reread the novel in 2000 or 2001, while studying for my PhD comprehensive exam. I'd taped my Penguin copy together as best I could, but trying to read a thousand-page book that was falling apart at the seams was impractical, and I replaced it. Still, my second reading of the book was colored from the outset by that physical reminder of the story's central event, and I found myself shrinking from what was to come in much the same way that David does as he begins the chapter containing it:

> A dread falls on me here. A cloud is lowering on the distant town, towards which I retrace my solitary steps. I fear to approach it. I cannot bear to think of what did come, upon that memorable night; of what must come again, if I go on.
>
> It is no worse, because I write of it. It would be no better, if I stopped my most unwilling hand. It is done. Nothing can undo it; nothing can make it otherwise than as it was. (382)

It's a passage I didn't especially remember from my first reading of the novel; I was, on that occasion, experiencing the story as the *narrated* David experiences his life, knowing what's past but not what is to come. But it hit me hard my second time through because I was now experiencing the story as the *narrating* David does, knowing what is to come, anticipating the shock that his past self felt when it did come, and also, crucially, reexperiencing that shock. The jumbling of tenses in this passage is typical of the syntax used to describe moments of stress in *Copperfield*, particularly in the first half of the book. The first sentence's present tense clearly belongs to the recollecting, narrating David. But the second sentence's present tense is harder to parse: there is a metaphorical cloud, synonymous and contemporaneous with the dread the narrating David feels in the previous sentence; but as we learn two paragraphs later, that night was a wild one, so there's also a literal cloud that existed in the past but is reexperienced by the narrating David as if he were the narrated David walking toward Yarmouth. The present tense in the second half of that sentence is just as muddled. Dickens wrote "retrace" in the manuscript, and modern scholarly editions often privilege that reading. But the original compositor, understandably confused by the passage, substituted "retraced," and Dickens, who closely revised the proofs of the novel, didn't catch or correct the change, which thus appeared in the first edition and all subsequent ones in his lifetime. Neither reading is obviously the right one, because David is both remembering the walk back to Mr. Peggotty's house and viscerally reliving it. He frets about "what must come again, if I go on," but it's impossible to say whether the "going on" refers to his past feet taking "solitary steps" or to his present "unwilling hand" moving the pen.

Such jumbling of tenses, which is clearly indebted to Wordsworthian ideas about a poet's uniquely intense memory, occurs over and over in the novel. The most amazing example comes at the end of chapter 11, when David, winding up his—and Dickens's—traumatic memories of the blacking warehouse, thinks about London streets, "the stones of which may, for anything I know, be worn at this moment by my childish feet" (145). Are the stones worn down in the present because he trod them in the past? Is the adult David's memory so intense that even his mental image of past feet can start physically eroding stones in the present? Are the ten-year-old David's haunted walks through London the real present tense of the novel, and everything that happens afterward, up to and including the writing of this passage, just a proleptic daydream running through his mind as he wanders? These temporally complex passages have become important to me because on every reading of *Copperfield* since that second one, I feel something similar: an intense emotional experience that's compounded because I'm identifying with both the older David, who knows about and dreads Steerforth's betrayal, and the young David, who gut-wrenchingly experiences it for the first time at the end of the tenth number.

My career path changed after my second reading of the novel, just as it had after my first. I'd thought I was going to write a dissertation about the influence of Evangelical thought on the narrative structure of Victorian poetry, but after rereading *Copperfield*, I came to feel about that topic the way I'd started to feel about my history major in 1995: it was not very hard to get sufficiently far away from it to refer to it with composure. I've been a Dickensian ever since. And *Copperfield*'s midpoint became crucial to my understanding of nineteenth-century literature. One of the questions on my comprehensive exam asked me to outline a survey of the period and to discuss one text that would serve as a centerpiece of the course. I chose *Copperfield* and talked about how the end of the tenth number is the midpoint of the novel (it has twenty parts), of Dickens's career (it comes halfway through the eighth of his fifteen novels), and of the century (the tenth number was published on January 31, 1850). I argued that the book's center is useful for teaching the shift from the romantic (the heroic Steerforth, the idealized Dora, the dreamy *Arabian Nights* retelling of eighteenth-century novels) to the Victorian (the pragmatic Traddles, the practical Agnes, the earnest composition of original and socially engaged fiction). And I wrote about how the betrayal is a crucial turning point between the autobiographical first half of the novel, which is similar to Wordsworth's *Prelude* in many ways, and the very different second half, which multiplies and intertwines plotlines in a dry run for *Bleak House* and much other mid-Victorian fiction. I wrote a chapter on the book for my dissertation; I've published on it; I've taught it more than any novel other than *The Woman in White*, despite the practical difficulties of assigning a thousand-page monthly-part novel in the confines of a sixteen-week semester.

My belief in the narrative thus hasn't prevented a critical perspective on it. I am able to get sufficiently far away from the novel to see things that neither the narrated nor the narrating David can. But I do not find it easy to get that distance. I've read the novel, as far as I can figure, nearly a dozen times, and it doesn't matter whether I'm teaching it in a survey of British fiction, a single-author course on Dickens, or a seminar on serial technique: every time I read it, I find myself becoming more and more deeply attached to Steerforth as I get closer to that tenth number, feeling sick to my stomach when I reach his betrayal, and mourning the fact that I'll never again see him alive as I move on to the second half of the narrative. That emotional echo of my first time through the book is what makes it my Victorian novel.

But *Copperfield* teaches differently now than it did even five or ten years ago. When I reach the tenth number in class, I sometimes ask my students how they responded to it, and offer up my own first experience with the book. No one has ever admitted to having the visceral reaction I did to either the novel as a whole or the betrayal scene in particular (which is okay, because no one ever loves your favorite book as much as you do, and you don't really want them to). But over the twelve years of my career, my students' typical response to my first reading of *Copperfield* has shifted away from bemusement and toward bewilderment, and when I last taught the novel to a mixture of graduate students and advanced undergrads in the fall of 2017, the class as a whole was simply incredulous. How on earth, they objected, could I have failed to see the seduction coming given

David's dark hint about Em'ly's future in chapter 3, or Steerforth's predatory wish that David had a sister in chapter 6, or Agnes's overt warning about Steerforth in chapter 25? They were all reading the novel for the first time, just like I'd been. Most of them had no more experience with Victorian literature than I'd had. But they'd picked up on enough hints to see the seduction coming. How could I have failed to do so?

Obviously, my students are correct in asserting that there are lots of places in the book where David reveals upcoming plot points—not through veiled or symbolic foreshadowing, though there is some of that, but in overt proleptic pronouncements. Such pronouncements are not solely concerned with the climactic betrayal: the narrating David discloses Em'ly's dark future in the first monthly number (31), but he also reveals that "by-and-by" his aunt will appear in the narrative, that his mother will be altered for the worse and then die, and that in going with Peggotty to visit Yarmouth, he is leaving his happy home forever (2, 21, 23). The novel admits right away that it is a retrospective narrative and conditions readers to expect occasional revelations of the future. But all these other revelations are short-term prolepses. David's aunt appears in the narrative just three paragraphs after he says she will, presides over his birth, walks off, and, David says twice, "never came back" (11). It's entirely possible that, at this point in the novel's composition, Dickens didn't envision Miss Betsey playing any bigger role in the plot than does the caul of the novel's first page, and that he had nothing but this scene in mind when he has David say that she'll appear "by-and-by." David's happy home has crumbled by the end of the first number. His mother is already being crushed by Murdstone's firm hand in the very first pages of the second, and she dies in the third, following another short-term proleptic statement that David's happy afternoon with her on his returning home from school was "the last of its race, and destined evermore to close that volume of my life" (99). If readers are conditioned by such passages to expect that the narrating David will occasionally reveal what is to come, they are also trained to expect that the future will follow its revelation in fairly short order. They are not trained to remember such revelations for hundreds of pages, as they need to do if they are to anticipate the seduction of Em'ly.

Dickens also works to efface the warning about Em'ly immediately after David sounds it, in a technique that is repeated over and over in *Copperfield*. In the third chapter of the novel, Em'ly runs out onto a jagged timber overhanging the North Sea; the narrated David fears she is "springing forward to her destruction," and then the narrating David inserts his proleptic thoughts:

> There has been a time since—I do not say it lasted long, but it has been—when I have asked myself the question, would it have been better for little Em'ly to have had the waters close above her head that morning in my sight; and when I have answered, Yes, it would have been.
>
> This may be premature. I have set it down too soon, perhaps. But let it stand. (31)

The narrating David's decision to let it stand is what first alerts my students to the coming seduction. But as portentous as the passage is, the paragraphs following it tend to obscure it as they recount the true, tender, pure, disinterested love of the young narrated David for Em'ly, and wind up with the reflection, "As to any sense of inequality, or youthfulness, or other difficulty in our way, little Em'ly and I had no such trouble, because we had no future. We made no more provision for growing older, than we did for growing younger" (32). Immediately after the narrating David prematurely looks ahead, he asks readers to join him in not looking ahead.

The passage about Steerforth that ends the second number may ominously note that for the narrated David, "[n]o veiled future dimly glanced upon him in the moonbeams. There was no shadowy picture of his footsteps, in the garden that I dreamed of walking in all night" (76). But at proof stage Dickens deleted an additional phrase—"the garden that I picked up shells and pebbles in, with little Em'ly, all night" (76n2)—which would have made it easier for readers to connect Steerforth with Em'ly at this point. And then the third number, which drops plenty of hints showing that the narrating David can see Steerforth's character flaws, insistently follows each one with the narrated David's adoration of him. Steerforth laughs in church, but David wishes that he, not Traddles, could have had the honor of covering for him (78–79). Steerforth inconveniences David by making him, Scheherazade-like, recount his favorite books, but David's admission of the drawbacks of this arrangement are followed by an account of its benefits, and his confession that the storytelling encouraged him to be romantic and dreamy is obscured by the subsequent analysis of the boost it gave to his self-esteem and energy (80–81). In the scene where Steerforth denounces Mr. Mell, almost every instance of hesitation about the propriety of Steerforth's behavior is followed by a description of how noble and gallant he is, and the narrating David effaces the scene's final word of pity for Mr. Mell with the admission that the narrated David "soon forgot him in the contemplation of Steerforth" (87). So does the narrating David, and so do his readers—Mr. Mell is not mentioned again until the penultimate chapter of the book, which was originally published a full sixteen months after the confrontation scene.

Agnes's warning about Steerforth is where the novel's pattern of obscuring its own premonitions is most structurally prominent. The eighth number ends with David getting drunk at the dinner party he throws for Steerforth; the ninth begins with a chapter titled "Good and Bad Angels," in which David makes it quite clear that Agnes is his good angel and she warns him that Steerforth is his bad one (312–13). This conversation, my students felt, should have warned me about Steerforth's upcoming treachery, even if nothing else had. But it is followed by the narrated David's insistence that "[i]t was a great relief to me . . . to enlarge on the obligation that I owed to Steerforth for his care of me when I was unable to take care of myself" and then by an abrupt shift to the revelation of Uriah Heep's revolting scheme to marry Agnes, which occupies the remaining nine-tenths of the chapter (314). The narrated David finds this plan so abhorrent that he fantasizes throwing a bootjack at Uriah and running him through with a poker (323, 326, 328), and, crucially, imagines him as "some meaner quality of devil" or an "evil genius," in the sense of a ministering spirit (328, 330). The narrated David's visceral loathing of Uriah, in other words, turns Uriah into the "bad angel" of the title and lets Steerforth, whom readers have been explicitly warned against, slip from view. Dickens's note to himself in his plans for the ninth number—"No Steerforth this time. Keep him out" (app., 764)—literally underscores what a conscious decision this was: the novel's readers are being manipulated toward a position where the betrayal will come as a surprise, even though it really shouldn't.

The tenth number keeps the pattern going to the very last minute. In chapter 29 the narrating David unmistakably reveals that a rupture with Steerforth is about to take place:

> He was fast asleep; lying, easily, with his head upon his arm, as I had often seen him lie at school.
>
> The time came in its season, and that was very soon, when I almost wondered that nothing troubled his repose, as I looked at him. But he slept—let

> me think of him so again—as I had often seen him sleep at school; and thus, in this silent hour, I left him.
>
> —Never more, oh God forgive you, Steerforth! to touch that passive hand in love and friendship. Never, never, more! (373)

But chapter 30 again keeps Steerforth out, and distracts David with the sentimental death of Mr. Barkis. As in the previous number, immediate emotion felt by the narrated David is used to obfuscate rational knowledge possessed, and revealed prematurely, by the narrating David.

When my students expressed incredulity about my first reading of *David Copperfield*, the unspoken subtext was surprise that a PhD and professor could have been such a poor reader of the novel. (To which one obvious response is, no one was always a PhD.) But I would like to suggest that my initial reading was not poorer than theirs—it was just different. The narrator of *Copperfield* occupies what should be two antithetical positions: the narrating David employs a series of cues that serve as forewarnings of upcoming plot events, but he also uses cues that invite readers to emotionally identify with the narrated David and thus to experience plot events as if they were complete surprises. I and my students each responded to one set of cues, and deemphasized, effaced, or forgot the other.

The nature of memory and its relation to *David Copperfield*'s narrative structure and voice is a longstanding critical concern, but examinations of forgetting in the book are rarer. Nicholas Dames's *Amnesiac Selves* argues that midcentury fictional autobiographies like *Copperfield* were heavily influenced by nineteenth-century associationist psychology. They're built around the assumption that events in a person's life that recur, or that parallel other events, or that turn out to be predictive of future events, will be the ones that stick in that person's memory. Trivial, random, or otherwise unassimilable events (those that aren't "associated" with other events) will be forgotten. The literary result of these assumptions is that in novels written from a retrospective first-person point of view, memory works teleologically. The events that David remembers are the ones that will be relevant to the plot and/or to the formation of his single, integral self as he understands it at the time of writing: Agnes's warning is remembered because it predicts the climactic betrayal and teaches David that an aristocratic dilettante like Steerforth must be a bad angel to the earnest bourgeois writer David prides himself on becoming. Unassimilable events may be remembered by pathological characters such as Mr. Dick, who can't keep the figure of King Charles out of his head, but they will be simply forgotten by healthy characters like David.[2] Moreover, Dames argues, these fictional autobiographies train readers in the same art of selective forgetting practiced by the narrators: any thousand-page novel is bound to have unassimilable material, but readers are taught to nostalgically remember only "a carefully whittled-down, diluted set of vague facts that then work retrospectively to cast a haze over the mistakes, chaos, and loss that might have been a part of the narrative's fabric."[3]

The argument doesn't match my experience with *Copperfield*. I remember precisely the mistakes, chaos, and loss that Dames says nostalgic readers are trained to forget. His assertion that associationist psychology always recognizes the past as past, and thereby clearly distinguishes Dickensian retrospection from Wordsworthian memory, takes into account none of the syntactically and temporally tangled passages that have so attracted me since my second reading of the book. My *David Copperfield* is better described by an opinion Robin Gilmour put forth long ago in a formative article about the novel: he felt that the structural bent of the book may be teleological, focused on showing how David becomes a good Victorian middle-class man, but that its emotional core resides in those places where the narrating David loses himself in the immediacy of remembered emotion or in the confusion of memories he has trouble assimilating into his bildungsroman.[4]

On the other hand, Dames's argument that associationist novels train readers to view them nostalgically does explain the way my students read the Steerforth plot. I don't want to imply that what those students remember are "vague facts," because they can point to very specific proleptic passages. But they absolutely suppress "mistakes" such as the narrated David's defenses of Steerforth in favor of teleological passages that display the narrating David's knowledge of the betrayal. Dames's ideas fit my students' responses to other parts of the novel as well. Every time I teach the book, my classes seem more eager to discuss the four "retrospective" chapters, which Dames points to as perfect examples of associative memory boiling down the messy details of life to only those events that propel the protagonist forward toward his future self. And they typically have difficulty approaching chaotic moments like the passage about David's childish feet wearing the stones of London's streets.

The thing is, Dames's argument really shouldn't explain the way my current students read *Copperfield*. He reminds us that associationist psychology was scientifically obsolete by the early twentieth century, and that from the modernist period on, literature has presented "fictional or autobiographical consciousnesses" that are "temporally, and perhaps temperamentally, closer to us"—by which he means that Proust, for instance, better understands the uncontrolled, unassimilated presence of what we currently call traumatic memories.[5] I don't want to claim that my first reading of *Copperfield* rises to the level of trauma, but the continual re-eruption of my initial response to the novel is something that can be understood and anticipated via twenty-first-century theories of memory. My twenty-first-century students, however, are reading like what Dames describes as a nineteenth-century audience well trained by associationism.

In the brief conclusion to his book, Dames tries to explain such paradoxes by saying that the distance of modern readers from comfortingly teleological associationist understandings of memory and self is precisely what makes such readers nostalgic for novels that model nostalgia.[6] But I wonder whether a more direct argument might be made—whether my current students are actually returning to an associationist way of thinking rather than speeding away from it. After all, these students have grown up in a world where the primary site of autobiography is social media, which Dames couldn't have foreseen in 2001 and which would have sounded like science fiction to me in 1995 (email only arrived on campus six months after I first read *Copperfield*).

It may seem odd to suggest that students who've grown up in the world of Web 2.0 are conditioned to read a Victorian bildungsroman from a nineteenth-century perspective and to deemphasize its unassimilable material, which we might have expected them to be more comfortable with than were Dickens's original readers. But media scholars argue that around 2008, social-networking sites began a structural shift away from user-managed databases, which allow the nontemporal presentation of multiple selves, toward algorithm-generated narratives, which tell teleological stories about singular, unified selves. That is, they began a shift toward something like electronic versions of associationist memory. Facebook features prominently in accounts of this shift. Its real-name policy was famously defended by Mark Zuckerberg in 2010 under the rationale that "[y]ou have one identity. . . . Having two identities for yourself is an example of a lack of integrity." And its rollout of Timeline in 2011 (right about the time that my current students were entering their formative teen years) reorganized everyone's page into a chronological format and used proprietary algorithms to decide which past data was most important: older content, Zuckerberg explained, would be summarized so as to reflect "only the most important things from your life." Facebook keeps its algorithms secret, but Zuckerberg's brief account of them suggests that they work teleologically, analyzing a mass of present data and then selectively forgetting past data that doesn't appear to be associated with it.[7]

Clearly those algorithms can make choices that don't match users' own narratives about their pasts. Since 2012, when Facebook started showing users their Years in Review, we've all heard stories about people being forcibly reminded of things they would have preferred to forget—romantic breakups, for instance. (The last spate of complaints occurred in the fall of 2017, after Apple's iOS 11 started spontaneously showing users packaged Memories—picture albums that it had assembled by algorithmically selecting and editing what it saw as important photos on their phones. The operating system was thus deciding not only what users should remember, but also when they should remember it. This was happening just as my students were arguing that I hadn't read *Copperfield* teleologically enough.) The speed with which these outcries die down, however, suggests that we are coming to accept an enforced teleological paradigm that puts us "in a place where the self is paradoxically always unfinished and about to be contributed to by multiple authors and agents, but also cloaked in the illusion of a timeline that neatly plots life according to earmarked highlights, low points, and milestones."[8]

The increasingly linear narratives spun by social media might help explain why, over the last ten years, my students have increasingly privileged the teleological passages of *David Copperfield* over the unassimilable ones. David's proleptic statements about Steerforth's seduction of Em'ly presage an appalling betrayal, but they also demonstrate David's reassuring ability to incorporate that betrayal into a controlled narrative pointing toward a future, coherent self: the seduction prods David to stop imitating Steerforth's dilettantism and to turn instead toward a bourgeois work ethic. The increasing linearity of social media might help explain why my last group of students were so focused on the teleological passages that one of them could tell me—even after the revelation of his plot to marry Agnes—that she wasn't convinced Uriah Heep was a villain, since the narrating David had never given her any proleptic warnings about him the way he does about Steerforth. (It's hard for me to express how bizarre that sounded to me. I still squirm, just as the narrated David does, at the mere thought of Uriah's clammy hands.) It might help explain why today's students are so drawn to the retrospective chapters, which, of course, are not all that different from Facebook's Years in Review.

The overshadowing of the traditional humanist self, usually thought of as autonomous, by the modern digital self, liable "to be contributed to by multiple authors and agents," might also be relevant to my current students' reading of *Copperfield*. When I teach the book in my survey of the British novel, as I did in the fall of 2017, I typically draw on my comprehensive exam and call attention to the way the bildungsroman of the first half morphs into a multiplot structure after Steerforth's betrayal. In the past, students haven't seen this on their own; they have tended to assume, thinking back to the novel's opening words, that David is the hero of his own life and that his hesitation to formally anoint himself with that label is just modesty. But once I draw attention to the chapter where it falls to Mr. Dick to reconcile Doctor Strong and Annie because David thinks his suspicion of her infidelity is "[t]oo delicate and difficult a subject" for a respectable middle-class man to interfere in, they're usually quick to recognize how marginalized David becomes in the second half of the novel (558). Mr. Peggotty and Martha find Em'ly because David claims he wouldn't know where to look for prostitutes in London (577); Mr. Micawber and Traddles unravel Uriah's plots by themselves, even though David claims to "assist at an explosion" (633) and does not correct Uriah's belief that he is "the prime mover in the discovery" (646); Ham has a final engagement with Steerforth in the tempest while David runs "wildly up and down along the beach, crying for help where no help could be" (679).

In the fall of 2017, however, my students didn't much care whether David was personally involved in the legal maneuvers to unmask Uriah. David was invited to be at "the explosion," he attended it, was gratified by it, and, most importantly, recorded it, and that was enough for them to accept that he was the hero of the scene. That response is surely inflected by their own self-narratives on Facebook or Twitter, which are full of points, not where they've personally done something, but where they've liked, retweeted, or commented on something done by a friend they're following. To students who've spent most of their lives as networked selves, David's move into a similar kind of identity doesn't signal a loss of autonomy; the book appears under his name, and that makes him its hero even if he's less active than other characters within its pages.

David's network functions in another way that should feel right at home to today's social media users. He is famously reticent about his career as an author:

> In pursuance of my intention of referring to my own fictions only when their course should incidentally connect itself with the progress of my story, I do not enter on the aspirations, the delights, anxieties, and triumphs, of my art. That I truly devoted myself to it with my strongest earnestness, and bestowed upon it every energy of my soul, I have already said. If the books I have written be of any worth, they will supply the rest. (723)

I've always accepted at face value David's assertion that his autobiography avoids the subject of his literary work, but on rereading the book while thinking about social media culture, I find myself reassessing. David may not talk much about the aspirations, delights, or anxieties of his writing career, but the second half of the novel is significantly more forthcoming about his triumphs. Not much of the evidence comes in David's own words, to be sure, but as he is "liking" other people's actions in the book's multiplot second half, he makes absolutely sure that we know how many people "like" him back. Mrs. Steerforth (575), Mr. Micawber (598, 746–47), Mrs. Micawber (601), Mr. Omer (627), Agnes (698, 721), Traddles (704), and Mr. Chillip (712) all comment about how famous David has become, as do various unnamed English travelers who visit him during his three-year retreat in Switzerland (699). David also informs us that he gets fan mail by the bushel (723). Only Agnes, in obliquely implying that David's books are social-purpose novels, says anything even remotely substantive about their content (722). The rest of the characters merely testify in an agglomerative way to David's popularity, in the same way a like count or a follower count does in social media. David's autonomous self may be diffused among a network of friends in *Copperfield*'s second half, but his networked self gains authority because of just how widely he has been diffused.

All this makes me wonder how I appear when I "like" the novel in a class full of students raised on social media. I rarely discuss my personal feelings about what I teach. (I doubt that I'd be able to get students all the way through *Pamela*, for instance, if I told them how insipid I find it.) Does that reticence make me a curmudgeon who is too frugal with his Like button? Does my "liking" *Copperfield* come off as transactional, teaching it as I do at the end of a semester, when students are getting ready to fill out online evaluations—which are in large part just opportunities for them to "like" me? When I do talk about my love for this novel, I feel that I'm making an intimate and qualitative confession; are my students reducing this to one impersonal tick, a single "like," in what for them needs to be a collective, quantitative judgment about the value of the novel?

And if my current students are being conditioned by social media to read retrospective narrative from an associationist viewpoint, how might that affect their understanding of the story I'm telling them about my own past? After all, I'm talking about my personal history and experience, just as David is. I'm asserting that my initial reaction to Steerforth's betrayal persists as an emotional echo when I reread the book, just as David is claiming that his childhood feelings come flooding back when he reviews his own life. But my students are increasingly privileging the forward-looking cues in *David Copperfield*, and either effacing the unassimilable ones in which David loses himself in his past experiences, or reading them as simple mistakes that need to be grown out of and learned from. Does that mean that they're also likely to efface my admission about my emotional initial reading, or to understand it as just a phase that needed to be overcome before I could go on to a PhD?

The very qualities that make me like *David Copperfield*, then, have made it an increasingly tricky book to talk about liking. I'd be especially disappointed if my graduate students thought that an emotional reaction of the sort that Dickens describes in his preface—believing in a book, finding it hard to get sufficiently far away from it—is something to be outgrown on a teleological trip toward a doctorate. I could never have taught *Copperfield* effectively after just that first emotional reading. I needed to get more distance from it than I had when my interest in it was so recent and strong. But I wouldn't have wanted to teach it as often as I have, had the emotional impact of that first reading not come back to me anew every time I've approached the book. I'd much rather that my students view my initial faith in Steerforth the way the narrating David does his love for Dora: "There is no doubt whatever that I was a lackadaisical young spooney; but there was a purity of heart in all this still, that prevents my having quite a contemptuous recollection of it, let me laugh as I may" (336).

## NOTES

1. Charles Dickens, *David Copperfield*, ed. Nina Burgis, 59. Further references will be given parenthetically.

2. Nicholas Dames, *Amnesiac Selves: Nostalgia, Forgetting, and British Fiction, 1810–1870*, 125–48.

3. Dames, *Amnesiac Selves*, 237–38. Dames makes a related argument in *The Physiology of the Novel: Reading, Neural Science, and the Form of Victorian Fiction*, 73–122.

4. Robin Gilmour, "Memory in *David Copperfield*."

5. Dames, *Amnesiac Selves*, 126–27, 164–66.

6. Dames, *Amnesiac Selves*, 236–37.

7. Laurie McNeill, "There Is No 'I' in Network: Social Networking Sites and Posthuman Auto/Biography"; José van Dijck, "'You Have One Identity': Performing the Self on Facebook and LinkedIn"; José van Dijck, *The Culture of Connectivity: A Critical History of Social Media*, 54–56; Andreas Kitzmann, "The Machines That Write Us: Social Media and the Evolution of the Autobiographical Impulse."

8. Kitzmann, "Machines," 425.

## WORKS CITED

Dames, Nicholas. *Amnesiac Selves: Nostalgia, Forgetting, and British Fiction, 1810–1870*. New York: Oxford University Press, 2001.

———. *The Physiology of the Novel: Reading, Neural Science, and the Form of Victorian Fiction*. New York: Oxford University Press, 2007.

Dickens, Charles. *David Copperfield*. Edited by Nina Burgis. Oxford: Clarendon, 1981.

Dijck, José van. *The Culture of Connectivity: A Critical History of Social Media*. Oxford: Oxford University Press, 2013.

———. "'You Have One Identity': Performing the Self on Facebook and LinkedIn." *Media, Culture & Society* 35.2 (2013): 199–215.

Gilmour, Robin. "Memory in *David Copperfield*." *Dickensian* 71 (1975): 30–42.

Kitzmann, Andreas. "The Machines That Write Us: Social Media and the Evolution of the Autobiographical Impulse." In *A History of English Autobiography*, edited by Adam Smyth, 417–31. Cambridge: Cambridge University Press, 2016.

McNeill, Laurie. "There Is No 'I' in Network: Social Networking Sites and Posthuman Auto/Biography." *Biography* 35.1 (Winter 2012): 65–82.

CHAPTER TWELVE

# Endless Circling, Perpetual Beginning

Tom Ue

## On *New Grub Street* by George Gissing

Early on in Gissing's *New Grub Street* (1891), the narrator describes an experience with which writers can readily relate:

> There were floating in his mind five or six possible subjects for a book, all dating back to the time when he first began novel-writing, when ideas came freshly to him. If he grasped desperately at one of these, and did his best to develop it, for a day or two he could almost content himself; characters, situations, lines of motive, were laboriously schemed, and he felt ready to begin writing. But scarcely had he done a chapter or two when all the structure fell into flatness. He had made a mistake. Not this story, but that other one, was what he should have taken. The other one in question, left out of mind for a time, had come back with a face of new possibility . . .
>
> For months he had been living in this way; endless circling, perpetual beginning, followed by frustration. A sign of exhaustion, it of course made exhaustion more complete.[1]

Edwin Reardon's writer's block arises out of a surplus of ideas, out of his dissatisfaction with his current writing and the lure of alternative storylines. Outside of his fiction, he searches similarly for the life that he might have led. He suspects, some pages later, that he and Amy could have endured poverty had it not been for their child, Willie: "It is natural in a weak and sensitive man to dream of possibilities disturbed by the force of circumstance. For one hour which he gave to conflict with his present difficulties, Reardon spent many in contemplation of the happiness that might have been" (188–89).[2] He returns to this particular counterfactual following

Willie's death: "Poor little Willie had been the cause of the first coldness between him and Amy; her love for him had given place to a mother's love for the child. Now it would be as in the first days of their marriage; they would again be all in all to each other" (438). Reardon imagines a future by means of envisioning, and returning to, an alternative past. Neither he nor we, as readers, will ever know if the lives that he did not lead would have been as successful as he expects, but it is the plurality—in these two scenes and beyond—that first attracted and that has continued to attract me to Gissing. His concerns regarding the survival of art in an increasingly commercial age are strikingly contemporary: Jasper Milvain in his disregard for ideals would have been at home in the publishing world of Joël Dicker's *The Truth about the Harry Quebert Affair* (2012) and its adaptation for television (2018); and Dan Gilroy's new film *Velvet Buzzsaw* (2019) finds a supernatural agency preying on those who try to profit off a deceased artist's works.[3] The notion of returning to one's past, as Gissing conceives it, is universal: we all wonder, perhaps less ruefully and regularly than Reardon, about the decisions that we have made and that have led us to the present.

Part of the reward of reading Gissing stems from his play on, and resistance to, stable meanings. In what follows, I revisit some of my own experiences with studying, and now teaching, *New Grub Street* to foreground some of the demands that it makes, and to suggest some of the ways in which it invites reading and rereading. I begin by examining Gissing's approaches to the life of writing, before attending to his engagement with the past, his experiments with form, how our reading is shaped by new developments, and finally some of my experiences with teaching the novel. My central claim is that the novel, in its hospitality to diverging interpretations, thematizes the reading process and thus challenges us to revisit the novel and see the extent to which our readings have held up. *New Grub Street* was written during a period of intense creativity and productivity for Gissing, and it speaks to his bookish inclinations, which were developed from an early age. The eldest of five children, Gissing was educated at Lindow Grove in Cheshire (1871–1872) and at Owens College (1872–1875). Not only was Gissing well taught in languages ancient and modern, but he was also actively involved in extracurricular activities: he directed and performed school productions, and wrote and delivered scholarly papers. His academic career was terminated prematurely when, on May 31, 1876, he was apprehended for stealing from Owens College's locker rooms: these funds were meant for Marianne Helen ("Nell") Harrison, a young prostitute. Following his imprisonment, he went to America, where he taught French, German, and English in Massachusetts. Through Whelpdale's adventures in *New Grub Street*, Gissing would revisit some of his adventures in Chicago, where he found himself desperate and penniless, and where he published a number of short stories. Gissing returned to England in 1877, and married Nell in 1879. Often working as a private tutor, he wrote a succession of powerful working-class novels, including *Workers in the Dawn* (1880) and *The Nether World* (1889). Gissing and Nell separated in 1884, and she died in a Lambeth slum in 1888. In 1891, Gissing married Edith Underwood, an uneducated young woman who became mother to his children, Walter and Alfred.

I first encountered Gissing and *New Grub Street* in an undergraduate course on the Victorian novel after 1860 at the University of Toronto Scarborough (UTSC). The book provided us with a useful point-of-entry into the historical period: Gissing was an astute social commentator, and he productively incorporates conversations as a means for dramatizing different viewpoints on contemporaneous issues. In a chapter titled "Married Woman's Property," for instance, he specifically addresses the act of 1882, prior to which "all of a woman's property passed into the legal possession of her husband upon their marriage" (357n1).[4] Gissing brings together a number of opposing views. At this stage in the novel, Amy has separated from Reardon, and so she is pleased with the act when she learns that she has inherited ten thousand pounds from her uncle. However, her immediate reaction gives way to kinder feelings—"The thought of her husband in his squalid lodgings tempted her to forget injuries and disillusions, and to play the part of a generous wife"—alternating with skepticism "that he would lapse into a life of scholarly self-indulgence, such as he had often told her was his ideal" (358). In further conversations with Mrs. Carter, Amy complains about the limited ability of married people to separate and to have their premarital freedoms restored. Amy dismisses Mrs. Carter's qualms that "it would lead to all sorts of troubles":

> "So people say about every new step in civilisation. What would have been thought twenty years ago of a proposal to make all married women independent of their husbands in money matters? All sorts of absurd dangers

> were foreseen, no doubt. And it's the same now about divorce. In America people can get divorced if they don't suit each other—at all events in some of the States—and does any harm come of it? Just the opposite I should think." (359)

As scholars such as Stephen Arata have remarked, divorce remained uncommon in England even after the divorce act of 1857, and the only grounds for it were a wife's adultery or adultery combined with intensified cruelty by the husband (359n1). Neither Amy nor any other character in the novel needs divorce—Amy reunites with Reardon prior to his death—but, as we see here, Gissing dexterously explores a contemporary issue which lends itself to multiple, conflicting perspectives, and provides us with an index into his characters' psychology.

Alongside my scholarly work, I was developing an interest in journalism, and I became a regular contributor to *The Underground*, the UTSC's official student newspaper. Accordingly, my investment in the novel is more specific. I was drawn to the dichotomy established early on regarding literary and commercial success, concretely embodied in Reardon's and Milvain's writerly missions. Readers will recall how Milvain distinguishes himself from Reardon: "He is the old type of unpractical artist; I am the literary man of 1882. He won't make concessions, or rather, he can't make them; he can't supply the market. . . . Literature nowadays is a trade. Putting aside men of genius, who may succeed by mere cosmic force, your successful man of letters is your skilful tradesman" (56). Milvain assumes that writers before his time were less aware of, and less responsive to, their markets, whereas success in the 1880s necessitated complicity with the terms of the establishment. Nineteenth-century literature abounds with writer characters, from David Copperfield to Jo March, and from Bartleby the scrivener to John Watson. What distinguishes Gissing's novel is the questions that it raises regarding the life of writing, many of which continue to be resonant: What kind of writer, I wondered, would I become? In what ways are my choices predetermined by the contexts and the genres in which I work? Does one necessarily have to compromise his or her integrity, as Milvain suggests, to be successful? To what extent is Gissing's view of the literary world affected by his own personality and experiences? As a budding journalist, I share Milvain's concerns regarding the marketplace: a writer's projects are constrained by pressing deadlines and he or she necessarily writes to capture and sustain an audience's interest. But surely, I pondered, one can also challenge and move the reader, just as Gissing's novel has me. Both *New Grub Street* and my experiences reveal how much messier the dichotomy invoked by Milvain is than he assumes. Reardon conceives of himself as a proponent for literary value, yet Gissing's choice of words in his description of Reardon's books casts doubt on the character: Milvain describes how "one book had a sort of success" (54); how his books "are glaringly distinct from the ordinary circulating novel" (75); and how, "after one or two attempts, he made half a success" (75). The more impartial narrator praises Reardon's books for their promise, rather than their accomplishment:

> Those two books of his were not of a kind to win popularity. They dealt with no particular class of society (unless one makes a distinct class of people who have brains), and they lacked local colour. Their interest was almost purely psychological. It was clear that the author had no faculty for constructing a story, and that pictures of active life were not to be expected of him; he could never appeal to the multitude. But strong characterisation was within his scope, and an intellectual fervour, appetising to a small section of refined readers, marked all of his best pages. (104)

Reardon's follow-up may be a significant "improvement on its predecessors, and the reviews were generally favourable" (105), but this sequence of qualifications—"a sort of success," "half a success," "within his scope," "marked all of his best pages," and "improvement"—is unencouraging. As Robert L. Selig finds, "neither [Reardon nor his friend Biffen] comes anywhere near his goal of creating great art: at best their careful work ranks slightly above average."[5] Gissing similarly spurs us to reassess Milvain, the entrepreneurial journalist who professes to Reardon and Amy that he shall never "do anything of solid literary value; [and he] shall always despise the people [he] write[s] for" (115). Milvain's output includes a proposed article on the characteristics of the new generation of Board schoolchildren (80); one that "consist[s] of sketches of typical readers of each of the principal daily and weekly papers" (114); and one that celebrates Reardon's novels in such a way that "[t]he praise was not exaggerated, yet all the best points of Reardon's work were admirably brought out" (450). Such articles may not have substantial literary value but, if done properly, they could be of significant cultural and historical insight. In fact, Milvain's study of the readers of periodicals thematically likens him to the literary veteran Alfred Yule, who wrote a monograph on English prose in the nineteenth century. This latter work differs from Milvain's chiefly in its animosity: "The final chapter dealt with contemporary writers, more especially those who served to illustrate the author's theme—that journalism is the destruction of prose style: on certain popular writers of the day there was an outpouring of gall which was not likely to be received as though it were sweet ointment" (195). Yule's strategy prevents sustained engagement from friends and foes alike and it reduces the rhetorical function that his scholarship might serve, regardless of how convincing his arguments might have been. Nevertheless, in characters such as Dora Milvain, Gissing provides a positive model. The end of the novel finds her, now Mrs. Whelpdale, writing with autonomy: "Dora was writing; she had no thought of entirely abandoning literature, and had in hand at present a very pretty tale which would probably appear in *The English Girl*. Her boudoir, in which she sat, could not have been daintier and more appropriate to the charming characteristics of its mistress" (489). Dora's comfort and her laboring over a tale that would likely—though it need not—appear in a particular periodical separate her from Milvain, who writes always with his readers in view. She writes with greater autonomy than the ideal writer that Milvain describes in the novel's opening.

In my course essay, I examined some of these dynamics in connection to Shakespeare, and in my undergraduate thesis, I analyzed how Gissing incorporated Shakespeare's language in a number of poems and novels. I was particularly struck by a pair of scenes wherein Reardon and Biffen draw on *The Tempest*. On his deathbed, the former begins to quote to his friend: "We are such stuff as dreams are made on, and our—" (442). Reardon's words become "indistinguishable" (442) and Biffen, before poisoning himself, completes this image:

> We are such stuff
> As dreams are made on, and our little life
> Is rounded with a sleep. (476)

At first glance, such allusions seem incongruent: What do Shakespeare and Prospero have to offer these writer characters in their most desperate moments? What do they tell us about Gissing as a reader? How does Gissing's reading deepen our understanding of Shakespeare? Shakespeare shows us how heavily the past weighs on the present and the ways in which the past can operate as a point of comparison in *New Grub Street* and in Gissing's larger oeuvre. Milvain, as we have seen, defines the writer of 1882 against those of earlier times. As he encourages his sister Maud to write Sunday-school prize-books, for example, he says: "I tell you, writing is a business. Get together half a dozen fair specimens of the Sunday-school prize; study them; discover the essential points of such composition; hit upon new attractions; then go to work methodically, so many pages a day. There's no question of the divine afflatus; that belongs to another sphere of life. We talk of literature as a trade, not of Homer, Dante, and Shakespeare" (60). Milvain foregrounds the propensity of genre to constrain—his instructions concentrate more on repetition than on original creation—but, in so doing, he overlooks and obscures the potentialities it offered and continues to offer writers.[6] Accordingly, my thinking about Gissing and Shakespeare has prompted me to consider my roles as a critic and as a teacher, where I am routinely arguing for the value of studying historical literatures. Milvain may hold Shakespeare at a distance in his romanticizations, but Gissing engages with the past in more complex ways. In his unfinished novel *Veranilda* (1904), for example, Gissing takes us to Rome in the sixth century. Consider how he depicts the monks who are laboriously preserving literature in times of war:

> All at once the life of this cloister appeared before him in a wider and nobler aspect. In the silent monks bent over their desks he saw much more than piety and learning. They rose to a dignity surpassing that of consul or praefect. With their pens they warred against the powers of darkness, a grander conflict than any in which men drew sword. (306)

In my ruminations on form in *New Grub Street*, as this manifests both in large-scale narrative structures and in small-scale allusions and repetitions of particular words and phrases, John Peck's seminal article offered important interlocution. Writing in 1978, Peck attributes the formalist critics' resistance to the novel to Gissing's realism, the significant gap between the middle-class narrator and his working-class characters, his prose style, and his reliance on literary sources. Peck's article opens up new avenues for approaching the novel formally: it perfectly illustrates "the problems about novel-writing raised in the content of the novel." In looking at Reardon's first appearance in chapter 4, Peck contrasts the stillness of the episode with the novel's relentless pacing: "The formal originality is that

Gissing has dared to present the sterility of so much of the process of writing by bringing the novel to a complete halt, so that the only encounter is between a man and a blank piece of paper." Reardon's (in)activity, as we have seen, is inhibited by his propensity for counterfactuals. Peck draws attention to Gissing's ironic narrator, who prevents us from romanticizing his character: "We are never allowed to lose sight of Reardon's egotism, his selfishness, his readiness to blame others for his failure."[7] Gissing's irony manifests, more prominently, in his treatment of dialogue. As both Gissing and Reardon recognize, it monopolizes significant narrative space, yet it also enables the former to remark on social and cultural differences, and how characters cope with them: the self-consciousness that Mrs. Yule is made to feel because of her accent and bearing prevents her from speaking to Marian "with a mother's freedom; one might have taken her for a trusted servant waiting upon her mistress" (125). Citing the novel's depiction of the dome in the British Library's Reading Room, the rooms, the streets, and London, Peck argues persuasively for the importance of symbolic patterning to Gissing's creative vision: "The alternative mode of ordering in the book is symbolic, but not the rather forced symbolic moments, rather a more thoroughly integrated symbolic structure."[8]

I would go further by turning to a pair of scenes, the first of which Peck remarked on in passing. In one of their earliest meetings, Milvain and Marian watch as the London express passes by. Milvain feels invigorated by this synecdoche of progress and modernity: "If I were ten years younger. . . . I should say that was jolly! It enspirits me. It makes me feel eager to go back and plunge into the fight again" (78). The sight rejuvenates Milvain by reminding him of the train that had taken him to London to live independently when he was a lad of eighteen. Conversely, it ages Marian: "Upon me it has just the opposite effect" (78). This scene economically evokes the differences in their temperaments and foreshadows their doomed romance. After he leaves Marian with Yule, Milvain heads into a field, where he "observe[s] a poor worn-out beast, all skin and bone, which had presumably been sent here in the hope that a little more labour might be exacted from it if it were suffered to repose for a few weeks" (79). Although we know that Milvain sees the horse, it is unclear if we are being given Milvain's and/or the narrator's perception, and our interpretive decision here will influence our ethical evaluation of the character: Does Milvain pity the horse ("[t]here were sores upon its back and legs; it stood in a fixed attitude of despondency, just flicking away troublesome flies with its grizzled tail" [79])? Or does he disparage the beast's inability to survive in a competitive climate—as Milvain does Reardon only pages before? Does he identify in the horse a bad omen, that is, a possible future for himself should he follow his romantic inclinations? Or does the solitary horse impress upon him the value of a sympathetic partner? This narrative ambiguity translates into an ethical one. How we view this scene—including whether or not we view it as an instance of pathetic fallacy—will determine the extent to which we sympathize with Milvain and, indeed, the novel's central concerns; and thus Gissing unassumingly opens up a range of interpretative possibilities. My reading has not only spurred me to rethink how I practice literary criticism—Gissing's experiments with form encourage me to test its boundaries in my own articles when I actively use journalism to further my scholarly inquiries—but also, as we see here, to think about the ethical implications of reading and writing.

During my PhD program, postdoctoral fellowship, and visiting fellowships, I began to gather material for a new edition of Gissing's *The Private Papers of Henry Ryecroft* (1903), in some ways a kind of spiritual sequel to *New Grub Street*. This latter work opens with a preface, wherein an editor, "G. G.," reminisces about his friend, the titular character, whose papers have fallen into the editor's hands. Both the entrepreneurial editor and the jack-of-all-trades Ryecroft would have been at home in *New Grub Street*. Ryecroft and the editor first met when the former was forty. By then, Ryecroft had already been living off his writing for twenty years: "Many forms of literature had he tried; in none had he been conspicuously successful; yet now and then he had managed to earn a little more money than his actual needs demanded, and thus was enabled to see something of foreign countries." As time went on, Ryecroft worried about the future: "In moments of depression he spoke of his declining energies, and evidently suffered under a haunting fear of the future." Such fears were alleviated when, at the age of fifty, he was bequeathed a life annuity of three hundred pounds, following the death of an acquaintance. Ryecroft moved from his London suburb to a cottage near Exeter, where he made his home. Unbeknownst to him, however, he suffers from a heart disease, and so, one evening, after a long walk, he lies down on the sofa of his study and dies. The editor "came upon three manuscript books which at first glance seemed to be a diary; a date on the opening page of one of them showed that it had been begun not very long after the writer's settling in Devon." *Henry Ryecroft* poses a challenge to genre and it recalls *New*

*Grub Street* in its play on meanings: "When I had read a little in these pages, I saw that they were no mere record of day-to-day life; evidently finding himself unable to forego altogether the use of the pen, the veteran had set down, as humour bade him, a thought, a reminiscence, a bit of reverie, a description of his state of mind, and so on, dating such passage merely with the month in which it was written."[9]

The arrival of film and radio projects introduced Gissing to a wider audience, encouraging us to approach his writing in new ways and enabling me, by means of exploring them through reports and interviews in magazines and academic journals, to bring together my journalistic and scholarly interests: I had become a regular contributor to *Film International* and wrote also for periodicals such as the *Times Literary Supplement*.[10] In 2016, Gissing appeared onscreen, for the first time, in *The Limehouse Golem*, a film adaptation of Peter Ackroyd's 1994 neo-Victorian novel *Dan Leno and the Limehouse Golem*. Director Juan Carlos Medina introduces us to the pre-*Grub Street* Gissing, by allowing us both to *see* and to *hear* a version of Gissing. The principal events of the film unfold during an early chapter in Gissing's career, shortly after the publication of his first novel, *Workers in the Dawn*, and two years before *New Grub Street* opens. The film juxtaposes the (apparent) murder of John Cree (Sam Reid) by his wife, Elizabeth (Olivia Cooke plays the older Elizabeth and Amelia Crouch the younger), with the mystery of the Limehouse Golem, a serial murderer whose name is on every Londoner's lips. The snippets that we see of Gissing (Morgan Watkins) reveal his proximity to the protagonist of *Workers*: as numerous scholars have remarked, he and Arthur Golding are both in troubled marriages, and the wall between the writer and the character is at times precariously thin. In the film, Gissing is suspected of being the Golem because he is one of four men who had access to the book on which the Golem had written. Gissing may play a relatively minor role as red herring, yet Medina does more when he depicts Gissing at work in the British Museum, rubbing shoulders with literary and cultural giants such as Karl Marx (Henry Goodman) and Dan Leno (Douglas Booth).

Medina demonstrates, to remarkable effect, the fertile intellectual environment wherein Gissing was reading and writing and, for students and scholars of Gissing and Victorian studies, beckons fresh historicizations. My scholarly work has examined Gissing's connection to, and his reading of, many contemporaries, including George Meredith and Walter Besant. The experience of engaging with the writer onscreen was an entirely new

Gissing and his contemporaries at work in the British Museum in Juan Carlos Medina's *The Limehouse Golem*. Courtesy of *The Limehouse Golem*/Number 9 Films Ltd.

and exciting one: it offers a useful counterpoint to our reading, for instance, of his letters and diary, where we learn of his thoughts about other writers and their projects. We do well to contrast Medina's and Gissing's depictions of the literary scene, as this manifests in the Reading Room. Where Medina prioritizes the circulation of ideas, Gissing inclines more heavily toward the toiling writers. Marian, readers may recall, is temporarily elated by the advertisement for a "Literary Machine." What she hoped would be "some automaton to supply the place of such poor creatures as herself, to turn out books and articles" transpires to be a machine "for holding volumes conveniently, that the work of literary manufacture might be physically lightened" (143). Rather than lessening the workload of writers, the device ironically enables writers like Marian to labor more efficiently and for longer periods—in sum, to become more machine-like. Hundreds of pages later, Marian has not abandoned her idea, and she imagines herself in mechanistic terms: "She did her best, during the hours spent here, to convert herself into the literary machine which it was her hope would some day be invented for construction in a less sensitive material than human tissue" (454).[11]

Perhaps more significantly for the reader of *New Grub Street*, Gissing occupies a central role in two programs on BBC Radio 4. The third adaptation for this radio channel, *New Grub Street* is in two hour-long episodes and it aired on September 3 and 10, 2016.[12] This production was directed and produced by Gary Brown, and it stars Christopher Douglas, who adapted the novel for the program, as Gissing; Henry Lloyd-Hughes as Milvain; Sam Alexander as Reardon; Emily Pithon as Amy and Edith; and Olivia Hallinan as Marian. Douglas interweaves the stories of the biographical Gissing and those of his characters. The link is established, for instance, by the doubling of Douglas both as Gissing and his narrator, and by the doubling of Pithon as Amy and Gissing's wife, Edith. Some months later, on February 27, 2017, BBC Radio 4 aired *The Wells Way*, an original forty-five-minute drama to mark the seventieth anniversary of H. G. Wells's death. Directed and produced by Tracey Neale and written by Martyn Wade, this program traces Gissing's and Wells's friendship from their first meeting at a dinner organized by the Omar Khayyám Club, on November 20, 1896, until Gissing's death; and it explores, to some extent, the antagonism between Wells and Gabrielle Fleury, Gissing's romantic partner in his final years and the French translator of his books. Like *The Limehouse Golem*, the program shows Gissing in active conversation with his contemporaries and encourages us to think more about the exciting, imaginative environment in which they were working. As the title *The Wells Way* suggests, however, the program is neither *The Gissing Way* nor *The Gissing-Wells Way*: it is relayed entirely from Wells's perspective, which, in turn, frames our reading experience. The criticisms leveled at *Veranilda* owe entirely to the differences between Gissing's and Wells's interests and values. In Wade's program, Wells confides privately to his wife, Jane, "Romans and Goths—whether Visi or Ostro—they aren't my cup of tea at all. If he must write novels, Gissing should stick to realism. But he'd read heaps and heaps on the ancient topic, and he was very keen. It would have been cruel to put him off."[13]

As a professor at Dalhousie University, in one of the oldest English departments in Canada, I am working collaboratively with Dalhousie University Libraries to digitize and transcribe the *Fortnightly Review* version of *Henry Ryecroft* (1902–1903), making this text available for contemporary readers. In winter 2019, I taught, for the first time, *New Grub Street* in a fourth-year undergraduate seminar on modernisms and masculinities. My students are completing their degrees in arts, biology, contemporary studies, English, early modern studies, and neuroscience. This course studies some of the conversations regarding masculinity as they manifest in literature from the 1890s to the 1950s: we attend to Conan Doyle's definitions of honor, gentility, and masculinity, before examining the troubled relations between agency and action in Gissing's and James Joyce's fiction; how men coped with war and peace in movies by William A. Wellman and fiction by Virginia Woolf; and finally E. M. Forster's treatment of homosocial and homosexual relations. Prior to our first meeting about *New Grub Street*, I asked my class whether they identify more with Milvain or Reardon. The responses are illuminating. Charlie Hook, for one, finds such identification difficult. Where, in the early chapters, "Milvain comes off as self-important and condescending towards his sisters and his mother," Reardon shuns Amy despite her attempts to help him get on with his writing: "He appears to wallow in his own self-pity, and expects his wife to pick up his emotional slack." As I have been arguing throughout this essay, Gissing's novel advocates a kind of pluralism: it constantly invites, rather than offers, interpretation, and his narrative voice is regularly critical of *both* Reardon and Milvain. On Gissing's seemingly straightforward prose style, Brennan McCracken, another student, makes a number of insightful observations. Gissing seems to tell readers what they need to know about characters, though McCracken "wonder[s] if there might be a larger metafictional resonance between the schematic development of his characters and the climate of the literary world from which (and *about which*) Gissing himself was writing." By this, McCracken refers to the proximity between Gissing's and his characters' style: "Perhaps *New Grub Street*'s simple, prosaic style aligns it more with Milvain's articles than with Reardon's artistry? Might Gissing be mimicking the style of emerging 'economical' writing in order to ultimately subvert (or at least challenge) it through the novel's plot—a sort of sly literary trick?" Fresh queries arise as we discuss the novel and seminal works of criticism, and I find myself circling back to Gissing's writing, beginning afresh. *New Grub Street* could ostensibly have ended with Reardon's and Amy's reunion in part 4: what is the significance of presenting, and juxtaposing, two endings in parts 4 and 5? The novel closes with Milvain learning that he is to replace Clement Fadge as *The Current*'s editor and so he is married to both Amy and his readers: Milvain, in his effort to get ahead, contributes to the capitalist system that deprives him and his fellow writers of the autonomy that they cherish. Does Milvain's hubris prevent him from realizing that he has become the Literary Machine that Marian had imagined? Thirteen years after my first encounter with the novel, I eagerly await my return to Gissing's *Grub Street*.

## NOTES

This essay is dedicated to Pierre Coustillas, who was encouraging and supportive from the very beginning and under whose shadow generations of Gissing scholars work. I thank Annette Federico, Diana Maltz, and the reviewers for their incisive reading. Rohan Maitzen and Monique R. Morgan were important interlocutors and warm supporters, as were the students in the Department of English at Dalhousie University. I am grateful to the staff of the Dalhousie University Libraries for their help.

1. George Gissing, *New Grub Street*, ed. Stephen Arata, 156–57. Further references will be given parenthetically.

2. See Andrew H. Miller's illuminating analysis of counterfactual narratives in *The Burdens of Perfection: On Ethics and Reading in Nineteenth-Century British Literature*. I examined *New Grub Street* in relation to some of these concerns in "Moral Perfectionism, Counterfactuals, and the Inky Line in Besant's *All in a Garden Fair* and Gissing's *New Grub Street*."

3. On Gissing's and Dicker's depictions of the commercialization of art, see my forthcoming essay "Marcus the Magnificent: Closure and Resolution in Joël Dicker's *The Truth about the Harry Quebert Affair*."

4. See also chapter 1 of Annette Federico's *Masculine Identity in Hardy and Gissing* for an account of some of the quantifiable social changes that brought about "the ferment of ideas about sexual relations and the nature of the sexes, provoking men to meditate upon their patriarchal inheritance." *Masculine Identity in Hardy and Gissing*, 19.

5. Robert L. Selig, *George Gissing*, 52.

6. Caroline Levine has usefully distinguished genre from form: "Genres . . . can be defined as customary constellations of elements into historically recognizable groupings of artistic objects, bringing together forms with themes, styles, and situations of reception, while forms are organizations or arrangements that afford repetition and portability across materials and contexts." *Forms: Whole, Rhythm, Hierarchy, Network*, 13–14.

7. John Peck, "*New Grub Street*: Some Suggestions for an Approach through Form," 5, 6–7, 8.

8. Peck, "*New Grub Street*," 9–12.

9. George Gissing, *The Private Papers of Henry Ryecroft*, viii, ix, xi, xi–xii.

10. I have traced some of these new developments in the *Times Literary Supplement*, "New *New Grub Street*." See also my interviews with Morgan Watkins and Christopher Douglas. I have discussed Martyn Wade's program in "Gissing Laughs, Wells Sighs: *The Wells Way* on BBC Radio 4."

11. As Zena Meadowsong argues, Marian's attempt to escape the literary labor through marriage to Milvain can ironically be read in mechanical terms: "[T]his form of emancipation must be purchased—depends upon her inheritance of several thousand pounds—and thus requires Marian's functional objectification all

over again: she can only leave the literary factory by becoming the material basis of Jasper's success in it. . . . Reducing both women [Amy and Marian] to interchangeable love objects with the heartless efficiency of the factory system Marian seeks to escape, Jasper not only accentuates the effects of her drudgery, but seems to doom her to its perpetual extension." *Narrative Machine: The Naturalist, Modernist, and Postmodernist Novel*, 82.

12. Christopher Douglas, *New Grub Street*.

13. Martyn Wade, *The Wells Way*.

## WORKS CITED

Ackroyd, Peter. *Dan Leno and The Limehouse Golem*. 1994. London: Vintage Books, 2007.

Annaud, Jean-Jacques, dir. *The Truth about the Harry Quebert Affair*. MGM Television. 2018.

Dicker, Joël. *The Truth about the Harry Quebert Affair*. Translated by Sam Taylor. London: MacLehose Press-Quercus, 2012.

Douglas, Christopher. *New Grub Street*. Unpublished radio script. 2 vols. London: n. pag., 2016.

Federico, Annette. *Masculine Identity in Hardy and Gissing*. Rutherford, NJ: Fairleigh Dickinson University Press, 1991.

Gilroy, Dan, dir. *Velvet Buzzsaw*. Netflix. 2019.

Gissing, George. *George Gissing, "The Private Papers of Henry Ryecroft."* Edited by Tom Ue. Edinburgh: Edinburgh University Press, forthcoming.

———. *The Nether World*. Edited by Stephen Gill. Oxford: Oxford University Press, 2009.

———. *New Grub Street*. Edited by Stephen Arata. Peterborough, ON: Broadview, 2007.

———. *The Private Papers of Henry Ryecroft*. Westminster: Archibald Constable, 1903.

———. *Veranilda*. Edited by Pierre Coustillas. Brighton: Harvester Press, 1987.

———. *Workers in the Dawn*. Edited by Pierre Coustillas. Brighton: Harvester Press, 1985.

Levine, Caroline. *Forms: Whole, Rhythm, Hierarchy, Network*. Princeton: Princeton University Press, 2015.

Meadowsong, Zena. *Narrative Machine: The Naturalist, Modernist, and Postmodernist Novel*. New York: Routledge, 2019.

Medina, Juan Carlos, dir. *The Limehouse Golem*. Number 9 Films Ltd. 2016.

Miller, Andrew H. *The Burdens of Perfection: On Ethics and Reading in Nineteenth-Century British Literature*. Ithaca: Cornell University Press, 2010.

Peck, John. "*New Grub Street*: Some Suggestions for an Approach through Form." *The Gissing Newsletter* 14.3 (July 1978): 1–13.

Selig, Robert L. *George Gissing*. Rev. ed. New York: Twayne-Macmillan, 1995.

Ue, Tom. "George Gissing On-Screen: An Interview with Morgan Watkins on *The Limehouse Golem*." *Film International* 15.4 (December 2017): 138–40.

———. "Gissing Laughs, Wells Sighs: *The Wells Way* on BBC Radio 4." *Gissing Journal* 51.2 (April 2017): 1–6.

———. *Gissing, Shakespeare, and the Life of Writing*. Edinburgh: Edinburgh University Press, forthcoming.

———. "Marcus the Magnificent: Closure and Resolution in Joël Dicker's *The Truth about the Harry Quebert Affair*." In *The Map and the Book: Cartographic and Topographic Turn in Literature and Culture*, edited by Monika Szuba and Julian Wolfreys. Leiden, Netherlands: Brill, forthcoming.

———. "Moral Perfectionism, Counterfactuals, and the Inky Line in Besant's *All in a Garden Fair* and Gissing's *New Grub Street*." In *Walter Besant: The Business of Literature and the Pleasures of Reform*, edited by Kevin A. Morrison, 205–23. Liverpool: Liverpool University Press, 2019.

———. "New *New Grub Street*." *Times Literary Supplement*, October 6, 2016.

———. "The Roads to Gissing's Grub Street: An Interview with Christopher Douglas." *Journal of Adaptation in Film & Performance* 9.3 (December 2016): 287–92.

Wade, Martyn. *The Wells Way*. Unpublished radio script. London: n. pag., 2017.

CHAPTER THIRTEEN

# Let to a Single Gentleman

Lillian Nayder

## On *The Pickwick Papers* by Charles Dickens

In what proves to be a pivotal chapter of *The Pickwick Papers* (1836–1837), Dickens dramatizes a scene in which the novel's hero, Samuel Pickwick, offers the job of manservant to Sam Weller, the "boots" at the White Hart Inn. Mr. Pickwick acts "with the concurrence" of his followers and fellow club members, Tracy Tupman, Nathaniel Winkle, and Augustus Snodgrass. He has already met Sam—when he and Mr. Wardle tracked to the White Hart Wardle's sister Rachel, on a runaway match with Alfred Jingle. Having invited Sam to his lodgings in the hopes of hiring him, Pickwick opens the negotiations, supported by his three friends:

> "We want to know . . . whether you have any reason to be discontented with your present situation."
>
> "Afore I answers that 'ere question, gen'lm'n," replied Mr. Weller, "*I* should like to know, in the first place, whether you're a goin' to purwide me with a better."
>
> A sunbeam of placid benevolence played on Mr. Pickwick's features as he said, "I have half made up my mind to engage you myself."
>
> "Have you, though?" said Sam.
>
> Mr. Pickwick nodded in the affirmative.
>
> "Wages?" inquired Sam.
>
> "Twelve pounds a year," replied Mr. Pickwick.
>
> "Clothes?"
>
> "Two suits."
>
> "Work?"
>
> "To attend upon me; and travel about with me and these gentlemen here."

> "Take the bill down," said Sam, emphatically. "I'm let to a single gentleman, and the terms is agreed upon."[1]

Promptly measured for his new set of clothes and dressed in a grey coat, a pink striped waistcoat, a black hat with cockade, and a Pickwick Club button, Sam is a "suddenly-transformed individual." Although he wonders what, precisely, he is meant to be, whether "a footman, or a groom, or a gamekeeper, or a seedsman," he is delighted with his new position: "There's change of air, plenty to see, and little to do; and all this suits my complaint uncommon; so long life to the Pickvicks, says I!" (236).

In March of 1983, as a third-year graduate student at the University of Virginia, I, too, was "let" to a new employer and brought into the orbit of Mr. Pickwick—as pleased with my new job as Sam Weller could be. A professor at another university was seeking a research assistant for an annotated bibliography of *The Pickwick Papers* and would be coming to Charlottesville to interview candidates. Whomever he hired would be sent to London at his expense to work at the Dickens House (now the Charles Dickens Museum) and the British Library that summer, locating, examining, and describing various editions of the novel as well as the many adaptations and ephemera to which it gave rise.

The popularity of *Pickwick* from the late 1830s onward would make this a substantial task. The novel was Dickens's first monthly serial and his first tremendous success—originally intended by publishers Chapman and Hall to showcase the illustrations of Robert Seymour, who committed suicide shortly after commencing his collaborations with Dickens in 1836. In addition to the novel's own sales, its runaway popularity took the form of Pickwick quadrilles and waltzes, instrumental pieces, dramas and farces, club satires, spin-offs, parodies and continuations, and a wide range of material objects and souvenirs.

In mid-February of 1983, I received a letter informing me that, based on my written application, I had made the first cut:

> Dear Ms. Nayder:
>
> Thank you for applying for the position of research assistant in London. I received eighteen applications and found yours to be among the five best suited for the position. I would like to meet with you for an interview and shall be on campus on Wednesday, March 9 from 12:30 until 3:00. Professor

> [X] has the schedule which you should sign at a convenient time slot; please see him to do so.

By the end of March, I had been offered the position—and, like Sam Weller, would be a "transformed individual" as a result.

The work I was about to start would stretch over a period of three years, my research on *Pickwick* expanding to include annotations of *all* critical studies on the novel and continuing at Alderman Library in my fourth and fifth years of the PhD program. It was to help pay my bills at a time when I was earning very little money as a graduate instructor—hence my surprise at finding an uncashed check for $425, dated August 8, 1986, among the papers, notes, and correspondence in my *Pickwick* box when I began to outline this essay. But my new position proved most profitable because it brought me to London for the first time in my life; provided me with access to some of the world's most important archives and introduced me to the kind of research conducted in such places; immersed me in the world of Charles Dickens; and sealed my fate as a Dickens critic. From 1983 through 1986, I would examine and describe in detail twenty-seven editions of *The Pickwick Papers*, five of them published in Dickens's lifetime; read and describe more than three hundred works of criticism on *Pickwick* and discover what dozens of critics had written about the novel in their dissertations as well as their published books and articles; and learn about Victorian material and popular culture by annotating imitation sequels of *Pickwick* as well as musical, dance, and stage adaptations. Twenty years before I became a Dickens family biographer, recognized Henry Burnett as the novelist's brother-in-law—the husband of Dickens's musical sister Fanny—and examined the pair's student work at the Royal Academy of Music, I had annotated Burnett's vocal adaptation of *Pickwick*, "Oh, A Dainty Plant Is the Ivy Green," part of the Dickens House collection.

By means of the articles, books, and chapters that I annotated for the bibliography, I first "met" a number of the Dickens critics and biographers who are my friends today. And combing through adaptations of *Pickwick* in what then served as the research area of the Dickens House—the basement room at the bottom of the stairs—I met several Dickens critics in the flesh. I was also introduced to Cedric Dickens, the great grandson of the novelist, as he prepared to meet the members of the Tennessee

Pickwick Club. Until the summer of 1983, I had no idea that such people or organizations existed.

A few of my notes on *Pickwick* criticism for the annotated bibliography. Photo courtesy of the author.

For a graduate student working in archives for the first time, the pairing of the Dickens House and the British Library, then still a part of the British Museum, was fortuitous, revealing the range of practices and expectations established in such places—and the range of negotiating skills required of researchers as well. The Dickens House was a domestic space—granted, a domestic space with remarkable manuscript holdings—and attracted visitors as the home of Charles Dickens. It showcased artifacts relating to the novelist's life as well as manuscripts and publications charting his literary career, as it does in expanded and perfected form today. For better or for worse, there was no surveillance of researchers at the time; materials were made available to me quite freely, in boxes and large files, and I was left to do at least some of the work that would have been performed by staff members in stacks and behind counters at larger, more institutional repositories. The space allotted to researchers was limited to that single basement room; everyone sat at one large wooden table, with seats for five or six at most, surrounded by rows of tall bookshelves. Work halted for twenty minutes or so each afternoon so that we could walk down the hall to the kitchen for tea, which we brought back with us to the research table. These practices have changed since 1983—wisely so, of course, though the space for researchers has grown even smaller than it was then, as it has moved upstairs—but the trust extended to me by the curator and staff and the domesticity of the place were essential parts of my early experience there and its value to me.

When I shifted from one archive to another midway through my time in London, my research experience took a turn. If the curator of the Dickens House appeared to me like a generous host serving up a feast of nineteenth-century material, the head of conservation at the British Library seemed more like a dragon at the gate. When I arrived in the Reading Room and duly submitted my request for the original monthly parts of *The Pickwick Papers*, it was promptly and curtly refused. The material was extremely rare and highly fragile, I was told, and unavailable for research. Only after the head of conservation had descended from the upper reaches of the Reading Room and listened as I strenuously made my case were the monthly numbers warily made available to me. In fact, no one could have treated them with more care or reverence than I did, seated for the first time at a table at the British Library. I had already studied the complicated publishing history of *Pickwick*, including the struggle to find an illustrator whom Dickens would find satisfactory after Seymour's suicide. Now I was face to face with the monthly numbers documenting that struggle as well as Dickens's rise to dominance from the third number onward, the emphasis clearly shifting from illustrations to printed text. Seven of Seymour's plates are divided between the first two monthly numbers, the second number announcing the artist's "melancholy death"; two illustrations by R. W. Buss appear in the third, and two by Hablôt Knight Browne in the fourth and each of the following numbers. Adding to the allure of the monthly parts, they had a distinctly acrid and musty smell, no doubt familiar to others who have done similar research on Dickens.

Although this was my first day with the original monthly numbers, my relationship with *Pickwick* had already come a long way. I had first read the book in my graduate course The Victorian Novel in February 1982, almost a year before I was hired as a research assistant. It was a somewhat inauspicious start to what has become my professional life with Dickens. The syllabus also included *Jane Eyre*, *Bleak House*, and *Middlemarch*, along with *Mary Barton*, *The Mayor of Casterbridge*, and *The Odd Women*. *Pickwick* was second in the sequence, immediately following *Jane Eyre*. I was on firm ground with Brontë: *Jane Eyre* made perfect sense to me, even when it shouldn't have. But *Pickwick* was a very different story. What exactly *was* this book? Was it really a novel? And where were all the women? In a work centered on an exclusively male club, and following, as Dickens puts it on his title page, the "perambulations, perils, travels, adventures and sporting transactions" of a roving band of amateur English gentlemen and bachelors, it was difficult for me to find a comfortable point of entry into this fictional world, despite its celebrated humor—to respond to it as I did most nineteenth-century novels. Critics such as Steven Marcus, assigned alongside Dickens, might characterize the hero of *Pickwick* as "unaggressive" and define him against the "insistently masculine" Jorrocks of Robert Smith Surtees's *Jorrocks's Jaunts and Jollities*, one source for Dickens's novel. But I found little consolation in that fact.[2]

My problem with *Pickwick* reflected my sense that I had entered a modern-day clubland of sorts in graduate school—that for a number of the professors in my program, graduate study was itself an exclusively male club, or *ought* to be. When I entered graduate school in the fall of 1980, there were only two women on the large faculty of the English department, only one of whom had tenure. During my first year, I learned not to linger by the Xerox machine; if I did so, I might be handed material to copy by a renowned scholar who mistook female graduate students for departmental secretaries or simply thought all women were fair game. My own advisers were enormously generous and equitable in their work with graduate students, regardless of gender, and I remain immensely grateful and indebted to them. Nonetheless, my life as a literary critic had its start in a general atmosphere in which women faced unequal odds and gender inequities could be stark. I was pointedly told that I could have either a career or a family, though one of the two women on the faculty would soon give the lie to that claim; and I learned that my "sentimental" responses to American fiction were "just what had been expected" of me as a woman. In more than one class, female students were "corrected" for comments that would then be praised as insightful when repeated nearly verbatim by the men in the room.

Faced with Dickens's fond portrait of male fellowship within the Pickwick Club—and the mayhem created when male allegiances are interrupted by, or mistaken for, heterosexual ties—I took refuge in the structure of the novel. When asked to write about *Pickwick*, I could simply bypass questions of gender, I then thought. In my one-page essay on the novel intended for class discussion, which I recently rediscovered in my notebook from the course, I focused on the problem of interpolation. "The issue of integrating the 'embedded' tales with the frame is deliberately avoided," I noted, my use of the passive voice marking my own distance from the novel. "It is left to the reader to 'integrate' these tales with the larger framework of *The Pickwick Papers*. To what extent is this possible? In view of the light tone of the work . . . what is the reader to 'do' with this tragic and, at times, grotesque material?" My interest in Dickens's interpolations and structure—what seemed to me the strange heterogeneity of the work—would circle back to questions of gender after our two weeks on *Pickwick* were up and we moved on to *Bleak House*, its dueling narratives giving shape to the gender divide in that novel. As I read more and more of Dickens, I would come to see that the narrative interpolations and quarantine in *Pickwick* are crucial and recurring elements of his writing, and are inseparable from conceptions of gender throughout his work.

By the time I started my London research in 1983, I was more at ease with the "Pickwickian sense" of things, thanks largely to my better knowledge of Sam Weller and his service to readers as well as club members. Sam celebrates the Pickwickian ("long life to the Pickvicks, says I!") and is faithful to it, getting his employer out of various scrapes, testifying in his behalf in the breach-of-promise suit brought against Pickwick by Mrs. Bardell, and accompanying Pickwick to the Fleet Prison when he refuses to pay damages to her. Yet Sam is also the wise cockney whose experience and humor expose the illusions of the gentlemen he serves. At best, he has one foot inside this club that women never enter. His wry recognition that Pickwickian territory could be alien ground echoed my own, even as the manservant is naturalized to it.

To a female graduate student hoping to make her way in what was still largely a masculine realm, Sam was particularly appealing—a working-class figure who repeatedly satirizes the gentlemen's club in which he is both servant and honorary member. Whether or not Sam believes that "all women was alike" (542), a proposition that he questions at one point in the novel, he is keenly aware of class differences among men—reminded that his place is in the kitchen while Pickwick and the others dine upstairs.

Critics often identify Sam as the knowing character who foregrounds the "innocence" of the Pickwickians, and a number of the articles and chapters I annotated for the bibliography make exactly that point. But from his first appearance in the story, Sam points to the class assumptions and privileges that underlie Pickwick's behavior, calling into question the very innocence that he allegedly validates. Enraged by Alfred Jingle and his disparaging treatment of Tracy Tupman, his romantic rival, for example, Pickwick throws an inkstand at the strolling actor at the White Hart Inn, earning Sam's respectful reproof: "'Hallo,' said that eccentric functionary, 'furniter's cheap where you come from, sir. Self-acting ink, that 'ere; it's wrote your mark upon the wall, old gen'lm'n" (210). When Sergeant Buzfuz asserts, during the trial of Bardell against Pickwick, that Sam's work as manservant means "little to do, and plenty to get," Sam counters the claim: "Oh, quite enough to get, sir, as the soldier said ven they ordered him three hundred and fifty lashes" (572–73).

If Sam functions as an affectionate critic of the Pickwick Club and its "Transactions" (67), Martha Bardell, Mr. Pickwick's landlady, is more direct and accusatory in her critique, though nearly as comic. Her response to her bachelor tenant—her blindness to the homosocial and its primacy for Pickwick—helped win me over to the novel. Having a clear sense of the injuries she has suffered at Pickwick's hands, Mrs. Bardell brings an action for breach of promise against him, encouraged to do so by Dodson and Fogg, who take the case "on speculation," asking for £1,500 in damages (446). In the chapters that follow her faux engagement, Dickens discredits her and her case: she has presumably misunderstood the hero and, as a consequence, errs in her claims against him, suffering as much, if not more, than he does because of the mistake she has made—imprisoned, like Pickwick, in the Fleet, but unable to pay her way out of it because Pickwick refuses to pay the £750 in damages the court has awarded her. But to my thinking at the time, the novel defended Mrs. Bardell as fully as it dismissed her. Not only does her alleged mistake seem virtually inevitable as Dickens constructs the scene, but also Sam views Pickwick's claims of innocence skeptically, encouraging readers to doubt them. His "Wellerisms" often expose the injustice that women suffer at the hands of men, bolstering Mrs. Bardell's case—as do other comically incriminating features of Pickwick's behavior.

Sam Weller and Martha Bardell first converge in the scene in which Sam is hired, as Dickens develops the counterpoint between the manservant and the landlady. Dickens identifies the chapter in which Sam is "let" as an "epoch" (229) in the novel not only because it brings him into Mr. Pickwick's orbit but also because it effectively confuses him with Mrs. Bardell, laying the groundwork for the breach-of-promise lawsuit. Pickwick approaches his landlady at the start of the chapter in question, hoping, he later explains, to gauge her views on his plans to hire a manservant. But she interprets his behavior, and the position he seeks to fill, very differently than he intends—as an offer of marriage.

Before Pickwick "engages" Sam as his manservant, he seems already to have promised the spot to Mrs. Bardell, though on substantially different terms. "Do you think it a much greater expense to keep two people, than to keep one?" he begins.

> "La, Mr. Pickwick," said Mrs. Bardell, colouring up to the very border of her cap, as she fancied she observed a species of matrimonial twinkle in the eyes of her lodger; "La, Mr. Pickwick, what a question!"
>
> "Well, but *do* you?" inquired Mr. Pickwick.
>
> "That depends—" said Mrs. Bardell, approaching the duster very near to Mr. Pickwick's elbow, which was planted on the table—"that depends a good deal upon the person, you know, Mr. Pickwick; and whether it's a saving and careful person, sir."
>
> "That's very true," said Mr. Pickwick, "but the person I have in my eye (here he looked very hard at Mrs. Bardell) I think possesses these qualities; and has, moreover, a considerable knowledge of the world, and a great deal of sharpness, Mrs. Bardell; which may be of material use to me."
>
> "La, Mr. Pickwick," said Mrs. Bardell; the crimson rising to her cap-border again.
>
> "I do," said Mr. Pickwick, growing energetic, as was his wont in speaking of a subject which interested him, "I do, indeed; and to tell you the truth, Mrs. Bardell, I have made up my mind."
>
> "Dear me, sir," exclaimed Mrs. Bardell.
>
> "You'll think it very strange now," said the amiable Mr. Pickwick, with a good-humoured glance at his companion, "that I never consulted you about this matter, and never even mentioned it, till I sent your little boy out this morning—eh?"
>
> Mrs. Bardell could only reply by a look. She had long worshipped Mr. Pickwick at a distance, but here she was, all at once, raised to a pinnacle to which her wildest and most extravagant hopes had never dared to aspire. Mr.

> Pickwick was going to propose—a deliberate plan, too—sent her little boy to the Borough, to get him out of the way—how thoughtful—how considerate! (230–31)

Promising to "take more trouble to please [him] . . . than ever," Mrs. Bardell pronounces herself "a very happy woman," assuming they are engaged. She calls Mr. Pickwick a "kind, good, playful dear," flings her arms around his neck as he "struggl[es] violently" against her, and faints in his arms (231–32). The two are found in this compromising position by Tupman, Winkle, and Snodgrass, who enter Pickwick's apartments immediately afterward, followed by Sam Weller, whom Pickwick hopes to hire.

With few exceptions, the critics whose work I read and annotated for the bibliography referred to Mrs. Bardell's "misunderstanding" of Pickwick, emphasizing her misperception of his behavior and the "injustice" done him by the landlady. Tracing the "elements of epic" in *Pickwick*, for example, Joseph Kestner compared Mrs. Bardell to a siren; Ross H. Dabney paired her with Jingle as a mercenary character hoping to marry for money. Among all the critics I read, only one, E. A. Lewis, came to Mrs. Bardell's defense—but on grounds far from palatable to my taste: she deserved to be defended because of her good looks, her clean home, and her temperate taste for tea instead of gin. "Had Mr. Pickwick been of another mind and married her," Lewis conjectured, "I do not doubt that she would have made him a model wife."[3]

What none of the critics seemed to acknowledge or consider was the *logic* of Mrs. Bardell's reaction to Pickwick and his cues—her understandable inference that he was proposing marriage, and hence the justification of her breach-of-promise suit. Neither did the critics appear to consider the irony of Pickwick's implicitly confusing (and hence also identifying) a potential wife with a potential manservant when he makes his overtures to each, despite the different services they provide. At the outset of the chapter, in fact, Dickens teases readers with the possibility that Pickwick might be about to propose to his landlady, noting his "mysterious and unaccountable" behavior as "he paced the room to and fro with hurried steps" before approaching her; and Pickwick waits until after she believes they are engaged and has left the room to explain to his friends that he "had merely announced to her [his] intention of keeping a man servant," thereby disabusing us of what she believes while keeping her in the dark (230, 234). The interpolated tale that follows shortly afterward, "The Bagman's

Story," serves to corroborate the reasonableness of Mrs. Bardell's thinking by reminding us of how appealing widows like Mrs. Bardell could be on the matrimonial market—because of their personal property as well as their personal attractions. In the story, Tom Smart outwits a rival to win the hand of a young widow who, like Mrs. Bardell, is a landlady (an innkeeper, in this case): "[B]efore long, [the rooms] and their contents would be his property," Smart rightly thinks (269).

Sam Weller and Mrs. Bardell have their obvious differences—differences captured late in the novel when the two come face to face in the Fleet. Catching sight of the landlady, Sam "[takes] his hat off with mock reverence, while his master turn[s] indignantly on his heel," the manservant's mock chivalry reinforcing the gender differences at play here (747). Yet the fact that the questions Pickwick seems to pose to Mrs. Bardell romantically apply equally well to Sam and his service highlights the similarities between the two figures and the work they perform. Both wife and manservant would be "kept" by Mr. Pickwick, for example, and both would prove of "material use" to him, the wife even more subservient than a paid domestic could be (230–31).

These connections help to explain Sam's evident willingness to speak on Mrs. Bardell's behalf and on the part of women more generally—to counter the misogyny his father, Tony, espouses even as he sometimes invokes it himself and to question Pickwick's claims to innocence with women. "'Rum feller, the hemperor,' said Mr. Weller . . . 'Think o' his making up to that ere Mrs. Bardell—vith a little boy, too! Always the vay vith these here old 'uns hows'ever, as is such steady goers to look at'" (327). Sam's jokes often depend on double meanings in which he both supports and threatens the women he addresses; throughout, he plays on our understanding of coverture, which transformed wives into the property of their husbands: "I wish I was *the* Weller as owns you," he tells his stepmother, in what the narrator terms "a double-barrelled compliment" (451). "All I can say is, that I wish you *may* get it," he tells Mrs. Bardell, equating her being awarded the damages she seeks with her receiving the corporal punishment he suggests she deserves for pursuing the compensation (446). When Tony Weller rails against "widders," warning Pickwick against them ("I hope you han't got a widder, sir" [353]), Sam counters with a quip about Bluebeard, the serial wife murderer. Referring to his father, who has married a widow, Sam reminds us that, in most cases of connubial "wictimization," sympathy for the husband is utterly misplaced:

"Mrs. Bardell encounters Mr. Pickwick in the Prison," steel engraving by "Phiz" (Hablôt K. Browne), August 1837. The Victorian Web, scanned image by Philip V. Allingham.

"I think he's the wictim o' connubiality, as Blue Beard's domestic chaplain said, with a tear of pity, ven he buried him" (355).

And so I settled on a reading of *Pickwick* in which Dickens effectively comes to Mrs. Bardell's defense, despite the novel's protestations to the contrary. But my understanding of the work took a different turn once my years as research assistant were over. When the volume was finally published and the portions I had written appeared in print, my name was wholly absent from it, my contributions unacknowledged in any way. While few English graduate students in the 1980s would have expected to be acknowledged as coauthors or contributors under the circumstances in which I had been hired, most expected to be recognized as research assistants at the very least, that position being understood to cover duties as broad as Sam's: not those of "footman . . . groom . . . gamekeeper . . . seedsman," but of secretary, researcher, writer, editor—"a sort of compo of every one on 'em," as Sam puts it (236). While no promises had been made to me about the recognition of my work—and hence no promises breached—I was still struck by the omission. My reaction was sharpened by my having become an assistant professor by this time, more confident and ambitious as a Dickens critic and better able to recognize inequities in the profession for what they were. My sense of the matter was reinforced by the shocked reaction of a Dickens critic and friend to whom I confided the story years later, once my own books and articles on Dickens had appeared.

When I reread *Pickwick* for new research projects after my first venture into Dickens scholarship had ended, the meaning of the novel seemed to have shifted significantly. Having sought, as a graduate student, to *justify* Mrs. Bardell in her claims against Pickwick—to show that breach of promise, what she and her friend Mrs. Cluppins considered the "law for us women," applied in her case (445)—I now understood her to have made a lucky escape in the first place; remaining a widow, she averted the loss of identity and rights that remarriage would bring. From this perspective, breach of promise—that very "law for us women"—provided a dubious advantage at best, inviting female agency but promoting an ideal of female dependence, as historian Ginger Frost has argued.[4] In much the same way, the opportunity I had been given as research assistant allowed me to work as a Dickens critic while also obscuring my earliest contributions to the field.

In one of the more memorable scenes in *The Pickwick Papers*, Sam Weller composes a valentine to Mary, his "first love," a servant in the household of Mr. Nupkins (441). Understanding that you "never sign a walentine with your own name," Sam suppresses his identity when he signs his composition with the phrase "Your love-sick Pickwick" (543). In a novel that explores the meanings of shared or corporate identity, its appeal and its dangers—whether in club membership, marriage, or authorship—Sam becomes "a Pickwick" yet remains himself, his originality recognized by his readers and his employer. As Pickwick observes to Peter Magnus in response to Sam's "Wellerisms," "he is my servant, but I allow him to take a good many liberties; for, between ourselves, I flatter myself he is an original, and I am rather proud of him" (381). While Pickwick takes some credit for employing a clever manservant, he recognizes Sam as "an original" nonetheless.

Were Mrs. Bardell to become "a Pickwick," however, the same would not be true in her case. When, as a widow, Mrs. Bardell ventures into authorship, her composition gains public recognition—when Sergeant Buzfuz explicates for the jury her wording on the placard that "she placed in her front parlour-window," advertising her furnished apartments and bringing Mr. Pickwick to her door (559). But as "Mrs. Samuel Pickwick," she would have had no claim to the originality Dickens parodies in this courtroom scene, whether she was to become author, wage earner, or mother, for as Sir William Blackstone explains of the workings of coverture in his *Commentaries on the Laws of England*, "the husband and wife are one person in law," with "the very being or legal existence of the woman . . . incorporated and consolidated into that of the husband."[5] Even as *mother*, her identity and originality have been subsumed by those of her late husband, a custom-house officer and exciseman—for as Sergeant Buzfuz puts it in describing the birth of Master Bardell, "Some time before his death, [the late Mr. Bardell] had stamped his likeness upon a little boy"—the metaphor of "stamping" drawn from the father's profession and reflecting his rights under common law (559). The pitfalls of such "shared" identity, which have proved especially hazardous for women and which appear in the foreground of my most recent Dickens scholarship—my portrait of Catherine Dickens's life—are among the lessons I've learned from my work on *The Pickwick Papers*.[6] So, too, is my sense that we can best make ourselves visible and become full members of our profession not by seeking to join "the club" but by working to eliminate it altogether.

## NOTES

1. Charles Dickens, *The Pickwick Papers*, ed. Robert L. Patten, 235. Further references will be given parenthetically. My tattered copy of Patten's edition, which I used again while working on this essay, dates from my days as a graduate student.

2. Steven Marcus, *Dickens: From Pickwick to Dombey*, 26.

3. Joseph Kestner, "Elements of Epic in *The Pickwick Papers*"; Ross H. Dabney, *Love and Property in the Novels of Dickens*; E. A. Lewis, "In Defense of Mrs. Bardell," 208.

4. Ginger Frost, *Promises Broken: Courtship, Class, and Gender in Victorian England*.

5. William Blackstone, *Commentaries on the Laws of England*, 1:441.

6. See Lillian Nayder, *The Other Dickens: A Life of Catherine Hogarth*.

## WORKS CITED

Blackstone, William. *Commentaries on the Laws of England*. 12th ed. London: T. Cadell, 1793.

Dabney, Ross H. *Love and Property in the Novels of Dickens*. Berkeley: University of California Press, 1967.

Dickens, Charles. *The Pickwick Papers*. Edited by Robert L. Patten. New York: Penguin, 1981.

Frost, Ginger. *Promises Broken: Courtship, Class, and Gender in Victorian England*. Charlottesville: University of Virginia Press, 1996.

Kestner, Joseph. "Elements of Epic in *The Pickwick Papers*." *University of Dayton Review* 9 (Summer 1972): 15–24.

Lewis, E. A. "In Defense of Mrs. Bardell." *Dickensian* 38 (1941–1942): 208–9.

Marcus, Steven. *Dickens: From Pickwick to Dombey*. New York: Basic Books, 1965.

Nayder, Lillian. *The Other Dickens: A Life of Catherine Hogarth*. Ithaca: Cornell University Press, 2011.

CHAPTER FOURTEEN

# Bedtime Reading

Narin Hassan

## On *Dracula* by Bram Stoker

My first memory of reading Bram Stoker's *Dracula* (1897) is from the age of thirteen, when I found a frayed, well-read copy of the novel on a bookshelf at home. I grew up in a house pretty full of books and was often intrigued by the ones my parents owned, and as an only child and eager reader, I frequently entertained myself with novels. I remember being impressed by this book's graphically striking cover, with the black-and-white image of a face with a bright red rivulet of blood running down from the mouth to the edge of one bottom corner. I've looked for that old paperback more than once, but it may have been discarded in one of our many moves. I had heard of *Dracula* through popular culture, images, and films, and was curious about the original story and how it would unfold. Part of my attraction to this text—along with its bold cover—was that it was the kind of book I probably wouldn't have been allowed to read at a younger age. While I didn't know a lot about the story, it intrigued me, especially since my parents had been quite strict about my film-viewing and book-reading options. By this point, I loved Ouija boards and ghost stories, so off I went, book in hand, to begin *Dracula* as my bedtime reading.

I was drawn into the narrative very quickly as it traced Jonathan Harker's journey to Transylvania and introduced the characters Mina and Lucy. However, Harker's seduction by the three vampire women at the Count's castle confirmed the need for my parents to be cautious about my reading choices. That scene was haunting to me and resulted in restless sleep for several nights after. The vividness of Stoker's descriptions, particularly his representations of the female vampires and their desire, stuck with me for a long time. Harker's claims were chilling and frightening: "I was not alone. . . . I could see the floor, the brilliant moonlight, my own footsteps where I had disturbed the long accumulation of dust . . ."[1]

His description of the three women and their "great dark piercing eyes, that seemed to be almost red when contrasted with the pale, yellow moon," along with their "silvery musical laugh," was jarring—the scene comes quite early in the novel and establishes Stoker's ability to push the boundaries of Victorian culture by presenting subversive female characters and a weakened male, Jonathan Harker, who is simultaneously attracted to and repulsed by these figures. He claims that "there was something about them that made me uneasy, some longing and at the same time some deadly fear. I felt in my heart a wicked, burning desire that they would kiss me with those red lips" (69). These words, often quoted by scholars, reflect the uneasiness produced by the novel and its engagement with the tensions of fear and desire. They also reflect my own quandary with the novel at the time—I was simultaneously drawn to and fearful of it.

*Dracula* made me unsettled in my own surroundings; the dark scenes of the novel and the depictions of "gloom-haunted rooms" reappeared within familiar spaces (68). I remember that among the various art pieces hung in our house were a series of portraits of women (not women we knew) painted in hues of blue and green. In the daylight, these images didn't bother me, but at night the eyes and faces glowed, resembling Stoker's depiction of the vampire women, with their piercing eyes, lending an even more creepy aspect to the hallway outside my room. The book seemed to have a powerful effect even as it sat, unopened, at my bedside, as if it could permeate my dreams just by being in proximity. I didn't know a lot about Victorian culture at this stage of my life, but I had seen plenty of images of polite Victorian ladies and gentlemen in films and popular culture. This book provided a different glimpse of the period—its dark, gothic, and sometimes transgressive scenes were enticing but also frightening. This was my introduction to the now commonplace trope of combining scenes of horror with references to sexuality and desire. As a thirteen-year-old girl, I didn't make it to the end of *Dracula*.

To write about "my Victorian novel" is a daunting task—I've always struggled with choosing "favorite" things—and *Dracula* isn't typically the kind of novel that would make this list. I love the Victorian period for so many reasons, but especially because its novels often draw me into a series of relationships and engagement with carefully crafted characters that resonate with my life in some way. The first two possible books I think about when I think of my Victorian novel are Charlotte Brontë's *Jane Eyre* and George Eliot's *The Mill on the Floss* because I identify with their central figures—with Jane's rebelliousness and her winding path through life, and with Maggie's struggles to be understood, always torn by ambivalent emotions. Brontë and Eliot present female characters who might be like me, through generational shifts and through a range of situations. They are characters we can connect with through various phases and situations, and these novels situate them within contexts that can be familiar and emotive. Both of these books tug at my heart a little, and my rereadings reveal new ways to ponder them, and to *feel* them.

Bram Stoker's *Dracula* is in another universe from these morally secure, heroine-centered stories. It isn't a novel one wants to hug tightly for reassurance, or find by one's pillow at night. *Dracula* doesn't make us feel warm and loved, or attract us strongly to its characters, or even to its settings and themes. It is a more fragmented, cold text—one that makes us wonder and worry, as it winds us through multiple settings, characters, and media to tell its tale. Yet it is a novel that has unfolded quietly and steadily for me for many years and continues to haunt and connect me to the Victorian era in powerful ways. *Dracula* takes me into the late nineteenth-century moment widely and with open parameters—it presents a global world of shifting boundaries and also frames "other" worlds of the spiritual and the supernatural. It evokes questions about life and death, and also about the margins of the body and our humanity.

My relationship to the novel has been a long and tortuous one—it is a strange book and has traveled with me in various ways, from my initial attempt at reading it as a teenager in Saudi Arabia to other partial readings while finishing high school in Boston. I didn't read the novel all the way to the end until I was in graduate school in upstate New York. Initially, in my early teenage years, it was a book that made me feel like I was growing up—reading its sometimes daunting pages felt like a rite of passage to adulthood. My full reading coincided with the heady time when I was deciding to pursue Victorian studies. Now, as a book I teach regularly at Georgia Tech, it evokes thought-provoking class discussions through its references to science, technology, gender, and empire. While it's not a novel I cherish through warm childhood memories, or through readings where I feel an immediate connection to the narrative and characters, it is one that I have grown to love, and that has in many ways marked phases of growth—both in terms of my scholarly development and my travels. *Dracula* increasingly shapes me intellectually and correlates to the larger research questions I address in my work. It is my Victorian novel because of the ways that it has intrigued me and emerged to enlighten me at various critical stages of my life, and because of its capacity to repeatedly entice me and connect me more deeply to the Victorian era. My trajectory with the novel is also marked by various migrations of my own—geographically and culturally, as well as intellectually. In this way, the novel's engagement with space, imperialism, and nation echoes my development as a child who moved frequently and as a scholar studying the Victorian novel and the British empire.

My parents served as Pakistani diplomats and I grew up in several countries, moving every three years or so. My sense of "home" was often shifting and I had to adapt to different locations, to understand new languages and cultures. Many of the regions in Europe and the Middle East (the former Czechoslovakia, Yugoslavia, Turkey, Iraq) where we lived are located geographically close to the settings of the novel and have gone through political, social, and cultural transformation and upheaval that echo the disorderly aspects of the vampire's influence. I realize now, though I may not have as a teenager, that part of the reason *Dracula* is "my" novel is that it captures that sense of movement, travel, and disorder so aptly as it represents late Victorian urban and global expansion. Border crossings were a large part of my childhood, and the novel's emphasis on permeable boundaries, shifting geographic turns, and the vampire's ability to disrupt or circumscribe limits intrigued me then, and continues to now. I was drawn to the story's development as a journey, with Harker "leaving the West and entering the East," because I knew such metaphorical and physical journeys firsthand (31). I found Stoker's ability to intertwine the form of the novel with the travel narrative, a writing style that gripped so many Victorians, particularly effective, especially for an opening scene. The focus upon shifting locations and interconnected geographies made the narrative relevant and timely as I was living in an increasingly globally interconnected world and journeys were a large part of my own life.

My initial fascination with this novel was, as I've noted, due to its allure as a frightening and forbidden text. It presented not only scenes of horror but also vivid images of the body—as sexual, reproductive, desiring, hungering, and potentially empowering and evolving. The vampire women in

Dracula's castle represented a kind of illicit female sexuality and hunger that was slightly shocking but also thrilling to read at thirteen, as were the more veiled but still hungering qualities of Mina and Lucy. As Mina notes in one of her first journal entries, "[W]e would have shocked the 'New Woman' with our appetites" (123). The novel presents both characters at the brink of selecting life partners and depicts images of desire and (in the case of Lucy) flirtatious femininity. We are introduced to Lucy as she consults with Mina about her three suitors through her letters: "[W]hy can't they let a girl marry three men? Or as many as want her and save all this trouble? But this is heresy, I must not say it" (91). At an awkward age of discovering boys and experiencing changes in my body, I was struck by Lucy's desires and indecision and her ability to say what should not be said. At that age, I felt that these early chapters of the book served as a warning to me about the dangers of unchecked, audacious flirtation. I identified most closely with Mina, but Lucy, the more flighty, adventurous victim of the novel, evoked the risks of promiscuity and desire.

The novel was an entry for me not only to the Victorian era and fin de siècle attitudes but also to European culture as a whole—pop culture images related to *Dracula* connected me to Western culture as I lived an expatriate lifestyle in the Middle East. I attended a British school in Saudi Arabia for a few years in my early teens, and many of my friends lived in British or American compounds related to their embassies—we were all living in an exploding, oil-rich nation in the middle of the desert, but we were exposed (through video and cassette tapes) to American culture and to British books. *Dracula* was one of the more fascinating of these because it inspired so many popular representations and because it had a subversive quality. It presented a Western culture not enclosed within the distant scenes of Brontë and Eliot but instead more hybrid, fluid, and immanent in the life I was living in between cultures abroad.

After my initial, limited reading of the novel as a thirteen-year-old, I attempted to read the book again several times as a teenager, but never made it past the halfway point, often stalling and then beginning from the first chapter all over again. *Dracula* was a novel I really wanted to read, but I hit stumbling blocks with its intensity and the structure of its narration and intertwining locations. Stoker's writing style, with multiple narrators and fragments of information gathered from journals, letters, and other media, didn't initially lure me to continue the book. I found other

Victorian novels readable because I could easily immerse myself in the characters' worlds via the realistic narratives and linear perspectives, and through stories that were often about a coming of age or an exploration of human identity and connection. And yet, I kept going back to *Dracula*, thinking of it as a novel that I needed to finish—as if it represented for me a challenge to conquer my childish inability to get past the scenes that haunted me. I hadn't seen many vampire films and the internet hadn't arrived yet, so most of the frightening images were produced by my own imagination. It was Stoker's attention to detail, and the vivid and unearthly descriptions from those early scenes in Dracula's castle, that held me in the grip of the novel for several years. The enticing cover of the book was an entry point for me to the "original" story that had inspired so many other texts and images.

This was the early 1980s, a time when I was discovering pop culture and music, and, like the songs that made it onto my listening list—Duran Duran's "Hungry Like the Wolf," for one, and a number of Madonna's songs soon after—*Dracula* presented scenes of desire and hunger that aligned with the pop culture and music of the time. The *Halloween* and *Friday the 13th* series would soon become the iconic teen/young adult films of the period, and *Dracula* seemed timeless as its themes fit with those visual representations. But, while the pop culture images related to and surrounding *Dracula* seemed almost comical, the novel itself was more frightening than I expected, especially in its description of Lucy's transformation as a vampire. I was drawn into the friendship between Mina and Lucy, and fascinated by Mina's journal, which captures the various phases of Lucy's demise—from the "two little red points like pin pricks" and the "drop of blood" Mina records (127), to Lucy's "uncanny laugh" (133), and finally to the letters Lucy writes soon after she leaves Whitby (127–30, 132–33). These chapters coincide with our introduction to Dr. Seward's asylum and the character of Renfield. At the time, I found these characters and Dr. Seward's scientific recordings tedious to read, but the increasingly creepy and uncanny references to Lucy intrigued me even as they made me uneasy. I was particularly struck by the details of the repeated transfusion of blood, which Dr. Seward describes as a "ghastly procedure" after it has been performed by Lucy's suitors over the course of her decline (186). The image of Lucy's body being alternately pumped with the blood of her three suitors and drained by Dracula was unlike anything else I had ever read, and while Stoker was representing the transfusion scenes as a method of "fighting" the vampire, my needle-phobic, hospital-fearing teenage self was queasy from the starkness, detail, and repetition of those scenes.

After a gap of about ten years, finally reading the novel through to the end was pivotal to my graduate school experience. In that moment, it opened up to me the richness and diversity of Victorian studies and inspired me to pursue advanced research in the field. As a graduate student in the 1990s, I was delving into the rapidly evolving field of colonial and postcolonial studies, and critics of the novel were often noting its references to travel and empire. I had taken several seminars that dealt in some way with the nineteenth century, but in Anita Levy's graduate seminar Fictions of Illicit Reproduction at the University of Rochester I engaged more deeply with *Dracula*, along with several other Victorian novels, including Brontë's *Villette*, Braddon's *Lady Audley's Secret*, and Wilde's *The Picture of Dorian Gray*. The course focused on forms of reproduction (physical and metaphorical) in Victorian culture, paying attention to themes of "illicit reproduction" and to the surfaces and layers of various kinds of Victorian fictions. As I experienced the book more intimately and in its entirety, I recognized the similarity of its gothic and sensational qualities to those of other Victorian novels. I read it alongside critical material by Foucault and discussed it in relation to a range of critical feminist and postcolonial works that were being published at the time. The novel produced an open field for conversations about gender and sexuality, power, reproduction, and empire and inspired me to pursue theoretical work in these areas. Unpacking the novel at this moment coincided with my entry to the American academy and also what felt like my transition to the United States as "home." As an interdisciplinary scholar whose work, in addition to literary studies, often addresses issues related to the body and medicine, I saw in the book a treasure chest of material to teach and research. The very aspects of the novel that I found hard to digest in earlier readings, such as the scientific references in Seward's records and the descriptions of Lucy's bodily changes in Mina's diary, became the aspects of the novel that were most interesting to me, especially as I became more deeply immersed in feminist and literary theories.

As I've noted, a large part of my connection to *Dracula* has to do with how it dismantles the neatly defined borders of England and disrupts boundaries themselves. As a graduate student, I became more aware of how Stoker plays with space and geography as he depicts Dracula's movements to and through London. I was particularly intrigued by how spatial and physical metaphors function in the novel and by Stoker's representation of the fluidity and intermixing of blood and earth. From those early pages of Harker's journal to the multiple foreign characters represented—from the eccentric Van Helsing of Amsterdam to the cowboy Quincey Morris to Dracula himself—the book relies upon a sense of the intricately entwined nature of peoples and cultures. And the vampire figure represents that conglomeration of bodies and identities by his consuming and continuously digesting the blood of others—regardless of race, gender, class, or nationality. I discovered how the novel has garnered attention in terms of its relationship to colonial histories and postcolonial theories, with critics tracing its allusions to various forms of "otherness" and its expression of colonial tensions linked to an old and diverse British empire farther east. As Stephen Arata and other scholars have noted, the novel exemplifies the anxieties of a waning empire and a sort of "reverse imperialism" when it depicts Dracula and his primitive past entering England and wreaking havoc upon the systems of a modern, civilized, industrial society.[2]

Scholars such as Patrick Brantlinger have analyzed the text in terms of its fin de siècle cultural fears of degeneration, claiming that, like other late Victorian gothic invaders, "Dracula threatens to create a Demonic empire of the dead from the living British Empire."[3] Other scholars, such as Ernest Fontana, trace Stoker's rendering of Dracula to Victorian depictions of primitive "types" and to Cesare Lombroso's descriptions of criminal physiognomy.[4] In the novel, the Count is represented as an atavistic criminal whose sharp nose and beady eyes match the images that criminal anthropologists such as Lombroso represented in photographic and sketched classificatory images. In addition to such anthropological considerations, I was drawn to readings of the novel that considered its gender politics—references to the New Woman and to illicit sexualities—and to the multiple metaphorical readings of the vampire figure in relation to reproduction.[5] The malleability and readability of *Dracula* at this stage of my life was a contrast to earlier readings—I now found the text much easier to read and was drawn to the ways the novel (and the vampire himself) could be so widely symbolic, and could shift and produce multiply layered meanings and interpretations. The dark and strange qualities of the novel converged with my own slightly gothic sensibilities, and I found that it was not only more readable but even inspiring.

*Dracula* continues to intrigue me as it resonates with our current global, technological, and scientific tensions. Stoker's fin de siècle novel, with its depiction of an increasingly urban and technologized, but also vulnerable, society is still highly relevant, and gives us opportunities to question topics related to social justice, cultural difference, and technology in our time. On a personal level, too, *Dracula* especially feels like my Victorian novel now: it is an apt intellectual companion for me at Georgia Tech, where many of my students and colleagues study science and technology and my classes are sometimes the only space where students can engage with literature and history. We have a growing major in literature, media, and communication, but many of my students aren't focusing on nineteenth-century studies, and often my courses are the first and only place where they are introduced to the depth and richness of the period. *Dracula* usually excites my students, and the novel's references to technology—in the form of communication technologies such as stenographs and telegraphs and transportation systems such as shipping and railroads—open up lively discussions about all the forms of technology that emerged in the late nineteenth century. In a cultural moment when students are often inundated with various forms of visual media, from films and television shows to YouTube channels and video games, *Dracula* functions as a highly mediated and relatable text. My students seem more willing to engage with the multiple forms and narrators of the text than I did as a teenager, and they adapt to the varying perspectives and the shifts in time, location, and information more readily than I did at their age. Indeed, Jennifer Wicke's groundbreaking article "Vampiric Typewriting: *Dracula* and Its Media" is one I often reference in my teaching, as it illuminates how the book functions as a conglomeration of mediated forms. Wicke reads *Dracula* as "the first great modern novel in British literature" and investigates the "narrative patchwork" of the book and its links to mass culture, ultimately concluding that "the reading of the mass of typewriting is the labor of consumption the text requires of us. This mass is vampiric typewriting, this vampire is modernity, we are vampires at a banquet of ourselves, we are Dracula and Madame Mina, the one who bites and the one who is bitten, the one who types and the one who is typewritten."[6] Wicke deftly reveals how *Dracula*'s structural nature mirrors the figure of the vampire as a mass of information and a driver of mediated forms produced and employed by the characters. Along with being particularly drawn to the various media forms of the book, my students often engage with *Dracula*'s juxtapositions and its patterns of time and space, particularly as it is organized as a cluster of letters, journal entries, newspaper accounts, and more.

My students regularly come up with creative readings of *Dracula* that link it to current issues and to technology. Their responses to the text have evolved over the past fifteen years of my teaching it, and increasingly the text inspires them to connect aspects of the novel to modern forms of visual culture, media, and communication. Growing up in a highly saturated information age, they engage with questions of "information" gathering in the novel and produce their own unique informational projects. For example, a recent summer class took on the project of re-creating *Dracula* as a social media chain of information—they created a Twitter feed with the narrative of the novel juxtaposed with posts and announcements. Another group created a Pinterest page with dialogue from various crucial passages (such as the transfusion scenes and descriptions of Lucy as a vampire) rewritten as contemporary conversation. They produced dialogue related to the novel as a text message chain and described in messages how the characters would use abbreviations and text messaging to communicate critical moments of excitement and horror in the novel. In the chain, characters such as Van Helsing, Mina, and Jonathan Harker took on personas from today. The students creatively used the medium of text messages to create humorous abbreviated forms of communication and also to track the pace and suspense of the novel through short texts between characters. While my own work doesn't focus specifically on digital media and digital technologies, projects like these by twenty-first-century students have opened up my readings of the novel and made me see how applicable it is to modern technologies and innovations. What I've noticed in these teaching moments is that this novel, like the vampire, often consumes the class energy in terms of creative projects—in a recent summer class, more than half the students ended up working on projects related to *Dracula* and also described it as the Victorian novel that most captured their attention. So it was "their Victorian novel" as much as it was mine, and it inspired a rich series of projects and analyses. After teaching the novel several times in the past few years alone, I see it as a malleable text. Students get creative with it because its style allows for permeable and shifting interpretations and inspires the production of mediated and creative forms—again, like the vampire himself. As Christopher Keep argues, "[I]t is Stoker's *Dracula* that most effectively dramatizes the relationship between the new communication and transportation technologies and the unmanageable problem of 'information.'"[7] The novel has an aspect of reproducibility—allowing students to take liberties with the narrative to build their own creative forms by reproducing the vampire through new kinds of impressions, interpretations, and productions.

My own reading of *Dracula* has shifted in recent years—I find the novel timely and also find myself more intrigued by Stoker's use of technologies to create pacing and suspense. As happens with most professors, I have found that teaching my Victorian novel has deepened my appreciation for it. My rereadings, influenced by my students' contemporary renderings, have given me opportunities to read it more fluidly and openly and to find the more warm and tender moments within it. Mina's friendship with Lucy, framed in the early chapters of the novel, juxtaposed with scenes of her comforting Arthur after Lucy's death, for example, allow us to see the softer side of these characters and the strange and contradictory nature of human relationships. After the intense scene where Arthur puts a stake into the vampire Lucy's heart (she is described as a "Thing" that writhes as he performs this difficult and hideous task), he finds comfort in Mina, and in an awkward scene she describes him as "overwhelmed with grief" and "quite hysterical" (268). She then writes in her journal, "I felt this big sorrowing man's head resting on me as though it was that of the baby that may someday lie on my bosom" (268). Stoker's vampire reveals the vulnerability of English masculinity and brings together various characters through their contact with Mina, who, as the novel progresses, is an increasingly vital connection between Dracula and the men hunting him. Scenes like this one and the scene soon after of Mina sucking at Dracula's breast showcase the perplexing boundary-crossing qualities of the book. These are the scenes I always share in my classes as they exemplify Stoker's ability to create subversive and unsettling images of Victorian culture that challenge and complicate our understanding of the period. These scenes also expose the fluidity and shifting nature of the terms "science" and "spirituality" in the nineteenth century.

*Dracula*'s exploration of the uneasy boundaries of science and spirituality make this "my novel" at this stage of my life. Much of my intellectual work in my career has addressed gender and medicine in the nineteenth century, but my newer interests are engaged with the fine line between science and pseudoscience in the period and the questions related to spirituality, psychology, and neurology that intrigued Victorians and still resonate with people now. Some of my recent thinking about the novel relates to questions regarding supernatural and spiritual environments and experiences that can come from a deep study of yoga and meditation, which is currently both an intellectual and a personal pursuit for me. The novel asks us to be open to esoteric and supernatural possibilities and to expand our notions about the nature of the mind and its powers. Its inclusion of Dr. Seward and his asylum references the development of psychological theories, and other aspects of the novel consider topics such as hypnotism and mesmerism that excited Victorians. *Dracula* reminds us that there is still much that is unknown when it comes to our understanding of the human brain and perception, and the possibilities of worlds beyond what we can easily perceive. So much of the novel engages with the tensions between Dr. Seward's scientific methods and Van Helsing's arcane and idiosyncratic techniques of vampire hunting. Dracula himself represents an obscure and ancient past, and his methods include powers of the mind, such as telepathy. As I practice teaching yoga and meditation—which includes the study of yoga philosophy and theories of energy—I find myself more deeply interested in Stoker's representation of Dracula's ability to build connections with his victims through hypnosis, mesmerism, and telepathy. Through these intuitive mental powers, as well as his ancient and "undead" persona, Stoker's vampire transcends our concepts of time and space. His intrusion is not just physical, but also mental and spiritual. The vampire, and the novel's pursuit of him, thus expresses the convergence of emerging psychological theories with spiritual philosophies.

I now read the novel's engagement with foreign spaces and characters as also engaging with Eastern philosophies related to mental and spiritual energies, which began to spread to British and American readers during the period after the Parliament of the World's Religions in Chicago in 1893, when Swami Vivekananda more openly and actively presented yoga as a practice and a philosophy. Queen Victoria also became increasingly interested in the work of sages such as Shivapuri Baba—a Nepali mystic who is said to have lived over a hundred years, traveled across the globe on foot, and taught the queen meditation techniques. The theosophical ideas proposed by Madame Helena Blavatsky also intersected with yoga philosophies and presented notions of science and superstition simultaneously—in much the same ways that Van Helsing proposes. Other novels of this period, such as Florence Marryat's *The Blood of the Vampire* (1897), published in the same year as *Dracula*, presented the energetic and psychic components of vampirism—Marryat depicts a main character who psychically drains the energy of her lovers, and this female vampire's powers rely upon psychic energy. Some popular novels, including Marie Corelli's *A Romance of Two Worlds* (1886), referenced Eastern philosophies and imagined exoticized and transcendental worlds of the mind that connected with aspects of meditation and exploring astral planes.

Further, Van Helsing's eccentric approach to fighting the vampire evokes the possibilities of the unknown and supernatural that were being acknowledged at the end of the century. Stoker offers a medley of characters who present a wide range of sometimes conflicting philosophical and scientific theories. As Anne Stiles has recently discussed, the novel engages with neurology quite extensively, and Stoker's "composition notes for *Dracula* include typewritten pages on somnambulism, trance states, and cranial injuries."[8] The novel brings together vast and varying theories of the mind and contrasting ways to address the expanding influence—mental and physical—of the vampire figure. In this way, *Dracula* presents confusion and conflict combined with elements of the unknown that suggest the vast capabilities of the brain and its capacity to know and to perceive. It also presents flexible versions of vampiric horror—Lucy's victimization functions very differently from Mina's, and in the gripping scene toward the end of the novel when Mina is sucking from Dracula's breast, the inversion of the schema with her consumption of Dracula's fluids suggests the capability of the vampire to subvert bodily processes and challenge gender binaries. The tie between Mina and Dracula, which bears more meaning as the novel progresses, also presents us with a supernatural kind of linkage that highlights Mina's intuitive behaviors in terms of her connection with all the male figures in the novel.

By the end of *Dracula*, we see that supernatural efforts beat scientific ones. As Van Helsing notes, modern scientific progress doesn't protect us from the effects of a powerful supernatural and primitive force: "A year ago which of us would have received such a possibility, in the midst of our scientific, matter-of-fact nineteenth century?" (278). While Stoker presents the modern asylum and emerging technologies as central within the novel, it is the use of garlic, wooden stakes, and intuitive awareness that ultimately conquers Dracula. The author points out the limits of modernity and the need to balance scientific knowledge with other, less understood but powerful traditional ways of knowing. Further, the novel shows how Victorians were curious about the brain and psychological theories but limited in their knowledge of them, something that still rings true today as we live in an age where the possibilities of our mental capacities continue to be studied and may yet be largely unknown. In this way, Stoker's novel is particularly timely as we enter a moment of renewed interest in aspects of neurology and psychology, and as practices such as astrology, energy reading, and tarot, which have been categorized under broad terms such as "metaphysics" and "the occult," become more mainstream or at least accessible more widely through the internet and other forums. Our current culture of "self-care," "self-help," and "life coaching" also encourages more and more aspects of building intuition and finding connections between mind and body, to understand both personal and organizational behaviors more fully. *Dracula*, with its convergences of personalities, their instinctive bonds, and the "typewriting" or mediated forms of communication that they produce, presents us with a mass of text that we as readers need to decipher both literally and intuitively over time with a sense of emotional and mindful intelligence.

I can say the novel has become my Victorian novel because of the long relationship I've had with it and the various ways it has intrigued me and inspired my teaching. But even as I make that claim, I continue to hold *Dracula* at arm's length because it provides so many layers that I still need to unpack. It's surprising that, for a novel I've read and taught many times, I rarely write critically about it. Instead it has inspired connections to related topics in the period, about which I do write critically. Even as I worked on this essay, one that I struggled to write in some ways, I found myself approaching the novel guardedly, still cautiously trying to figure out its story for me—how it might intersect with my current interests in yoga philosophy, mindfulness, and meditation. Thus, my relationship with this novel is a complicated but contemplative one that feels mediated through the shifting forms and stories the novel itself tells. It's like a puzzle I'm feeling my way through, and the pieces of information the narrative provides inspire me to pursue new possible meanings and connections.

Right now, those connections have to do with the novel's allusions to concepts related to Hindu philosophies of reincarnation and to practices of meditation and yoga that were, in the nineteenth century, themselves global movements combining ancient Indian texts and philosophies with European concepts of gymnastics, body strengthening, and scientific theories of mental conditioning. My current readings of the novel are also influenced by research on the theosophical movements of the nineteenth century and their attempts to claim and embolden spiritual and supernatural practices through scientific rationality. *Dracula*, like these movements, presents us with a global conglomeration of forms and philosophies that reproduce and circulate—as does the vampire. My relationship with the novel shifts and recharges through various readings, influencing and inspiring my thinking, but also perplexing me and preventing the production of clean and seamless conclusions. To write about this novel in a more personal way as "my story" is to write about it with some caution—for fear of limiting it, or being further consumed by it. As Mary Shelley famously, in her 1831 introduction to *Frankenstein*, bids her "hideous progeny [to] go forth and prosper," I see the power of *Dracula* in its ability to keep returning and reproducing itself through various forms, creating global impact with its reach to many different kinds of readers.[9] "My" novel, then, is a story that reflects the tense but triumphant qualities of Victorian horror. While not a tender tale, the story of *Dracula* is one that inspires through its acts of reproducibility and expansion—and its ability to reveal the complexities of the Victorian age.

## NOTES

1. Bram Stoker, *Dracula,* ed. Glennis Byron, 68. Further references will be given parenthetically.
2. Stephen Arata, "The Occidental Tourist: *Dracula* and the Anxiety of Reverse Colonization."
3. Patrick Brantlinger, *Rule of Darkness: British Literature and Imperialism, 1830–1914*, 234.
4. Ernest Fontana, "Lombroso's Criminal Man and Stoker's Dracula."
5. Carol A. Senf, "*Dracula*: The Unseen Face in the Mirror"; Christopher Craft, "'Kiss Me with Those Red Lips': Gender Inversion in Bram Stoker's *Dracula*."
6. Jennifer Wicke, "Vampiric Typewriting: *Dracula* and Its Media," 467, 492.
7. Christopher Keep, "Technology and Information: Accelerating Developments," 151.
8. Anne Stiles, "Cerebral Automatism, the Brain, and the Soul in Bram Stoker's *Dracula*," 131.
9. Mary Shelley, *Frankenstein: or, The Modern Prometheus*, xii.

## WORKS CITED

Arata, Stephen. "The Occidental Tourist: *Dracula* and the Anxiety of Reverse Colonization." *Victorian Studies* 33.4 (1990): 621–45.

Brantlinger, Patrick. *Rule of Darkness: British Literature and Imperialism, 1830–1914*. Ithaca: Cornell University Press, 1988.

Craft, Christopher. "'Kiss Me with Those Red Lips': Gender Inversion in Bram Stoker's *Dracula*." *Representations* 8 (Autumn 1984): 107–33.

Fontana, Ernest. "Lombroso's Criminal Man and Stoker's Dracula." *Victorian Newsletter* 66 (1984): 25–27.

Keep, Christopher. "Technology and Information: Accelerating Developments." In *A Companion to the Victorian Novel*, edited by Patrick Brantlinger and William B. Thesing, 137–54. Hoboken: Blackwell, 2002.

Senf, Carol A. "*Dracula*: The Unseen Face in the Mirror." *Journal of Narrative Technique* 9.3 (Fall 1979): 160–70.

Shelley, Mary. *Frankenstein: or, The Modern Prometheus*. London: Colburn & Bentley, 1831.

Stiles, Anne. "Cerebral Automatism, the Brain, and the Soul in Bram Stoker's *Dracula*." *Journal of History of Neurosciences* 15.2 (July 2006): 131–52.

Stoker, Bram. *Dracula*. 1897. Edited by Glennis Byron. Peterborough, ON: Broadview, 1998.

Wicke, Jennifer. "Vampiric Typewriting: *Dracula* and Its Media." *ELH* 59.2 (Summer 1992): 457–93.

CHAPTER FIFTEEN

# The Hand of Fate

Annette R. Federico

## On *Wuthering Heights* by Emily Brontë

> Soul, self; come, poor Jackself, I do advise
> You, jaded, let be; call off thoughts awhile
> Elsewhere; leave comfort root-room . . .
>
> Gerard Manley Hopkins

There are transitional objects that bridge the space between inner and outer reality, and then there are objects of almost occult suggestiveness, when a work of art seems to possess talismanic significance. The psychoanalyst Christopher Bollas has described this kind of experience as being "captured in an embrace that is an exercise of being rather than mind, rooted in the total involvement of the self rather than objectified via representational or abstract thought." We can feel "held by the object's spirit." The work engenders a conviction that it has selected us for its message. It appears, says Bollas, as "the hand of fate."[1]

When I was in my twenties, Emily Brontë's *Wuthering Heights* (1847) bore a strange immanence for me. It seemed a part of my personality was hidden inside this book. I didn't consciously identify with either heroine, the first Catherine or the second Cathy. I am not sure I even liked any of Brontë's characters, with their inexplicable needs and frenzied sensitivities, the opposite of my tentativeness. Yet I recognized them. Not only Catherine and Heathcliff, but also Nelly Dean and Lockwood, Hareton and Cathy. I knew them all. Emotionally, intuitively, I was a secret sharer in their selfish, hungry lives.

*Wuthering Heights* is structured in dualities. Lord David Cecil set the template, in 1934, with his classic interpretation of the struggle between two cosmic forces in the novel: there are the children of storm and the children of calm. And in a chapter on Brontë's novel in his *Fiction and Repetition*, in 1982, J. Hillis Miller showed that *Wuthering Heights* is everywhere separated by "patterns of sameness and difference." These dualities are "within the self, within the relation of the self to another, within nature, within society, and within language," and whatever unitary force generated them remains hidden in shadows, just out of cognitive reach.[2] In *Wuthering Heights*, something strange and very powerful exists alongside or underneath the routines of ordinary life. The novel is a masterpiece of nineteenth-century realism, geographically accurate, historically definite, perfect in its internal logic, with a painstaking chronology that is verifiable with the use of an almanac. But the pull of the aberrant and the disturbing—the gothic dimension—is also quite real. And what, after all, is reality? The imagination has its own universe. At age sixteen Brontë noted in her diary, "[T]he Gondals are discovering the interior of Gaaldine[.] Sally Mosley is washing in the back kitchen."[3] In Nelly Dean's narration, household chores coexist with the defiant wanderings of ghosts. Obsession moles a tunnel under the ordinary rituals of courtship. Irrationality spreads its mists, settling uncomfortably on everyone's version of the facts of the case, their explanations for things, their reasons.

When I read *Wuthering Heights* in my twenties, I was pulled in by its complex of emotions, the combinations of affection and fear, scorn and pity, awe and revulsion. I must have recognized in its pages the dramatic props of my own feeling of duality—the security of family unsettled by loneliness and alienation, claims of belonging to the group undermined by slights and belittlements. Within me, kindness warred against willfulness, layers upon layers of obedient denial and bargaining to achieve the medal of goodness competed with a hunger for something else, something more.

After forty years, how do I begin to cut a path back to *Wuthering Heights*? "Do point out some landmarks by which I may know my way home," begs Lockwood in chapter 2. "Take the road you came," mutters Cathy. "It is brief advice but as sound as I can give" (13).

I first read *Wuthering Heights* in English class at my Catholic all-girls high school in suburban Cleveland—a surprising curricular decision, perhaps, but Sister Carla was an inspired and progressive educator. It is not a vivid reading memory, though, compared to those of other books we studied. I can recall reading *Macbeth*, *Romeo and Juliet*, *Frankenstein*, *Dubliners*, *The Scarlet Letter*, *The Great Gatsby*, and, I think, *The Return of the Native*. *Wuthering Heights*, though, has slipped through the nets of memory. All I remember from that first reading is the weather and the geography—a gloomy, remote place in England, with something called moors.

Throughout my adolescence, and well into my adulthood, I kept diaries. When I was growing up, writing was an outlet for me, a way to work through the infinite confusions of adolescence. I developed a habit of copying quotations I liked, recording my thoughts about everyday things—maybe confessions of crushes I had, or frustrations with school, all harmless enough. And yet, when I was a high school senior, I gathered together all my diaries, a collection of perhaps ten small notebooks, buried them in black plastic garbage bags, put those bags inside more bags, tied them tightly, and when no one was at home, stuffed them into the bottom of the trash bin in the garage to be picked up and incinerated the next day. I am not sure exactly what event triggered this gesture of destruction, but I think, now, I made this purge of my writing for two reasons. One was that, probably like many adolescent girls in the 1970s, I just did not like myself. Impermissible feelings, so ugly and disgusting once they were actually written down, had to be banished forever. The other reason may be that once, during a conversation about parental rights, my mother had said firmly that she would have no scruples about reading her child's private diary if, in her opinion, it was for the child's own good. There was no hiding place secret enough in the room I shared with my older sister. I destroyed my diaries partly to keep my inner world safe. Did I say anything in them about reading Emily Brontë? Alas, the record of my feelings about *Wuthering Heights* as a teenage girl is lost in oblivion.

My reading of *Wuthering Heights* in the fall of 1980, at twenty, on the other hand, is etched into my memory. I was a wide-eyed college English major doing my junior year abroad at a small college in Carmarthen, Wales. It is possible for me to say now that it was the most romantic time of my life. Living in Wales was like watching a play, in which wonderful, funny people act out their eccentricities, performing their roles with genuine and transparent pleasure. In *David Copperfield*, when Mr. Micawber turns up suddenly, David exclaims, "It was Mr. Micawber! It was Mr. Micawber, with his eye-glass, and his walking-stick, and his shirt-collar, and his genteel air, and the condescending roll in his voice, all complete!"[4] I was like David Copperfield that year, seeing people as marvelous types, and taking them delightedly and unsuspiciously exactly as they presented themselves.

I studied Victorian literature under four Welsh professors. There was Mr. Bevan, a cheerful, abrupt, slightly untidy man with a reedy voice. He shared his class on nineteenth-century British literature with three other lecturers. One of them was Mr. Raymond Garlick, an accomplished poet and editor, and an ardent Welsh nationalist. He was compact and birdlike, charmingly and artificially formal. He always wore a bow tie. Another teacher, Mr. Thomas, I don't quite remember. But then there was Mr. Binding: large, messy, awkward, and jaded. With his sweater vests, wild gray hair, chalky trousers, and the gap in his front teeth, Mr. Binding was the picture of an eccentric British literature professor, all complete. Mr. Garlick, Mr. Thomas, and Mr. Binding traded off teaching Victorian fiction, and Mr. Bevan lectured on the poetry. He described the Pre-Raphaelites as a little gang who unabashedly promoted themselves. They painted fantasies of the Middle Ages—without the plague, and with drainage. Mr. Bevan taught me that bad Arnold isn't as bad as bad Tennyson, but that both poets have the same message: life is grim. Robert Browning trampled on Victorian bric-a-brac and wrote poems with his mouth full of boiled beef and pudding. Christina Rossetti, ethereal and morbid (and the poet I secretly adored), was a devout young woman who became a neurotically devout old woman. Mr. Bevan was well loved by the American students.

Mr. Binding taught *Wuthering Heights*. On the first day, he told the class, not at all condescendingly, considering his audience, that the novel was about young love and how daft it is. We had to write a paper on the question "Is *Wuthering Heights* a great love story?" I argued that the novel was a great *tragic* love story, and consulted a book of literary terms to support my point. In my conclusion, I wrote this: "*Wuthering Heights* is a great love story, a tortured love story, which eclipses the romances of other Victorian novelists, and succeeds in revealing more about the strange and various forms love may take, and the desolation which can be the result of idealized human passions."

How could I have written that at the age of twenty? Surely this was unconscious theft. I had read almost no other Victorian novels to compare against the romance in *Wuthering Heights*, and it is hard to believe I would select the word "eclipses" on my own. I knew absolutely nothing about tortured love or the strange forms love may take—and far from idealizing my own passions, I was about to subdue and domesticate them. Before I had departed to go abroad for two semesters, I accepted an engagement ring from my boyfriend, Steve, as a kind of security deposit on our relationship.[5] Steve was a year older, in his senior year at another university. He was a kind, dependable person, a business major, and he already had a job in a bank lined up after graduation. We had been dating since my junior year in high school. Although he had no authority over my decision to go to Wales, he asserted an emotional claim I didn't have spirit enough to fight. It was an implicit deal: I could go to Great Britain for nine and a half months on the condition that I marry him after graduation. Supposedly the ring would help us avoid the complications and conflicts that might follow from our situation as parted lovers.

I wrote many, many letters to Steve describing my adventures in Europe. I joyously crammed every inch of those light-blue, folding airmail envelopes with my small handwriting, the tiniest script possible, all around the edges. I had so much to say! I must have imagined I was sending love letters, sentimental missives from an exciting world "abroad." Steve told me later that after a while he stopped reading even my postcards, and he threw the letters into the trash, the blue envelopes I thought of as speeding to him across the ocean still sealed, unopened.

I wonder what effusions failed to reach Steve in April, when I hitchhiked to Yorkshire, Brontë country, with my new friend Laurie. Laurie was from St. Louis, and like me she was an English major, a journal keeper, and a voracious reader. I will never forget the sense of freedom and adventure we shared hitchhiking through England during Easter week—hunting out youth hostels, getting lifts from lorry drivers, tramping through empty villages in search of tea and hot cross buns. In Haworth, we took foggy, atmospheric black-and-white photographs of the Black Bull Inn, where Branwell Brontë drank himself to death; of the farmhouse ruin on Top Withens, believed to be the inspiration for Wuthering Heights; and of the grazing sheep on the moors. How insanely I loved sheep that year abroad! I have one photograph of Laurie striking a moody pose in the churchyard of St. Michael and All Angels' Church, where the Brontës lived in the parsonage, as we played the role of ironic young Americans amused by the droll customs of the old world. My letters and postcards to Steve were probably ironic, too, a way of distancing myself from the power those places had over my imagination. A way of reassuring him that nothing very life-changing was happening there, without him.

Laurie standing among the tombstones at the St. Michael and All Angels' churchyard, Haworth, UK, April 1981. Photo courtesy of the author.

Laurie sitting at the farmhouse ruin on Top Withens and the surrounding moor, April 1981. Photo courtesy of the author.

If I was slightly guarded in those letters and postcards, in my journals I was ebullient. How blissfully enthralled I was by the romance of literary Britain! It was indescribably evocative to be near these literary landmarks. Actual history was all around me, but nothing felt as real as what happened in the otherworldly universe of British Literature. I remember reading somewhere that, on a trip to Lyme Regis, Tennyson told someone irritably, "Don't talk to me of the Duke of Monmouth. Show me the *exact spot* where Louisa Musgrove fell!" I was like that in 1980 and 1981, reading literature on the exact spots where everything actually happened.

Haworth was peculiarly spellbinding: being there was like stumbling upon a landscape I had experienced in a dream or seen in a movie. Laurie and I rambled the moors—yes, we *rambled* them—for hours and hours and never saw another human being, even on the paths designated for walkers. We laughed with fury and amazement at the mad passions of Brontë's characters, their hunger, their huge demands. But the churchyard and the parsonage felt truly uncanny. To stand quietly and respectfully inside the very rooms where the Brontë sisters wrote their stories was, at my impressionable and romantic age, simply unearthly—I almost want to say it was a spiritual experience, the endpoint of a kind of pilgrimage. The brown and violet moors, the heather, the low skies and silent village streets, and *Wuthering Heights* itself, all rattled me. Why did I feel all of this concerned me? I had written in my essay for Mr. Binding, "Emily Brontë wrote a great love story—but she dealt with love of such extreme devotion that it transcends ordinary love. The understanding between Heathcliff and Catherine lies on another plane. Their love cannot be described in any ordinary domestic terms." There must be a kind of love that carries people right out of the world. You could be possessed by the conviction that you would die without the presence of your beloved. "I *cannot* live without my life! I *cannot* live without my soul!" (129). It was the love story that had me by the throat that year. Was this what it meant to love someone?

No one says "I love you" in *Wuthering Heights*. Instead, they say this:

> "I cannot express it; but surely you and everybody have a notion that there is, or should be, an existence of yours beyond you. What were the use of my creation were I entirely contained here? My great miseries in this world have been Heathcliff's miseries, and I watched and felt each from the beginning;

> my great thought in living is himself. If all else perished, and he remained, I should still continue to be; and if all else remained, and he were annihilated, the Universe would turn to a mighty stranger. I should not seem a part of it." (64)

Catherine Earnshaw makes this speech to Nelly Dean in chapter 9. The person who should have heard her has already slipped away, and the person who does is disdainful: "I was out of patience with her folly!" Catherine has revealed a profound secret, and she only tells Nelly on the condition that she "will not mock at me." But Nelly refuses to listen, calling it "nonsense" and lecturing Catherine about the duties of marriage. "But trouble me with no more secrets," she says. "I'll not promise to keep them" (64–65).

Freud thought that normally people are protective of the boundaries of the ego, the source for making sense of the frightening world we are thrust into. But there are rare times in life, he conceded, when it is possible to feel tied to something so great that the ego-self evaporates in the certainty that there *is* an existence of yours beyond you, a transcendent, supercharged conviction of meaningfulness. This, perhaps, explains the "oceanic" feeling that is the source of religious energy. But there is another state, Freud said, "admittedly an unusual state," in which the ego's line of demarcation is blurred: "At the height of being in love the boundary between ego and object threatens to melt away. Against all evidence of his senses, a man who is in love declares that 'I' and 'you' are one, and is prepared to behave as if it were a fact." Freud also added (rather patronizingly) that, unusual as this experience may be, it is "not one that can be stigmatized as pathological."[6]

But it *is* stigmatized. When Catherine says, "Nelly, I *am* Heathcliff—he's always, always in my mind—not as a pleasure, any more than I am always a pleasure to myself—but as my own being," it is so taboo, so mad, so disruptive of social norms, that Nelly keeps Catherine's words at bay by all the unwritten laws of conventional courtship: "If I can make any sense of your nonsense, Miss . . . it only goes to convince me that you are ignorant of the duties you undertake in marrying; or else that you are a wicked, unprincipled girl" (65). When Catherine tries to tell her about a dream she has had—"I've dreamt in my life dreams that have stayed with me ever after, and changed my ideas; they've gone through and through me, like wine through water, and altered the colour of my mind"—Nelly won't hear it: "I was superstitious about dreams then, and am still; and Catherine had an unusual gloom in her aspect, that made me dread something from which I might shape a prophecy, and foresee a fearful catastrophe" (62). When Catherine sobs with "uncontrollable grief" at Heathcliff's disappearance, Nelly is "terrified" of her (69). Nelly is often the voice of self-discipline and reason. In chapter 9, she puts her catechism to Catherine "sententiously" (61). But she is also afraid, shaken by Catherine's self-exposure. She has had a glimpse of something outside the bounds of normal emotion, and she feels threatened by it, and, to her further dread, complicit in it. Nelly, perhaps, has had some frightening dreams of her own.

I wore Steve's engagement ring through my senior year of college. I wasn't proud of it, it wasn't a prize or a sign of feminine conquest. I felt guilty, embarrassed, and self-conscious. I loved my radical feminist housemates, their licentiousness and who-gives-a-fuck attitude. Being engaged made me feel ashamed, untrue to myself. But I was also afraid. I had no idea what I would do after graduation except get married to Steve, and this event was scheduled to occur in less than four months' time. One week before the wedding, my mother knocked on my bedroom door and discovered me in tears. I felt so ill from crying I could barely speak. "What's wrong?" she asked. "Don't you *love* Steve?" I could not answer. Could there be any question of loving Steve? I got married. I wore my mother's 1947 satin wedding gown, we had the traditional wedding in the Catholic Church,[7] we had the big Italian reception, we went on a honeymoon. Despite pressure from all sides, I kept my birth name (this decision was ignored by both our parents, who continued to address cards to "Mr. and Mrs. Steven Brown"). I moved into Steve's one-bedroom apartment and got a job at a bar around the corner, the kind of place that drew law students and yuppies enjoying the economic boom of the early 1980s. On weekends I would walk home at two or three in the morning reeking of cigarette smoke and alcohol, pile my tips on the bedroom dresser while Steve slept, and then sit alone in the living room, drinking wine and flipping through magazines, wanting nothing more than numbness. One afternoon, perhaps six months after the wedding, someone called asking for "Mrs. Brown." I thought it was a wrong number and apologized, wondering who would expect to find Steve's mother at my apartment. Then I realized that, to some portion of the world, *I* was Mrs. Brown. I became conscious of a small crisis, a little unraveling of identity. I had thoughts about my life now that were very different from those I had the year before. My real life was now something almost entirely internal. At the same time, it was something outside of myself, a force field between the two. I was having a private struggle that was both within myself and against something else, against people, against money, against pointless inevitabilities, Steve's promotion at the bank, vacations, buying a house, seeing friends who felt like strangers. I don't know what I wanted, authenticity, passion, beauty. Simply life. *A real life.*

After Steve and I were married, his mother gave me a beautiful two-volume set of *Wuthering Heights* and *Jane Eyre* published in 1943, with inspired woodcuts by Fritz Eichenberg (my university's library has recently acquired these same books for its special collections). I never thought to ask her how she got them or whether she had read them. I never thought this conventional, housewifely woman understood me, nor did I ever try to understand her. But her gift of these special books touched me. And perhaps my mother-in-law, Martha, saw something in me that Steve couldn't at that time. When his coworkers at the bank asked about his wife, Steve would say, "Well, Annette likes to read," which at that time was like saying, "Annette likes to breathe." (Once, I remember, he said to me, "Anyone can sit and read books.") Steve was a decent young man, he got along beautifully with my family, and he genuinely loved me. He had been on the cross-country team in college, and he remained a disciplined competitive runner, focused and determined. He was neither a simple nor a shallow person. When I look back at my journals from the years we stayed together, my heart breaks for us both, for our youth, ignorance, and loneliness. But marriage for me was like living in a fog. I couldn't lay my hands on it. "We have nothing in common," he said sadly after a year. The world was supposed to be cracked open for us to explore. Instead, it was more diminished. Living abroad had been a joy, the literature, the teachers, the kind people in the Carmarthen shops, the drunken Welsh students, the fields of little white birds on the road to town, even the cows that grazed outside the window of my dormitory, it all made me wildly happy. My senior year at college had also been intellectually intense. I wrote a thesis on Dostoevsky's novels, took a two-day comprehensive examination, received an academic award. My journals from my senior year are crammed with long quotations: Dostoevsky and nineteenth-century Russian writers, social philosophers such as Hannah Arendt and George Bernard Shaw, modernist poetry, Victorian sages, all of it promiscuously mixed with long reflections on daily life, and on the future I feared. In January I quoted someone called Dobrolyubov: "The most important thing is to follow the unbroken, harmonious, mighty, never-to-be arrested current of life, and to be alive, not dead." In February I was copying passages from my second reading of *The Brothers Karamazov*: "But in some cases it really is more creditable to be carried away by an emotion, however unreasonable, than to be unmoved." "I want another level. I want the level of poetry and I am a dried-up person," I wrote in March. "Lights are out in Cymru [Wales]." And in April: "Suddenly I feel I have lost track of something, some light, and now it seems blinking out, out of sight. Steve's boring too. Oh I don't like right now. But I don't like the future either."

Newly married, I had many hours to fill alone. I didn't have a car, so I stayed in our apartment all day reading, or I hung out at a local coffeehouse until I had to be at work. I wrote terrible poems, in something of a Sylvia Plath mode, and read the novels of Thomas Mann, which I did not at all understand, out of a desperate need to feel serious. The weightlessness of being married oppressed me, as did the buried grief I felt for my other self, my lost self, the girl who hitchhiked to Yorkshire with Laurie, the girl lightheaded from hours studying in the library. Two speeches twisted around in my head. One was from the end of Dostoevsky's *Notes from Underground*, when the peevish narrator jeers at his smug readers: "So perhaps I turn out to be more alive than you!" The other was Heathcliff's aggrieved accusation when Catherine is dying, from chapter 15 of *Wuthering Heights*: "*Why* did you betray your own heart, Cathy? I have not one word of comfort. You deserve this. You have killed yourself. . . . I have not broken your heart—*you* have broken it—and in breaking it, you have broken mine." My heart was being broken, and it was nobody's fault but my own. I did it, I chose it. Love was compromise, management, and constant negotiation. Its survival depended on not talking about my feelings, but even more, and worse, on not admitting them to myself. That was the hardest part about getting married at barely twenty-two, the automatic self-protection, and the self-betrayal. Out of which, inevitably, came the betrayal of the person I was supposed to love.

After a year, I went back to school. I told myself it would be practical to earn a master's degree in English, the only thing I was good at. I never thought of graduate school as a serious career move, or that I could study literature in a professional way. I only applied to one university, the one in my city. Steve and our parents assumed it was a stopgap until I found a real job—or, what would have been an undreamt-of disaster to me, became pregnant.

Graduate school was intimidating, but I was discovering a new community of readers, and it resuscitated me. My enthusiasm, though, was obnoxious to Steve. He was indifferent or hostile when I tried to explain what I was studying. "Talk normal, will you?" he said angrily once. My journals from those months reveal a truly astonishing capacity to deceive myself. Bitter outpourings of frustration, sadness, and rage are immediately covered over with apologetic assertions of love, moral self-accusations, sturdy resignation. "Pettiness and self-pity have begun to creep into my heart, and recognizing this I have become bored to a panic," I wrote in my journal. "I just hate myself for complaining. I hate myself for wanting more." I was, by everyone's standards, so lucky to be married to such a nice guy. Yet each day I was becoming more exasperated with this luck. I was torn between the need to feel some authentic emotion and the roles I had to play every moment of my life. At the bar where I worked, routine sexist verbal slights and physical incivilities (now called "unwanted touching") shook my efforts to be an intelligent human being. I offered Steve distracted and dutiful affection, but he was locked out of my private mental world, my real world of reading and thought. Then, in the spring, he began to suffer from mysterious and debilitating headaches that varied in intensity. One day he would describe the pain as being like a brick weighing on his skull, then it would be a knife twisting into his eyes. He had CAT scans and a spinal tap, and was hospitalized to undergo tests. Sometimes the headaches would disappear for weeks and everything would be normal. Then Steve would suddenly turn up at the apartment in the middle of the afternoon, unable to stay at work because the pain was so severe. This went on for months. The doctors could find no explanation. I knew they were my fault.

In the fall of 1984, I read *Wuthering Heights* twice. In less than two years, it had completely changed for me. It was not a story of transcendent love. That was not the secret buried and reserved for me in the passionate speeches of Catherine and Heathcliff, speeches that swell like arias throughout the novel. This speech, from chapter 12, now seemed the key to Brontë's vision:

> "But, supposing at twelve years old, I had been wrenched from the Heights, and every early association, and my all in all, as Heathcliff was at that time,

> and been converted at a stroke into Mrs. Linton, the lady of Thrushcross Grange, and the wife of a stranger; an exile, and outcast, thenceforth, from what had been my world. . . . I wish I were out of doors—I wish I were a girl again, half savage, and hardy, and free; and laughing at injuries, not maddening under them! Why am I so changed? why does my blood rush into a hell of tumult at a few words?" (98)

Catherine, confined to her room at the Grange, begs Nelly to open the window, but she again refuses, she doesn't want to listen, Nelly *never wants to listen*. Catherine drags herself from her bed, hangs out of the lattice, imagines she can see her old room at Wuthering Heights, the moors, the churchyard. She begs not to be buried in the church, but in the open air. "I'm sure I should be myself were I once among the heather on those hills," she says. Half delirious, Catherine stares at her face in the mirror. "Don't you see that face?" she asks Nelly. "Who is it?" (98). I wanted to recognize myself again.

In their feminist analysis of *Wuthering Heights* in *The Madwoman in the Attic* (1979), Sandra M. Gilbert and Susan Gubar present Brontë's novel as a rebellious revision of *Paradise Lost*, where hell and heaven are reversed: marriage, culture, womanhood, and gentility make up the prison that destroys Catherine's spirit. Gilbert and Gubar read Catherine's bloody ankle in the jaws of Skulker, the Earnshaws' bulldog, as a trope for the onset of menstruation, the end of savage girlhood and the beginning of the death of her soul in marriage and domesticity. She is taken into the Grange and nursed, finally civilized, her autonomy and her sexuality gently confiscated by Edgar's very genuine love.[8]

My first published academic essay was the paper I wrote on *Wuthering Heights* as an MA student. I was under the powerful sway of feminist criticism, and was breathless over Gilbert and Gubar. Yet in *my* reading of *Wuthering Heights*, I went against their emphasis on the first Catherine and focused instead on the second generation as the genuine story of growth. Cathy and Hareton, I argued, exemplify Brontë's ideal of mutuality in love. "The tortured first generation of *Wuthering Heights* fail to develop a mature understanding of themselves and others," I wrote. "In fact, Catherine and Heathcliff actually shrink from full participation in adult life, regressing into the adolescent preoccupation with self and the desperate need to feel love." The second Cathy was the true heroine, because her "acquired humility, patience, and affection yield what promises to be a satisfying marriage and a mutual broadening of experience." I also wrote this: "Rarely if ever is Catherine described as a loving person, one who is willing to give the self freely to another; even her professed love for Heathcliff is strangely qualified by her claim, 'I *am* Heathcliff!' He seems to be only a kind of narcissistic double."[9]

This could only have been written by someone determined to refuse the novel's moral challenges, a priggish scholarly exercise in self-discipline and mature resignation. My first college paper on the love story in *Wuthering Heights* was simplistic, but at least I was emotionally *inside* the book. My more critical response as a graduate student four years later was a screen for the difficulties I was experiencing as an adult. If I was obsessed with my own "desperate need to feel love," it must have been because I was stuck in adolescence. Cathy's "humility, patience, and affection" were precisely the virtues I had to cultivate to achieve a normal, rewarding relationship with Steve. I was married and had new responsibilities. I was older, the year in Wales was in the distant past. It was time to get real. Time to outgrow *Wuthering Heights*.

I wrote that essay for a class on the Victorian novel taught by an assistant professor who was as new to the department as I was. Richard was thirty-five, married, with a three-year-old son. I gave him my paper on *Wuthering Heights* in early October, two weeks before it was due. He praised my approach to the novel, and said the essay might be good enough for publication. I was a very quiet graduate student, the little graphomaniac who hardly looks up from her notebook during class. He told me he never really knew who I was until we spoke to each other in his tiny office, holding our marked-up copies of *Wuthering Heights* and talking about where to send my essay. I was enormously flattered that he thought I'd written something worthwhile about a work I loved so much—a book that, he said, was also one of the books of *his* life.

We started meeting for coffee, he gave me rides home from campus. Our conversations were about academic life, about life in our city, and, obsessively, about literature: Keats, Shakespeare, Dickens, Browning, Eliot, Yeats, Joyce, Beckett. I wrote nothing in my journal, *not a word*, for almost three months, refusing to admit even to myself that something exciting and frightening was happening to me. I finally poured out my confusion in a drunken scrawl at 3:30 a.m. after work at the bar—disbelief, fascination, bewilderment, and, of course, emotional denial. "You're not in *Wuthering*

*Heights*!" I reminded myself in my journal. Yet I was overwhelmed by the intensity of this man's focus on me.

All that fall and winter, we would take walks in urban parks, or drive all over the city in his unreliable '74 Dodge Dart, always talking, talking about life, books, music, poetry. In his class, we read *The Egoist*, *The Heart of Midlothian*, *Jane Eyre*, *Middlemarch*, *Bleak House*, long, staggering novels I had never read closely before. Outside of class, he would say things to me like, "There's a Brontë-esque moon tonight," or when he couldn't track me down he would leave a note in my mailbox: "I have been walking all over this godforsaken campus like Lady Dedlock." He joked that he was like Fred Vincy trying to impress Mary Garth: "When a conversation has taken a wrong turn for us, we only get farther and farther into the swamp of awkwardness." It was courtship through books—through Victorian novels, of all things! I had no close friends and it was impossible to share my mental life with Steve. And although I knew that I should do something, stop meeting him for coffee, stop taking walks with him, I also felt a gathering determination to live my own life, and to allow that I had a right to this friendship.

In the first five weeks of the next semester, I read almost everything by William Blake, as well as *Frankenstein* again, D. H. Lawrence's poetry, *The Awakening*, much Yeats, *Great Expectations*, both *A Room of One's Own* and *Jane Eyre* again, *The Last Temptation of Christ*, several works by Christa Wolf, and more theory and criticism than any human could digest. My journal is full of quotations. I cite Denis de Rougemont on "the triangle of adulterous desire" and the Tristan myth, and George Meredith's *Modern Love*, about marital infidelity: "Come, Shame, burn to my soul! and Pride and Pain— / Foul demons that have tortured me, enchain!" I quote Charlotte Brontë's letters: "[A]nd as to intense passion, I am convinced that that is no desirable feeling. In the first place, it seldom or never meets with a requital; and in the second place, if it did the feeling would be only temporary." I was also rereading *Notes from Underground* and identifying very strongly with the obnoxious narrator: "Whether it's a good thing or a bad thing, smashing things is also sometimes very pleasant."

In January 1986, I was immersed in a seminar on the Brontës. (This was also about the time I discovered Kate Bush, whose hit single "Wuthering Heights" and *all* the songs on *Hounds of Love* became the soundtrack to my inner drama.) The instructor, a young woman, an adjunct, talked about the Brontës as if she yearned to get to the heart of their writing. She gave us everything: novels, criticism, biographies, letters, juvenilia, poetry. That month I reread *Jane Eyre* for the fourth time in two years. I was also feeling nostalgic about my trip to Yorkshire with Laurie and made plans to visit her in St. Louis during spring break. I wrote in my journal,

> I felt deeply moved, even haunted, in Haworth. Especially entering the village, taking that long long deserted road at twilight, feeling tired and excited, curious and bold, and also frightened at the haunted quality of the scene—there were the moors, and we hadn't yet approached Haworth, so there were few houses, and no traffic. Passed a row of houses and a cat moved and we jumped. Too afraid to knock at a door and ask directions, we kept imagining someone like Joseph in *Wuthering Heights* answering the door, speaking in an incomprehensible Yorkshire accent. Coming into the village a big hill, a few shops, and only later the parsonage. I wish I remembered it more clearly. I mourn my lost memories. I would do almost anything to return to Haworth, above all other places. Above all other memories, to retrieve that one—and to be different about it, to be solemn.

I mentioned Emily Brontë often in my journal in February. I think she represented transcendence, fierceness, and I needed to be fierce. "She had a dog, Keeper," I wrote, "that she beat with her fists to tame him. She had a hawk. They called Emily 'The Major.' She safeguarded her inner life. Emily Brontë doesn't care if *Wuthering Heights* makes us well or not." Then, on February 24, I made this note to myself: "I love Emily Brontë like a goddess. So read her one novel again and again."

Steve found my journal in March—ambushed me with it, quite spectacularly, when I came home from dinner with a high school friend. He later told me he was stunned to discover that those college-ruled, spiral notebooks were filled with deeply personal reflections, thick with analyses of feelings and experiences. "I always thought you were just writing about your books," he whispered, crushed. What he read was shockingly intimate, and released a stampede of conflicting feelings: relief, shame, anger, disgust. There was some mild violence—he threw a couple of glasses against the wall, ransacked my dresser drawers, broke a kitchen chair, vandalized Richard's car, and said many hateful sexual things, but I felt I deserved it, the screaming, the heartache and destruction. And after it was over, wasn't I free to be with the man I wanted, the man I said I was in love with? Our parents were hurt, but I don't think they were very surprised. My mother located the source of all my problems in the very thing that kept me alive: "It's those books you read! It's those books!" I lived with my parents for a few weeks until I found a dirt-cheap apartment within walking distance of the university. And I carried on with those dangerous books. In the next two months, I read *Shirley*, *Villette*, Emily Brontë's poetry, Edith Wharton's short stories, Margaret Drabble's *The Waterfall*, Zola's *Thérèse Raquin*, more literary criticism, and *Sons and Lovers*, *Aaron's Rod*, *The Rainbow*, and *Women in Love*. I was in a mind-blowing seminar on D. H. Lawrence. In my journal I noted that "*Sons and Lovers* is related to *Wuthering Heights*." My pantheon now included William Blake, D. H. Lawrence, and Emily Jane Brontë.

Richard and I were now thrown together in a new and frightening way. We had brought into existence something startling to us both, and it tied us to one another. Yet through all of it I had discovered a longing for myself that was almost elemental, surging and irrepressible. I wanted freedom, I wanted my own life, and I wanted to figure things out for myself, from a solid core that was both deeply intuitive and coldly deliberating. I was looking at the world defensively, and with a reasoned eye. My next reading of *Wuthering Heights*, that March, during a weeklong visit with Laurie in St. Louis, was accordingly cold and critical. I took sanctuary from the turbulence of the past weeks in her bohemian apartment in a working-class neighborhood called Dutchtown. It was a relief to be with another woman who understood what I was going through (Laurie had married at twenty-three and divorced at twenty-five). Her single life looked fabulous to me, and now I, too, was going to be independent. During the afternoons, when she was at work, I explored the neighborhood or hung out in her apartment with her two cats. I was reading Sartre's *Nausea* along with *Wuthering Heights*, vacillating, appropriately, between an existentialist and a mystic. I remember lying on a mattress on the floor at midnight reading *Wuthering Heights* while Laurie slept, bristling with intolerance over Brontë's insane characters. I was even exasperated with the narrative frame! I wrote in my journal that the novel was "often clumsy, and too too intense—unbelievable, farfetched." The only character I cared about was Hareton, whose basic goodness had, in every other reading, been drowned out by the egomaniacs around him. Poor Hareton. When Heathcliff dies, he is the only mourner. Nelly says, "He sat by the corpse all night, weeping in bitter earnest. He pressed its hand, and kissed the sarcastic, savage face that every one else shrank from contemplating; and bemoaned him with that strong grief which springs naturally from a generous heart, though it be tough as tempered steel" (256). Hareton sees the beauty in the savage and lonely man, just as he sees the ugly wound lying deep within Cathy, a young and beautiful woman. That spring in St. Louis, Hareton was my hero, for despite all his disadvantages, he managed to protect his "generous heart," the hidden tenderness and responsiveness inside himself. Suddenly it seemed that Hareton's story mattered most, and I had missed it. As for Catherine and Heathcliff, I was unaccountably impatient with them; everything in *Wuthering Heights* seemed overdone and contrived. I resented it.

When I was an undergraduate, Brontë's prose sank into the soil of my becoming and gave voice to extremes that were frightening and unfathomable to me but that I was convinced could exist, did exist, in certain kinds of people. They existed in *me*, didn't they, or how would I have been able to respond so viscerally to this imagined world? At that time in my life, I didn't see how determined adults can be about containing emotional irruptions, supervising whatever is volatile, confusing, or borderline. And I couldn't see that I was on my way to becoming just such an adult. In 1986, when I read my beloved novel in the darkness and silence of Laurie's St. Louis apartment, *Wuthering Heights* brought me face to face with things I didn't want to see, failures of feeling and conviction I couldn't honestly confront. I had abdicated my marriage, and I was frightened of my new responsibilities toward someone else. I wasn't even sure now that I did love Richard. I just felt relieved to be free. As practical Nelly says, "Well, we *must* be for ourselves in the long run; the mild and generous are only more justly selfish than the domineering" (72). Well, I was justly selfish. All the players in my self-involved drama now felt like distant strangers.

What happens to Catherine and Heathcliff always takes place in the presence of perplexed and exasperated witnesses. Their speeches are delivered with unprotected conviction before uncomprehending people, as if those people did not even exist. Catherine and Heathcliff dash their heads against a tree or a table edge, groan, wail, howl like wild animals, throw objects, gnash their teeth, foam at the mouth, grip each other's wrists and hands, heave, bite, pinch, seize one another's hair, stare with eyes that seem to burn out of their sockets. How is it that no one in the novel really gets what is happening between them?

The philosopher Martha Nussbaum has written about the compromise *Wuthering Heights* makes with conventional Christian virtues. She notes, as many critics have, how Lockwood and Nelly Dean self-protectively avoid the risks of knowledge and of love, how they crawl into a shell to escape from hearing and seeing the painful human drama unfolding before their eyes. Nelly doesn't want to hear Catherine's explanations, just as Lockwood tries to block out the cries of the orphan ghost in his dream, stopping his ears "to exclude the lamentable prayer" (21). For Nussbaum, onlookers such as Nelly and Lockwood point to our own lives, as we watch at a safe distance the sufferings of other people, then congratulate ourselves for our virtuous docility. "We think that we are people of sympathy and charity; we think that we love and permit ourselves to be loved," she says. "Chances are we really don't. Chances are that we, like so many others, are hedging our bets." I was learning that I was more like Nelly and Lockwood than I thought, turning the other way, avoiding uncomfortable truths and unpleasant scenes, looking out for myself. Heathcliff is the only character in the novel who is not ashamed to love, and he loves Catherine without conditions or limits. "The love of Heathcliff for Cathy contains the total exposure of self to other from which Lockwood shrank in fear and in shame," writes Nussbaum. "Only Heathcliff permits his very soul to be at risk."[10] Depressingly, I realized that, like Lockwood, maybe I could not stand to be *seen* through the eyes of love. Steve, Richard—I kept them at arm's length, I hid from their gaze. I began to fear that I would never really love another person completely and entirely, with total surrender and without stipulations. I would never risk my soul that way.

Heathcliff's love *is* unsettling. I can't count how many times students have argued that Heathcliff's feeling for Catherine should not even be called *love*—it is a sickness, a psychosis, an obsession, he is a stalker and a necrophiliac. The ferocity of his passion for Catherine doesn't characterize the caring and supporting behaviors that define true love, at least not for many sensible young college students. One young woman, though, I will never forget. In the spring of 2005, I designed a general education course called Love and the Novel—a form of self-therapy after the end of my relationship with Richard. As the class argued back and forth about

Heathcliff's mental health, Mindi, who had been a shy student all the way through the semester, stilled and stunned the room when she raised her hand and said, in almost a whisper, "There's nothing wrong with the way he loves her. That is how we should love." For me, after I had again failed at love, her quiet certainty felt like an accusation.

Heathcliff lives according to his own law, his own being. He is taken over, it is true, by a need for vengeance, and he is driven by vindictiveness. But even in this, there may be a radical self-acceptance, a refusal to reform or justify his love for Catherine. Mindi saw that we have no business judging Heathcliff's feelings just because we can't understand them, because he doesn't fall back on conventional pieties to defend himself. Heathcliff mocks Edgar's subservience to moral precepts: "And that insipid, paltry creature attending her from *duty* and *humanity*! From *pity* and *charity*! He might as well plant an oak in a flower-pot and expect it to thrive, as imagine he can restore her to vigour in the soil of his shallow cares?" (120). Heathcliff never says, as Joseph and Nelly do, that love for our fellow man is the only redemption from human isolation, or that love of God supersedes other worldly attachments. He does not love Catherine in an abstract and proper way. He loves her body and soul. He loves Catherine because he sees himself in her wild and disobedient spirit. Just as Hareton, who sees himself in Heathcliff, is his only mourner, Heathcliff is the only person who is able to comprehend Catherine's suffering when her father dies. And Catherine loves Heathcliff because she sees herself in *him*, in his wolfishness and resentment. A person like Lockwood—for Nussbaum, a person like most of us—refuses to admit that the desperation, hunger, longing, and rage of people like Catherine Earnshaw and Heathcliff could also be in oneself. So Lockwood brutalizes the waif in his dream until her blood soaks the bedclothes.

"The acceptance of oneself is the essence of the whole moral problem and the epitome of a whole outlook on life," wrote Jung.

> That I feed the hungry, that I forgive an insult, that I love my enemy in the name of Christ—all these are undoubtedly great virtues. What I do unto the least of my brethren, that I do unto Christ. But what if I should discover that the least among them all, the poorest of all the beggars, the most impudent of all the offenders, the very enemy himself—that these are within me, and that I myself stand in need of the alms of my own kindness—that I myself am the enemy who must be loved—what then?[11]

"I *am* Heathcliff" is a breathtaking statement, but not because a girl of nineteen thinks she has found her soulmate. It is a courageous statement because this young girl, Catherine, who is *about to marry Edgar Linton*, has seen with utter clarity that her selfhood contains dark impulses that she is never going to get rid of. She knows that her soul will be torn asunder if the Lintons press down on that part of her emotional life. There is little pleasure in that dark self. No one wants to be Heathcliff all the time. But he is a part of her being, and no matter how dutifully she performs as Mrs. Edgar Linton she had better learn to love that darker part of herself or she will figuratively and really die, become the orphaned waif wandering the moors, perpetually asking to be let in, looking for the lost part of herself. Maybe *Wuthering Heights* is not about loving someone else, but about loving the enemy within, about how very hard it is to love and accept oneself. A tenet of psychoanalysis is that without self-acceptance and self-forgiveness, we won't be able to see others in their prismatic complexity, the evil and the good. We won't be able to fully love another, with genuine openness, if we don't welcome the demons inside our own hearts.

Catherine says she loves Edgar because he is "handsome, and pleasant to be with," "young and cheerful," and "he will be rich." Deadliest of all, she says she loves him "because he loves me." Edgar is a presentable man, there is nothing wrong with him, and Catherine does love Edgar for these things, as I loved Steve, and Richard, for these things. But she loves Heathcliff because "he's more myself than I am." Catherine commits a terrible crime against herself, as Heathcliff, her shadow self, tragically knows. She thinks she can tidy up her divided feelings, keeping some of them on the surface for everyone to approve of and leaving others to growl in the depths. Most of us do this all the time, girls and women especially. In so many ways, *Wuthering Heights* is about growing out of those supposed virtues, and learning to accept the existence of opposing emotions within oneself. This can take a lifetime to understand. The waxing and waning of parental authority pull a child's feelings like the tides. Often there is a turning off of shameful emotions—rebellious anger, or a desire for self-assertion, or guilt. Other people are idealized as happier and better, a habit develops of seeing everyone else as full of the deepest wisdom. The real self, Janus-faced, torn by opposites, stays exiled in the cold, outside the casement, feared and unwelcome. I had adapted as a young woman so well to what Alice Miller, in *The Drama of the Gifted*

*Child*, calls "the impossibility of consciously experiencing certain feelings . . . such as jealousy, envy, anger, loneliness, impotence, and anxiety" that half of my emotional life was under lock and key.[12] Although with other people I accepted dubious opinions and silly actions forgivingly, without judgment, I applied the severest standards to my own thoughts and feelings. It seemed my feelings were wayward, they were wrong, I was "a wicked, unprincipled girl." Why was this so? For as it turns out, I was not as alone as I thought. "I feel like my whole life has been to learn all of this, that I and my feelings are just fine, not wrong or even remarkable. I wonder what I might have learned if I had started with that?" Laurie, my Haworth companion, my wise friend and confidant for close to forty years, sent these words to me in an email just a few months ago. To feel your feelings, to give yourself permission to love or to hate, to just be yourself. Such a cliché! "Perhaps this sounds very simple," Jung says, "but simple things are always the most difficult."[13] To just accept who I was. Could it have been as simple as that?

In writing this essay, I have sometimes been condescending toward my younger self, with all her *sturm und drang*, her foolishness and seriousness. She thought books were talismanic objects, that Emily Brontë was a goddess. But a part of me has held that young woman protectively close. She didn't know what she didn't know. Some things she knew without knowing she knew them. Even now, as I write this, I cannot be sure my self-diagnosis is correct. Just as my judgments of the people in *Wuthering Heights* changed over the years, my judgments of the people in my own story may be wrong and one-sided. *Wuthering Heights* has taught me this lesson, too: every story is partial, in both senses of the word—just one part of a larger story, and unavoidably limited by bias. When I run out of explanations for the flatness of my life and can't find any more people to blame, what rattles the casements outside my safe and fortressed house are the stories I have reread over so many years, the stories I think I know well until the next reading, after the years have wrought changes within and without. The Victorian novels I love the most, *Dr. Jekyll and Mr. Hyde*, *Great Expectations*, *Middlemarch* and "the hand of fate," *Wuthering Heights*, are among the greatest myths of the self ever imagined. These books must have found my young heart because I had great need of them. And still have need of them.

## NOTES

1. Christopher Bollas, *The Shadow of the Object*, 31–32.
2. David Cecil, *Early Victorian Novelists*, chap. 5; J. Hillis Miller, *Fiction and Repetition: Seven English Novels*, 68.
3. Emily Brontë, diary entry, November 24, 1834, in *Wuthering Heights*, ed. Richard J. Dunn, 261. Further references to the novel are from this edition and will be given parenthetically.
4. Charles Dickens, *David Copperfield*, 266.
5. Some of the names in this essay have been changed.
6. Sigmund Freud, *Civilization and Its Discontents*, trans. James Strachey, 13.
7. There was also the rigmarole of attending a weekend "retreat" for engaged couples, and we had the obligatory cross-examination with the monsignor at our parish. To say I was a "lapsed Catholic" at this point is more than an understatement, and I am appalled at how nicely I swallowed my integrity. (I drew the line, however, at signing a statement promising that we would raise our children in the Catholic Church.) After the legal divorce, Steve sent me a formal letter of annulment authorized by the bishop of our district. So according to the Church, we never married, and none of this ever happened.
8. See Sandra M. Gilbert and Susan Gubar, *The Madwoman in the Attic: The Woman Writer and the Nineteenth-Century Literary Imagination*, 248–308.
9. Annette R. Federico, "The Waif at the Window: Emily Brontë's Feminine *Bildungsroman*," 26, 28.
10. Martha Nussbaum, "*Wuthering Heights*: The Romantic Ascent," 381, 373.
11. Carl Jung, *Modern Man in Search of a Soul*, trans. W. S. Dell and Cary F. Baynes, 235. Gerard Manley Hopkins's piercing poem "My own heart let me more have pity on" speaks to this same truth.
12. Alice Miller, *The Drama of the Gifted Child*, trans. Ruth Ward, 9.
13. Jung, *Modern Man*, 235.

## WORKS CITED

Bollas, Christopher. *The Shadow of the Object*. New York: Columbia University Press, 1987.

Brontë, Emily. *Wuthering Heights*. Edited by Richard J. Dunn. New York: W. W. Norton, 2003.

Cecil, David. *Early Victorian Novelists*. London: Collins, 1934.

Dickens, Charles. *David Copperfield*. Harmondsworth, UK: Penguin, 2004.

Federico, Annette R. "The Waif at the Window: Emily Brontë's Feminine *Bildungsroman*." *Victorian Newsletter* 68 (Fall 1985): 26–28.

Freud, Sigmund. *Civilization and Its Discontents*. Translated by James Strachey. New York: W. W. Norton, 1961.

Gilbert, Sandra M., and Susan Gubar. *The Madwoman in the Attic: The Woman Writer and the Nineteenth-Century Literary Imagination*. New Haven: Yale University Press, 1979.

Hopkins, Gerard Manley. *The Poems of Gerard Manley Hopkins*. Edited by W. H. Gardner and N. H. Mackenzie. Oxford: Oxford University Press, 1970.

Jung, Carl. *Modern Man in Search of a Soul*. Translated by W. S. Dell and Cary F. Baynes. New York: Harcourt, 1933.

Miller, Alice. *The Drama of the Gifted Child*. Translated by Ruth Ward. New York: Basic Books, 1981.

Miller, J. Hillis. *Fiction and Repetition: Seven English Novels*. Cambridge: Harvard University Press, 1982.

Nussbaum, Martha C. "*Wuthering Heights*: The Romantic Ascent." *Philosophy and Literature* 20.2 (October 1996): 362–82.

# Notes on Contributors

**Jonathan Farina** is an associate professor of English at Seton Hall University and president of the Northeast Victorian Studies Association. He is the author of *Everyday Words and the Character of Prose in Nineteenth-Century Britain* (Cambridge, 2017), which received Honorable Mention for the Sonya Rudikoff Award for the best first book in Victorian Studies, and many articles on Victorian fiction and criticism.

**Annette R. Federico** is a professor of English at James Madison University in Harrisonburg, Virginia. She is the editor of *Gilbert and Gubar's "The Madwoman in the Attic" after Thirty Years* (Missouri, 2009) and the author of *Idol of Suburbia: Marie Corelli and Late-Victorian Literary Culture* (Virginia, 2000), *Engagements with Close Reading* (Routledge, 2016), and *Thus I Lived with Words: Robert Louis Stevenson and the Writer's Craft* (Iowa, 2017). She has published many articles on Victorian writing.

**Michael J. Flynn** is an associate professor of English at the University of North Dakota. He has written about the strained relationship between Dickens and Thackeray and its intersection with issues of intertextuality, fictional form, and the social status of literature in early Victorian England, and about other aspects of the professionalization of nineteenth-century writing.

**Mary-Catherine Harrison** is an associate professor of English and chair of the Department of English at the University of Detroit Mercy, where she also serves as the executive director of Rx for Reading Detroit, a nonprofit literacy program focused on expanding access to children's books and supporting low-income families in reading with their children. Her research has appeared in the journals *Narrative*, *Poetics Today*, and *Journal of Family Theory and*

*Review*, and in an edited collection, *Rethinking Empathy through Literature* (Routledge, 2014). She is past president of the Midwest Victorian Studies Association.

**Narin Hassan** is an associate professor in the School of Literature, Media, and Communication at Georgia Tech. Her book, *Diagnosing Empire: Women, Medical Knowledge and Colonial Mobility* (Ashgate, 2011), traces the figure of the woman doctor in the context of Victorian colonial and scientific expansion. She has published essays in *Women's Studies Quarterly*, *Nineteenth-Century Gender Studies*, *Mosaic*, and *Nineteenth-Century Contexts*, as well as in a number of book collections. She coedited the anthology *Consuming Culture: Narratives of Consumption in the Long Nineteenth Century* (Lexington, 2007) and a special issue of *Nineteenth-Century Contexts* on the topic "Nineteenth-Century Mobilities." She currently serves as vice president of Interdisciplinary Nineteenth-Century Studies.

**Sara Malton** received her doctorate from the University of Toronto in 2004. Following a postdoctoral fellowship at Cornell University in 2005 she joined the Department of English Language and Literature at Saint Mary's University in Halifax, Canada, where she is a professor of nineteenth-century literature. Her articles have appeared in such journals as *Studies in the Novel*, *Victorian Literature and Culture*, *Nineteenth-Century Studies*, and *European Romantic Review*. Her book, *Forgery in Nineteenth-Century Literature and Culture: Fictions of Finance from Dickens to Wilde*, was published by Palgrave Macmillan in 2009. She is the current secretary of the Dickens Society.

**Deborah Denenholz Morse** is the Sara E. Nance Eminent Professor of English at The College of William & Mary. Her books on Anthony Trollope include *Women in Trollope's Palliser Novels* and *Reforming Trollope: Race, Gender, and Englishness in the Novels of Anthony Trollope*, as well as the coedited volumes *The Politics of Gender in Anthony Trollope's Novels* (Routledge, 2009) and *The Routledge Research Companion to Anthony Trollope* (2016). She is the lead editor of *COVE*'s online edition of *The Way We Live Now*, a novel she wrote about for *BRANCH* (2014). Her most recent essay on Trollope is forthcoming in *Victorian Handedness: Essays on Nineteenth-Century Manual Culture*, edited by Pete Capuano and Sue Zemka (Ohio State). In recent years, she has written on the Brontës. She is finishing a monograph on their work as well as editing their poetry for the Cambridge Complete Works.

**Lillian Nayder** is a professor of English and chair of the Humanities Division at Bates College, where she teaches courses on nineteenth-century British fiction. Her books include *Unequal Partners: Charles Dickens, Wilkie Collins, and Victorian Authorship* (Cornell, 2002) and *The Other Dickens: A Life of Catherine Hogarth* (Cornell, 2011), and she has edited *Dickens, Sexuality and Gender* (Routledge, 2012). She is writing the group biography *Charles Dickens: A Life with Brothers*. Her articles and essays on Dickens, Collins, Braddon, and Stoker, among other Victorian writers, have appeared in a range of journals and collections.

**So Young Park** is an associate professor of English at Gustavus Adolphus College, where she teaches courses in nineteenth- and twentieth-century British literature. She has published on Victorian poetry and fiction, as well as on Korean popular culture. As an Andrew W. Mellon Digital Humanities Fellow, she developed a course on Korean drama and its transnational contexts that used digital media tools to analyze popular culture. Her research in Victorian studies focuses on women writers of the 1890s, collaboration, and the visual arts.

**Beverley Park Rilett** is a research assistant professor and lecturer in English at the University of Nebraska–Lincoln. She is the inaugural editor of the *George Eliot Archive*, an extensive digital repository of writings and research materials by and about the author, as well as the *George Eliot Review Online*, which hosts all digital editions of the journal from its inception in 1970. She is vice president of the George Eliot Fellowship. She has published several articles on aspects of the author's life and works and is currently completing a revisionist biography of George Eliot.

**Terrance Riley** (1951–2019) was a professor of English at Bloomsburg University in Bloomsburg, Pennsylvania. His articles have appeared in many scholarly journals, including *Americana: The Journal of American Popular Culture*, *Neo-Victorian Studies*, and *European Romantic Review*.

**Catherine Robson** is a professor of English at NYU, director of NYU London, and longtime faculty affiliate of the Dickens Project. Her essays have appeared in *PMLA*, *Victorian Literature and Culture*, *Dickens Studies Annual*, and *Journal of Victorian Culture*. Her first book, *Men in Wonderland: The Lost Girlhood of the Victorian Gentleman* (Princeton), was published in 2001; in

2003 she joined the *Norton Anthology of English Literature* as coeditor of *The Victorian Age*. Her second book, *Heart Beats: Everyday Life and the Memorized Poem* (Princeton), received the North American Victorian Studies Association's 2012 Best Book of the Year award.

**Ellen Rosenman** is a professor emerita of English at the University of Kentucky. She is the author of, among many other publications, *Unauthorized Pleasures: Accounts of Victorian Erotic Experience* (Cornell, 2003), which was nominated for the Morris D. Forkosch Prize. She has coedited *Other Mothers: Beyond the Maternal Ideal* (Ohio State, 2008) and *Provocations: A Transnational Reader in the History of Feminist Thought* (California, 2015), and has published in *Victorian Studies*, *Signs*, and *Victorian Literature and Culture*. Her scholarly interests include gender, sexuality, social class, and the novel.

**Andrea Kaston Tange** is a professor of English, chair of the English department, and director of Digital Liberal Arts at Macalester College. She is the author of *Architectural Identities: Domesticity, Literature, and the Victorian Middle Classes* (Toronto, 2010) and coeditor of *Children and Empire* (Routledge, 2012). Her work has appeared in *Nineteenth-Century Contexts*, *Victorian Literature and Culture*, and *Nineteenth-Century Literature*, among other journals and edited collections. Her current research focuses on Victorian travel and empire. She has served as the president of the Midwest MLA and chair of the MLA Committee on Academic Freedom, Professional Rights and Responsibilities, and she is currently on the Executive Board of the Midwest Victorian Studies Association.

**Tom Ue** researches and teaches courses on nineteenth-century British literature, intellectual history, and cultural studies at Dalhousie University. He is the author of *Gissing, Shakespeare, and the Life of Writing* (Edinburgh, forthcoming) and *George Gissing* (Liverpool, forthcoming), and the editor of *George Gissing, The Private Papers of Henry Ryecroft* (Edinburgh, forthcoming). Ue has held the prestigious Frederick Banting Postdoctoral Fellowship and is an Honorary Research Associate at University College London.

# Index

Page numbers in *italics* refer to illustrations or their captions.